CRISIS, MIRACLES,
AND BEYOND

Dedicated to the memory of Leslie C. Eliason

CRISIS, MIRACLES, AND BEYOND

Negotiated Adaptation of the Danish Welfare State

Edited by
Erik Albæk, Leslie C. Eliason, Asbjørn Sonne Nørgaard
and Herman M. Schwartz

Aarhus University Press |

Aarhus University Press
Langelandsgade 177
DK-8200 Aarhus N
Denmark
www.unipress.dk

Gazelle Book Services Ltd.
White Cross Mills,
Hightown
Lancaster,
LA1 4XS
www.gazellebooks.co.

The David Brown Book Company (DBBC)
P.O. Box 511
Oakville CT 06779
USA
www.oxbowbooks.com

PREFACE

Like the crisis of the welfare state, this book has been underway for a long time! But, unlike the welfare state, and particularly the Danish welfare state, this book has finally come to an end! The papers in this collection of essays first saw the light of day in 1995, at a time when the Danish economy had just found its feet after a decade of turmoil and adjustment. At that time the authors of this book came together to explain how it was that Denmark, widely proclaimed to be riding a fast train to a macroeconomic hell (albeit in the first class coach), had somehow not only avoided going over the brink but had also reversed direction.

More than ten years later the Danish economy is one of the strongest in Europe. Unemployment is low, the budget is in surplus, foreign debt is at manageable levels, and people are generally happy with the economy and the welfare state. We hope that this book will provide some insight into why this came to be so. We found there was no magic policy or miracle that cured Denmark's ills. Indeed, one major point is that a changing external environment helped a Denmark that simultaneously changed domestic public policy in incremental but ultimately positive ways. These deliberate changes were specific to discrete policy areas, which is why the collection surveys health, education, and daycare in addition to the usual macroeconomic policy issues. But the collection also looks at the actual operation of and politics around local government, as well as relations between central and local government, because in Denmark local government funds and delivers the bulk of welfare state services. We argue that the cost efficiency and political legitimacy of these services is what makes or breaks a welfare state, not the generic external economic environment.

We also hope this collection sheds some light on the differences among the Scandinavian political economies and welfare states and also those between Scandinavia and the other advanced economies. As Lars Mjøset argued back in the 1980s, there were really five Scandinavian models, not one. The Danish model, despite a flurry of articles in the late 1990s and early 2000s, remains relatively unknown in English language publications. While the OECD routinely lauds the Danish mortgage finance system as a model for the rest of Europe, and also recommends Danish active labor market practices, much of the Danish welfare state remains *terra incognita* outside of Scandinavia. While we hope that there is something to be learned from the Danish experience, one major point that emerges from our analyses is how much the working of these successful policies is tied up with a set of attitudes that is hard to transport across borders, and with a specific set of environmental conditions that will not necessarily be encountered again.

This is not to say that there are no transferable lessons, though. The central problems of the Danish welfare state in the 1980s and 1990s were political problems – enduring problems of governance and governability that transcend any specific polity. Could political actors shift the welfare state's funding priorities if and when the demand for services changed or as social demographics changed? Could political actors prevent welfare state producers from putting their own interests ahead of their clients' interests? Could political actors structure transfers in ways that maintained social solidarity and a willingness to work; or to put it in terms of the foregoing question, in ways that prevented rent seeking not by producers but by concentrated groups of clients? We think the chapters here speak to these core political questions in ways that matter for the durability of other welfare states.

We wish to extend our gratitude to Aarhus University Research Foundation for providing funding for the initial conference in 1995, and to the Danish Social Science Council for providing financial support for the publication of the book. Special thanks to the contributors and the publisher for their patience with the editing of the book, and to Annette Andersen for her efficient secretarial assistance in the preparation of the manuscript. And finally, Herman Schwartz would like to thank Eve Schwartz for understanding that the US Customs Department would not have allowed him to take an entire cake from her favorite Danish confectioner back to the USA after the 1995 conference!

Our great pleasure in seeing this project finally in print is overshadowed however by the untimely death of our co-editor Leslie Carol Eliason in 2004. Leslie received her BA from the University of Virginia and her PhD from Stanford. She taught at the Department of Scandinavian Studies and at the Evans School of Public Policy at the University of Washington, and then at the Monterey Institute for International Studies. Her love for Denmark started when she was a high school Rotary exchange student in Holstebro, and her impeccable command of the Danish language was fortified by a Marshall Fund Fellowship to study at the University of Aarhus, and a return visit as a Fulbright scholar. Her academic work focused on public policy and in particular the comparison of welfare states. But she clearly cared much, much more for her students, who remember her as an inspiring and committed teacher and trainer. We remember Leslie as a spirited and loyal colleague, who cared deeply about her students and inspired other women in her field. While on a Fulbright Fellowship to Hungary and Bosnia she was diagnosed with melanoma and passed away shortly after. Leslie played a key role in motivating this project and we dedicate this book to her memory.

Erik Albæk, Asbjørn Sonne Nørgaard, Herman M. Schwartz

August, 2008

CONTENTS

PREFACE   5

INTRODUCTION   11
Erik Albæk, Leslie C. Eliason, Asbjørn Sonne Nørgaard and Herman M. Schwartz

1   KEEPING THE BUMBLEBEE FLYING   33
Economic Policy in the Welfare State of Denmark, 1973-99
Peter Nannestad and Christoffer Green-Pedersen

2   PUBLIC SUPPORT FOR THE DANISH WELFARE STATE   75
Interests and Values, Institutions and Performance
Jørgen Goul Andersen

3   THE WELFARE STATE AND THE LABOR MARKET   115
Per H. Jensen

4   PUBLIC EXPENDITURES   146
Is the Welfare State Manageable?
Peter Munk Christiansen

5   SMALL STEPS, BIG CHANGE?   171
Continuity and Change in The Danish Social Security System
Jon Kvist and Niels Ploug

6   DANISH LOCAL GOVERNMENT   201
Poul Erik Mouritzen

7   HEALTH CARE IN DENMARK   227
Adapting to Cost Containment in the 1980s
and Expenditure Expansion in the 1990s
Thomas Pallesen and Lars Dahl Pedersen

8   GROWTH BY RULES   251
The Case of Danish Day Care
Jens Bejer Damgaard

CONCLUSION   277
Erik Albæk, Leslie C. Eliason, Asbjørn Sonne Nørgaard and Herman M. Schwartz

CONTRIBUTORS   305

INTRODUCTION

Erik Albæk, Leslie C. Eliason, Asbjørn Sonne Nørgaard and Herman M. Schwartz

What explains the remarkable resilience of the Danish welfare state, and what does this tell us about the future of the welfare state in general? How did this welfare state survive a quarter century that saw the collapse of its economic foundations in Keynesian demand management and full employment, and the erosion of its political foundations in the face of a fairly successful and OECD-wide ideological challenge to the whole idea of the welfare state from the political right? In order to answer these important questions, this volume presents a comprehensive account and analysis of the institutional structure of the Danish welfare state.

The focus of the book

The book focuses on four narrower sets of questions. The first is simply an empirical question: what is the institutional and political structure of the Danish welfare state? Surprisingly, there has been no comprehensive survey of the Danish welfare state since Lars Nørby Johansen's chapter in Peter Flora's path-breaking *Growth to Limits*. But Johansen presented a dry, empirical, and quite brief survey of changes in spending levels, programs, and clientele. His analysis suffered from a lack of attention to the actual bureaucratic structures that delivered services, the economic sustainability of rapidly rising spending, and the political basis of welfare state support. Although Gøsta Esping-Andersen presented a roughly contemporaneous analysis of the political basis for the Danish welfare state in *Politics Against Markets*, this too suffered from a marked defect. Esping-Andersen more or less elevated Sweden as the exemplar of the Scandinavian social democratic welfare state. Denmark thus appeared to be a lesser or defective version of the Swedish model; the preeminence of the Swedish model obscured the details of the Danish system. The first task this book takes up is thus a comprehensive survey of the Danish welfare state. Naturally we examine some of the core social services and transfers: on the service side, health, and daycare; on the transfer side, pensions, unemployment insurance and some smaller programs.

Second, we ask how these various pieces fit together with each other, with the broad macroeconomy and with political dynamics. Rather than simply surveying the core social services and cash transfers, we also show how these services and transfers are governed by central and local decision-makers, how they interact with labor markets, and what their macroeconomic consequences are.

The third question turns from empirics to dynamics: given its foundation in a small, open economy, how is it that the Danish welfare state is economically sustainable and that spending does not spiral out of control? This involves us in an exploration of both the supply of and demand for cash: how was the macroeconomy and budget regulated so as to prevent an erosion of the state's capacity to tax, and why is it that citizen demands for services and transfers has not spiraled out of control?

Finally, the fourth question similarly turns to political dynamics: given a polity characterized by highly organized economic interests, corporatist control over most institutions, and producer control over welfare state services, how is it that the welfare state remains governable and retains public support? Why don't producers abuse their position of control within state institutions that deliver services? Why do citizens willingly accept some of the highest average and marginal tax rates in the OECD? Why do they tolerate substantial state intrusion into their lives? The briefest possible answer to all these questions is that the Danish institutional structure and moral economy permits a "negotiated adaptation" by Denmark's welfare society to a large number of internal and external stresses. The very institutional structures, which theories of welfare state crisis see as the causes of decay, are also the sources of resilience in the face of internal and external challenges.

What the studies in this book reveal is a much more varied and complex picture of the predicaments and problems of the welfare state than most generic theories suggest. Our research on the Danish welfare state demonstrates a need to reexamine the theoretical underpinnings of contemporary welfare state research. From the point of view of those who see the welfare state as perpetually mired in self-destructive tendencies, or from the point of view of those mired in Esping-Andersen's triad of ideal types, Denmark remains an inexplicable phenomenon. Thus, we consider Denmark a critical test case for, rather than an exception to, these arguments.

Over the years Denmark has been struck by most alleged symptoms of welfare state crisis. As a small country with an open economy, Denmark was severely affected by changes in the international economy and the recessions of the 1970s. EC/EU harmonization policies have been part of the Danish political landscape for more than 35 years. Minority governments and corporatism are dominant features in Danish policy making; and Denmark was one of the very few countries where a protest party managed to capitalize on a tax-welfare backlash. And yet Danish policy makers managed to overcome or contain such "crisis" tendencies.

Similarly, viewed from the perspective of comparative welfare state research, the Danish welfare state has been presented as institutionally less developed and more compromised by its relatively stronger element of Liberalism than other Scandinavian social democratic welfare states. Our approach has been to subject these assumptions to empirical analysis. Rather than hypothesizing on the inherent weaknesses that drive the politics of welfare state change, we have redirected our attention to the questions of whether and how welfare states have the capacity to adapt institutionally to changes in their international and domestic environments.

The problem?

We ask the above questions because the Danish welfare state resembles the bumblebee: theoretically neither should fly, yet both seem to do pretty well despite the predictions of theories of the welfare state and aerodynamics respectively. Three decades of welfare state research and theorizing beginning in the 1970s suggest that the extensive – and expensive – Scandinavian service-heavy social democratic welfare states should encounter economic and political difficulties.

The Danish welfare state in particular should have had the hardest time surviving, compared to its Scandinavian neighbors. Not only is the generous, universal Danish welfare state expensive, absorbing roughly 45 pct. of GDP, it is also largely financed by highly visible progressive personal income taxes. The Danish public sector therefore should be the most likely candidate for a tax and welfare backlash (Wilensky, 1984). Second, the political basis for the welfare state is weaker than in the rest of Scandinavia. The Danish Social Democratic Party has always had a smaller vote share than its Scandinavian counterparts, and its share has eroded more rapidly than theirs (Esping-Andersen, 1985; Svensson, 1989). Weakness in the traditional working class vote was not offset by new white-collar middle adherents. On both the left and the right the Danish Social Democrats face well organized parties that attract considerable white collar support, and various tax protest and anti-immigrant parties have sometimes attracted more working class voters than the Social Democrats themselves. In turn this created minority coalition governments whose ability to steer the economy and polity should have been quite limited.

Externally, changes in the global economy as well as in supranational political institutions such as the European Union seem to have curtailed policy makers' opportunities to develop or even sustain their national welfare states (Keohane & Milner, 1996). The European Exchange Rate Mechanism (ERM), the European Central Bank, and the Euro all constrain or curtail local monetary policy autonomy, while calling into question the utility of local corporatist arrangements. Some research suggests that corporatist bargaining is more difficult to sustain in a deregulated economy. Kitschelt (1994), Piven (1991), and Pontusson (1992) each argue that the strength and solidarity of organized labor, a critically important component of the corporatist bargaining structure, have been undermined by increasing market integration and exposure to more intense international competition. This means that national corporatist arrangements may be less effective as mechanisms to negotiate public sector expenditure control and reorganization.

All these tendencies can be seen in Denmark's unfolding economic crisis during the 1970s and 1980s. Like other Western countries, these years confronted Denmark with serious problems and challenges: persistently high unemployment, slow rates of growth in public sector efficiency, and what appeared to be a very low capacity to change policy and spending priorities. All of these might well have cumulated into a serious welfare state crisis. Thus, for example, in the so-called "landslide election" of 1973, Denmark became the first Western democracy to experience a tax revolt and a corresponding reaction against welfare spending. But intense voter concern with taxes was short-lived, and twenty years later popular support for the welfare state is as strong as ever (cf. Goul Andersen, below).

Similarly, the first international oil crisis provoked a serious recession that then turned into the devastating combination of high inflation, growing unemployment, and stagnating economic growth. These problems ramified into spiraling budget and balance of payment deficits. However, since the beginning of the 1990's the Danish economy has improved substantially. Indeed, by the end of the 1990's, observers were speaking of a "Danish Miracle" paralleling the "Dutch Miracle."

Meanwhile, neither tax revolt nor economic stagnation did much initially to inhibit the growth of the Danish welfare state. Indeed, after the 1973 election, Danish public expenditures grew faster than all but one other OECD welfare state in the 1970s. However, in the 1980s public expenditure growth was brought under control and the Danish rate was significantly below the 1970s rates and significantly below rates in other OECD countries. From 1986 to 1991 the share of national income consumed by the public sector actually decreased, and then remained stable through the 1990s. Remarkably, politicians achieved macroeconomic stabilization and reductions in public expenditure growth without major cuts in the levels or content of social welfare services and transfers. The same occurred in most countries where welfare state expenditures continued to grow parallel to, or faster than, GDP. According to Alber (1988: 463), "[t]his suggests an interpretation of the recent period as a phase of consolidation rather than of welfare state dismantling." So the much-heralded "fiscal crisis of the state" (O'Connor, 1973), while not an illusion, proved to be a manageable problem.

Similarly, Denmark's membership in the EU and ERM has not led to welfare state downsizing or affected the level, content, organization and financing of the Danish welfare state. Although some have argued that "the movement towards integration will carry with it a gradual erosion of national welfare state autonomy, increasingly embedding national regimes in a complex, multi-tiered web of social policy" (Liebfried & Pierson, 1995: 2), Denmark has adjusted relatively painlessly to – indeed, perhaps has benefited from – the demands of the internal market program. With social policy explicitly excluded from European cooperation and reserved to individual member states' jurisdiction, direct intervention from the supranational level remains unlikely. And Denmark has famously rejected both the Maastricht Treaty and the Euro without visible consequence.

Finally, partly in response to theories of the welfare state that saw it as generating contradictions for capitalism (for neo-Marxists see Offe, 1984, for neo-Conservatives see Bell, 1978, and for neo-Liberals, see Brittan, 1975), and partly in response to the obvious empirical challenge posed by the continued growth of social welfare spending, a whole series of investigations have shown that different parts of the welfare state are not only a benign force, but indeed a positive one for capital accumulation. The "varieties of capitalism" literature (Soskice & Hall, 2001; but see also Iversen, 1999) argues that welfare state inputs are an essential part of a strategy for differentiated quality production and thus the very world market competitiveness that the welfare state allegedly undermines.

Denmark's thirty year cycle from crisis to miracle merits explanation, and not just because Denmark seems to have pulled itself back from the brink of disaster. Rather, the whole cycle suggests that the rhetoric of both crisis and miracle is overblown. Given the almost unanimous predictions of crisis in welfare state theories, why didn't Denmark experience a fundamental and general crisis of the welfare state? Given the fact that the state took few if any heroic measures to save the economy, how was crisis turned into miracle? These questions suggest that we should apply normal social science to Denmark and the problems of the welfare state. As with most normal social science, the answers are much less shocking than one might think. The problems of the Danish welfare state – and probably most welfare states – resolve into problems of the governability and governance of large-scale organizations. The remainder of this section thus focuses on those theories of welfare state crisis that address governance issues, rather than the generic theories of internationalization, Europeanization, fiscal crisis, or contradictions of capitalism cursorily dismissed above.

Public choice theorists squarely address the issue of welfare state governance by suggesting two different axes for welfare state decay. First, welfare service producers, politicians, and bureaucrats for different reasons should seek budget growth, and different client groups should seek increased spending on services and transfers (Kristensen, 1987; Niskanan, 1971; Mitchell & Simmons, 1994). The inherent asymmetries of interests between the better organized and concentrated interests advocating increased spending and the broader, more diffuse support for controlling taxes should combine to produce a ceaseless expansion of the welfare state that is economically unsustainable and democratically unwarranted (Kristensen, 1987).

Second, the public sector has a principal-agent problem that should create popular dissatisfaction with the public provision of services as producers arrange services to suit their own rather than the clients' needs. Bureaucrats' and service producers' capture of welfare agencies disconnects the quality and quantity of welfare services from consumer and/or voter preferences and willingness to pay. In theory, these twin forces should create a trilemma that can only be resolved with great difficulty. A fiscal crisis ensues because the state becomes a drain on the economy; the management and steering capacity of policy makers is impaired; and the popular willingness to pay for public expenditures declines.

Contrary to this explanation, we find that Danish institutional dynamics provide a partial explanation for the absence of a general crisis rather than its presence. Our examinations of a wide range of policy sectors show that the entrenched institutions of the Danish welfare state impede any radical departure from past practices and policies, particularly if they involve targeted cuts in budgets or programs. However, these institutional dynamics could not prevent a crisis if institutional rigidity also inhibited any necessary changes in response to internal and external political and economic pressures. Thus, institutional dynamics must allow for some capacity for steering and adaptation. Contrary to what is often claimed, the norms embodied in the institutions of Danish corporatism generate precisely this kind of adaptive capacity. The collectivist democratic norms embedded in Danish corporatism have proved durable enough to maintain some degree of solidaristic support for welfare provisions and the acceptance of some sacrifices if privileged professional groups as well as clients perceive them as fair. While the adaptations of policies and programs are not dramatic, their effect has been sufficient to sustain the welfare state in Denmark.

But institutional dynamics provide only a partial explanation for the absence of crisis. Popular support – as the principal-agent version of public choice crisis theories suggests – is another critical factor. As Goul Andersen's chapter shows, the Danes generally like their welfare state. For the modern Dane – or perhaps more accurately, the modern Danish family – the welfare state and its institutions have become necessary and integral parts of their day-to-day existence. There is little support for fundamental changes in the present, familiar welfare system. At the same time, Danes willingly accepted cutbacks in welfare spending when these were understood to be unavoidable in a period of fiscal crisis. Thus, the Danish political economy is embedded in a moral economy: the norms of solidarity can be invoked and utilized by policy makers in the service of public policy, in particular if policy makers can invoke a crisis consciousness (Petersen et al., 1987, 1994; Goul Andersen, 1994).

Even though the dominant "normative bounds" of the moral economy are "enforced by institutional and/or spontaneous collective intervention that overrides what self-interest and market power alone would dictate" (Svensson, 1989, 3), these very same institutions simultaneously shape the interests and strategies of welfare state producers and consumers by providing incentives for rent seeking, opportunism, and exploitation of the institutions which have granted them a privileged position in the management of the welfare state in the first place. This explains the presence of continuous problems of governability. Although the policy makers are capable of some steering and adaptation, the chapters demonstrate that administrative reform and redistribution are hard to execute and that the prospects for improving public sector efficiency or making major changes in policies and priorities are difficult at best.

Ironically, the Danish welfare state's capacity to adjust was enabled by some of the very structural features that rational choice theory argues contribute to the collapse of the welfare state. The multi-leveled corporatist structure of Danish politics and governance along with the widespread popular support of the welfare state have prevented major distributional changes like those in the U.S., Britain, New Zealand, and lately, parts of Canada. Interest groups, including public sector groups, are highly organized, well-represented through a wide range of corporatist fora, and in many ways more powerful than the minority political coalitions that typically make up the cabinet. To avoid repeals after a shift in power on election day, most significant reforms are negotiated with, or tacitly approved by, organized groups involved in their implementation and usually passed by large parliamentary majorities. According to public choice theory, this should lead to a disastrous deadlock. However, when organized interests must trade off long-term institutional power to achieve short-term budgetary gains, they choose the former over the latter. This situation tends to occur in times of budgetary scarcity and when institutional privileges themselves become politicized. Politicization and the chance of a repeal of their privileges help to focus the attention of institutional actors on their fundamental goals (Dunleavy, 1980).

The privileged position of organized interests and the autonomy of local governments became objects of political debate in the 1980s. In that context, both were willing to make economic sacrifices in order to maintain their institutional privileges. Thus the recurrent negotiations among central state bureaucrats, local politicians and their interest organizations, and strong professional organizations became a key arena for national policy makers to pursue their goals of budgetary restraint and increased public sector productivity. In times of scarcity and perceived crisis, the local flexibility and adaptiveness of the Danish welfare state increased because norms reinforced the desirability of a negotiated outcome and prior practice permitted one. Although a dominant feature of Danish policy making, the terms and effectiveness of "negotiated adaptation" vary across time and policy sectors. Politics change the terms of the game.

The Danish puzzles

The analyses presented in this volume take these theories of welfare state crisis as their point of departure and critique them. They demonstrate that generic theories of welfare state crisis – whether based on international competitive pressures accentuated by the liberalization of trade and capital flows, EU convergence criteria and other supranational demands, immanent fiscal crisis tendencies, or ebbing political support and polarization – cannot account for the Danish case. However, the chapters also suggest that the Danish welfare state has survived *despite* policy failures, the prevalence of incremental change rather than effective reform, and, most significantly, until recently continuing high broad unemployment.

Each chapter identifies various political-institutional capacities for adaptation. They emerge from both popular and institutional norms as well as from a number of structural characteristics of the Danish polity, including localization of public consumption production and financing, public sector corporatism, and weak minority coalition governments. We use the term "negotiated adaptation" to denote these capacities and indicate that these changes were not the product of ineluctable structural forces, but rather resulted from the interactive bargaining of various political actors. In the 1980s and 1990s, "negotiated adaptation" permitted politically acceptable, most often incremental, but occasionally more radical changes in the welfare system that allowed the system to regain its economic and fiscal viability despite unresolved problems and challenges.

The chapters address our two general quandaries about the absence of crisis despite the persistence of governability problems. From different theoretical perspectives, analyzing various levels and sectors of government, utilizing different concepts and methodologies, each study gives partial answers to these questions. Taken together, however, they not only analyze aspects of the Danish welfare state and its shortcomings previously inaccessible to a broader international audience, but they also indicate that to grasp and explain the problems of highly institutionalized contemporary welfare states we must investigate a range of sectors and levels of government in more detail and apply different methods of inquiry. Much of the existing literature on welfare state crisis emphasizes macrodynamics and micromotives, but fails to analyze how these dynamics are connected and mediated by intermediate institutions, particularly within the state.

The Chapters

The book is structured so that the chapters move from the general to the specific, and so that each chapter leaves an unanswered question picked up by the subsequent chapters. We begin with a broad picture of the macroeconomic constraints facing the Danish welfare state, particularly those expressed in fundamental tradeoffs between inflation and employment and in the 1980s between trade and fiscal deficits. Nannested and Green-Pedersen's contribution on macroeconomic constraints is balanced by Goul Andersen's analysis of popular support for and the legitimacy of the welfare state. Subsequent chapters consider the ways in which those economic and political constraints are translated politically into budget constraints, into decisions about transfer and social service expenditures, into state-local negotiations over local fiscal behavior, and into adaptation in labor market policy. The last two chapters look at specific welfare sectors, showing the connections between the behavior of professionalized public sector organizations and macroeconomic and budgetary choices. Dynamics at the lower levels sharply constrain what is possible at the higher levels, yet pressures emanating from the top because of tough macroeconomic and political choices also shape the options available at lower levels.

Peter Nannestad and Christoffer Green-Pedersen's chapter shows that politics did matter for macroeconomic policy. In 1982, the new Conservative-led coalition government moved decisively away from the existing policy mix of inflation, devaluation, and high interest rates. Instead it subjected the Danish economy to the fiscally conservative, market-oriented German economic policy by pegging the Danish Krone to the German Mark. The coalition rejected demand-stimulating policies in favor of a policy emphasizing supply side measures. When unemployment fell and budgets moved into surplus in the mid-1980s, the fiscal policy became less coherent and somewhat laxer, but the government never abandoned its commitment to the fixed exchange rate and low interest rates. Also the social democratic-led governments in the 1990s stuck to this goal, and they managed to lower unemployment without creating other macroeconomic imbalances during the economic upturn in the late 1990s. Although international economic pressures and later EU convergence criteria provided strong incentives to maintain this economic policy, this was a deliberate policy choice on the part of successive Danish governments, rather than an automatic result of policies imposed by external actors or conditions. Other countries chose differently: neighboring Sweden, also a small state with a small open economy, decided not to accommodate these international pressures. EU members like Italy, Great Britain, Spain and Portugal also resisted, even though they must have known that the financial markets might subsequently punish them ruthlessly because of their lenient fiscal policy – as they did in 1992.

Nannestad and Green-Pedersen highlight three macroeconomic policy issues, which are examined in subsequent chapters. First, despite the tight fiscal policy, the welfare state was not rolled back. Rather than subordinating welfare state policy to economic policy, successive coalition governments used economic policy as a means to preserve welfare state policies that enjoy nearly universal support. As Jørgen Goul Andersen's chapter shows, this policy was not only the most popular one, but also the easiest choice for Danish policy makers. The second issue in Nannestad and Green-Pedersen's analysis is labor market and income policy. While the Conservative-led coalition's policy of "politics according to markets" led it to abandon further economic equalization, this paradoxically did not lead to increasing income inequality. The largely unsuccessful income policy of the seventies was abandoned, but even though rigidities in the labor market were – and still are – widespread, the government launched few targeted initiatives to reduce unemployment. Per Jensen picks up the labor market theme in a subsequent chapter and analyzes the incentives of Danish labor market policy in more detail. The third thread identified by Nannestad/Green-Pedersen is the implication that tight fiscal policy requires control over public expenditures (and/or public revenues). Peter Munk Christiansen's chapter analyzes the extent to which budgetary constraints were translated into cuts in welfare state programs.

Why didn't Danish politicians try to dismantle the welfare state? Jørgen Goul Andersen's chapter shows that macroeconomic policy making remains constrained by widespread popular support for the welfare state. Elected officials have little to gain and much to lose from attacking the welfare state. Goul Andersen's data shows that assertions of dwindling welfare state legitimacy and growing polarization between employed and unemployed find little support in the Danish case. Negligible differences in welfare state attitudes divide the privately and publicly employed or supported. Only the young show signs of increasing polarization between insiders and outsiders. With two thirds of the population receiving their main source of income from the state (either through transfer payments or public sector employment), and the remaining third receiving substantial, concentrated benefits for prolonged periods during some part of their life cycle, any tinkering with the basic building blocks of the welfare state will affect almost every voter at some point. Does this mean that Danes suffer from fiscal illusion? Despite a healthy vigilance against fraud, corruption, and perceived bureaucratic inefficiencies, Danes not only want to spend the same or even more on education, elder care, and health care; the vast majority are also willing to pay the taxes to finance all this.

Goul Andersen's study indicates that the polarization predicted by public choice theory is swamped by the pro-welfarist attitudes generated by life in the system. Danish welfare policies and institutions may provide short-term incentives for self-interested behavior. But these policies and institutions also mold people's social and life experiences. Shared experiences in school, on the labor market, in hospitals and day care all help forge a shared identity and identification with these institutions (cf. Wildavsky, 1987; Pierson, 1993). These shared experiences and identification with welfare state institutions contribute to a moral economy "constrained by values and traditions" that shape the interaction between the political elites and subordinate groups (Svensson, 1989, 12). Goul Andersen suggests that with two thirds of the population receiving their income from the public sector, the policy positions derived from self-interest and solidarity have become indistinguishable. In addition, most people have organized their family and work life in a way that takes an extensive and generous welfare state for granted. The pro-welfare state attitudes of the Danish electorate definitely constrain the politicians' behavior.

If the welfare state is popular and pervasive, why do Danes work, and how does the welfare state structure the nature of the labor market? Per Jensen argues that the welfare state structures the labor market in three ways. First, the public sector is large, and the public sector workforce is predominantly female: approximately one third of the labor force and half of all working women are public employees. The public sector's rapid expansion into "reproductive" activities – health care, child care, social work, etc. – shifted women's work from the unpaid informal economy to the formal paid economy. Thus female labor force participation rose rapidly, as did the number of women with children in the labor market, and the percentage of women engaged in full-time employment outside the home.

Second, the welfare state dramatically restructures incentives affecting the demand and supply of labor through generous income maintenance programs, including early retirement schemes, unemployment benefits, and paid leave. Neo-classical economics would predict that the expansion of labor market exit options through early retirement schemes and high and easily obtained unemployment benefits should have produced inflationary pressures. But in Denmark, the correlation between inflation and labor market policies is spurious: high benefits have reduced wage dispersion without causing a general upward drift in nominal wages.

Third, the welfare state's need for high levels of taxation and the composition of these taxes also affect the demand and supply of labor. Again, neoclassical economics would suggest that high taxes and generous unemployment insurance would spill over into moonlighting and under-the-table employment and into either a diminished supply or demand for labor. But again, empirical evidence does not support the prevailing wisdom. While Denmark has quite generous unemployment insurance, labor law also permits firms to hire and fire easily. Therefore, Danish workers as well as employers defy, respectively, economic disincentives to work and not to hire workers.

If most people of working age work, the state can collect taxes to pay for those who don't. But even if it collects those taxes, can it allocate them in a reasonably rational way and also prevent itself from spending too much? Peter Munk Christiansen's chapter on the manageability of the welfare state shows that budget restraint was achieved without implementing tough budgetary decisions. Christiansen's thesis about differential capacities to control spending at different levels of government explains why the Conservative-led coalition governments from 1982 to 1993 succeeded in controlling budgetary growth while failing to make good on campaign promises of targeted cuts in the public sector. The Social Democratic governments of the 1990s replicated this story. At the micro or organizational level, the government failed to improve public service efficiency, as the sectoral chapters show. For the Danish public service sector, second in size only to Sweden's, (improved) efficiency has become an essential concern. However, professional autonomy, public sector corporatism, lack of competition, the complexity of most public services, and other characteristics of service delivery make it almost impossible for politicians to control efficiency at the organizational level. Public choice theory would also predict a limited capacity to change priorities at the meso-level – i.e., across sectors and programs – because the asymmetrical distribution of benefits and costs and disparities in the capacity of various affected interests to organize produces fierce resistance to reallocation of appropriations. While scarcity requires a government to develop the capacity to control appropriations, the dynamics of interest representation by and large only permit incremental cuts in programs and across the board reductions according to Wildavsky's "fair share" principle (Wildavsky, 1987). Not surprisingly, sectors in which producers are weaker and less professionalized received the deepest cuts. The capacity to control public expenditures at the macro level is not constrained to the same degree. As long as policy makers make equal cuts while avoiding redistributional battles among public sector unions and their political advocates, even minority coalition governments have been able to reduce the growth rate of public expenditures. Negotiations based on shared sacrifice allowed the central government to keep public sector spending at a constant percentage of GDP between 1982 and 1999.

This aggregate picture of restraint conceals a major theoretical puzzle for public choice theory. During the decade from 1982 to 1992, transfer payments grew at a much greater rate than programmatic expenditures. As public choice theory would predict, elected officials, experiencing temporary relief from budgetary exigencies in the mid-1980s could not resist the temptation to buy votes with further spending. But public choice theory suggests that professional service providers are even better positioned to escape cuts and bolster budgets compared with the larger, more diffuse and relatively unorganized interests of transfer payment recipients. Apparently it was easier for politicians to control service providers than to control themselves. Why?

This unexpected pattern of expenditure growth reminds us that, institutions notwithstanding, budgetary politics is a political game. Second, it directs out attention to the possible economic, political and institutional changes that facilitated control of service providers' demands during the 1980s. Christiansen points to the institutional linkages between the central state and local governments that provide the lion's share of social services. Institutionalized annual budget negotiations between central state officials and local government associations date back to the late 1970s. The importance of these negotiations increased throughout the 1980s due to institutional innovations in response to economic and political pressures. Their tenor also shifted as the central government dedicated itself to expenditure control, and local governments confronted resource scarcity without the possibility of a central government bailout. Despite the comparatively high degree of local autonomy, the kind of embedded state corporatist negotiations between representatives of the central state and those of the association of local governments allowed for successful budgetary adaptation to control expenditures without major programmatic cuts. This success, it should also be noted, also depended on convergent preferences for budgetary constraint shared by central and local officials.

Christiansen's discussion of control capacity raises three issues that are examined in subsequent chapters. First, the increase in transfer payments and cash benefits invites further inspection of the composition and causes of growth. Ploug and Kvist partly explain growth by pointing to changing demographics and business cycle trends, as well as policy. Second, the macro-level capacity to keep public expenditures from spiraling upwards was to a considerable extent the result of successful intergovernmental negotiations. Mouritzen investigates the links between local and central government. His discussion of macroeconomic management reinforces Christiansen's conclusions. He explores a number of other issues related to local autonomy that help fill in the picture of change at the local level.

The third issue arising from Christiansen's chapter involves the persistent problems of public sector efficiency and the difficulties encountered in trying to change the relative priority of various service sectors. This aspect also reinforces the precarious and political nature of the success of negotiated adaptation. The system has demonstrated only a modest capacity to prevent uncontrolled budget growth. Two sector-based chapters – Pallesen and Pedersen's dealing with the health care system and Bejer Damgaard's on day care – identify many of the critical institutional constraints that operate on different levels in different policy sectors. These factors contribute to the limited capacity of central state authorities to introduce greater manageability into the system.

Niels Ploug and Jon Kvist discuss the organization, provision and financing of various social transfer payment schemes. Although some programs have been modified, the basic contours of the Danish cash benefit system remain relatively unchanged. Much as public choice theory predicts, controlling the growth of transfer payments to individuals is difficult at best. Once granted, benefits come to be seen as established rights. Over the decade from 1982 to 1992, the Danish government increased unemployment benefits by 10 pct., expanded child allowances to all families regardless of income, expanded access to parental leave, increased government grants to students by 30 pct., and in the early 1990s introduced paid work leave.

Ploug and Kvist show that the Danish system conforms to the generic Scandinavian model of universal, flat rate, tax-financed social transfers (Esping-Andersen & Korpi, 1984; Esping-Andersen, 1990; Baldwin, 1990). They also explore the implications of recent reforms. The expansion of means testing, supplementary labor market pensions and compulsory social security contributions in combination with changes in the social policy discourse may indicate a slow, but perceptible shift in the principles guiding Danish welfare provision. Ploug and Kvist echo concerns voiced in the international literature on transfers by noting that current fiscal stress will only be exacerbated by continuing high levels of unemployment and an aging population. This may necessitate some rethinking or reinvention of the Danish welfare state. The creation of some new programs and the contraction of other existing programs during the 1980s and 1990s have not produced major changes in the main structure of the Danish welfare state (cf. also Nannestad and Green-Pedersen). One in four persons of working age receives his or her main income from cash benefits or publicly subsidized job programs.

The Nordic countries, more than other OECD countries, rely on local authorities to implement welfare policies. The expansion of the Scandinavian welfare states coincided with the municipalization of public spending, suggesting that it may be more appropriate to refer to these countries as "welfare municipalities" rather than welfare states. With more than half of all public expenditures and three quarters of public employees connected with local government, the problems of the welfare state have become the problems of the local state – and vice versa.

Poul Erik Mouritzen asks whether the broad formal autonomy granted to local governments after the comprehensive reforms that consolidated local governments in 1970 resulted in greater variation in services and taxes across municipalities and counties. Most of the variation in taxes, budget composition, and service provision are largely explained by "objective" factors such as fiscal stress, the wealth of the community, the composition of needs among residents, and related socioeconomic conditions. Partisan politics appear to matter only in times of abundance and in more weakly organized, politically insignificant policy areas. This means that citizens can choose between different welfare mixes by "voting with their feet," thus putting competitive pressure on local governments. But once an individual or family has chosen a place of residence, there is little room to influence the mix by casting their voting at the ballots.

What happened when this local autonomy was challenged by a center seeking fiscal restraint? Mouritzen concurs with Christiansen's finding that annual negotiations have turned into an important element in the center's fiscal control capacity. This conflicted somewhat with norms supporting local autonomy and flexibility to respond to shifting local demands. But the center found ways to make its increased control more palatable by shifting from specific per capita grants and reimbursement for services to block grants that allowed local governments greater discretionary authority. The central government also added credibility to its threats against overspending by punishing profligate localities with grant reductions. This allowed central policy makers to reduce aggregate state subsidies without formally infringing on the widely endorsed norm of local autonomy. Local officials, fearing reductions, had a strong incentive to comply with central government demands. While local politicians could not make delivery systems more efficient, they could use the central state's budget pressure to lengthen voters' short-term outlook and to contain producer demands for larger budgets. By shifting the blame to the central state, local officials could execute their own policy preferences, play hardball with the professional unions of state employees while reducing the political costs of these actions. This outcome does not appear to have been reproduced elsewhere. For example, U.S. states responded to federal budget cuts by increasing their own spending (see also Lotz, 1990).

In 2007 the Danish system of local government once again underwent a major reform, among other things reducing the number of municipalities from 275 to 98 and the 14 counties into five regions. Mouritzen discusses the reform process, its rationale and results.

The two chapters prior to the conclusion pick up on Christiansen's discussion of the inability of public sector organizations to increase their own efficiency and responsiveness to user demands, as well as the difficulties in redistributing public expenditures across various sectors and activities. The chapters demonstrate why reforms are hard to implement. Public service institutions are deeply entrenched in a complex system of national rules and regulations, working norms set by national corporatist organizations, and local traditions of cooperation and negotiation among local officials and professional organizations representing service providers. Information asymmetries and preference intensities in combination with institutional privileges accorded resourceful groups give organized interests a strong voice in Danish policy formulation and implementation.

Consequently, the authors conclude, decentralizing spending authority in hospitals and strengthening the "exit" and "voice" options in day care institutions have had little effect on efficiency and responsiveness. Although public choice theory provides an adequate explanation for these outcomes, the chapters presented here show that even in highly institutionalized, corporatist, and professionalized welfare states, there is no inherent logic of continuously rising costs. At various points in the 1980s, depending on sector-specific circumstances, it was possible to contain costs and even, as Bejer Damgaard shows in the case of day care, to stem further productivity decline.

The power conferred on insiders by public sector corporatism does not necessarily preclude short-term economic sacrifice or budgetary restraint. While professional service producers seek economic gains – i.e., bigger budgets, higher wages, and improved working conditions – these are all predicated on the survival of their organizational and professional privileges. When politicization of an issue threatens both their future-oriented demands and their existing privileges, they are likely to back off their demands in order to retain their preferential access to the decision-making process, since this is in their long-term interests. Precisely because corporatism establishes iterative bargaining games as part of the decision-making routine, participants tend to develop longer time horizons with respect to their demands, and this also tends to make them attentive to the sources, rather than the fruits, of power. How did this work in specific policy sectors?

Thomas Pallesen and Lars Dahl Pedersen attack two prevailing myths about Danish health care. Danish health care is neither the "best socialized system" in the world, nor the "cheapest." With its mix of privately and publicly financed and organized services, the Danish health care system is only partially socialized. It is difficult to establish empirically that it is superior in quality to the health care systems of other advanced welfare states.

The bulk of their chapter focuses on the cost myth. Despite methodological problems in generating comparable statistics for Denmark and four other European states (Germany, the Netherlands, Sweden and Britain), they do find a general pattern in cost containment efforts. Costs, particularly hospital costs, were roughly comparable in all five countries. Each country, but especially Denmark, succeeded in slowing the rate of growth in costs in the 1980s. Hence political priorities can overcome the upward expenditure pressures of technological advances generating demand for new equipment and new procedures, increasingly sophisticated consumers, and bureaucratic politics. But this political dominance comes with its own cost: the countries that succeeded in reducing costs also saw higher reductions in output. The price for successful cost containment in the health care system seems to be a drop in productivity. According to some measures, this decline was more dramatic in Denmark than in the other four countries. Thus Denmark is unlikely to have the least expensive health care system, especially if efficiency and quality of care are taken into consideration.

Denmark differs on two other counts. First, very few reform efforts have succeeded. Despite the formal freedom to experiment, few serious attempts were made to alter the prevailing public integrated hospital services model. As in other sectors, it is difficult to reorganize without the consent and participation of professional organizations. Even when they are excluded from policy formulation, these groups can derail a reform at the street level, i.e., during implementation. This points to a second difference: more so than in other countries, Danish professional groups, especially physicians and certified nurses, have expanded their turf and increased employment at the expense of other employee groups. The increasing professionalization of Danish health care, unmatched in any of the other four countries, may have improved the quality of care. But it also demonstrates that adaptation to changing circumstances at the organizational level is a distributional battle between strongly organized groups defending their privileges. Furthermore, during the 1980s, nurses expanded their organizational privileges to include a kind of corporatist representation in the executive management committees of hospitals. Thus, in the health care sector, it has been much harder to increase productivity and make institutional reforms than to contain total costs. As described in Mouritzen's chapter in the 2007 local government reform the 14 Danish counties were amalgamated into five regions whose main responsibility is health care. Contrary to their predecessors, the new regions do not have the right to levy taxes. At the moment it is unclear how this will affect costs in the health care sector.

Jens Bejer Damgaard presents an analysis of the multilayered public sector corporatist system that governs the day care sector. The array of institutional actors resembles the health care sector, particularly in their ability to forestall reforms that would increase managerial discretion to implement reforms to increase efficiency and productivity. Using a public choice theory framework,

Bejer Damgaard demonstrates how the day care professionals' union uses its access to multiple "veto points" to its advantage as it participates in simultaneous bargaining games at different levels of the system. Unions bargain with the Local Governments Denmark (LGDK) concerning working conditions, productivity norms, and salary; unions and the LGDK meanwhile lobby Parliament concerning national regulations; local authorities regulate their day care sectors; and negotiations between local bureaucrats, elected officials, union representatives, and to some extent users, all add to the national agreements about the provision of day care. In this context, administrative reforms intended to decentralize budgetary responsibility and (even if only marginally) to strengthen voice and exit options for users, produced little change.

Bejer Damgaard's chapter offers important evidence bearing on the normative and positive theories of institutions. Although normative transaction cost theory suggests that introducing competition in the day care sector would produce efficiency gains, the theories fail to predict or explain what happens in the real world. Despite inefficiencies in the current arrangements, the hierarchical, corporatist governance structure in Danish day care gives none of the relevant actors incentives to change the status quo. Given the existing range of options, parents seem quite content with the public day care system. Day care professionals have strong incentives to defend their collective bargaining gains. Local politicians sensibly ignore diffuse voter preferences and acquiesce to the demands expressed by professionals and parents. Local bureaucrats, caught between politicians, unions, and parents, see no reason to upset any of their principals. Politically, the status quo constitutes a plus-sum game for all relevant actors even if suboptimality prevails economically. Hence Bejer Damgaard demonstrates that an analysis of focusing on how institutions and incentive structures influence actor preferences and power is more effective in explaining political outcomes than are normative theories of institutions.

Combined, the chapters demonstrate major anomalies in contemporary welfare state crisis theories. The Danish welfare state provides a crucial case for examining the empirical evidence needed to confirm the crisis literature's claims. The absence of a systemic crisis suggests that a revision of the current prevailing wisdom is needed. First, we must consider the social relations that have shaped the emergence and development of political institutions and that continue to influence – and in turn are influenced by – the dynamics described by public choice theory. This approach allows us to observe the interaction of organizational and electoral politics in determining the fate of the modern welfare state. Second, comparative studies based on aggregate measures at the systemic level must be supplemented by more detailed, in-depth explorations of individual welfare states. As the analyses presented here clearly demonstrate, the explanation for why the Danish welfare state has survived cannot be captured by statistics alone, and neither by examining only economic and labor market policy. The welfare state is comprised of a wide range of interdependent policies and programs benefiting individuals and families at different times in their lives and as a function of their personal circumstances. Thus we need to weave together a wide range of policy arenas and institutional perspectives to understand the welfare state's durability as well as its vulnerabilities. Explanations that remain only at the level of national politics and political structures miss one of the most important dynamics of the Danish welfare state: the relations between the central and local governments. Similarly an approach that compares inputs (demands and supports) to outputs (policies, programs, and expenditures) can never capture the process of adaptation and the structural opportunities that make bargaining among various actors and interests possible.

Such an ambitious enterprise required a team of researchers open to a variety of analytical perspectives. We were fortunate to engage many of the foremost researchers on Danish politics and public policy in this project. By capturing the central findings in their particular fields of research and casting them into the context of our two central puzzles, each author has contributed a vital element to a more holistic treatment of a single case. While there are several valuable studies of the Swedish and Norwegian cases available to an English language readership, few serious political analyses of the recent dynamics of the Danish welfare state are available in English. Thus we hope to make a contribution to the broader debate about the developmental tendencies of social democratic welfare states and at the same time offer a fairly comprehensive examination of the major policy elements that comprise the Danish case. The result is a volume that covers many policy areas and several levels of the institutional structure of the welfare state and its relationship to Danish society. Taken together the chapters reveal many important aspects of the policy system that both impede and, in some important instances, enable actors to negotiate adaptations that redefine incentive structures without destabilizing the overall organization and structure of the welfare state. Whether this approach to innovation and change will be adequate to sustain the Danish welfare state in the years to come remains to be seen. But at least so far, the system has proved its capacity to find relatively stable compromises that addressed some if not all of the challenges it faced. Institutionalized negotiations have prevented radical restructuring and held back major improvements in efficiency, but they have also provided an arena for aggregating interests to control budgets and address the critical fiscal problem of deficit spending. Seen from a comparative perspective, this is no small feat and is one that is worthy of greater attention from the international scholarly community.

References

Alber, Jens (1988). "Continuities and Changes in the Idea of the Welfare State." *Politics and Society* 16, 4: 451-468.

Baldwin, Peter (1990). *The Politics of Social Solidarity*. Cambridge: Cambridge University Press.

Bell, Daniel (1978). *The Cultural Contradictions of Capitalism*. New York: Basic Books.

Brittan, Samuel (1975). *Participation without politics: an analysis of the nature and the role of markets*. London: Institute of Economic Affairs.

Christiansen, Peter Munk (1990). "Udgiftspolitikken i 1980'erne: Fra asymmetri til asymmetrisk tilpasning." *Politica* 4: 442-456.

Dunleavy, Patrick (1980). *Urban Political Analysis: The Politics of Collective Consumption*. London: Macmillan.

Esping-Andersen, Gøsta (1985). *Politics against Markets: The Social Democratic Road to Power*. Princeton: Princeton University Press.

Esping-Andersen, Gøsta (1990). *The Three Worlds of Welfare Capitalism*. Princeton: Princeton University Press.

Esping-Andersen, Gøsta & Walter Korpi (1984). "Social Policy as Class Politics in Post-War Capitalism: Scandinavia, Austria, and Germany," in John Goldthorpe (ed.), *Order and Conflict in Contemporary Capitalism*. Oxford: Clarendon Press, pp. 179-208.

Goul Andersen, Jørgen (1994). "Samfundsøkonomi, interesser og politisk adfærd," in Eggert Petersen et al. (eds.), *Livskvalitet og holdninger i det variable niche-samfund*. Århus: Department of Psychology and Aarhus University Press, pp. 15-136.

Iversen, Torben (1999). *Contested Economic Institutions: The Politics of Macroeconomics and Wage Bargaining in Advanced Democracies*. Cambridge: Cambridge University Press.

Keohane, Robert & Helen Milner (eds.) (1996). *Internationalization and Domestic Politics*. New York: Cambridge University Press.

Kitschelt, Herbert (1994). *The Transformation of European Social Democracy*. Cambridge: Cambridge University Press.

Kristensen, Ole P. (1987). *Væksten i den offentlige sektor. Institutioner og politik*. Copenhagen: Jurist- og Økonomforbundets Forlag.

Leibfried, Stephan & Paul Pierson (1995), "Multi-Tiered Institutions and the Making of Social Policy," in Stephan Leibfried & Paul Pierson (eds.), *European Social Policy*. Washington, D.C.: Brookings Institution Press, pp. 1-40.

Lotz, Jørgen (1990). "Controlling Local Government Expenditures: The Experience of Five European Countries," in Rémy Prod'homme (ed.), *Public Finance with Several Levels of Government*. Brussels: Proceedings of the 46th Congress of the International Institute of Public Finance, pp. 249-262.

Mitchell, William & R.T. Simmons (1994). *Beyond Politics: Markets, Welfare, and the Failure of Bureaucracy*. Boulder: Westview Press.

Niskanen, William A. (1971). *Bureaucracy and Representative Government*. Chicago: Aldine, Atherton.

O'Connor, James (1973). *The Fiscal Crisis of the State*. New York: St. Martin's Press.

Offe, Claus (1984). *Contradictions of the Welfare State*. Cambridge: MIT Press.

Petersen, Eggert et al. (1987). *Danskernes tilværelse under krisen II: Studier i den politisk-psykologiske udvikling 1982 til 1986*. Århus: Aarhus University Press.

Petersen, Eggert et al. (1994). *Livskvalitet og holninger i det variable nichesamfund*. Århus: Department of Psychology, University of Aarhus.

Pierson, Paul (1993). "When Effect becomes Cause: 'Policy Feedback' and Political Chance." *World Politics* 45, 4: 595-628.

Piven, Frances Fox (ed.) (1991). *Labor Parties in Postindustrial Societies*. Cambridge, UK: Polity Press.

Pontusson, Jonas (1992). *The Limits of Social Democracy: Investment Politics in Sweden.* Ithaca: Cornell University Press.

Statistisk Tiårsoversigt (1994).

Swensson, Peter (1989). *Fair Shares: Unions, Pay, and Politics in Sweden and West Germany.* Ithaca, NY: Cornell UP.

Soskice, David and Peter Hall (eds.). *Varieties of Capitalism: The Institutional Foundations of Comparative Advantage.* Oxford University Press, 2001.

Wildavsky, Aaron (1987). "Choosing Preferences by Constructing Institutions: A Cultural Theory of Preference Formation." *American Political Science Review* 81: 3-21.

Wilensky, Harold L. (1984). "Leftism, Catholicis, and Democratic Corporatism: The Role of Political Parties in Recent Welfare State Development," in Peter Flora & Arnold J. Heidenheimer (eds.), *The Development of Welfare States in Europe and America.* New Brunswick: Transaction Publishers, pp. 345-382.

1   KEEPING THE BUMBLEBEE FLYING

Economic Policy in the Welfare State of Denmark, 1973-99

Peter Nannestad and Christoffer Green-Pedersen

Introduction

A recurring theme in the long-standing 'crisis of the welfare state' debate has been the question of the economic viability of this construction, not least its Nordic or Social Democratic subspecies, to which Denmark belongs (Esping-Andersen, 1990). In a rare display of consensus, critics from the right as well as from the left have argued that in the long run, the welfare state would ruin the economy, thus undermining its own material basis (Offe, 1984). The persistent economic troubles in Denmark during the 1980s and the near-collapse of the Swedish economy in 1993 may well have reinforced this point of view.

The case of the Danish welfare state challenges this consensus. While welfare state critics might draw additional confirmation of their skeptical view of the long-term compatibility between a developed welfare state and a stable economy, our inspection of Danish macroeconomic developments during the period from 1960 to 1982, along with subsequent economic developments makes such a view more difficult to sustain. Actually, developments during recent years directly contradict the well-established perspective of the welfare state critics.

In many important respects, the modern foundations of today's Danish welfare state were created during a 'golden age' of high growth and low unemployment that began in the late 1950s. Long uninterrupted economic boom and rapidly growing wealth provided the material circumstances to support a series of comprehensive social reforms devised and implemented in such a way that various social services and institutions greatly expanded. But the Danish economy experienced only a brief period of overall macroeconomic balance (around 1960), when both unemployment and inflation rates were low, with the current account as well as the public budget in balance (Pedersen, 1994: 1). Apart from this short spell, the Danish economy was constantly troubled by macroeconomic imbalances until only recently. Table 1 provides a snapshot of the economic situation at four crucial points in time: 1971, prior to the commodity price shocks of the 1970s; 1982, when the era of Social Democratic governments ended and a decade of Conservative-led governments began; 1993, with the return of a Social Democratic government coalition, and 1999.

TABLE 1:

Indicators of macroeconomic imbalances 1971, 1982, 1993 and 1999

	Real GNP growth (pct.)	Unemployment (pct.)	Consumer price inflation (pct.)	Current account (pct. of GNP)	Saldo, public budget (pct. of GNP)	Public debt (pct. of GNP)
1971	2.7	1.6	5.8	-2.4	3.4	13
1982	3.0	9.8	10.1	-4.0	-9.1	59
1993	0.0	12.1	1.3	3.3	-2.9	66
1999	1.6	5.5	2.5	1.1	3	53

Source: OECD Economic Outlook no. 44 and 67; Statistisk Tiårsoversigt 1981, 1984, and 2000; Statistisk Årbog 1995; Statistiske Efterretninger, Offentlige finanser 2000:12.

Between 1971 and 1982, existing imbalances (inflation and the current account deficit) grew and new problems surfaced: unemployment, the budget deficit and public debt. By 1982, the Danish economy had slipped into a serious crisis, resembling in many respects the crisis that befell the Swedish economy a decade later. But, as we argue below, the Danish economic crisis of the 1970s was not the unavoidable consequence of a welfare state that overburdened the economy and stifled growth. Rather, it was the direct outcome of a series of economic policy failures. Inappropriate solutions to the adaptation problems facing the Danish economy in the wake of the two oil price crises in the 1970s were largely to blame.

This point of view is corroborated by subsequent economic developments. As can be seen from Table 1, a number of the imbalances that existed in 1982 had been redressed or defused by 1993. In the late 1990s, scholars began to discuss Denmark's economic 'miracle' (Schwartz, 2001; Hemerijck & Schludi, 2000). Furthermore, as will be shown below, this remarkable economic recovery was not brought about by rolling back or dismantling the welfare state. Once again, economic policies played a decisive role.

The chapter presents a straightforward, narrative account of some main aspects of macroeconomic developments in Denmark during each of the sub-periods (1973-82, 1982-1993, and 1993-1999). We focus on the main economic strategy applied by successive governments facing changing economic situations, looking for possible relationships between policy outputs and policy outcomes. This provides part of the political background for the Danish welfare state's economic ups and downs since 1973.

The account is based on two implicit assumptions. First, we assume that economic policies may indeed have real impacts on the macroeconomy. This assumption obviously runs counter to the modern macroeconomic theory's assumption of policy inefficiency. It is well-known, however, that the policy inefficiency perspective is premised on rather restrictive assumptions. These include, among other things, complete and symmetric information and the absence of reaction lags due to overlapping contract periods, which are hardly adequate descriptions of reality. Second, we assume that although the Danish economy is small and open, its course is not entirely determined by international economic developments. While the international economy certainly constrains the choices open to national economic decision-makers, and conceivably increasingly so due to the growing integration and internationalization of financial markets, nevertheless some leeway for national choices remains. In fact, during the 1970s, Denmark managed to do considerably worse economically than comparable small, open economies like Austria and Sweden (Nannestad, 1991). During most of the 1980s, the Danish macroeconomic trends were in important respects out of phase with international economic trends. Finally, in the last half of the 1990s when the Danish economy experienced a remarkable recovery, many other countries struggled with slow growth and high unemployment.

To the brink of the abyss ... : Social democratic economic policy 1973-82

OVERALL DEVELOPMENT

With the wisdom of hindsight, an account of Danish economic policy in the aftermath of the first and the second oil crises must be judged a prolonged story of failures or near-failures. A casual inspection of the main conventional indicators of economic performance (i.e., outcomes; see figure 1) supports this assessment. With respect to policy outputs, 'too little, too late' would probably be the most fitting description. Thus from the outset, the Danish experience during this period would seem to contradict Katzenstein's thesis that small, open countries adapted more easily to the economic shocks of the period than did larger countries (Katzenstein, 1985).

The pattern of growth in the Danish economy, as shown in Figure 1, exhibits some fluctuations around a computed stable growth line for the whole period 1971-93. The impacts of the two oil price shocks in 1973-74 and in 1979-80 are clearly visible in economic growth performance. Apparently the negative impact of the first oil price shock in 1973-74 was overcome more rapidly than the subsequent shock of 1979-80. Two years after the first oil price shock, the GNP growth rate returned to the average level or somewhat above average. In contrast, following the second oil price shock, economic growth did not return to its average level within a three year period.

Developments in the Danish unemployment rate also mirror the impact of the period's two external shocks. From a level below 2 pct. prior to 1974, unemployment skyrocketed to a level around 6 to 7 pct. after the first oil price shock. With the second oil price shock, unemployment took still another upward leap to a new level of 9 to 10 pct. Thus unemployment exhibited an ominous, cumulative tendency: it rose with every external shock, never reverting to previous levels in the interval between the shocks.

The impact of the two oil crises on consumer prices can also clearly be seen in Figure 1. The immediate inflationary impact was reinforced by the automatic cost-of-living (CoL) indexation of wages. These changes occurred with only a short delay and coverage was broad. The impact of the first oil price shock was considerably stronger though than that of the second. One possible explanation is that incomes policies became more restrictive in the time between the two shocks, and the CoL indexation coverage was reduced. Consequently, the price-income spiral gained less momentum after the second oil price shock. Unemployment was considerably higher at the time of the second oil price shock. The sudden drop in the inflation rate during the first quarter of 1976 was 'artificial', however, in the sense that it mainly reflected a temporary reduction in the VAT rate.

FIGURE 1.

Main economic indicators, quarterly data, 1971-1982

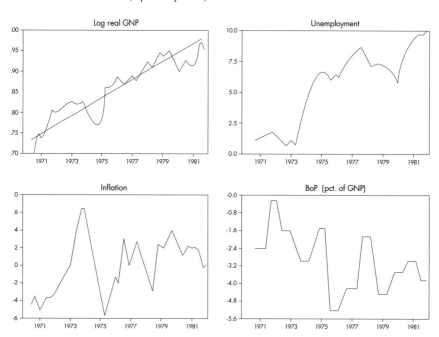

Source: OECD Historical statistics.

CRISIS, MIRACLES, AND BEYOND

Taken together, the patterns of unemployment and inflation suggest stagflationary tendencies in the Danish economy from 1975 onwards, not the classical Phillips curve relationship between unemployment and inflation (cf. Fig. 2). By 1975, inflationary expectations appear to have changed quite dramatically.

The current account of the balance of payments, finally, was in the red for the whole period, with a marked tendency to deteriorate over time. The deficit reached its maximum in 1976 (in the vicinity of 5 pct. of GNP). This was largely the result of a political attempt to improve employment by stimulating domestic demand through Keynesian fiscal policy.

Obviously the overall tendencies in the main economic aggregate indicators in Denmark during the period from 1971 to 1982 resemble those that can be detected in many other Western economies. All had to cope with the direct impact of the oil price shocks and the ensuing recessive tendencies in the world economy. Most faced the danger of stagflation. Nevertheless, especially when compared to other small, open economies, like the other Nordic countries or Austria (Scharpf, 1987; Nannestad, 1991), Danish economic policy did a remarkably poor job in dealing with the economic disturbances and challenges of the period. The poor performance of the Danish economy did not have exclusively external causes (Hoffmeyer, 1993: 75). Inadequate domestic economic policy responses and outright policy failures played their part, too.

FIGURE 2.
Relationship between annual rates of unemployment and inflation (CoL) 1971-1982

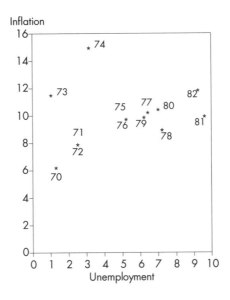

Source: OECD Historical statistics.

Between 1974 and 1982, the main economic strategy of the government went through three distinct phases. Both the interpretation of the economic situation and the evaluation of the effectiveness of various policy instruments had to be revised several times. From 1974 to 1976, the government followed a conventional Keynesian stop-go policy; from 1976 to 1979, policy makers attempted to enact a combination of 'demand twist' and incomes policy; during the period from 1979 to 1982, they used a 'braking strategy' based primarily on strategic devaluations, tight incomes policy and tight fiscal policy, although this policy was not pursued consistently. Table 1 in the Appendix provides an overview of major economic policy measures enacted during the period 1974-82. Two trends stand out. First, economic policy became more comprehensive over time as a broadening range of instruments were applied. In the second place, some of the policies also were more forcefully applied.

1974-76: (Keynesian) politics as usual

Initially the recession following the first oil price shock 1973-74 was generally expected to be short, calling mainly for Keynesian counter-cyclical measures. Thus from 1974 to 1976, a stop-go type of fiscal policy was enacted. The first impact of the oil price shock was an increase in inflation, while the economy as a whole continued to boom. Fiscal policy was therefore tightened early in 1974. When, beginning by the middle of 1974, the employment effect became visible, the government turned to an expansive fiscal policy, primarily through the combined effect of a reduction in personal taxes in 1975 and a temporary reduction of the VAT-rate effective from September 1975 to February 1976. Policy makers hoped an international economic recovery would do the rest of the job after that.

At the same time, the government left the cost side of the economy largely unattended. From 1974 through 1976, nominal wages rose about 45 pct., far outrunning wage increases in other countries as well as domestic inflation. Trade unions and employers tried to wring compensation for the rising costs of energy from each other. A distributive struggle ensued, preventing strategic coordination and, as in any prisoners' dilemma, both sides lost relative to the cooperative solution. Furthermore, with the Danish krone tied to the Deutschmark in the European currency 'snake', the Danish currency appreciated by about 8 pct. in the same period. The combined effects on competitiveness of exploding wage rates and an appreciating currency was serious.

The international recovery never materialized. The government's expansive fiscal policy and near-total neglect of the cost side of the Danish economy resulted in a severe deterioration of Denmark's competitive situation which decimated the country's balance of payments in 1976, while unemployment continued to grow. The lesson was clear: if not supported by an effective incomes policy, the Danish unemployment problem could not be solved just by stimulating domestic demand, especially not while the dominant OECD-countries prioritized fighting inflation.

1976-79: 'Demand twist' and incomes policy

Given the results of economic policy during the previous two-year period, the economic strategy from 1976/77-79 necessarily had to focus on the balance of payments problem. In the first place, the strategy aimed at improving Denmark's competitive position by incomes policy measures which, if successful, would bring Danish wage developments more into line with foreign wage increases. In the second place, the policy was designed to curb import-heavy demand in favor of types of demand with lesser impacts on the balance of payments. In practice this demand twist strategy meant curbing private and expanding public consumption.

The main incomes policy initiatives normally came through statutory wage settlements that were imposed when the biennial negotiations of economy-wide wage contracts broke down – as they did regularly starting in 1975. The central aim was to bring down the rate of wage increases. It had to be done in a 'socially acceptable' way, however, with the greatest wage increases granted to the lowest paid. This put a heavy strain on the solidarity of higher-paid wage earners who had to refrain from attempting to restore previous wage differentials through wage drift. Solidarity rarely triumphed. The CoL-indexation of wages was also repeatedly reformed in various respects, but in all cases with an eye to reducing the coverage of wage-indexation.

As a whole, the incomes policy initiatives of this period were not very successful. The government never got away with bringing down wage increases below ca. 10 pct. per year (Hoffmeyer, 1993: 75), which was far above the targets publicly pronounced. These wage increases remained higher than wage increases in relevant countries abroad.

To a minor degree, the effects of the high wage increase rates in Denmark were mitigated by exchange rate policy. Beginning in 1976, the Danish krone was depreciated relative to the DM in several small steps. Between 1976 and September 1979, the krone was depreciated vis-à-vis the DM by 26 pct. (Hoffmeyer 1993, 74-75).

The demand twist policy apparently was quite successful in curbing private consumption, mainly through increased taxation. In 1977, 1978 and 1979, real private consumption expenditure grew at an average rate of only 1.1 pct. a year, compared to an average of 3 pct. during the three preceding years. In the same period, the tax burden rose from 41.7 pct. of GNP in 1976 to 44.7 pct. in 1979. Most of this increase came from indirect taxation. Real public consumption expenditures, on the other hand, grew by an average of 4.8 pct. per annum, compared to 3.3 pct. in the preceding three-year period. Employment in the public sector grew from 28.9 pct. of all wage earners in 1976 to 31.2 pct. in 1979. Thus, a shift in demand growth in favor of the public sector did in fact occur.

Taken together, the results of the economic strategy from 1976 to 1979 – a combination of incomes policies and demand twist policies – were not impressive. Opinions differ as to the real employment effects of the demand twist strategy, with estimates running from no net effect to a reduction of about 10 to 15,000 a year in registered unemployment (Nannestad, 1991). Actually, annual unemployment figures continued to increase until 1979, and the reduction that year was primarily due to an early retirement scheme that became effective on January 1, 1979. Despite the creeping depreciation of the krone, the competitive situation was not decisively redressed either. The balance of payments, while improving relative to the all-time low in 1976, stayed firmly in the red (cf. figure 1). As a consequence, aggregate foreign net debt kept increasing, too. In 1979, it amounted to about 22 pct. of GNP. Interest payments became a growing burden. For this reason, as the National Bank pointed out, "it was extremely dangerous to aim at a slow reduction of the balance of payments deficit" (Hoffmeyer 1993, 75).

Despite the tax increases that were part of the demand twist strategy, state budgets remained in deficit throughout the period. As a result, state sector domestic debt roughly doubled from 1976 to 1979, when it amounted to about 20 pct. of GNP (Pedersen, 1994: 36).

1979-82: Incomplete adjustment and the end of the Social Democratic era
The imbalances in the Danish economy had thus by no means been redressed, when the second oil price shock hit in 1979-80. Quite to the contrary: at the eve of the shock already the Danish economy seemed to be trapped in a situation characterized by low growth, high unemployment, high inflation and growing foreign debt (Hoffmeyer, 1993: 75). The second oil price shock aggravated these pre-existing problems.

The impacts are clearly visible in Figure 1. Unemployment shot up to a new level (ca. 10 pct.); inflation increased. Another serious deterioration in the balance of payments occurred, and real economic growth turned negative in both 1980 and 1981.

The most noteworthy element of Danish economic policy from 1979 to 1982 was an initial dramatic reduction in disposable real income that was successfully brought about in order to improve the competitive situation. Through a combination of repeated depreciations of the krone, combined with a tightening of incomes policies and fiscal policies in late 1979, real disposable income was forced down by 12 to 15 pct. per year, most strongly in 1980-81.

But after this remarkable achievement, fiscal policy was relaxed again in 1981, against stern warnings that it was much too early to stop the ongoing adjustment process. The government decided not to heed the advice. Instead of an unconditionally restrictive fiscal policy, they announced a two-pronged strategy: public expenditures that would further necessary structural adjustments of the Danish economy would be allowed to grow, while other types of public expenditures would have to be kept within a constant budgetary ceiling.

In practice this distinction never worked as intended. New, costly employment programs and other emergency measures were repeatedly introduced to slow down the growth in unemployment. The tax burden was kept approximately constant. As a consequence, the public sector budget deficit rose from 2 pct. of GNP in 1979 to 9 pct. in 1982. Inflation and the balance of payments also headed the wrong way.

INTERPRETATION

Several factors contributed to the unfortunate developments in the Danish economy following the oil price shocks. Some were beyond the control of the government; others were not. Here we shall concentrate on the domestic policy failures.

The Danish politico-economic malaise during the period from 1974 to 1982 was at heart the result of repeated failures to solve 'the Keynesian co-ordination problem' (Scharpf, 1987) properly. The oil price shocks of 1973/74 and 1978/79 exposed the Danish economy to a double shock. In the first place, they led to a drop in effective demand both at home and abroad, due to the vastly increased costs of oil products, thus threatening growth and employment. Simultaneously, there was a direct as well as indirect effect on price levels, threatening to fuel domestic inflation. Thus the central problem became how to avoid stagflation. If the government tried to combat unemployment by the usual Keynesian recipes, inflation might accelerate to levels making this policy unsustainable. Soon the economy would return to the previous level of unemployment, only with higher inflation rates.

The only way to escape from either horn of this dilemma would have been a close coordination of the economic strategy of the government, the wage strategy of the labor unions, and the price setting behavior of firms. This would require that the government could trust the unions to accept the welfare loss (temporarily) brought about by the oil price shocks, rather than trying to wring compensation from the employers. In addition, firms would have to restrict themselves in their prices to passing on only the actual increases in energy prices. If both these objectives could be secured, then the inflationary impacts of the oil price shocks could be insulated and would eventually dissipate. Then there would have been room for expansive measures to bolster employment, without the risk of fueling ongoing wage-price inflation. In the language of rational expectation economics, what was needed in order to keep the expectation-augmented Phillips-curve in place, or even haul it back towards the origin, was a credible commitment of the economic agents to behavior that would curtail the development of inflation. Such a strategic coordination was not entirely utopian: it was achieved, after some initial fumbling, in Austria (Scharpf, 1987; Nannestad, 1991).

Theoretically, the necessary coordination could have come about in two ways. It could have been the result of voluntary action by those involved, and it could have been enforced by the government. In practice, Denmark saw neither voluntary nor enforced strategic coordination. Why?

Seen from the perspective of the Danish labor unions, a voluntary coordination would have implied the acceptance of some kind of distributional consensus or at least distributional truce. Unlike their Austrian counterparts, however, Danish labor unions – by virtue of tradition, ideology and organization – lacked incentives to enter into a voluntary coordination of strategies with, primarily, the government.

Instead, the oil price shocks initially resulted in increasing wage pressures. In part, the wage pressure was generated automatically by the existing CoL indexation of wages. At the same time that Denmark lost, in effect, about 4 pct. of its GNP to the OPEC countries in 1973-74, the Danes compensated by allowing each other nominal wage increases in the vicinity of 20 pct. per year! The wage reaction to the second oil price shock was up to a point more appropriate, thanks to changes in the coverage of the CoL-regulation of wages, among other things. Nevertheless, yet another price-wage spiral was set in motion.

Conceivably, one incentive might have bought the consent of the unions to a more restrictive wage strategy. It was the enactment of a scheme for 'Economic Democracy', as demanded repeatedly by the unions in their negotiations with the government and the employers. The Social Democrats and the Danish trade union federation (LO) had put an 'economic democracy' proposal on the political agenda in 1972. Its main element was a centralized wage earner fund to which employers would contribute. The funds would be under trade union control and re-invested in business as risk-bearing capital.

Politically, the idea was stillborn. In parliament, the Social Democrats found themselves totally isolated on the issue. All other parties, both left and right of the Social Democrats, denounced the idea, albeit for somewhat different reasons. Judging from public opinion polls, popular backing for the scheme was lacking as well. In fact, opposition at the mass level was strong, especially toward the idea of the central, trade union-controlled wage earner fund – the very heart of the whole plan (Buksti et al. 1978: 3-10). Thus even if the government could have gained the voluntary strategic cooperation of the trade unions in return for economic democracy, neither the public nor the parliament was inclined to support the trade-off.

An enforced coordination of strategies, on the other hand, would have required that the government impose and maintain very tight wage controls. The main problem with this solution was that it would have been politically very costly for the Social Democrats. The party would have almost certainly been flung into internecine conflict with the trade unions. Even the half-hearted incomes policy measures actually taken were sufficient to put a heavy strain on the relationship between the Social Democrats and the trade union movement. Most Danish unions are politically affiliated with the Social Democrats, and this close relationship between party and labor unions is an important part of the party's power resources. Whatever the outcome, a full-fledged conflict could easily threaten to seriously weaken the Social Democrats' relationship with the unions and thus compromise the party's strength. It would also have exposed the Social Democrats' left flank to attacks from left-wing parties.

In comparison, the political cost to the government of growing unemployment quickly turned out to be remarkably modest. Even though unemployment rose from 1 pct. to 10 pct. of the labor force throughout the period from 1973 to 1982, the Social Democrats did not lose votes or popularity on that account. On the contrary, except, possibly, for the election of 1981, the Social Democrats were not punished at the polls (Paldam & Schneider, 1980; Nannestad, 1991). No party was able to exploit politically the employment situation. In the eyes of the voters, the bourgeois opposition lacked a credible commitment to the full employment goal. The left-wing opposition lacked a credible strategic alternative. Even if voters might have disapproved of the way the government handled the unemployment problem, they were trapped. The government had only weak political incentives to enforce a strategic coordination that would have allowed it to decisively combat unemployment without inflationary consequences.

In this situation, the government chose the path of least resistance. On the one hand, the government tried – with due respect to the pain threshold of the unions – to contain wage inflation by enacting a series of incomes policy measures. On the other hand, within the constraints soon placed upon it by a chronic and growing balance of payments deficit, the government attempted to accommodate the wage development that it could not control and thereby offset the adverse effects on employment. The result was an incoherent and at times even inconsistent policy mix, unsuited to attain either the employment or the inflation goal.

The continuous attempts to attain the primary economic goals in a way that would, at the same time, result in ever-greater economic equality in society added another inconsistency to the government's economic policy. Leveling of wage differentials was a central concern to the government, but attempts to achieve it compromised other goals. Thus the introduction of a minimum wage and its gradual increase have been pointed to as the main reasons for the increasing and persistently high levels of unemployment among unskilled workers, women and the young (Albæk et al., 1992).

Finally, the political situation after the 'landslide election' of 1973 was hardly conducive to devising and enacting coherent economic policies. The elections left the parliament severely fragmented, making majority formation an arduous and time-consuming exercise for the governing minority. Policy necessarily came to reflect compromises between the various points of view of, normally, four to six parties with often rather diverging ideas on how to solve Denmark's growing economic problems.

... and back: Non-socialist economic policy 1982-92

OVERALL DEVELOPMENT 1982-92

By 1982, the economic situation looked even bleaker than ever. Unemployment and inflation each stood at the 10-pct. mark. Long-term nominal interest rates were close to 20 pct. Private investments were at an all-time low. The balance of payment deficit was 4.5 pct. of GNP, and the foreign debt was exploding. So were interest payments on foreign credits as a proportion of the total government budget. The budget deficit had grown to about 10 pct. of GNP, with no end to its continued growth in sight. There was real anxiety that the imbalances in the Danish economy were getting out of control. As a former Social Democratic minister of finance remarked already in 1979, Denmark was standing on 'the brink of the abyss'.

In this situation the Social Democratic minority government formed after the general election of 1981 found itself unable to marshal further parliamentary support for its economic strategy. The other parties turned down a proposal for still another comprehensive plan. After abandoning the braking strategy (despite its initial success), the Social Democrats failed to inspire confidence or convince the public that they really had the stomach to implement the necessary tough measures. The Social Democrats resigned in September 1982, and a Conservative-led government took their place. Conservative-led governments managed to stay in office for the following decade.

As the main economic indicators in Figure 3 show, the period from 1983 to 1992 included two clearly different sub-periods, each characterized by different economic trends. The watershed separating them occurred around 1987.

From 1983 to 1986, Denmark experienced a period of rather strong economic recovery. This development was eventually aided by international trends, but the Danish recovery preceded the OECD recovery (Pedersen, 1994, 35). The average real GNP-growth from 1983 to 1986 reached 3.7 pct. p.a. (strongest in 1985 and 1986), compared to an average 2 pct. growth for the decade from 1972 to 1982. Unemployment reached its peak in 1983 (10.5 pct.) and declined steadily thereafter to 7.9 pct. in 1986. And this time the improved employment situation did not accelerate consumer price inflation rates. On the contrary, inflation rates continued the downward trend begun in 1982; they dropped from 6.8 pct. in 1983 to 2.9 pct. in 1986.

The downside of the picture was the development in the balance of payments, which deteriorated steadily from 1983 to 1986. Unfortunately, the Danish economic boom of these years derived most of its momentum from rising levels of activity in the private non-tradables sector and from a sharp drop in the Danish private sector savings rate.

FIGURE 3.
Main economic indicators, quarterly data, 1983-1992

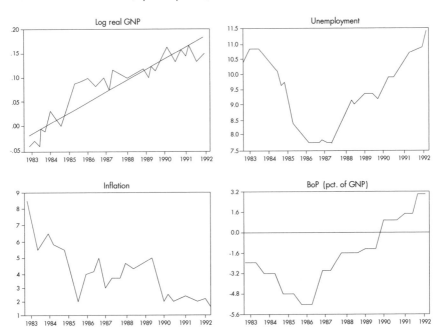

Source: OECD Historical statistics.

In many respects, the period 1987-92 was the exact counter image of the period 1983-86. The severe deterioration in the balance of payments, reaching its maximum deficit of about 5 pct. of GNP in 1986, triggered political measures that abruptly and quite literally turned a number of the previous years' economic trends upside down.

From record-high real GNP growth rates, the Danish economy sank to growth rates close to zero. For the whole period 1987-92, average real growth hovered around a meager 1 pct. This brutal economic braking process occurred well ahead of developments in the global economy. As a consequence of the economic slow-down, Danish unemployment soared from 1988 onwards and reached a new peak in 1992. On the other hand, after a short interlude, inflation rates steadily declined.

The balance of payments improved markedly after 1986. In 1990, for the first time since 1962, a surplus was registered on the current account. Even bigger surpluses were recorded in 1991 and 1992. German unification was an important contributing factor in this development.

STRATEGIES

Unlike the Conservative takeovers in Great Britain (1979), the United States (1981) and Germany (1982), the Conservative-led bourgeois coalition that came to power in Denmark in late 1982 did not produce a radical shift in the economic regime and rhetoric. The new Danish government had no blueprint for rolling back, let alone dismantling, the welfare state. Whether the bourgeois government formulated its economic policies within a single, consistent macroeconomic frame of reference is open to debate. The policies drew generously from Keynesianism as well as supply-side and neoclassical economics. This pragmatism may well reflect the fact that the Conservative-led governments, as was the case for its Social Democratic predecessors, remained minority coalitions throughout the entire period. Thus they had to obtain support for their economic policies from parties not represented in the cabinet. In spite of these obstacles, changes nevertheless soon emerged in the prioritization of economic policy goals, in some of the instruments to achieve them, and in policy style.

An overview of the timing of major economic political measures implemented by the Conservative-led government is provided in Table 2 (see Appendix). Initially, the new government emphasized eliminating the two big and longest lasting deficits: the budget deficit and the balance of payments deficit. These goals, the government acknowledged, would not be achieved immediately, though. They referred to 'the long, tough haul' their policies would require and that their goals would not be achieved until some time in the middle of the decade.

Controlling inflation constituted another important goal, but this was promoted as a prerequisite for improving international competitiveness, and hence a necessary component of the strategy to achieve the balance of payments goal. Similarly, curbing the growth in public expenditures was an important goal, but primarily because a balanced budget required it. Thus neither reducing inflation nor controlling expenditures were presented as ideologically motivated anti-welfare state goals in and of themselves.

Improving the employment situation would have to be the product of private sector initiatives and not an expanding public sector or artificial employment schemes. Policy makers expected activity in the private sector to pick up if and when the deficits were brought under control, which would, among other things, lower interest rates and encourage investment activity. While the Social Democratic demand twist strategy was designed to tackle the unemployment problem by crowding out, the new government planned to alleviate unemployment by crowding in. Moreover, employment would improve when private sector competitiveness improved through controlling wage increases.

On the other hand, the new government had no intention of accommodating wage policy set by the labor unions, as the Social Democrats did whenever feasible. Thus the employment goal had clearly taken a backseat to the goal of redressing the two big deficits to 'resurrect' the Danish economy.

Perhaps the most visible and most highly politicized difference between the economic-political priorities of the Conservative-led government and its Social Democratic predecessor was the question of economic equality. To the Conservative-led governments, this was not a high-priority goal. Early on, modest cutbacks in social expenditures were no longer taboo. Little wonder, then, that some of the fiercest clashes between the new government and opposition were fought over the issue of economic equality.

The new government also changed some of the instruments of economic policy. Most importantly, it denounced the Social Democratic policy of 'creeping devaluations' of the Danish krone from the late 1970s and 'strategic devaluations' from the early 1980s. Instead, the new government announced the shift to a fixed exchange rate policy, pegging the krone to the Deutschmark. Initially, it also resorted to imposing much tougher incomes policy measures than previously seen.

Still another difference was a change in the government's policy making style. The Social Democratic government had normally considered consultation with the labor unions and – to a lesser degree – employers' organizations as a necessary step in economic policy formation. Normally the government sought the consent of at least the labor unions. However, under the new government, a 'shut up' style became more common (Damgaard 1989). The main economic interests could no longer count on automatically being consulted, or even informed, in early stages of economic policymaking. This policy style was made possible, at least in part, by the 'rally around the flag' sentiment the government initially drummed up among the public by pointing to the serious nature of the challenges facing the country. Moreover, the Conservatives argued that there was no alternative to the government's cure, exploiting the urgency of the problems inherited from the luckless Social Democrats and pointing to their voluntary, ignoble retreat from power and responsibility.

In other respects, the differences between the Conservative-led and the Social Democratic governments' policy means turned out to be surprisingly small. Most noteworthy, the Conservative-led government did not refrain from introducing new taxes or raising existing ones in order to balance the budget; from 1982 to 1993, the total tax-pressure actually grew from 47 pct. to 51 pct.

The 'long tough haul' to resurrect the Danish economy: 1982-87

In his opening speech to the Danish Folketing on October 5, 1982, the new Conservative Prime Minister Poul Schlüter announced economic measures to be undertaken immediately and sketched the medium-term prospects. As did its Social Democratic predecessor, the government would rely mainly on fiscal policy and incomes policy to redress the main imbalances in the Danish economy.

But in marked contrast to the Social Democrats' exchange rate policy since 1976, and against the advice from the Council of Economic Advisors (Laursen, 1987, 241-42), the new government refrained from beginning its period in office with a sizeable, strategic devaluation. Instead, a fixed exchange rate regime was proclaimed, meaning that the government ruled out depreciation of the Danish krone as a policy tool. The government stuck to this new line even when the krone came under pressure early on, first in the wake of a huge Swedish devaluation and subsequently when the parliamentary fate of the government's consolidation initiative appeared uncertain. Having weathered these storms, the fixed exchange rate policy gradually gained credibility, although the process was slow (Andersen & Sørensen, 1993). Hence the gap between Danish and German interest rates remained sizeable, indicating the international financial markets remained skeptical of the government's ability and willingness to stick to the fixed exchange rate regime and support it with the necessary fiscal and incomes policy measures.

Up until 1986, fiscal policy was tightened considerably in order to reduce the budget deficit and to stop the growth in public debt. A budget deficit of 9.1 pct. of GNP in 1982 was transformed into a surplus of 3.4 pct. of GNP by 1986. During the period from 1983 to 1986, Denmark experienced the tightest fiscal policy since 1960 (Christensen, 1993: table A.2.1).

The government realized that fiscal austerity policies might have adverse short-term effects on real growth and employment. But growth and employment were expected to pick up again after a while, thanks to lower interest rates and an improved competitive position for Danish businesses as a consequence of flanking incomes policy measures. Thus the government hoped for crowding-in effects as a result of its fiscal policy in the longer run (Damsgård Hansen et al., 1988: 147). This effect materialized sooner than expected.

Expenditure cuts, tax increases and the improving economic climate contributed to the swift closing of the budget deficit. Although in his opening remarks to parliament, the prime minister declared that his government did not consider tax increases a suitable means to bring down the budget deficit, a temporary tax on pension benefits was introduced in 1982 and a new 'real interest tax' adopted in 1983 taxed away pension fund returns in the excess of a long-term real yield of 3.5 pct. on the capital stock. This contributed about 8 billion krone of additional revenue. Moreover, thanks to the incipient economic recovery and the drop in unemployment that came along with it, state expenditures on unemployment benefits soon started to fall.

Incomes policy was designed to curtail inflationary expectations and bring Danish wages into line with international trends. In 1982, existing automatic wage regulation schemes were either suspended or revoked. Thus the CoL-indexation of wages was suspended and the automatic regulation of public sector wages linking them to wage developments in the private sector was abolished. These were the most far-reaching and austere incomes policy measures ever enacted in Denmark in peacetime. Employers and unions went along, and the collective wage agreements that were concluded in early 1983 cut the wage increases to half the previous years', thus contributing to closing the gap between wage developments in Denmark and abroad.

In a number of respects, economic aggregates reacted as expected. In the words of the prime minister, "things were going well, beyond comprehension" – or so it seemed. In line with international trends, Danish inflation rates slowed and long-term interest rates dropped from 22 to about 14 pct. Despite the tight fiscal policy, economic growth was high and unemployment fell. Only the balance of payments kept moving in the wrong direction.

By 1984, crowding-in effects had become much stronger than expected. Private consumption reacted strongly to lower interest rates and increasing private wealth. The strong growth in private consumption was reflected in a dramatic drop in private sector savings. Net savings in the private sector dropped from about 15 pct. of net disposable income in 1983 to about 5 pct. in 1986. Much of the Danish economic recovery between 1983 and 1986 was actually fueled by loan-financed private consumption.

The statutory wage settlement of 1985 severely restricted wage increases in the private sector, and public employees received only minor wage increases. The annual unemployment rate hovered between 7 and 8 pct. But by 1986 as bottleneck problems developed in the labor market, wage increases in the private sector started to accelerate, leading to widespread wage drift. The competitive situation once more deteriorated. Furthermore, private consumption remained high. These developments contributed to a steady deterioration of the current account.

The growing balance of payments deficit led to further restrictive fiscal measures, increasing tax pressure still more. By March 1986, indirect taxes were increased by 10 billion DKK. This measure had only limited impact on private disposable income. Energy taxes were the main contributor, and the hike in energy taxes was by and large offset by the declining energy prices on international markets. Thus to restore the balance of payments, a bundle of initiatives nicknamed 'the potato cure' and designed specifically to encourage private savings and reduce loan-financed consumption was enacted later in 1986.

Soon after, however, the government loosened incomes policies. Specifically, it did nothing to prevent the 'wage feast' reflected in the collective wage settlements concluded in the labor market in early 1987. Wages grew by more than 10 pct., after four years of extremely limited wage increases. As it was, these wage agreements were totally inappropriate, given the economic situation, and constituted a considerable deterioration in Danish wage competitiveness.

Part of the reason why the government allowed this to happen might well have been that 1987 was to be an election year. The increasing tax burden, and especially 'the potato cure' of late 1986, had not contributed to the government's popularity (Nannestad & Paldam 1994); neither had the income tax reform. There was good reason to do something to make the electorate happy, especially public sector employees who in 1985 had been forced to accept wage increases that were less than the ones conceded to private sector employees.

The years of fatigue and fumbling: 1987-92

The contradictory policies of 1986-87 – curbing consumption through fiscal policy and then letting wage developments get out of hand – may be considered a watershed in the Conservative-led governments' economic policy. The government never reestablished the consistent policies it had exhibited during the first years. Elements of muddling-through and stop-go strategies proliferated. Economic activity slowed, unemployment soared, and growing expenditures on unemployment benefits contributed to refueling budget deficits starting in 1989. On the other hand, inflation fell to record-low levels, and the balance of payments recovered strongly.

The 'potato cure' curbed growth in private consumption from 1987 on and reversed the downward trend in the private savings rate. By 1990, private savings crossed the 15 pct. mark and continued to increase throughout 1992 (Hoffmeyer, 1993: Figure IV.6).

A comprehensive reform of private income tax legislation that took effect in January 1987 influenced the economic climate and consumption behavior in Denmark. This tax reform had a profound, albeit apparently not entirely expected, effect on the economic behavior of many homeowners. It significantly reduced the deductibility of interest payments on home mortgages. Given the situation in early 1986, when the reform was adopted, this might have appeared a sensible step to reduce loan-financed consumption. But it also reduced homeowners' disposable income. Moreover, real estate prices dropped sharply as the reduced tax-deductibility of interest payments was capitalized in prices. As a consequence, many homeowners suddenly found themselves in a state of technical bankruptcy because the market value of their real estate was less than what they owed on their mortgages. In the wake of the tax reform, the number of foreclosures skyrocketed.

Beginning in 1987, fiscal policies were again liberalized somewhat in a number of small steps. In December 1987, a number of earlier cuts in social transfers were restored, and transfers to families with children as well as grants to students were raised substantially in 1987-88. Budget surpluses fell steadily, and from 1989 the budget was in deficit once more. Even after correcting for the effect of rising unemployment, the fiscal policy had a slightly expansive effect. The loosening of fiscal policy was especially marked in 1988 and was primarily the result of the sizeable increase in the rates of various transfer payments. In 1990, public transfers to households were linked to the development in workers' annual wages, thus reintroducing part of the automatism that had been abolished with great fanfare in 1982.

Faced with rising unemployment, the government introduced a labor market package in May 1992. It was the only major labor market policy initiative taken during the period of Conservative-led governments. Most importantly from the perspective of later developments was the introduction of a job-rotation scheme. On the other hand, the government refrained from taking initiatives that would result in more far-reaching structural reforms of the labor market, even though the experiences from 1986-87 indicated that structural unemployment (NAIRU) had risen to 7 to 8 pct. This meant that even a new economic upswing would eliminate no more than about one-third of the Danish unemployment problem.

In November 1992, nevertheless, the government chose a fairly traditional policy of demand stimulation for 1993 which included, among other things, increased capital spending by the central government. The stable surplus in the balance of payments meant that these measures were deemed affordable. But in January 1993, the government was forced to resign due to a political scandal unrelated to economic policy management, and a decade of Conservative-led governments had come to an end.

If one compares the economic situation inherited by the Conservative-led government in 1982 to the one it left to its Social Democratic successor in 1993, a number of problems in the Danish economy appear to have been solved during the Conservative-led reign. By 1993, the Danish economy had moved away from 'the brink of the abyss' it faced in 1982. The most spectacular economic results have been the reduction in the rate of consumer price inflation to a record-low figure sustained since the end of the 1980s, and the change from a chronic balance of payments deficit to a stable surplus from 1990 onwards, cf. figure 3. Moreover, budget deficits were significantly reduced and public debt stabilized. Nevertheless, three important qualifications have to be added to this rosy picture.

In the first place, turning the balance of payments deficit into a surplus proved in the end to take considerably longer than the two to four years initially envisaged by the government and exacted a considerably higher price than expected. When the goal was finally achieved in 1990, it came at the expense of a substantial slump in the Danish economy which was, at least in part, home-made and preceded the onset of the global recession by a couple of years. This slump is most clearly seen in changes in real GNP-growth and in the unemployment figure.

In the second place, after the initial improvement in the employment situation up to the middle of the 1980s, unemployment rose to new heights in the early 1990s. Thus the Conservative-led government did not exactly solve the problem of how to achieve high economic growth and employment together with a balanced foreign account. Rather it had been forced to sacrifice, at least temporarily, growth and full employment in order to solve the balance of payment problem. Even so, a balance of payments surplus was actually achieved at a level of unemployment that had been associated with a sizeable balance of payments deficit only about ten years earlier.

In the third place, initial achievements in reducing the budget deficit turned out to be unsustainable in the longer term. While the government succeeded in closing the budget deficit sooner than expected, primarily through implementing the tightest fiscal policy in thirty years, budget deficits reappeared in the second half of the 1980s, although on a smaller scale.

Still, one may ask why the Conservative-led governments' economic strategy did succeed in a number of respects, while the Social Democrats' policies were an utter failure. A definitive answer to this question is hard to discern, but a few points are worth considering.

Changes in the global economy must have aided the Conservative-led governments' policies, but this explanation is insufficient. The timing of the trajectories of a number of main economic aggregates in Denmark during the period from 1983 to 1992 is sufficiently different from the international trends to reject any claim that the Danish economy reflected international developments. Both the economic recovery in the first part of the 1980s and the recession in the second half of the decade led rather than lagged international developments. Thus we have to focus on domestic causes related to the political economy. Four factors suggest themselves.

First, the Conservative-led government appears to have had a far better understanding than did the Social Democrats of the central role of expectations and credibility in effective economic policymaking. At least in the beginning, the government was able to promote credible expectations about its determination to combat the downward trends and this helped its policies to succeed. Its first policy measures very clearly aimed at breaking inflationary expectations and signaled the end of an accommodating economic policy that could be exploited by the wage setting strategy of the labor unions and employers. The government's stance in connection with the Swedish devaluation in late 1982 and international pressure on the Danish krone can also best be understood under the assumption that the government was determined to prove the credibility of its policy and let this concern dictate its decisions. To some extent, the government owed the successes of its economic policy to its success in changing expectations with respect to the Danish economy, both abroad and at home. The Conservative-led government was also able to capitalize on a widespread perception of crisis among the general public at the beginning of the period. At the same time, the government managed to instill optimism – possibly too much for its own good, as suggested by the drop in the private sector savings rate. In the second half of the 1980s, when both the sense of imminent doom as well as a bright future ahead had evaporated, the going turned much more difficult.

Second, the government did not attempt to swim upstream. Its economic priorities as well as its choice of instruments coincided with what in the 1980s had become a nearly universal international consensus on economic policymaking. If social democratic policy is 'politics against markets' (Esping-Andersen, 1985), the Conservative-led government replaced this with 'politics according to markets', international financial markets in particular.

Third, the Conservative-led government freed itself of one constraint on its economic policy by discarding economic equalization as a key economic goal. Previous Social Democratic governments had experienced grave difficulties in designing and implementing a consistent and efficient incomes policy that was compatible with their ideological commitment to economic equality (Nannestad, 1991).

The low priority assigned to the goal of promoting greater economic equality did not mean, however, that the Conservative-led governments were the uncaring monsters their left-wing critics liked to depict them as. The period of Conservative-led governments was not a period of massive redistribution from labor to capital, although the wage quota fell slightly (from about 65 pct. in 1983 to about 63 pct. in 1992). Nor did economic inequality significantly increase: with respect to disposable income, the Gini-coefficient changed little from 1983 to 1993 (Budgetredegørelse, 1994: Table 1.3.3.).

Although the average annual real growth in social transfers to households declined relative to the previous decade (1973-82), the Conservative-led governments did not significantly roll back the Danish welfare state as part of their economic resurrection strategy. Between 1982 and 1993, social transfers to households increased at an average annual rate of about 3.1 pct. in real terms, still far ahead of the period's average annual growth in real GNP (2 pct.). In part, this reflects the onset of the recession in the middle of the 1980s and the associated growth in unemployment. But it also reflects the fact that new kinds of social transfer payments were introduced and that entitlements under a number of welfare schemes increased or expanded substantially (see Christiansen in this volume).

Fourth, the Conservative-led governments went to far greater lengths than did their Social Democratic predecessors in coordinating economic strategy with expenditures and revenues in municipalities and counties. After all, local government spending accounts for about one-half of all public expenditures in Denmark. Through more or less voluntary agreements about local current expenditures, investments and tax rates, the government ensured that the effects of its fiscal policies would not be counteracted by local government decisions.

Old or new Social Democratic economic policy? 1993 – 1999

OVERALL DEVELOPMENT 1993-99

In January 1993, the last Conservative-led government resigned over a scandal involving the misadministration of legislation concerning refugees and immigrants by a former Minister of Justice. It was replaced by a government headed by the Social Democrats in coalition with three small centrist parties. By the narrowest possible margin, this was the first majority government since 1971. It lost this majority (and one of the centrist parties, which was ousted from parliament altogether) in the general election of September 1994, but continued as a minority government. Towards the end of 1996, another of the centrist parties left the government and the Social Democrats and the Social Liberals governed as a minority coalition until November 2001.

FIGURE 4.
Main Economic Indicators, quarterly data, 1993-1999.

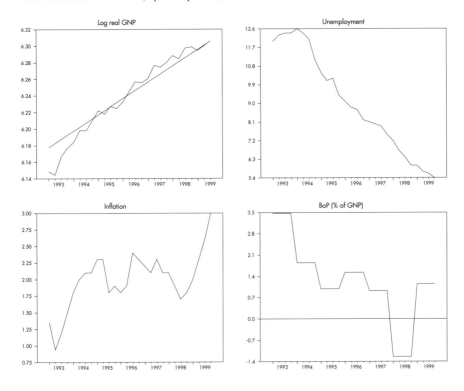

As Figure 4 shows, the new government inherited three interrelated economic problems, but in other respects a strong economy. The main problems were low economic growth, high and rising unemployment, and a growing budget deficit. On the other hand, the balance of payments surplus was high and stable, inflation rates were among the lowest in Europe, and interest rates were falling sharply. The new Social Democratic government quickly managed to improve growth rates, which have since declined somewhat, but remained at a higher level than in the second half of the 1980s and the beginning of the 1990s. Starting in 1995, unemployment steadily declined, and since 1997 public budgets began to show surpluses again. Thus, the Social Democratic-led governments managed to do something about the main problems they inherited. The booming economy since 1994 affected, of course, the balance of payments negatively, but with the exception of 1998, the Social Democratic-led governments had balance of payments surpluses and managed to keep inflation at an acceptable level. Thus for the first time since the beginning of the 1960s, the Danish economy did not show any major imbalances. It was this development that was described as the 'Danish miracle'.

The new government announced that improving the employment situation would be the main goal of its economic policy. This goal was to be attained primarily by a cautious return to Keynesian economic policies. According to a Social Democratic analysis, the budget deficit of 5.9 pct. of GNP was not structural and therefore left room for expansive fiscal measures (Finansrede-gørelse 1994, 313). For 1994, an economic stimulus in the magnitude of 14 billion DKK was to be injected into the economy by loosening fiscal policy, even at the price of a further increase in the budget deficit. The growth effect was expected to be 1.3 pct. of GNP. The aim was to kick start the economy well ahead of an expected international economic recovery. The anticipated effect of the fiscal stimulus on employment was to be aided by a 'labor market reform' emphasizing greater job rotation.

Both prongs of this strategy may be seen as a direct continuation of initia-tives taken by the Conservative-led government in May and November 1992, respectively (cf. Table 3 in the Appendix). The shift from a Conservative to a Social Democratic government had not yet resulted in a marked shift in eco-nomic policy. Quite the contrary, the Social Democratic government repeatedly pledged to continue the fixed exchange rate policy and controlling inflation.

An income tax reform adopted in 1993 and effective from January 1, 1994, was the central element in their stimulus package. The reform would be fully implemented by 1998, and by that time the impact would be neutral with respect to revenue, since a lowering of direct taxation on incomes would be balanced by a wide range of 'green taxes'. But in its first year (1994), the reform was underfinanced in order to generate higher disposable income for most taxpayers. This timing was also strongly influenced by the fact that general elections were to be held in 1994. The government did not try very hard to conceal that it hoped to reap political gains from making the voters financially better off just before the election. In the end, the payoff at the polls did not materialize.

Another means of increasing disposable income, and hence – it was hoped – private consumption, was a change in the rules for refinancing mortgages, especially on private homes. This change enabled home owners to convert high-interest mortgages from the 1980s to new mortgages at the lower inter-est rates of the 1990s. At the same time, the redemption period for mortgages could be extended to a maximum of 30 years. Thus the government quite openly invited homeowners to engage in loan-financed consumption.

Although to most observers the developments from 1985 to 1987 indicated severe structural problems in the labor market, the new government refrained from making structural reforms to improve employment levels. Instead the central element of its labor market reform became a series of schemes allowing wage earners to take a leave of absence paid for by unemployment benefits – either to take care of small children, for educational purposes, or (at a reduced rate of unemployment benefits) as a sabbatical. These benefits were also made available to the unemployed. The schemes would be effective for a three-year period beginning January 1994. But already in early 1994, the government committed itself to making them permanent after 1996, except for the sabbatical leave (see Kvist & Plough in this volume).

The results of these initiatives were slower than expected in materializing. But by the middle of 1994, signs of an economic recovery were finally surfacing in the figures for private consumption, investment and growth. During 1995, unemployment also started to decline and it became clear that the Danish economy had finally left the recession that began in 1987. The government had in fact managed to kick start the Danish economy. After this initial success, the Social Democratic-led governments focused their macro-economic policy on two goals. First, they wanted to ensure that the economic upturn would be more controlled than the one in the mid 1980s, and, second, a number of 'structural' reforms of the economy needed to be implemented.

Concerning the first goal, the governments were keen to avoid overheating the economy which would then require another 'potato cure'. They achieved this by tightening fiscal policy several times. Twice in 1997 the government raised green taxes and they also introduced a temporary pension contribution of 1 pct. of income from work. The most important measure was, however, the 'Whitsun' agreement struck by the government and its left-wing opposition in June 1998. The main element of this agreement was another tax reform that continued the line from the last two reforms by reducing personal income tax rates and reducing the value of the tax-deductibility of interests on private loans and mortgages. The reform simultaneously raised green taxes and made the 1 pct. pension contribution permanent.

As to the second goal, the Social Democratic-led governments were aware that policy measures other than tighter fiscal policy were needed. The two tax reforms aimed at reducing personal income taxes, financing this reduction through a broadening and 'greening' of the tax-base, constituted one type of 'structural reform'. The others relate to social security and labor market policy. The labor market reform passed in 1993 made Danish labor market policy more activist while also creating better possibilities for workers to exit the labor market. When the Danish economy began to boom, the government changed the content of its structural reforms of the Danish labor market. They intensified the active line, but the strategy concerning exit possibilities from the labor market was changed. A number of reforms were implemented, all aimed at reducing the number of people receiving social security benefits. Exit possibilities from the labor market were tightened. The first example was the second labor market reform passed in the autumn of 1995. This reform re-trenched unemployment benefits significantly. The maximum eligibility period was limited to five years, eligibility criteria were tightened, and unemployed youth without qualifying educations were forced into educational programs at a much lower level of benefits after six months of unemployment. In the autumn of 1998, a third labor market reform was passed which reduced the maximum unemployment benefits period to four years. Finally, in the fall of 1998, the government entered into an agreement with the right-wing oppos-ition concerning a major retrenchment of the early retirement scheme. This cutback was considered essential in order to achieve a higher average retire-ment age. Increasing the age of retirement would keep the labor force from shrinking too much as the 'graying' of the population set in.

In summary, the Social Democratic-led governments since 1993 in many ways continued the economic policy of their right-wing predecessors, for in-stance by unhesitatingly maintaining the fixed exchange rate policy. However, they also implemented a number of structural reforms of the Danish economy that were merely discussed under the right-wing governments. The best ex-amples are the retrenchments of unemployment benefits and early retirement benefits. Altogether, the economic policy of the Social Democratic-led govern-ments since 1993 has been very different from their fumbling policy of the 1970s.

INTERPRETATION

When the first Social Democratic-led government of the period took office in 1993, the Danish economy had already moved away from the 'brink of the abyss'. The Social Democratic led-governments further improved this situation. After the years of economic boom from 1994 to 1998, the Danish economy 'landed smoothly'. The 1999 growth rate was 1.6 pct., unemployment declined further to 5.5 pct., both the balance of payments and public budgets showed significant surpluses and inflation was at 2.5 pct. This sunny picture was expected to continue for the foreseeable future (Økonomisk Oversigt, August 2000).

How can we explain these successful outcomes? A number of factors outside direct governmental control may have played a role. First, international forces might have played a role, but this is not an obvious explanation. The Danish 'miracle' materialized at a time when few other OECD countries experienced favorable macro-economic conditions. Yet it does appear that higher economic activity among Denmark's main trading partners has played a role in reestab-lishing the balance payments surplus in 1999. Changes in the wage-bargaining system may also have played a role. As described by Iversen (1999: 119-165), Denmark has experienced a 'decentralized centralization' of wage bargaining since 1989 which has increased the impact of sector or industry based wage bargaining. This development may have facilitated wage moderation (Schwartz, 2001).

However, government policies have also played a role. From 1993 to 2001, the Social Democratic-led governments were able to pursue a very coherent macro-economic policy that combined a continuation of the Conservative-led government's approach with the will to implement a number of structural reforms. This policy mix differed radically from the one pursued by Social Democratic minority governments in the 1970s. Thus one of the factors behind Denmark's recent economic success was the new Social Democratic strategy. Economic democracy, the issue that dominated the Social Democratic agenda in the 1970s, vanished from the political agenda. The Social Democrats also downplayed the importance of achieving further income equality. Consequently there was little disagreement among the major political parties about macro-economic policy during the Social Democratic administrations of the 1990s. This meant a more coherent policy.

As suggested by Benner and Vad (2000), another factor facilitating the effective macro-economic policy was a change in parliamentary norms and the role of extreme-wing parties in Danish politics. In the 1970s, the four old parties of Danish politics were very reluctant to cooperate with the extremist parties that gained representation in 1973. This has gradually changed. The Progress Party became more influential during the ten years of Conservative-led governments, and since 1993, the extreme left-wing party, the Left Alliance, has played a crucial role on several occasions, most notably during the tax reform in the spring of 1998. The possibility of striking deals with parties like the Left Alliance has also been strengthened by changes in parliamentary norms. What the Danes term 'patchwork' agreements were concluded in connection with several of the budgets passed within the last years of the Social Democratic governments. In these cases, the government gained support from varying constellations of parties for different parts of its budget. Opposition parties could thus claim that they did not generally support the government, but only the policies they found sensible. This was of minor importance for the government as long as its policies are passed by parliament. Thus, the Danish party system has adapted to the new situation that emerged following the increased number and different types of political parties that gained representation after the 1973 landslide election.

Conclusion

The time after 1973 has called for far-reaching adjustments in the Danish economy, necessitated primarily by the supply shocks of the 1970s and the ensuing changes in the world economy. This process proved to be difficult to initiate and to steer politically, regardless of the partisan composition of government.

By and large, economic policy failed to bring about the required adaptation in the 1970s and prior to 1982, although some temporary progress was registered around 1980. The conventional optimism with respect to interventionist economic policy proved unfounded, as instances of inappropriate economic policy reactions multiplied. Against the backdrop of a fairly grave situation (the proverbial abyss that threatened), some progress was made between 1982 and 1986, but this upswing proved unsustainable in the longer term for political rather than economic reasons. Too quickly, the economic crisis was perceived to have been defused; economic discipline weakened, both among politicians and in the population, and some of the initial gains were allowed to slip away. But between 1987 and 1990, aided both by a sharp braking policy initiated in 1986 and 1987 and global economic trends, the current accounts deficit was eliminated, wage increases were curbed, inflation levels were dramatically reduced, and the debt situation stabilized. On this sounder basis, the early 1990s saw a cautious return to expansive policies aimed primarily at improving employment, first under the Conservative-led government and from 1993 to 2001 – and with much more vigor – under its Social Democratic successor. This strategy proved very successful and in the 1990s, unlike the mid 1980s, Danish governments proved capable of steering the Danish economy effectively through an economic upturn. They have even managed to implement a number of structural reforms.

While public expenditure growth rates were reduced in the 1980s and certain retrenchments were implemented in the late 1990s, neither Social Democratic nor Conservative-led governments made serious attempts to change drastically the size of the welfare state in order to redress imbalances in the economy. The political consensus held that the economy must be adjusted to support a viable welfare state in very much its present shape, rather than the other way around. There is also clear evidence that this is the strategy preferred by a sizeable majority of the electorate (Nannestad & Paldam, 1993). The lessons from the last twenty-five years or so of Danish economic policy indicate that it is possible to steer this course, but it requires prudent economic management. So far, the bumblebee has managed to stay aloft.

References

Albæk, Karsten, Erik Strøjer Madsen & Kurt Pedersen (1992). *Kampen mod ledigheden.* Copenhagen: Spektrum.

Andersen, Torben M. & Jan Rose Sørensen (1993). 'Valutakurspolitik, troværdighed og rentedannelse – nordiske erfaringer'. *Nationaløkonomisk tidsskrift* 131, 3: 300-13.

Benner, Mats Benner & Torben B.P. Vad (2000). 'Sweden and Denmark: Defending the Welfare State', in Fritz W. Scharpf & Vivien A. Schmidt (eds.), *Welfare and Work in the Open Economy*. Vol. II. *Diverse Responses to Common Challenges in Twelve Countries*. Oxford: Oxford University Press.

Buksti, Jacob A., Ole P. Kristensen, Karen Siune & Palle Svensson (1978). *ØD-undersøgelsen i Århus Kommune*. Aarhus: Arbejdernes Fællesorganisation i Århus.

Christensen, Anders Møller (1993). 'Finanspolitikken 1960-1990', in Erik Hoffmeyer, *Dansk Pengehistorie*, Vol. 5. Copenhagen: Danmarks Nationalbank.

Damgaard, Erik (1989). 'Crisis politics in Denmark 1974-87', in Erik Damgaard, Peter Gerlich & J. Richardson (eds.), *The Politics of Economic Crisis*. Aldershot: Gower.

Damsgård Hansen, E., Kaj Kjærgaard & Jørgen Rosted (1988). *Dansk økonomisk politik. Teorier og erfaringer*. Copenhagen: Nyt Nordisk Forlag Arnold Busck.

Esping-Andersen, Gøsta (1985). *Politics Against Markets*. Princeton: Princeton University Press.

Esping-Andersen, Gøsta (1990). *The Three Worlds of Welfare Capitalism*. Cambridge: Polity Press.

Finansredegørelse (1994).

Hemerijck, Anton & Martin Schludi (2000). 'Sequences of Policy Failures and Effective Policy Responses', in Fritz W. Scharpf & Vivien A. Schmidt (eds.), *Welfare and Work in the Open Economy*. Vol. 1. *From Vulnerability to Competitiveness*. Oxford: Oxford University Press, pp. 125-228.

Hoffmeyer, Erik (1993). *Dansk Pengehistorie*, Vol. 5. Copenhagen: Danmarks Nationalbank.

Iversen, Torben (1999). *Contested Economic Institutions*. Cambridge: Cambridge University Press.

Katzenstein, Peter J. (1985). *Small States in World Markets*. Ithaca: Cornell University Press.

Laursen, Karsten (1987). 'Perioden 1983-85: Det nye regime', in Det Økonomiske Råd, Formandskabet, *Råd og realiteter*. Copenhagen: Det Økonomiske Råd.

Nannestad, Peter (1991). *Danish Design or British Disease?* Aarhus: Aarhus University Press.

Nannestad, Peter & Martin Paldam (1993). 'The Demand for the Public Sector in the Rich Welfare State of Denmark: Two Polls from 1990', in Albert Breton et al. (eds.), *Preferences and Democracy*. Dordrecht/ Boston/London: Kluwer Academic Publishers, pp. 289-327.

Offe, Claus (1984). 'Competitive Party Democracy and the Keynesian Welfare State', in Claus Offe, *Contradictions of the Welfare State*. London: Hutchinson.

Paldam, Martin & Friedrich Schneider (1980). 'The Macro-Economic Aspects of Government and Opposition Popularity in Denmark 1957-78'. *Nationaløkonomisk Tidsskrift*: 149-70.

Pedersen, Peder J. (1994). 'Postwar Growth of the Danish Economy', Memo 1994-6. Aarhus: Institute of Economics.

Scharpf, Fritz W. (1987). *Sozialdemokratische Krisenpolitik in Europa*. Frankfurt a.M. 1987: Campus Verlag.

Schwartz, Herman (2001). 'The Danish "Miracle": Luck, Pluck or Stuck?' *Comparative Political Studies* 34, 2: 131-55.

Thygesen, Niels (1979). 'Udviklingstendenser i tilrettelæggelsen og virkningerne af dansk pengepolitik', in *Vækst og kriser i dansk økonomi i det 20. Århundrede*, Vol. II, Aarhus: Skrifter fra Aarhus Universitets Økonomiske Institut.

Økonomisk oversigt (May 1995). Copenhagen: J.H. Schultz Information A/S.

Økonomisk oversigt (August 2000). Copenhagen: J.H. Schultz Information A/S.

Appendix to Chapter 1

TABLE 1.

Timetable of major economic policy measures enacted

1 9 7 4 - 8 2

Date	Fiscal measures	Price and incomes policy	Labor market policy	Exchange rate policy
January 1974	* 1.55 bill Dkr. budget cut * Mandatory saving scheme	* Price freeze (Jan. – Feb. 1974) * Compensation to employers for CoL payment		
May 1974 ('Black compromise')	* Pers. taxes to be cut in 1975 * Indirect taxes up			
September 1974	* 7 bill. Dkr. pers. tax cut as per Jan. 1, 1975 * 6.7 bill. Dkr. budget cut from April 1, 1975			
February 1975	Budget cuts waived			
March 1975		Statutory wage settlement: * Contracts prolonged unchanged, * CoL regulation changed to flat-rate		
September 1975 ('September compromise')	* VAT temporarily reduced to 9.25 pct. * Compulsory savings from 1974 released	Declaration of intent: slowdown in wage growth	Special employment programs	
August 1976 ('August compromise')	Ind. taxes up 5 bill. Dkr.	(Non-binding) wage guidelines for 1977-79: * Max. wage increase 6 pct. p.a. * CoL portions in excess of 2 to be frozen in Suppl. Pension Fund	1 year employment program	

Date	Fiscal measures	Price and incomes policy	Labor market policy	Exchange rate policy
October 1976				Beginning of policy of gradual adjustments of exchange rate Dkr. / DM; total depreciation of Dkr. 26 pct. until Sept. 1979
December 1976		* Temporary price freeze * Wage increases obtained through wildcat strikes void		
February 1977	Ind. taxes up			
March 1977		Statutory wage settlement: * Introduction of minimum wage * CoL regulation limited to 2 portions p.a.		
August 1977 ('2nd August-compromise')	Ind. taxes up 7.3 bill. Dkr.		Employment program 1978-80, 10 bill. Dkr.	
September 1978	VAT rate raised to 20.25 pct.	Price and wage stop until March 1, 1979		
October 1978			* Job offer scheme for long-term unemployed * Early retirement scheme effective from January 1, 1979	
March 1979		Statutory wage settlement: *Minimum wage raised * 1 add. week paid vacation		
June 1979	* Indirect taxes up 4.5 bill. Dkr.		* Add. 1.35 bill. Dkr. for employment programs	

Date	Fiscal measures	Price and incomes policy	Labor market policy	Exchange rate policy
	* Budget cut 2.5 bill. Dkr. * 3 pct. ceiling on real expenditure growth in municipalities and counties			
November 1979		Comprehensive wage-price and profit stop until Dec. 31		5 pct. depreciation of Dkr. against other EMS currencies
December 1979		* Base of CPI reset * Fuel and energy prices removed from CPI * CoL regulation by Jan. 1, 1980 waived * Price stop, except for increases due to raw materials, until Feb. 28, 1981		
May 1980	* VAT up to 22 pct., indirect taxes up, 5 bill. Dkr. together * Budget cuts 4.5 bill. Dkr. * 2 pct. ceiling on real expenditure growth in municipalities and counties			
May 1981	* Indirect taxes up 2 bill. Dkr. * Gradual reduction of growth rate in public expenditures		Additional 5.6 bill. Dkr. for employment programs	
February 1982				3 pct. depreciation of Dkr. against other EMS currencies
June 1982	Indirect taxes up 3.8 bill. Dkr.		New and expanded employment programs aimed especially at young unemployed	

CRISIS, MIRACLES, AND BEYOND

TABLE 2.

Timetable of major economic policy measures enacted 1982-92

Date	Fiscal measures	Price and incomes policy	Labor market policy	Exchange rate policy
October 1982	* Contributions from employers and employees to unemployment insurance funds raised	* Total stop for wage and margin increases until Feb. 28, 1983		Declaration of intent: Fixed exchange rate, Dkr. pegged at DM
	* Reform of rules on payment of unemployment benefits to part time workers	* CoL regulation of wages suspended until 1985		
	* First day of sickness not covered by social security system	* CoL indexation of certain transfer payments abolished		
	* Size of old-age pension made dependent on income from work for people below the age of 70	* Semi-automatic regulation of public sector wages abolished		
	* Indexation of tax brackets and pers. allowances suspended	* Dividends etc. limited to 1981 level		
	* Tax ceiling raised from 70 to 73 pct.			
December 1982	Temporary 2.5 pct. tax on pension fund capitals			
March 1983				Central rate of Dkr. in the EMS revaluated 2.5 pct.
June 1983	Tax on interests in pension funds introduced: Interest in excess of an average real return of 3.5 pct. to be taxed away.			
September 1983	Grants to local authorities curbed by 1.4 bill Dkr.			
October 1983	Reduction in budget deficit approx. 5.5 bill. DKK through:			
	* Changes in tax scales and certain tax rules			

Date	Fiscal measures	Price and incomes policy	Labor market policy	Exchange rate policy
	* Contributions to Sickness Fund raised 1 percentage point			
	* 0.475 bill. Dkr. payments from Social Pension Fund waived for 1984			
May 1984	* Contributions to Sickness Fund up 0.15 percentage point	* Suspension of CoL indexation of wages prolonged until Jan. 1977		
	* Wage earners' contributions to Unemployment Insurance Fund up 16.7 pct.	* Cont. freeze on max. unemployment benefits		
	* Indirect taxes on beer and tobacco raised	* Invitation to tri-partite discussions to limit wage increases		
	* Freeze on real public expenditures 1984 to 1985			
March-April 1985	Corporate taxes raised from 40 to 50 pct.	Statutory wage settlement:		
		* Wage increases limited to 2 (1.75) pct. in 1985, 1.5 (1.25) pct. in 1986 in private (public) sector		
		* 1 hours reduction of weekly working hours from October 1986		
		* Margins etc. frozen		
		* Ceiling on price increases		
		* Employers' contribution to Social Security Funds reduced from Oct. 1985		
		* Mandatory saving scheme		
March 1986	Reform of personal income tax system, to become effective from Jan. 1987:			

Date	Fiscal measures	Price and incomes policy	Labor market policy	Exchange rate policy
	* Reduction in max. marginal tax rate * Broadening of tax-base * Reduction in tax deductibility of interests on private loans and mortgages. Indirect taxes up 10 bill. Dkr.: * Indirect taxes on energy and a number of consumer durables up * Indirect taxes on beer, liquor, tobacco etc. up			
April 1986				Realignment in the EMS: Dkr. revaluated 1 pct. vis-à-vis ECU
May 1986	Current expenditure by local government in 1987 and 1988 to average expenditures over preceding 2 years		Persons aged 60-67 may retire on part-time basis and receive corresponding public pension	
June 1986		CoL indexation abolished		
October 1986 ('Potato cure')	* 20 pct. tax on net interest payments on consumer credit * Reduced scope for installment purchases Premium on certain types of saving accounts * New rules for mortgage financing of housing investments: twist in time profile of payments * Energy taxes up to neutralize drop in energy prices			
January 1987				Realignment in the EMS: Dkr. devaluated 0.45 pct. vis-à-vis ECU

Date	Fiscal measures	Price and incomes policy	Labor market policy	Exchange rate policy
June 1987	Counties' tax rates frozen at 1987 levels	* Old age pensions up 5-7 pct. * Employers' Social security contributions abolished or to be compensated by the public * Employers' financial responsibility in connection with employees' sickness reduced	* Unemployment benefits and retirement pay up 10 pct. *Rules diminishing unemployment benefits after a certain period abolished	
December 1987	Levy of 2.5 pct. on VAT base (AMBI) to replace var. social security contributions by employers			
January 1988	Levy on net interest payments abolished for taxpayers with low net interest payments			
June 1988	Agreement with Association of Municipalities over budgets for 1989: * Taxes not to be raised * Ceiling on net investments * Current expenditures to be held at 1988 levels with certain adjustments			
November 1988	Taxation of net interest payments on consumer credits lowered or abolished			
December 1988	* Wealth taxation to be reduced over next three years * Employees contribution to labor market training fund to be doubled		*To discourage temporary layoffs, employers to pay unemployment benefits for first day of unemployment * Rules for supplementary unemployment benefits tightened	

CRISIS, MIRACLES, AND BEYOND

Date	Fiscal measures	Price and incomes policy	Labor market policy	Exchange rate policy
January 1989	Indirect taxes on certain consumer durables lowered to reduce incentives for across-border trade			
May 1989	Adjustment of excise taxes: Taxes on petrol down, on coal and electricity up			
June 1989	Agreement on local finances 1990: * County tax rates not to be raised * Municipality rates to be lowered 0.2 percentage points on average			
December 1989	1990 budget: * Corporate tax rate down to 40 pct. * Retroactive abolition of tax on net interest payments * Lowering of petrol taxes twice in 1990 * Lowering of excise taxes on goods subject to intensive border trade * Tightening of insurance company taxation * Increasing weight-based fees on automobiles * Increasing taxes on waste and raw materials * Restricting growth in public employment			
May 1990		Public transfers to households to be linked to raise in annual wages of workers		

Date	Fiscal measures	Price and incomes policy	Labor market policy	Exchange rate policy
January 1991	* Reduction of company and small enterprise tax * Reduction in excise taxes on goods subject to border trade / increase in tax on tobacco * Reduction of state subsidies to employers' con-tribution to work insurance: * Reduction in budgetary outlays for unemployment benefits			
June 1991	Agreement on unchanged local tax rates from 1991 to 1992			
May 1992			Labor market package: * More timely of-fers of temporary jobs or education to young welfare recipients * Introduction of job-rotation scheme * Increased subsidies to child-care and care for elderly by local authorities to pro-mote employment * Establishment of special condi-tion business zones in high-unemployment areas.	
November 1992	Stimulation pack-age for 1993: * Increase in capital spending by central gov-ernment (1.5 bill. Dkr.) * Increased sup-port for housing repairs and reno-vation (1.1 bill. Dkr.)		Education and labor market ini-tiatives (0.4 bill. Dkr.)	

Date	Fiscal measures	Price and incomes policy	Labor market policy	Exchange rate policy
	* Initiatives to encourage activity in small and medium-sized enterprises (0.4 bill. Dkr.)			
	* Easing of borrowing restrictions on local authorities			

TABLE 3.

Timetable of major economic policy measures enacted 1993-99

Date	Fiscal measures	Price and in-comes policy	Labor market policy	Exchange rate policy
June 1993	Temporarily under-financed tax reform * General reduction in personal income tax rates * Introduction of gross tax * Increased 'green'-taxes		Labor market reform: * Limitation of the maximum duration of unemployment benefits to 7/9 years * Significant improvement of temporary leave-arrangements for child rearing, education, and sabbatical purposes * Improved activation measures	
November 1994			Budget-agreement for 1995: *Leave arrangements for child rearing and education become permanent but benefits in the child rearing leave scheme are reduced. Leave arrangement for sabbatical purposes will end in 1999.	
June 1995	Agreement on local finances 1996: * Limitation of the growth in local spending * Income tax raises			
November 1995			Budget-agreement for 1996: * Maximum duration of unemployment benefits limited to 5 years * Tightened eligibility criteria in unemployment benefits * Mandatory education or activation of young unemployed after being unemployed for 6 months at a reduced level of unemployment benefits.	

Date	Fiscal measures	Price and incomes policy	Labor market policy	Exchange rate policy
			* Increased capacity at education institutions	
			* Enhanced job training	
November 1996	Budget agreement for 1997: *Increased green taxation			
May 1997	Package to avoid an overheating of the economy including increased 'green' taxes on cars and increased airport taxes		New social assistance law implying increased activation of recipients aged 25-30	
October 1997	Package to avoid an overheating of the economy including temporary pension contribution to ATP of 1 pct. of income from work			
October 1997	The government sells its remaining shares in Tele Danmark for 21 bill. Dkr.			
December 1997	Budget agreement for 1998 including higher indirect taxes		Tightened availability criteria for recipients of unemployment benefits	
May 1998		Statutory wage settlement to end a strike in the private sector. As a supplement to the agreement between trade unions and employers' association, the government introduces: * 2 extra holidays * 3 'caring' days for wage-earners with children under 14 * An additional pension contribution of 0.5 pct. instead of 0.9 pct.		

Date	Fiscal measures	Price and incomes policy	Labor market policy	Exchange rate policy
June 1998 ('Whitsun package')	Tax-reform: * 1 pct. pension contribution to ATP becomes permanent * Increased 'green' taxes * Lower marginal tax rates for low income groups * Reduction in tax deductibility of interests on private loans and mortgages. * Imputed rent tax replaced by local government property tax * Changed taxation of return of assets in pension funds			
June 1998	Four-year agreement on local finances: * Unchanged taxation * Expenditure growth of 1 pct.			
October 1998			New labor market reform implying among other things a maximum duration of unemployment benefits of 4 years	
November 1998	Budget agreement for 1999: * Cuts in housing allowance * Significant retrenchment of early retirement benefits including strong incentives not to enter the scheme before the age of 62 or later, increased contributions to the scheme, lowering of the pension age to 65			

2 PUBLIC SUPPORT FOR THE DANISH WELFARE STATE

Interests and Values, Institutions and Performance

Jørgen Goul Andersen

Introduction

This chapter presents an overview of popular support for the welfare state in Denmark, discussing the bases of welfare state legitimacy in terms of the interplay between interests, values, institutions and their performance. Whereas legitimacy problems were a main concern of studies of welfare state attitudes in the 1980s and early 1990s, the literature on welfare state retrenchment tended to regard the people's support for the welfare state as unconditional. This chapter builds on a notion of conditional support: In line with the welfare regime literature, we assume that attitudes are regime-dependent as the institutional configuration of the welfare state will tend to structure behavior, interests, as well as normative conceptions of welfare. Next, we suggest that support for the welfare state depends on what may be broadly labeled performance of the welfare state: (perceived) justice of distribution of taxes and benefits, efficiency, and sustainability. As several of these variables are not experienced directly by the individual, this leaves considerable room for political discourse.

While this macro level model cannot be tested systematically here, we shall test some of its implications and use it as a frame of reference for structuring our variables and interpreting our results; when operating in an analytical universe of individual level data, one may easily lose sight of macro level factors. However, we are also concerned with individual level variations. At this point, many propositions in the literature build on the premise that people act on the basis of self-interest; we balance this premise against cognitive, value-based and other normative interpretations. A particular area of interest here is the association between attitudes and people's position vis-à-vis the public sector; as more than one half of the Danish population receive their main source of income from the public sector, this association is anything but trivial.

In the next section, we briefly discuss theories of support for the welfare state and present a frame of reference for the discussion. This is followed by an overview of welfare state attitudes in Denmark and their change over time. The two following sections analyze the social variations in attitudes, in particular the division between privately employed, public employees and state dependents. Finally, we present some indicators of the sensitivity of welfare state support to the performance of the welfare state.

Conditional support for the welfare state

Throughout the 1970s and 1980s, innumerable studies prophesied a declining legitimacy of the welfare state. This is hardly surprising. One might indeed expect the legitimacy of the welfare state to be fragile in societies that compel their citizens to hand over half or more of their income in direct and indirect taxes. In Denmark, taxes are not only high; they are also extremely visible: Payroll taxes or social security contributions are almost absent and replaced by ordinary income tax.[1] In fact, Denmark *did* experience a tax revolt in 1973 when the anti-tax 'Progress Party' entered the Danish parliament with 15.9 pct. of the votes; since then, however, taxes have not been very a salient issue, and the Progress Party as well as its successor, the Danish People's Party, had to find another agenda issue (immigration) to survive the 1980s (Bjørklund & Goul Andersen, 2002).

Three classic types of legitimacy problems have repeatedly surfaced in discussions of the welfare state. They may take on new shapes from time to time, but the basic arguments – and counterarguments – are essentially the same. First, theories about modernization often claim that solidarity will decline as a consequence of increasing wealth, the decline of the working class, the development of a broad 'middle mass' (Wilensky, 1976), or the appearance of new, knowledge-based classes with individualist aspirations. However, such theories fail to acknowledge that in European welfare systems the middle class is about as much a part of the welfare state as the lower classes.

A second classic group of arguments encompasses various theories of 'colonization' or 'clientilization' of the welfare state (Habermas, 1981; Wolfe, 1989; Giddens, 1998). However, the claim that institutionalized solidarity in the welfare state will erode solidarity in civil society builds on a zero-sum assumption that is neither logically nor empirically well grounded (Rothstein, 2001; Juul, 2002). By the same token, the tendency to see users and clients as passive subjects is contradicted by the high levels of formal and informal user participation in the public sector (Goul Andersen & Hoff, 2001: Ch. 8).

---

1 This does not mean that taxes on labor are excessively high; if we add social contributions or employers' fees, which can be considered invisible income taxes, Denmark is close to the European average in its relative reliance on taxes on labor and considerably lower than countries like Germany or Belgium (OECD, 2004). It is high indirect taxes that distinguish Denmark. However, along with Sweden, Denmark has the most progressive income tax system.

A third cluster of theories concern demand overload or tax protest rooted in voters' 'fiscal illusions' – the belief that they can have it all for next to nothing (Citrin, 1979).[2] However, tax protest has become a rare phenomenon, and comprehensive empirical studies (e.g. Confalonieri & Newton, 1995) have consistently falsified theories of declining welfare state legitimacy. The evidence is so strong that Pierson's (1994, 1998) studies of welfare retrenchment simply took voter resistance for granted. However, like the fiscal illusion argument this position fails to acknowledge that learning processes and the mobilization of crisis awareness can sometimes make even retrenchment fairly acceptable (Petersen et al., 1987).

But legitimacy problems could also be rooted in changing social structures in other ways. In Denmark, about 30 per cent of the labor force are public employees. Unemployment, disability and early retirement have placed a growing proportion of the working age population outside the labor market, relying on social transfers for their income. Adding old age pensioners to this, we face a large majority of the adult population who receives its main income from the public sector. At this point, two potential conflict lines are imaginable. Either between the privately employed and those who receive their income from the public sector, or between the gainfully employed and those marginalized or excluded from the labor market. When unemployment is high, those who enjoy a safe labor market position are usually regarded as privileged. From a narrow perspective of self-interest, however, they could also come to see themselves as the 'victims' of an overtaxing, overly generous welfare state. Such a polarization would not necessarily lead to low aggregate support for the welfare state, but insufficient support among those who finance these programmes would certainly constitute a serious legitimacy problem. This question is examined below on the basis of data from the period when mass unemployment peaked in Denmark.

A common premise for most of the arguments above is that people, in their attitudes and overt behavior regarding the welfare state, act on the basis of self-interest, often narrowly conceived and short-sighted. Three criticisms may be leveled against this assumption. First, we might object on classical sociological grounds that behavior is determined more by norms or values, both generally shared norms of solidarity and norms or values associated with social class, sector, generation or gender. A second line of criticism would not attack the assumption of interest-motivated behavior as such, but rather its narrowness.

---

2 A classic shared by scholars to the left and to the right was 'demand overload' theories claiming that the welfare state's inability to satisfy rising expectations under conditions of limited economic growth would leave the government in a state of economic and moral bankruptcy (Habermas, 1975; Rose & Peters, 1978).

People learn through collective political mobilization, or through education, to act in more reflexive ways, for instance to be aware of collective interests.

The third line of criticism is institutional. Even if we assume that people act out of self-interest, it is difficult to specify what would constitute self-interest in an encompassing Scandinavian welfare state. In the first place, interest categories are blurred by the fact that most people have a family. This is particularly important in societies dominated by the dual breadwinner family pattern. For instance, 'unemployment homogamy' (Halvorsen, 1999) where both spouses are unemployed is rare. Further, interest categories are blurred by the redistribution over the life course. This means that interests should be defined by one's entire life trajectory rather than one's present position. In an institutional welfare state where the state provides a safety net for a very broad range of social risks, and where most of the 'risk pooling' of the welfare state includes the entire population, there are very few welfare areas where an individual can be entirely disinterested.[3] Even if people acted out of pure self-interest, they would find it difficult to calculate their exact self-interest except in rather extreme cases.[4]

Such 'extreme cases' do not include the majority of the low-income group, which is comprised of pensioners and young people, and neither group can be assumed to act very much in accordance with current self-interests. Apart from a small group of very marginalized people, the only group with unambiguous interests is a rather small group of individuals and families with the very highest incomes. For the majority among the middle classes, interests are blurred. Herein lies the paradox of the universal welfare states: They are by far the most redistributive states and therefore less beneficial to the upper middle classes than any other type of welfare state (Rothstein, 1998; Nolan et al., 2000). And yet, apart from those with the highest incomes, the upper middle classes can be expected to be quite happy about their situation.[5]

---

3 As pointed out by Esping-Andersen (1990) and others, only the most residual welfare states draw a clear dividing line between those who have a (potential) interest in expanding the welfare state and those who have an interest in keeping expenditure at a minimum.

4 Besides, the well-known phenomenon of risk aversion would make people care even less about costs and benefits, as long as they are adequately protected.

5 In Danish public debates, the middle classes' access to benefits from the welfare state has sometimes been referred to as a 'bribe' to ensure support. Needless to say, such thinking only makes sense within the mental confines of a residual welfare state. European welfare states – continental European as well as Scandinavian – are characterized by extensive public risk management, which normally includes the entire population (with varying degrees of solidaristic risk pooling between high risk groups and low risk groups). However, a truly residual welfare state which is not oriented towards risk management but only towards protecting the poor (leaving the middle classes to private insurance companies or private service providers) produces very visible divisions, and (to put it in rational terms) the information costs to calculate one's self-interest are considerably lower.

CRISIS, MIRACLES, AND BEYOND

Except for the richest, the information costs required for people to calculate their self-interest are so high that even self-interested people are not induced to take a stand on welfare issues on the basis of narrow self-interest. Instead, they must be assumed to take a stand on the basis of their everyday experience with the operations of the welfare state, and (in particular) on the basis of their experience of the welfare state as defined in public debates.

This leads to an institutional theory about the legitimacy of the welfare state. Support for the welfare state can be assumed to depend less on personal interests than on one's experience (personal or learned from the media and public debates) that it is *just* (just distribution of benefits and taxes, low levels of fraud and abuse), that it is *efficient*, and that it is *sustainable*. This argument rests on attributes of the entire welfare system rather than on variations among individuals, and its propositions are difficult to test on cross-sectional individual level data from one country, but at least we are able to provide some plausible evidence. Along with this argument, which is addressed below, we briefly discuss other macro level approaches that emphasize institutional factors and the importance of political discourse.

Unless otherwise indicated, the analyses presented below are based on data from Danish election surveys from 1969 to 2001,[6] and from 'Welfare Survey 2000'. All of these surveys were conducted using personal interviews with representative samples of the Danish population, typically some 2000 respondents in the election surveys, and 1235 respondents in the 'Welfare Value Survey'.[7] A few time series are updated by a mid-term survey conducted in 2003 and by a pre-election survey conducted during the 2005 election campaign. Both are telephone surveys with some 560 respondents.[8]

Basic support for the welfare state: an overview

Fundamentally broad support for the welfare state persists among the Danes. Different indicators cover various periods, but they reveal roughly parallel

---

6 For information about the Danish Election Project, see http://www.valg.aau.dk.

7 Fieldwork for the Welfare Value Survey was done by ACNielsen AIM, which also did the fieldwork in 1987/88 and 1998. For the other election studies, except from 1971 to 1973, fieldwork was conducted by the Danish Gallup Institute. The election surveys have all been financed by the Danish Social Science Research Council; the Welfare Value Survey was financed by *Ugebrevet Mandag Morgen* and the '2000 Foundation'.

8 The welfare survey and the 2003 and 2005 surveys were conducted by the author in cooperation with *Ugebrevet Mandag Morgen*.

trends. The best single indicator covering the entire period from 1969 to 2005[9] is a forced choice item in which the respondent is asked to choose between the statements: 'Social reforms have gone too far. More so than now, people should manage without social security and contributions from society', and, 'The social reforms that have been carried out in this country should be maintained at least at the present level'. In 2000, 69 pct. of the adult population answered that the reforms should be maintained at least at the present level, while only 25 pct. believed that reforms had gone too far (Table 1). In general, there is little support for welfare retrenchment.

TABLE 1.

Basic Welfare State Attitudes, 1994-2005. Percentages and PDIs (percentage difference indexes) in favor of the welfare state.

		Agree mostly with A	Agree mostly with B	Indifferent/ Don't know	Total	PDI (in favor of welfare state)
A: Social reforms have gone too far	1994	28	63	9	100	35
	1998	30	63	7	100	33
	2000	25	69	6	100	44
B: Social reforms maintained	2001	34	58	8	100	24
	2005	20	74	7	100	54
A: Prefer tax relief	1994	47	44	9	100	-3
B: Prefer improved welfare services	1998	41	54	5	100	13
	2000	40	55	5	100	15
	2001	45	51	4	100	6
	2003	34	61	5	100	27
	2005	35	61	4	100	26

*) Wordings:

1. 'First a question about government spending on social programmes.

A says: 'Social reforms have gone too far. More than now, people should manage without social security and contributions from society'

B says: 'The social reforms that have been carried through in this country should be maintained at least at the present level'. – Do you agree mostly with A or with B?''

2. 'If it becomes possible in the long run to lower taxation, what would you prefer: ...

A: Tax relief or B: Improved public services?'

Source: 1994, 1998, 2001: Election surveys (N=2000); 2000: Welfare survey (N=1235); 2003: Mid-term survey; 2005: Pre-election survey (N=560).

---

9 In an analysis conducted in cooperation with 'Huset Mandag Morgen' in 2000 (Mandag Morgen, 2000), we had the opportunity to test this item against various composite indexes. Although the indexes revealed a slightly higher explained variance due to the reduction of 'noise', the single item here fared surprisingly well (Goul Andersen, 2000). Therefore we can with confidence use this single indicator as our main measure of general welfare state support in the following, for the sake of simplicity.

This is also confirmed by another item that asks about *preferences* with respect to the trade-off between welfare and taxes. Even leaving out the possibility of retrenchment and asking about whether they would prefer tax relief or improved welfare services in the future, a small majority of the respondents in 2000 preferred improved welfare services. After the adoption of a tax relief in 2003, the majority for more welfare increased immediately to nearly two thirds. The demand for lower taxes among Danish voters is obviously not very strong.

TABLE 2.
Political agenda among Danish voters, 1971-2005. Percentages of answers given

	1971	1973	1975	1981	1987	1990	1994	1998	2000	2001	2005
1. Unemployment	3	1	40	44	16	29	24	7	3	3	16
2. Bal. of payment	5	3	2	8	21	8	3	1	1	.	.
3. Economics, else	19	14	30	20	10	11	12	6	3	4	3
4. Taxes	12	24	6	6	2	9	2	5	6	4	5
1-4. Total econ.	39	42	78	78	49	57	41	19	13	9	24
5. Environment	8	4	1	2	15	10	8	9	8	3	4
6. Welfare	26	14	4	8	15	20	38	47	47	55	53
7. Immigration	-	-	-	-	4	4	8	14	22	23	13
8. EU, foreign pol.1)	17	3	1	2	3	3	3	5	5	6	3
9. Else	10	37	16	10	14	6	2	62)	52)	4	3
Total	100	100	100	100	100	100	100	100	100	100	100

Wording: 'Now, I would like to ask which problems you consider the most important today, which politicians should handle?'

The table shows the distribution of all answers. On average, respondents gave 2.4 responses in 1998, slightly less than two answers in the 1970s.

1) Including defense.

2) Of which: Law and order 3 pct. in 1998 and 2001, 2 pct. in 2000.

Source: 1971-1990, 1998, 2001: Election surveys. 1994: calculated from Thomsen (1995). 2005 pre-election survey.

The response pattern revealed when voters are asked about what issues are most salient to them confirms the lack of interest in taxes (Table 2). Tax relief has been among the core issues in party competition, including several election campaigns, but it has not really been on the voters' agenda since 1973. In 1990, the bourgeois government called for an election on the issue of (largely unfinanced) tax relief. Not surprisingly, in the 1990 election survey, 54 pct. answered that taxation was the most important issue in the *electoral campaign in the media*. However, only a small minority among the voters regarded taxes as the most important problem, and the Social Democrats won by a landslide (Bille et al.,

1992: 89).[10] Also since 2000, the tax issue has repeatedly been on the media's agenda, and in the election campaigns it has played a significant role (van der Brugge & Voss, 2003). But it has attracted little interest among voters.

The questions about saliency also reveal that voters are not narrowly concerned with self-interest. If they were, they would mainly be concerned with welfare and taxes throughout the period as these are the issues that most directly affect themselves. However, voters' political priorities have fluctuated considerably. Since the end of the 1990s, welfare problems alongside immigration have been at the top of the agenda and economic problems at the bottom. But during the long economic crisis from the mid-1970s to the mid-1990s, unemployment and occasionally even the balance of payment deficit were the most important problems cited by Danish voters.

FIGURE 1.
Long term trend in support for the welfare state. PDI's in favour of welfare.

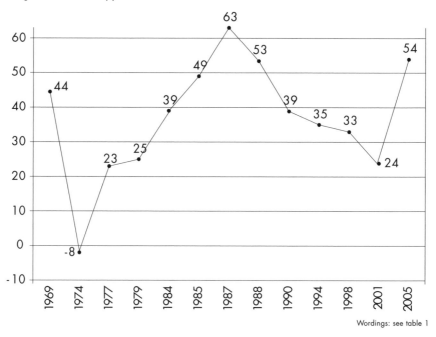

Wordings: see table 1

The long-term trend in support for the welfare state is presented in Figure 1. The figure confirms that there was a great backlash in 1973. It was short-lived, but some welfare skepticism remained throughout the 1970s. Considering the

---

10 Voters were very aware of their personal advantages (Goul Andersen, 1994: 85), but during the election campaign, the proportion regarding taxes as important dropped from some 20 pct. to 9 pct., and in the election survey immediately after the election, the proportion had declined further to only 6 pct.

CRISIS, MIRACLES, AND BEYOND

continued growth in public expenditures from about 50 pct. of GFI in 1972 to about 70 pct. in 1981 (see Goul Andersen & Christiansen, 1991), this is perhaps not so surprising. As a Conservative coalition government took office in 1982 with an (intended) zero-growth policy, sentiments began to change, however. When the prime minister announced in the mid-1980s that the economy had fared 'incredibly well', little support remained for welfare retrenchment. Ironically, the figures around 2005 are higher than in 1969 during the heyday of the welfare state. However, the welfare state that voters want to preserve today is considerably larger than the one voters supported in 1969.

Voter support for specific welfare programs is presented in Table 3, which describes spending attitudes during the period 1979 to 2005.

TABLE 3.

Attitudes towards welfare spending, 1979-2005. Percentages and balance of opinion (percentage points)

	2000: The state should spend ...				Balance of opinion: Spend more minus spend less								
	more	as now	less	Dk	79	85	90	94	98	00	01	03	05
Health care	77	21	2	0	28	61	61	73	77	75	67	49	55
Home help	73	23	3	1	.	.	.	73	69	70	69	61	70
Rest homes	75	23	1	1	.	.	.	.	.	74	.	.	.
Old age pension	60	37	2	1	56	64	57	51	42	58	46	38	41
Education	53	43	3	1	22	44	45	42	39	50	46	46	65
Kindergartens	49	42	7	2	20	24	29	32	36	42	33	.	.
Child allowances	16	62	20	2	.	.	.	0	0	-4	.	.	.
Leave programmes[1]	30	49	18	3	.	.	.	-20	-7	12	.	.	.
Activation of unemployed[2]	28	47	23	2	.	.	.	1	1	5	.	.	.
Unemployment benefits (level)	17	69	12	2	-42	17	2	0	-7	5	-1	.	.
Social assistance (level)	14	61	22	3	.	30	-11	-11	-19	-8	-13	.	.
Cultural purposes	12	40	46	2	-30	-12	-19	-34	-39	-34	-32	.	.
Aid to developing countries	12	42	44	2	.	.	-26	-35	-40	-32	-32	-12	5
Integration of immigrants	22	34	41	3	.	.	.	.	.	-19	.	.	.
Support for refugees/ immigrants					.	.	-30	-35	-41	.	-33	-13	-1

Wording 2000: 'Now, I'll ask about your view on public expenditures for various purposes. I should like to know whether you think government should spend: 1) much more, 2) a little more, 3) the same, 4) a little less, or 5) much less money on these tasks.'

1979-1998: '... I should like to ask whether you think, government spends: 1) too much, 2) appropriate, or 3) too little money on these tasks.'

Notes
1) 2000: Parental leave; 1994-1998: leave arrangements.
2) 1994-1988: Support to bring unemployed into employment.

Table 4 tabulates responses to a battery of questions on government responsibilities (from the ISSP 1996 survey, replicated in the 1994 election survey and the 2000 Welfare Survey), largely indicating a similar prioritization of tasks with a few remarkable exceptions.

TABLE 4.
Attitudes towards the scope of government, 1994 and 2000.
Percentages and average index values on a scale 1-4

To what extent should it be the government's responsibility to ...	Defi- nitely should be	Prob- ably should be	Prob- ably should not be	Defi- nitely should not be	Don't know	Index 2000 (1-4)	Index 1994 (1-4)
Provide health care for the sick	83	14	2	1	0	1.19	1.06
Provide a decent standard of living for the old	71	26	3	0	0	1.33	1.09
Provide child care for everybody who needs it	53	35	8	4	0	1.62	.
Provide a decent standard of living for the unemployed	33	48	16	2	1	1.88	1.53
Provide decent housing for those who can't afford it	39	45	12	3	1	1.78	1.63
Integrate immigrants	38	40	13	7	2	1.90	.
Provide good leisure facilities for children and young people	32	46	18	3	1	1.93	.
Provide leave arrangements for families with small children	30	46	15	8	1	2.00	.
Provide leisure facilities for pensioners	28	46	19	6	1	2.03	.
Provide a job for everyone who wants one	19	44	25	10	2	2.26	2.00
Reduce income differences between the rich and the poor	19	27	27	25	2	2.60	2.26

Unlike the 1994 survey and the ISSP, the 2000 questionnaire included the phrase 'to what extent' it should be the government's responsibility to take care of various tasks. This may have induced respondents to graduate their answers a little more, even though the response categories are identical. This assumption is confirmed by comparison with the 1994 Danish election survey.

Table 5 presents equivalent figures for other countries. The findings can be summarized as follows:

CRISIS, MIRACLES, AND BEYOND

TABLE 5.

Attitudes towards the scope of government, and 'non-financial work commitment.' Denmark 2000 and ISSP survey 1996. Proportions answering 'definitely' or 'probably should be'. Percentages

To what extent should it be the government's responsibility to ...	Denmark	Sweden	Norway	W. Germany	France	UK	USA
Provide health care for the sick	97	96	99	97	89	98	85
Provide a decent standard of living for the old	97	98	99	86	92	98	87
Provide a decent standard of living for the unemployed	81	90	93	80	81	79	48
Provide decent housing for those who can't afford it	86	82	74	78	87	89	67
Provide a job for everyone who wants one	64	65	81	75	69	69	39
Reduce income differences between the rich and the poor	47	71	73	63	74	68	48
Non-financial work commitment: Average on scale 1-5 (ISSP 1997).[1]	2.00	2.26	2.30	2.48	2.76	2.72	2.61
Agree/agree strongly (pct.)	78	61	61	70	53	47	50

1) Wording: I would enjoy having a paid job even if I did not need the money (strongly agree=1; strongly disagree=5).

Source: ISSP 1996, 1997, and Welfare Value Survey.

TOP PRIORITIES: HEALTH CARE, PENSIONS AND CARE FOR THE ELDERLY

With respect to these policy areas, public responsibility is absolute – as is the case in most other European countries (see also Taylor-Gooby, 1995, 1998) and public opinion supports this arrangement. Danes are clearly inclined to spend more money in these areas with the partial exception of old age pensions.[11] Again, this is not significantly different from attitudes in most other countries (Goul Andersen et al., 1999).

---

11 Attitudes towards pension spending are interesting because the introduction of labor market pensions may eventually 'crowd out' the universal, flat-rate pension system. However, it may be too early to read the data as an adaptation to such institutional change; improved pensions in 1988 and concern for the 'pension bomb' in the mid-1990s could be an alternative explanation. Data from 2000 based on a slightly different wording seems to indicate a new break – this time upwards.

From an interest perspective, this is sometimes explained by the fact that these welfare provisions are accessible to everyone. However, as argued above, universal access directly or indirectly pertains to most welfare provisions. It is also a well-known fact that young persons are not very much aware of the risk of becoming disabled and even less of the risk of growing old (i.e., they will tend to forget insurance and fail to make pension savings in time – these are classical arguments for public intervention). Note also that spending attitudes are not constant. In 1979, only a minority wanted to spend more on health care. The change that followed may be seen as a rational response to retrenchment in the 1980s,[12] and it also appears that after significant budget improvements around 2000-2003, the pressure for further increases again became more moderate – for a while, at least.

EDUCATION AND CHILD CARE

The questionnaire did not contain a question about public responsibility for education, but we can safely assume that this is also considered to be a fundamental task of government. Not surprisingly, this is also one of the areas where most people are inclined to invest more money. More surprisingly, provision of public child care is also considered a basic responsibility of the welfare state. We don't have any comparative data on this issue, but the omission of this item from the standard ISSP questionnaire may perhaps by itself be seen as an indicator that this is a Scandinavian characteristic.

HOUSING, UNEMPLOYMENT BENEFITS, AND INTEGRATION OF IMMIGRANTS

When it comes to decent housing, decent unemployment benefits, and integration of immigrants, we notice a marked difference between the questions about public responsibility and public spending. With respect to unemployment benefits, a huge majority wants to maintain the status quo in size of benefits (in contrast to 1979 when unemployment benefits were considered too generous), and until 2001, a very large minority wants to save on the costs associated with refugees and immigrants. However, these tasks, including integration of immigrants, range next to the 'most basic' tasks of government

---

12 Relatively speaking at least, retrenchment was quite harsh. Total public expenditure as pct. of Gross Factor Income (GFI) was nearly constant from 1981 to 1992 – 71.3 and 70.1 pct. respectively. But expenditure for health care declined from 7.0 pct. to 6.2 pct., and elderly care declined from 3.5 to 3.2 pct. (by 1987 – later statistics not comparable). Old age pensions declined from 6.0 pct. to 5.2 pct. (however, nearly one half of this decline is due to a formal change in accounting) (see Goul Andersen & Christiansen, 1991; Goul Andersen, 1998, 2001; see also Pallesen & Dahl in this volume.

referred to above. A plausible interpretation is that these tasks are essential for securing full citizenship for all inhabitants of the country, even though they are not placed as high in the spending hierarchy. It also shows that one should be careful not to extrapolate too far from the questions on expenditure.

It is also noteworthy that under the Liberal-Conservative government after the 2001 election, it only took moderate cutbacks in spending for immigrants and foreign aid to change the distribution of preferences considerably. By 2005, most voters were satisfied with the current level of spending, and only a small minority wanted further budget cuts in these fields. Again, we are reminded that people react to policies and not only automatically favor areas that serve their own interests.

OTHER WELFARE AREAS
Outside the 'basic' areas referred to above, the demand for public involvement is less strong, and especially in the field of culture, quite a large proportion of respondents want to cut public spending. Needless to say, people also want to save on public administration. It is remarkable also that leave arrangements (parental, educational and sabbatical leaves), which were introduced in the early 1990s, were not too popular – they probably enjoyed broad acceptance, at least in the beginning, but there has never been a broad popular demand to increase spending in such areas further.[13]

PROVISION OF JOBS AND REDISTRIBUTION OF INCOME
Finally, it is remarkable that the provision of jobs and redistribution of income are not listed among the fundamental tasks of government among Danish voters. This departs from the general Scandinavian pattern in which pursuing a policy of full employment is considered an important task for government; in Norway and Sweden, it is also among the most highly prioritized spending areas (Goul Andersen et al., 1999).

The findings here are in line with other surveys indicating a long-term decline in support for equality – or, more precisely, for *more* equality (see also Table 7 below). Apparently the 'passion for equality' (Graubard, 1986) is not so unambiguous in the Nordic countries; at least this does not seem to be the case in Denmark. It must be acknowledged that the responses probably also reflect the fact that unlike most other countries, Denmark was able to maintain or even improve equality during the 1980s and 1990s (Förster, 2000); one cannot infer from these findings that great inequality would be acceptable to the

---

13 The sabbatical leave was stopped already in the mid-1990s, and educational leave was terminated in 2000; in 2002, the parental leave programme was replaced by a prolonged maternity/paternity leave (52 weeks to be divided between both parents).

Danes. To take an example, there has so far been nearly unanimous opposition to lowering the minimum wage,[14] and comparing perceptions of proper income differentials, Danes resemble other Scandinavians in their preference for small differentials (Albrekt Larsen, 2006). Still, there does seem to be a long-term trend in attitudes revealing increasing acceptance of *some* inequality, perhaps a change towards an ideology of equality of opportunity rather than equality in results. Commenting on similar findings in Norway, Martinussen (1988) has described this mix of attitudes as 'solidaristic individualism'. Regardless of the exact interpretation of such findings, it would at least seem that equality may be a premise, but probably not the driving force behind the demand for welfare state expansion in recent decades.

UNUSUALLY HIGH WORK COMMITMENT?

To safeguard against erroneous interpretations, and to highlight the paradox, we note that attitudes towards government responsibility for employment do not reflect less emphasis on the importance of work. On the contrary, Danes have the strongest 'non-financial employment commitment', not only among the Nordic countries (Svallfors et al., 2001), but among all countries in the world where it has been measured. In effect, it is perfectly logical that a strong work ethic underpins the broad acceptance of generous social security; otherwise, suspicions of abuse would probably erode support for welfare arrangements that in some instances give small incentives to work.

A NOTE ON FISCAL ILLUSIONS, DEMAND
OVERLOAD AND CRISIS AWARENESS

As indicated, these results add some important qualifications to the idea of fiscal illusions, i.e., the assumption that voters want lower taxes while simultaneously demanding more services from government. In the first place, the premise that most people want lower taxes is wrong. In the 1990s, Danish voters were concerned about welfare *and* government debt. In 1994, 67 pct. agreed that 'In the present economic situation, we cannot afford to lower taxes'.[15] Furthermore, one should not assume people indiscriminately want more from government.

---

14 There is no minimum wage law in Denmark, but collective agreements in the labor market set an equally efficient *de facto* minimum wage, which is rather high in comparison with most countries. In the Welfare Values Survey 2000, 69 pct. disagreed with the statement that 'minimum wages should be lowered in order to improve employment opportunities for people without qualifications'. Even though the question explicitly referred to employment, only 17 pct. agreed.

15 The figures reflect a strong persuasion effect, but on an equivalent item concerning wage increases, there have been large fluctuations, including a majority expressing disagreement (Goul Andersen, 1994).

While this may hold true for interest associations, it is not true for ordinary Danes. In the question batteries about public spending referred to above, we actually find only a few areas where an absolute majority wants to spend more. Third, even if it is true that aggregating the spending preferences above would probably reveal a demand for spending that exceeds the willingness to pay taxes, we should not ignore that even within popular fields such as health care, there may be support for cost cutting measures or user charges within particular programmes (plastic surgery or refertilization are classical examples). Further, even if voters want 'more for less', this may also be an expression of a belief that productivity gains are possible and should be pursued. In the market, consumers are frequently able to get 'more for less', and it would be equally wrongheaded to assume that this is *not* possible in the public sector. As in the household, people may be surprised when they aggregate the economic consequences of their preferences. But one is equally struck by the 'realism' of Danish spending preferences. Given the unusually good shape of the Danish economy around 2000, demands actually appear quite modest.

Perhaps these modest demands reflect the lingering consequences of the mobilization of crisis awareness among Danes over the last two decades of the 20th century, especially in the early 1980s and around 1990 (Petersen, 1996). In 1979, the Social Democratic Minister of Finance had described Danish economy as 'balancing on the edge of the abyss' – which was no exaggeration. Throughout the 1980s the media focused on economic problems, heightening public awareness of the situation (Goul Andersen, 1994). Otherwise unpopular reforms such as cuts in public spending and abolition of the automatic indexation of wages became possible without much public outcry. Throughout the 1980s and 1990s, voters did not flock to parties advocating lower taxes. The assumption of 'demand overload' theories that people act mechanically, are unreceptive to political appeals about economic problems and unable to adjust their expectations simply does not hold up in the Danish case.

CONCLUSIONS

We have not tested every assertion about the legitimacy problems of the Danish welfare state, but already from the short overview above we can draw some general conclusions.

Basic welfare consensus persists. Changes in class structure and increasing individualism have not reduced support for the welfare state, nor have visible tendencies towards demand overload materialized among Danish voters. Most voters want to maintain public welfare at least at the present level and largely agree about the basic responsibilities of government, which also include provisions for immigrants, in spite of the dissatisfaction that prevailed with the level of expenditure on and other aspects of refugee and immigration policy in the 1990s.

People react to policy change. Time series data on health care and unemployment benefits, as well as on support for refugees and immigrants or for foreign aid clearly indicate that people adjust their demands to changing provisions.

Governability. The data lends no support to any idea that the welfare state has become ungovernable. In times of economic hardship, Danish voters can be persuaded to accept retrenchment – but not necessarily retrenchment of any kind.

This also indicates that people do not act mechanically on the basis of self-interest. This assumption is further explored in the following analysis of social variations in attitudes towards the welfare state.

Social variations

This section provides a brief overview of variations in general attitudes towards the welfare state across social categories. For the sake of simplicity, the overview is mainly based on responses to a single question (the forced choice question on social reforms having gone too far vs. should be maintained at present levels, as presented in the previous section). However, wherever necessary, we also report a few significant results from a full-scale analysis in 2000 of the subdimensions and overall composite indices.[16] We focus in particular on the debate about self-interest as a determining factor in welfare attitudes because so much of the research and analyses (both scholarly and popular) in the field is implicitly based on this assumption.

An overview of variations across social groups is presented in Table 6. Entries are percentage point difference between the proportion answering that 'social reforms should be maintained' and the proportion responding that 'social reforms have gone too far'. Beginning with *gender*, we find that women are slightly more positive. Even though the gender difference has increased somewhat since 2000 (Andersen & Goul Andersen, 2003), especially among the young, the gender gap on this general item is somewhat smaller than on concrete expenditure questions.[17] Still, the main gender difference is not in attitudes but saliency. When asked in 2001 about the most important problems, 61 pct. of the surveyed women pointed to a welfare issue; among men, the corresponding figure was only 39 pct. Conversely, only 7 pct. of the women surveyed indicated that taxes were the most important issue, while this issue was highly salient to 15

---

16 As compared to the analysis here, the full scale analysis largely reveals parallel trends on different subdimensions and more reliable findings on composite indices, resulting in a higher explained variance. However, the single question used here captures the main tendency and even competes well in terms of 'noise reduction'/explained variance.

17 Overall, men tend to be slightly less willing to spend more money *at all*. This corresponds with a similar gender difference in relation to taxes.

pct. of the men surveyed. Even larger differences are found on questions about overall economic strategies (e.g., to combat unemployment), where respondents were asked to choose between an 'export strategy' and a 'welfare strategy'; here gender differences tended to be even larger than differences across supporters of various political parties (Andersen & Goul Andersen, 2003).

TABLE 6.

Welfare attitudes, by social background factors and party choice. Balance of opinion in favour of the welfare state ('maintain social reforms' minus 'social reforms have gone too far'), percentage points. 2000

	Maintain social reforms (2000)	(N)
Men	40	622
Women	48	613
18-29 years	36	295
30-39 years	46	276
40-49 years	49	253
50-59 years	54	233
60 + years	38	179
basic education 7-9 years	54	401
basic education 10 years	45	471
High school exam	33	362
Unskilled worker	60	170
Skilled worker	55	160
Lower white collar	46	223
Higher white collar	41	235
Self-employed, Farmer	22	70
Private employees	42	446
Public employees	56	348
Left wing parties	76	111
Social Democrats	73	361
Center parties	40	108
Liberals, Conservatives	9	328
Danish People's Party/Progress Party	26	99

Source: 2000: Welfare value survey; 2001: see notes to Table 2.

Educational and class differences are also small,[18] except between the self-employed and wage earners; typically, if the group of 'higher' white collar workers is delineated more narrowly, they also reveal more welfare skepticism, especially the privately employed. But otherwise, differences are small, reflecting a broad welfare consensus. While it is reasonable to speak of a consensus across *social* groups, strong *political* divisions in attitudes remain. Among Social Democrats and left wing voters, support for the welfare state is nearly unanimous, and there is also overwhelming support among the adherents of the centrist parties. But among Liberal and Conservative voters in 2001, nearly one half of those who took a stand believed that welfare had gone too far. At this point, saliency largely corresponds with attitudes; among Social Democratic and left wing voters, only 6 and 3 pct. (respectively) mentioned taxation as an important issue in 2001 (Goul Andersen, 2001). Among voters supporting Denmark's 1973 tax revolt party and its successor, the Danish People's Party, taxation is no longer a salient issue. Only 6 pct. mentioned taxes as important, compared to 22 pct. among Conservative and Liberal voters, and 15 pct. among the centre parties' voters.

The three factors that relate most clearly to interests are age, employment sector, and income. According to an interpretation in terms of self-interests, the relationship between education, class and welfare attitudes would be mediated mainly by income and/or by actual or potential use of welfare programmes. As far as the employment sector is concerned, we should expect public employees to be 'budget maximizers', i.e. to be particularly keen about securing more resources for the public sector, or at least for the sector where they are themselves employed. However, data does not correspond very well with such expectations.

Beginning with age, an interest perspective would predict that the young and the elderly were most positively inclined towards the welfare state, i.e., we should find a 'U'-shaped relationship. However, we find exactly the opposite in the Danish case: the middle-aged are the most positive and the younger and the older age groups the most negative. This is a stable finding in all surveys around 2000, and a similar relationship is found on nearly all indicators. This is not difficult to explain: Voters aged 40 to 49 years in 2000 were socialized in the 1970s, a period marked by the political mobilization of new left values (Svensson & Togeby, 1986). This has had a generational effect on nearly all attitudes, as can be seen from Table 7. By 1979, the 18 to 29 year-olds were

---

18 The educational difference in Table 5 actually happens to be statistically significant. This is unusual, and we found no significant effects on the composite measures in the Welfare Values Survey; rather, the effects of the other background variables raise the value just above the significance level.

very positively inclined towards the welfare state, economic equality and state regulation of business. In 1998, the same cohorts had largely maintained these attitudes, while new cohorts hold more liberalist views. These findings do not exclude the possibility that, other things being equal, there might be a small life cycle effect in the predicted direction. But the point is exactly that other things are not equal, i.e. that interest effects are so small that they are completely overshadowed by value effects.

TABLE 7.

Attitudes towards the welfare state, economic equality and state control with business, by age. 1979, 1994 and 1998. PDI

	Maintain social reforms			More income equality			State control of business		
Age	1979	1994	1998	1979	1994	1998	1979	1994	1998
18-29	44	38	26	42	4	-14	19	-14	-20
30-39	30	52	35	23	13	6	-6	-7	-14
40-49	16	35	49	11	10	23	-29	-20	-11
50 +	19	25	27	12	8	4	-24	-42	-37

TABLE 8.

Political agenda, by age. Proportion of voters mentioning the issue as important. 2001 (1998). Percentages

	Tax 1998	Tax 2001	Welfare total 2001[1]	of which:			(N)
				Health care	Old age issues	Children and young	
Total	11	11	50	22	27	12	972
18-29 years	14	18	45	19	15	17	195
30-39 years	10	13	54	24	21	16	190
40-49 years	12	13	45	22	21	10	172
50-59 years	11	9	50	22	31	9	163
60-69 years	9	6	54	20	43	10	130
70 + years	5	2	55	27	40	8	121

1) As people may mention more than one welfare issue, totals are less than the sum of the following figures.

Source: Election survey and 2001 survey (see Table 2), see Goul Andersen (2001).

As far as saliency is concerned, the evidence is mixed (Table 8). In 2001, after an intense media campaign, the saliency of taxes simply followed age: the younger, the more concerned about taxes. This is difficult to explain from an interest perspective, but easy to explain as issue mobilization: Young people are more receptive to new ideas and new issues. The aggregate figures for saliency of welfare are unrelated to age, but when we turn to the specific welfare issues, we find a pattern that corresponds to what one should expect from an interest perspective. Especially the saliency of old age issues (care, pensions, etc.) is strongly related to age.

This is hardly surprising; more surprisingly, we do not find similar variations in attitudes when we look at particular spending areas (Table 9). Thus, we find almost no significant age differences in attitudes towards expenditure for the elderly (pensions, care and health care). As far as expenditure for the young is concerned (education, child care, child allowances and parental leave), figures generally do come out as predicted. But as to education, the association is weak, and some of the other associations may reflect generational experiences and expectations; a couple of decades ago, even the middle aged were reluctant to consider child care a task for the public sector (Goul Andersen, 1993), and we still encounter a marked decline of support among the elderly. Explaining attitudes about unemployment benefits and social assistance does not flow easily from an interest perspective; why are the young the most negative and the 40 to 49 year-olds the most supportive? Again, issue mobilization offers a more plausible explanation. Economic experts have advocated reducing these benefits – and tightening qualifications for benefits, too (Goul Andersen, 2002). Finally, we find persistent age effects on attitudes towards spending on immigrant integration; but this is part of a larger syndrome, which is outside the scope of this chapter. Overall, however, even those age differences that do conform to an interest interpretation are rather small.

TABLE 9.

Age and attitudes towards welfare expenditures, 2000.
Balances of opinion in favor of increased spending

	Age						
	18-29	30-39	40-49	50-59	60+	eta	beta
Health care	72	78	77	74	72	.05	.06
Home help	67	67	75	73	75	.07	.06
Rest homes	67	70	75	83	81	.13**	.10*
Old age pension	54	55	66	61	59	.09	.08
Education	49	49	55	56	40	.09*	.09*
Child care	53	56	39	26	22	.22**	.24**
Child allowances	9	-1	-8	-12	-15	.14**	.16**
Parental leave	14	33	12	0	-12	.21**	.22**
Unemployment benefits (level)	-7	4	15	12	4	.20**	.20**
Social assistance (level)	-23	-16	6	4	-4	.20**	.20**
Integration of immigrants	-8	-24	-16	-20	-39	.13**	.08*

Wordings: See Table 3. Beta coefficients refer to analyses of variance (controlled for education).

If self-interest explained the pattern of attitudes among Danish voters, then we would expect a strong negative association between income and welfare state support because the Danish welfare state is among the most redistributive in the world. Furthermore, as the highest marginal tax rate of some 62 to 63 pct. starts at a moderate income level (roughly equivalent to that of an average production worker), we should expect a sharp decline in welfare support around that level. However, our data do not confirm these predictions. As we can see in Table 10, there is no association between income and support for the welfare state for 85 pct. of the population. It is only when we come to the upper 15 pct. that an effect becomes visible, and it is only among the upper 1 to 2 pct. of respondents with household incomes above 1 million DKK that we observe a majority with negative sentiments.[19]

TABLE 10.
Family income and welfare attitudes. Balance of opinion. Percentage points

Household income (married/cohabiting only)	Maintain social reforms		Tax salient 1998	(N) 2000	(N) 1998
	2000	1998			
under 200,000	62	34	9	51	112
200-299,999	55	43	12	88	127
300-349,999	56	36	10	65	127
350-399,999	71	44	9	79	132
400-449,999	48	42	12	83	143
450-499,999	57	47	10	93	108
500-549,999	51	33}	12}	95	124}
550-599,999	56			79	
600-699,999	27	10	13	54	65
700-999,999	12	-6}	27}	60	66}
1,000,000 or more	-53			15	

The same basic pattern is found in the 1998 election survey data where the income variable is a little less detailed; we are not able to single out the very highest incomes, but again, variation is only found among the upper 10 pct. The 1998 survey also allows us to test the association between income and saliency. As far as the saliency of welfare issues is concerned, there is no association at all (data not presented). With respect to the saliency of taxes as a political issue, we find an association just above the significance level. Even here, there is no association with income until we reach the 700,000 DKK level.

---

19 The few other data sets with highly graduated income scales reveal a similar pattern with highly deviant attitudes among the upper 2 or 3 pct. (Goul Andersen, 1993).

Once again, it is only a small group (5 pct.) of high income earners that deviate from the rest of the population. To put it bluntly, *we do not find an association with income; we find a division between the social elite and everyone else*. Finally, there is the division between private and public employees. Not surprisingly, public employees are slightly more positively inclined towards the welfare state than privately employed, but the difference is small (Table 6). Turning to saliency (data not presented), we find no difference in the saliency of welfare issues. However, there is a significant difference in the saliency of taxation as 18 pct. of the privately employed consider taxes important, compared to only 7 pct. among public employees.

However, the latter finding is not so straightforwardly interpretable from an interest point of view. As taxpayers, private and public employees have the same immediate interests (and sector differences in income are not that big); it is only their producer interests that differ. Therefore there is some point in claiming that from an interest perspective, we should mainly look at job-generating public expenditures.

At any rate, since 1971 when there was virtually no sector difference in voting patterns, a marked political division has developed between the public and the private sector in Denmark. For instance, during the 1990s, the proportion of socialist voters among white collar workers in the public sector was twice that of private sector white collar workers (Goul Andersen, 1999). To some extent, this is a uniquely Danish phenomenon. The difference is visible, but much smaller, in the other Nordic countries (Holmberg, 2000; Aardal, 1999). The question is whether this is an expression of self-interest. As an alternative interpretation, Knutsen (1990) has proposed that it is post-materialist values in the non-market sector that distinguish public and private employees.

For the rank and file among public employees, self-interest may be operationalized as 'budget maximizing' behavior. Further, it may be argued that from an interest perspective, public employees in the health sector have little reason to support those in the education sector, so we have further disaggregated public employees into three sectors: health care and social institutions, education and culture (including child care), and all others. We also distinguish between services and transfers. In the field of transfers, we should not expect sectoral differences in attitudes towards the size of budgets; in the first place, few people are employed in paying out the transfers, and second, their working conditions probably do not depend on the size of the transfers to their clients. Finally, we have included a few expenditure items that do not affect the interests of public employees at all, but that are strongly related to values. From an interest perspective, we should not expect to find any sectoral differences here.

TABLE 11.

Attitudes towards public expenditures, among private and public employees.
Balance of opinion (spend more minus spend less). 2000. Percentage points

	Private employees (N=446)	Public employees (N=348)	Public employees in the sector	Difference public/private
Health care	77	76	79	-1
Education	50	56	60	6
Child care	45	46	49	1
Home help	70	71	74	1
Rest homes	74	75	79	1
Culture	-46	-21	-10	25
Child allowances	-1	-4		-3
Old age pension	61	58		-3
Parental leave	17	22		5
Unemployment benefits	3	12	Public employees, education/ culture:	9
Social assistance	-15	1		16
Aid to developing countries	-41	-24	-6	17
Integration of immigrants	-28	-9	13	19

Surprisingly, our data in Table 11 does not confirm that public employees act in a self-interested way.[20] The public/private divide in Danish politics appears to be more a matter of values. First, we generally do not find large differences in attitudes between public and private employees. Next, even if we compare the attitudes of private employees with those of people employed in the relevant public sector, we find only negligible differences – with culture as an exception. Third, we do not find that the public/private divide is larger in the field of services than in the field of transfers. Fourth, within the field of transfers, we find the most significant differences are in attitudes towards unemployment benefits and social assistance, which (if anything) may affect the interests of private employees more, due to reduced job security. And fifth, the biggest differences are found on issues of foreign aid and integration of immigrants where we should expect no differences from an interest perspective, but large differences from a value perspective. Some of the sectoral differences that were not expected from an interest perspective may be partly explained by differences in educational composition. But education is exactly the kind of 'value factor'

---

20 We are speaking here of public employees as voters. Obviously, interest associations and institutional interest groups should be analyzed from an interest perspective.

we mean in this context. And education only explains part of the difference. Thus, as far as public expenditures are concerned, we may conclude that the interest effects are close to zero, and that nearly all the sector differences can be explained by differences in values.

However, there are other areas where we do find significant sectoral differences that can be explained in terms of interests: attitudes to privatization – from contracting out and outsourcing to full privatization – are very different between the two sectors, and similar differences are encountered in attitudes towards new, more performance-related wage systems, etc. In short, resistance among public employees to market mechanisms of various sorts in the public sector is widespread. Although this is not exclusively a matter of interests, interests undoubtedly constitute a very important component. But the broader and more mechanical interpretation of public/private sector differences is not valid.

To conclude, in the Danish case, variations in attitudes towards the welfare state are difficult to explain in terms of narrow self-interest. Even public employees are not very different from private employees in their attitudes towards the welfare state – and to the extent that these two groups do differ, these differences must to a large extent be explained in terms of values rather than self-interest. This has implications for the question of conflict between those who receive their income from the public sector – the majority of the Danish population – and those who rely on the private sector for their livelihood.

State employment, state dependence and polarization

With the partial exception of public employment, the analysis above has followed a conventional perspective on social structure. However, it is sometimes argued that the divide between classes and income groups is less important than the impact of social structural changes related to the welfare state itself. The growing number of public employees and the growing number of people receiving their income as social transfers from the state are what make the difference. The political implications of this change have not been adequately studied to assess this hypothesis. From an interest perspective, if such a social structure is emerging, it would be cause for alarm. Together, public employees and the publicly supported constitute the majority of the adult population, and if they use their voting power to promote their own short-term interests, the economic sustainability and the political legitimacy of the welfare state may be in jeopardy. As we have seen, however, at the individual/voter level, public employee attitudes do not support the predictions of an interest-determined model. But is there a polarization between the employed and recipients of a transfer income from the state?

The idea of a 'new social conflict' (Dahrendorf, 1988) has resurfaced from time to time, both in the academic literature and in public debates. But the political implications of the growth in the number of people living on transfer incomes have not been examined in much detail (Goul Andersen, 1984; Bild & Hoff, 1988; Svensson & Togeby, 1991). In the 1970s, the focus was mainly on political distrust, protest or rebellion among those who were marginalized or excluded from the labor market. But, as it turned out, this group was 'politically harmless', so attention was directed more toward the willingness of the employed to pay for those supported by the state – a change in perspective that was also related to ideas about the welfare state inspired by neo-liberalism and rational choice theory.[21] From an economic perspective, and to some extent from a rational choice perspective, such a conflict may seem inevitable. From a sociological point of view, this is by no means obvious. Many types of transfer income are part of the life cycle – maternity/paternity and parental leave, early retirement allowance, old age pensions, and to some extent even disability pensions, etc. There is no reason to believe that receiving transfer payments should change one's political identity – and there is no reason to believe that those employed should feel that 'we' are paying for 'those people' (to borrow a famous quote from former US President George Bush Sr.).

Second, most unemployed are only unemployed for a short time, and many employed have experienced unemployment at some point. Third, the idea of a new conflict ignores the fact that most people live in families. If people are unemployed, their spouse will typically be working, and if people are employed, they will often have a close family member who has recently experienced unemployment. This means that the dividing line is blurred, and along with factors impeding organization, it contributes to explaining why no common identity has formed among people outside the labor market. Lastly, but not least, a relatively generous benefit system with high minima and long duration provides people with the economic resources to remain 'part of society' without becoming 'second class citizens'. In Denmark, economic security is the most basic determinant of well-being among the unemployed (Goul Andersen, 2002), and social exclusion in the meaning of a cumulative deprivation and spatial segregation – which can lead to a sort of 'underclass culture' (Littlewood & Herkommer, 1999) – remains a relatively rare phenomenon.

The general expectation in a Scandinavian type welfare system would be that working age persons who receive social transfers may be a little more inclined to defend these arrangements and may prefer more benefits, but we

---

21 In a Danish context, the theory of a new conflict has mainly been part of the 'folklore' in public debates. For an example in the academic literature, see e.g. Christoffersen (1995).

should not expect any decline in solidarity among the 'insiders' as long as the 'outsiders' remain part of society. In short, being employed or receiving transfer payments is mainly a matter of economic categorization, not sociological affinity in the meaning of group and identity formation. But what do the empirical findings tell us? How much of a divide is there between the employed and those receiving social transfer income, between those who earn their living in the private sector and those who receive their income (wage or transfer) from the public sector? And do such differences lead to legitimacy problems for the welfare state?

We have studied these questions in more detail elsewhere on the basis of information from 1994 (Goul Andersen, 1999) and shall focus here on the main lines presented in that research and on updated information. On the basis of detailed information in the 1994 election survey, it was possible to compile a picture of the social structure at the time when unemployment peaked (Table 12). The result was quite impressive. If we count students as publicly supported (they receive universal, generous allowances, but usually have a part-time job as well), some 66 pct. of the adult population at that time received its main income from the state, only 34 pct. from the private sector (including 1 pct. housewives). 55 pct. were employed, while 45 pct. lived on transfer payments from the state.

None of these contrasts are politically relevant, however. On the general item applied here, we found no aggregate difference in welfare state attitudes between the employed and the publicly supported (see Table 13), or between those with incomes from the private and the public sector. Election surveys continue to show that there are no major political differences. These groups are simply formal economic categories without sociological or political relevance. If the proposition has a rational core, it must be reformulated in a sociologically relevant way. Thus, we must leave out students and people more than 60 years old. Table 13 shows how this affects the results.

Among the working age population under 60, and leaving out students, we do find an effect on our main indicator of attitudes towards the welfare state: The balance of opinion among the employed is +38 compared to +62 among those publicly supported in 1994, and +45 and +63, respectively, in 2000. Thus, there are differences in the extent of positive opinion, but the effect is small, and we may further note that there was very little change from 1994 to 2000, indicating that attitudes did not polarize during the 1990s. To make an even more demanding test, we can look at attitudes towards unemployment benefits and social assistance in 2000. Even here, however, the contrasts are small. We do find a somewhat stronger leaning towards improvements among those living on transfer incomes rather than income from work, but both among employed and among transfer recipients around two-thirds simply want to maintain levels as they are.

TABLE 12.
The adult population, by source of income. 1994. Percentages

	Percentage of adults in survey[1]
State non-dependents, total	**34**
Employees	26
Self-employed, assisting spouse	7
Housewives	1
Public employees, total	**21**
Publicly supported/welfare recipients, total	**45**
Students, pupils (largely supported by the state)	7
Unemployed (unemployment benefits or social assistance)[2]	8
Leave (maternity, parental, educational or sabbatical)	3
Disabled	5
Early retirement allowance or transitional allowance	4
Old-age pensioners, state pensioners	17
Others	1

1) The sample is not perfectly representative. Privately employed and disabled seem slightly under-represented.

2) Including unemployed on parental leave.

Source: Election Survey 1994. N=2021.

TABLE 13.
Social reforms gone too far/should be maintained, by employment status. Balance of opinion in favor of maintaining welfare

	Social reforms gone too far?			Unemployment benefits, 2000		Social assistance 2000	
	1994: whole population	1994: age 18-59	2000: age 18-59	Balance of opinion	Per cent maintain	Balance of opinion	Per cent maintain
Employed	+37	+38	+45	+5	71	-11	61
Transfer income	+32	+62	+63	+30	65	+19	63
(N)	1109	1086	826	826		826	
	912	279	126	126		126	

Even replacing the category of the 'employed' with the category of 'employed in the private sector' has little effect on the results. But we may get a measure of the sharpest possible contrast by also including information on unemployment experience in the respondent's close family. Thus, on the 1994 data, we have distinguished between four groups:

- persons employed in the private sector, with no unemployment experience in close family during the last two years, and with no use of parental, educational or sabbatical leave;
- persons employed in the private sector, with some unemployment experience in close family (respondent, spouse, children or parents),[22] or with leave experience;
- public employees (regardless of unemployment record); and
- persons receiving public support.

TABLE 14.

Distribution of 18-59 year-olds (excluding students), according to labour market position, and welfare attitudes by labor market position. 1994

	Percentage of age group	Percentage of adult population	General welfare attitude[1]	Unemployment and social ass.[2]
Privately employed[3] without unemployment or leave experience in family	30	20	+25	-15
Privately employed[3] with some unemployment or leave experience	19	13	+37	-5
Public employees	31	21	+52	+2
Publicly supported	20	14	+62	+14
Total pct.	100	68		
(N)	1365	2021		

1) Entries are balance of opinion: Welfare should be maintained minus welfare gone too far.

2) Entries are averages of balance of opinion in relation to size of unemployment benefits and social assistance

3) Including housewives.

Table 14 shows the population distribution and welfare attitudes among these groups (for details, see Goul Andersen, 1999). Note that we are now contrasting those receiving transfers with a small minority of the working population. However, even though we do find a *difference*, the data reveals no polarization. Positive welfare state attitudes prevail even in the minority of privately employed unaffected by unemployment, and no grouping has a majority sup-

---

22 Under-reporting of unemployment among other family members is possible. If this is the case, there may be some respondents in the 'unaffected' group who are indirectly affected. However, we might infer that they are not greatly affected if they have forgotten about the unemployment of other family members. Thus, it has no bearing on the analysis here.

porting reductions in unemployment benefits or social assistance. Neither polarization nor legitimacy problems exist here.[23]

Institutions, performance and discourse

This analysis might seem to suggest that support for the welfare state rests on such solid support that a serious decline in welfare state support is highly unlikely. This conclusion would, however, be premature, perhaps even wrong. As with most studies based on individual level data, our analysis has been directed towards those problems that are somehow reflected in variation between individuals. Explanations in survey research can only account for variance among individuals. Lacking time series or comparative data, macro level factors are usually excluded from the analysis and perhaps even from the theories. We now turn to a macro level model, which we cannot test here. But we can illustrate how it might work, and we can discuss some possible sources of change.

The model is very simple (Figure 2). Inspired by Bo Rothstein's (1998) distinction between 'substantial' and 'procedural' justice, the model distinguishes between basic solidarity or support for welfare on the one hand, and trust in the practical operation of the system on the other. There is no question that basic solidarity is strong in Denmark. Here, it is difficult to think of any legitimacy problems. However, as will be described below, there may be some uncertainty about which principles of solidarity constitute the normative foundations of the welfare state. We return to this broader question below, but first we examine the main legitimacy problems on the implementation side of the welfare state.

The first implementation problem is the question of *reciprocity* or *trust in the fairness of the system*. This includes at least three elements: (1) perceived fairness in the distribution of the tax burden, (2) transparency, i.e., a clear set of rules about who is entitled to get what, and that everyone is treated equally, and (3) a shared perception that fraud and abuse are rare. All of these refer to a classical prisoner's dilemma problem. Even the most solidaristic persons are only willing to cooperate and contribute when they are reasonably certain that everyone else will do the same. The second challenge to legitimacy is that of *performance*. Do welfare programmes fulfil their goals?

Do citizens feel that they get 'value for their money'? Even the most solidaristic person is unlikely in the long run to contribute willingly to a system

---

23 As mentioned below, there was a public debate in 1996 that focused on 'uncontrollable' transfers and it did temporarily affect the legitimacy of the welfare state. However, this concern was no different among the employed and transfer recipients. This is an example of a macro level effect that cannot be measured by a one shot cross-sectional analysis of individual level data.

that he or she considers inefficient. The third problem is one of *economic sustainability* or affordability. Even the most solidaristic person cannot in the long run support welfare programmes that he or she considers unsustainable. If, for instance, the pension system is described by experts and others as impossible to finance in a future context of an ageing population, people are likely to be affected.

FIGURE 2.
A Macro-Level Model of Support for the Welfare State

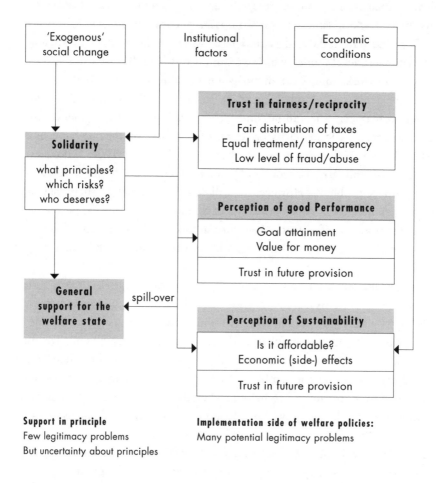

These matters involve not only objective fact, but also, and more importantly, perceptions. Typically, such perceptions rest on information received from the media, or more precisely, from the actors who define these problems in the media. We may also simply speak of political discourse. The final element in the model is a feed-back effect: If people experience problems on the imple-

CRISIS, MIRACLES, AND BEYOND

mentation side, this will, sooner or later, also have an impact on solidarity and general attitudes to the welfare state.

Political critics of the welfare state usually target implementation issues rather than the norm of solidarity per se. People are more receptive to such a message, especially about abuses (Svallfors, 1989, 1996). This model also provides some plausible explanations of earlier legitimacy problems. For example, the 1973 Glistrup-led tax rebellion was accompanied by the highest support ever measured for more progressive taxation (as measured by the item 'high incomes should be more fiercely taxed than today'). When politicians, in desperation over Glistrup's success in opinion polls, lamented the loss of solidarity, they misperceived the situation. The problem was not a loss of solidarity, but a loss of confidence in the tax/welfare system. When Glistrup revealed that he paid no taxes (and compared tax evaders with railway saboteurs during the German occupation because they undermined an immoral system), there was little legitimacy left for the tax system. The 1973 election survey also revealed the most widespread perception of social fraud ever measured. Public debate focused on arrogant behavior and laziness among public employees, and experts warned against continuing the rapid expansion of the public sector. In short, almost every conceivable dimension of welfare state implementation was criticized, undermining trust in the working of the welfare system.

This model also contributes to explaining why citizens in high tax universal welfare states are usually less worried about taxes than citizens in low tax residual systems. Apart from the fact that the latter will often need their post-tax money to buy those services and insurances which citizens in fully universal welfare states receive automatically, citizens in residual welfare states also have fewer reasons to trust the welfare state. The standard textbook arguments in favor of universalism, rather than residualism, flow from this same logic. Residualism allows discretion so that transparency is lost and it is difficult to see who gets what. Residual welfare states create stronger incentives for fraud and abuse. The interaction between taxes and means-tested social security can lead to perverse composite marginal taxes. And so on.

Turning to the efficiency dimension, when public attention is focused on inefficiency or problems of goal attainment, overall trust in the welfare state may be adversely affected, leading people to be more open to market alternatives. In Denmark, this occurred in the mid-1990s. Problems with home help for the elderly, criticism of basic education in public schools, long waiting lists for elective surgery, and declining quality of hospital care entered the public agenda at the same time. None of these problems were new, but they received little attention in the media until the mid-1990s. An overview of citizen evaluations from 1998 to 2001 is shown in Table 15.

TABLE 15.
Evaluations of the performance of the welfare state, 1998-2001. Percentage

		Very well	Quite well	Not so well	Badly	Don't know	Balance of opinion
Libraries	1988	56	34	2	1	7	+87
	2000	50	42	2	1	5	+89
	2001	47	28	2	1	21	+72
Childcare	1998	9	45	25	4	17	+25
	2000	10	56	22	3	9	+41
	2001	17	32	11	2	38	+36
Basic school	1998	6	42	38	6	8	+4
	2000	8	46	36	6	4	+12
	2001	14	36	17	5	28	+28
Hospitals	1998	8	26	45	19	2	-30
	2000	12	36	41	10	1	-3
	2001	24	35	21	9	11	+29
Home help	1998	4	16	44	26	10	-50
	2000	2	23	52	17	6	-44
	2001	9	20	19	12	40	-2
GP's	2000	23	57	16	3	1	+61
Tax administration	2000	13	60	16	6	5	+51
Social office	2000	7	46	20	5	22	+28
Employment office	2000	6	37	24	11	22	+8

Wording: Now, I should like to hear how well you think the public service is working in a number of fields.

Sources: Election Survey 1998, Welfare Values Survey 2000, and Mandag Morgen/ACNielsen AIM June 2001, in cooperation with the author.

It turns out that assessments of core welfare services were very bad around 1998, but they generally improved by 2001, especially as far as the health sector is concerned. This corresponds to voters' changing political agenda: Health care was the most important welfare issue in 1998, but elderly care was the most important issue in 2001 (Goul Andersen, 2001).

The usual immediate reaction to such problems once they are widely recognized – be they real or created by the media – is a general willingness to spend more money. However, in the long run, this may contribute to declining trust. If perceived problems appear to persist, people may begin searching for alternative solutions. This is sketched in Figure 3.

FIGURE 3.

Relationship between perceived problems and support for
increased spending: Positive and negative effects.

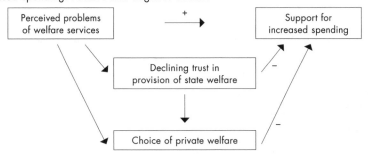

In Denmark, we have some information about such mechanisms. Thus the
perception of problems within each area can be correlated to the willingness
to pay. In 1998 and 2000, there was a positive association, but in most fields,
especially health care and elderly care, this association weakened considerably
from 1998 to 2000. Greater attention due to the elections might explain part of
the change, but the findings lend considerable plausibility to the explanation
offered above. In the long run, people may start looking for other solutions.
Finally, we have also observed a dramatic increase in private health care insurance (Goul Andersen, 2000). This is undoubtedly the consequence of heated
debates about the poor performance of the public health care system, especially
long waiting lists. More importantly, though, this type of insurance was introduced by employers or in collective agreements; no significant increase in
individual insurance has occurred. Our 2001 data also show that at least until
now, it is not the mechanism sketched in Figure 3 that is working here; there
is no correlation between perceptions of hospital performance and voters' attitudes towards private health care insurance.

Finally, we have some data concerning the issue of sustainability/afford-
ability and its effects. A long-running debate about 'uncontrollable' and unbearable increases in social transfer incomes (echoing the debate about public
expenditures in the 1980s and early 1990s) peaked in 1996.[24] This gave rise to

---

24 One may wonder about the timing. But controlling public consumption had been
    the main concern of the 1980s, while transfers received less attention. In particu-
    lar, reforms of student allowances, leave programmes and child allowances led to a
    marked increase in transfers. In the 1990s, this nurtured an erroneous belief that, due
    to unemployment and ageing, transfers were 'uncontrollable' (Goul Andersen, 1997).
    At any rate, controlling income transfers became a mantra of Danish politics in the
    1990s (with the predictable consequence that public consumption increased more
    than 20 pct. in real terms from 1992 to 2000).

a marked increase in the propensity to view current welfare programmes as unsustainable (see Table 16).

TABLE 16.
Opinions on the sustainability of the welfare state, 1994-2000.[1] Percentages

		Strongly agree	Agree	Neutral	Dis- agree	Strongly disagree	Disagree minus agree
Transfer incomes	1994	29	29	22	12	8	– 38
are becoming un-	1996	54	20	8	7	11	– 50
controllable	1997	27	36	10	15	12	– 36
	1998	21	26	32	14	7	– 26
	2000	17	36	28	13	6	– 34
In the long run,	1994	21	29	14	20	16	– 14
we cannot afford	1996	41	18	7	11	23	– 25
to maintain the	1997	28	28	5	18	21	– 17
welfare state as we	1998	12	22	21	26	19	+11
know it today	2000	12	33	21	23	11	– 11

1) In the second part of the 1994 survey and in 1996-1997 the option 'neither agree nor disagree' was not included. This af-fects the proportion of 'neutral' answers. But a comparison between the two parts of the 1994 survey indicates that the balance of opinion is not affected at all, whereas the proportion of 'strongly agree' went up by 3 percentage points and the proportion of 'strongly disagree' increased by 5, respectively 3 percentage points. Both the 1996 and 1997 surveys applied telephone inter-viewing but this probably had no effect. At any rate, the data collection methods in 1996 and 1997 were identical.

At the same time, there was a temporary decline in general support for the welfare state in 1996. And the two phenomena indeed seem to be related: The causal link was confirmed by a highly increased correlation between belief in sustainability and overall support for the welfare state in 1996, as compared with earlier and later measurement (Goul Andersen, 1997).

It is important to note that this increasing concern for sustainability and declining general support for the welfare state were found equally across all social groups, including those living on transfer incomes of all sorts. This is the acid test of the self-interest hypothesis and the idea of polarization. When the burden of financing transfer payments becomes a contested political issue, we might expect political polarization between the marginalized and the inte-grated on the labor market. But the data clearly shows that all groups, including those living on transfers, react as *citizens* to alarming new information about uncontrolled costs. Instead of asking, 'what do "we" do with "those people",' Danish citizens instead debated how 'we' should solve 'our' social problems.

What, then, are the institutional preconditions for one type of reaction rather than the other? We turn to this question below. These findings also illustrate the limitations of drawing conclusions about legitimacy problems

CRISIS, MIRACLES, AND BEYOND

from a single survey. Most macro level factors are not reflected in the data and are easily forgotten until we have time series or cross-national surveys.[25]

To sum up, the legitimacy of the welfare state appears to depend primarily on macro level factors such as trust in fairness, performance and economic sustainability. To a considerable extent, this is a matter of political discourse: A problem is not a problem until somebody defines it as a problem. In the short run, there is no necessary connection between problems 'out there' and what comes to be defined discursively as a problem. In the long run, problems and political debates are probably related, but not necessarily in a direct or obvious way.

Problems of fairness, performance and economic sustainability, in turn, are related to institutions, i.e., how welfare programmes are structured. Universalism, for instance, is generally believed to generate greater confidence in the fairness of the system than residualism does; on the other hand, there may be a tradeoff between fairness and sustainability as universalism is clearly more expensive.[26] However, if fairness is sacrificed in order to ensure economic sustainability and lower taxes, we should expect declining rather than increasing willingness to pay taxes. Danes are willing to pay high taxes because they trust that the system is fair, performs, and is economically sustainable.

Another reason for the willingness to pay high taxes is that people are not induced to think in terms of self-interest. If they were, and if they were able to calculate their interests, the (upper) middle classes would probably display greater dissatisfaction. Residualism tends to reinforce rational, self-interested thinking, while universalism leads people to think in terms of a big, collective insurance scheme where it becomes less relevant to calculate personal risk. The question of the durability of the welfare state from a public opinion perspective, therefore, is how stable this way of thinking is and how basic welfare values and institutions interact. This brings us back to the right side of Figure 2 above. Solidarity is unquestionably high. But what are the principles of this solidarity? At this point, Danes appear surprisingly ambivalent – not between corporatism and universalism, but between residualism and universalism. Should social rights be accorded to all citizens, or should they be targeted

---

25 This is a classic example. Another example is the positive correlation between knowledge about the EU and sympathy for the EU. Of course we cannot infer from this that information campaigns are an adequate method to improve Danes' sympathy for the European Union. It may even be counterproductive.

26 It should be noted, though, that apart from possible distortions associated with high levels of taxation, universalism is a welfare model quite compatible with the market – probably more than other welfare regimes (residualism often produces perverse incentives, and corporatism produces insider/outsider divisions both in an economic and a sociological sense).

towards those in greatest need? In principle, a majority of Danes answer that social rights should be targeted towards those in need; in practice, the majority tends to support the structure of existing welfare programmes (the main exceptions are universal child allowances and free home care for the elderly).

However, institutions teach people to see the world in a particular way. There is no reason to believe that demands for institutional change should come from Danish citizens. The question is whether institutional change could take place for other reasons, and how voters would react. One possibility is a model of counter-reaction. Most proposals to alter the welfare state die before they ever reach the political agenda because voters resist. And if politicians were to succeed in adopting changes, sustained voter resistance would soon force them to modify or abolish the reform (like the freezing of unemployment benefits and social assistance 1982/83-1985/86), unless they manage to obfuscate the decision or introduce 'reform by stealth'. This is the standard model of 'voters as veto point' assumed in the retrenchment literature (Pierson, 1994).

The other possibility is that voters *learn* to interpret the world differently and see the reforms as part of the 'natural' order. These alternatives are equally logical and plausible, but they lead to very different outcomes. The once highly celebrated Danish 'old age pension', a political sacred cow, is now being crowded out by 'labor market pensions' and other occupational or private pensions. The policy response has been to broaden the incomes-tested part of the old age pension and to change the indexation scheme. Further change is likely. Public discourse about the old age pension is increasingly framed in the language of residualism. The first step is to remove all sorts of 'special arrangements' for pensioners that not so long ago were considered basic rights. This helps reduce the minimum efficient pension. The non-means tested part of the old age pension has already been repeatedly reduced and might even be phased out. Eventually the public pension may become insignificant – a basic support for the poor and a supplement for those with below average incomes. Whether the new pension mix (which actually solves the ageing problem) will be 'functionally equivalent' to its precursor remains to be seen. So far there are no indications of increasing inequality among pensioners (Ministry of Finance, 2000). But more regulation will probably be required to maintain current equality levels. And people learn to think about pension in a more privatized way. Could this spill over to other areas of welfare state activity? Until recently, it was completely unthinkable to break with universalism in health care. And any such move would undoubtedly face fierce resistance. But even though it is not likely, it is at least becoming conceivable that the gainfully employed could be insured by their employers, either as a simple fringe benefit or as a part of a collective agreement. Logics of new welfare mixes and compensation for the (perceived) inadequacy of public programmes are conceivable in other policy fields as well. By and large, any dramatic development in such a direction is not very likely. But it is possible to imagine a situation where people find themselves largely outside the welfare system while still paying high taxes to pay for services and income transfers for 'those people' who are dependent on the welfare state. This situation – if it were to emerge – would certainly test the limits of social solidarity.

Conclusions

The speculations stop here. We do not seek to envisage an alternative future for the Danish welfare state, but rather to illustrate how the question of public support for the welfare state should be phrased in terms of interactions between institutional change and changing perceptions and behavior. As far as we can judge from our data, we should not look for dynamics of change in 'exogenous' change among citizens (such as changes in the social structure, changing values etc.), but rather in 'endogenous' factors related to the welfare state itself. These factors are by definition contextual and macro level; they enter survey analysis rather indirectly. But they appear to be more powerful explanations than those we can immediately detect at the level of individual voters/citizens.

As to the latter, we found strong evidence that thinking about the welfare state is to a surprisingly limited degree structured by self-interest. This invalidates many theories about the sources of legitimacy problems for the welfare state. The limited influence of self-interest in shaping Danish public opinion is explained in several ways. First, we suggested that many of the dimensions of a narrow economic self-interest perspective do not contribute to identity formation. Further, we found little or no interest effects in many instances where we might otherwise expect them to emerge. Our main explanation is institutional. In a comprehensive, universal welfare state, people are not induced to think in terms of costs and benefits, and even if they were, the information costs in calculating costs and benefits would inhibit them from doing so. Only among the very obvious big losers (far more than among the obvious winners, as this is often a transitional stage) in the public redistribution game should we expect to find any larger effects. This was confirmed, and so was our assumption that the public/private divide, as far as welfare expenditure is concerned, is mainly (though not exclusively) a matter of values.

For the reasons indicated above, we found no indication of polarization between those inside and those outside the labor market – and very little even between the 'core insiders' and the marginalized; there were differences, but no sign of low or declining willingness to pay for any of the groups outside the labor market. In short, the question is not whether there is support for the welfare state and not even what changes among voters might alter the situation. The question is what institutional and policy changes might bring about a decline in support. Here we pointed to the implementation side of the welfare state – its institutional effects as well as performance – as possible sources of change, and we found some evidence to substantiate this hypothesis. The other potential source of change is the conjunction between ambivalent welfare values (in relation to the principles of social rights) and 'exogenous' institutional change. At this point, the argument is purely speculative, as we lack adequate data to test the hypothesis.

In spite of strong evidence for high and stable welfare state support in Denmark around 2000, our conclusion is *not* that support for the welfare state is unshakeable. It is hardly as strong a 'veto point' as sometimes described, and we should not generalise too far from current high levels of support. In particular, we should look for potential sources of change in the interplay between voters' (somewhat ambivalent) values, institutions and policy performance, broadly conceived.

References

Aardal, Bernt (1999). *Velgere i 90-årene*. Oslo: NKS-Forlaget.

Albrekt Larsen, Christian (2006). *The Institutional Logic of Welfare Attitudes. How Welfare Regimes Influence Public Support*. Aldershot: Ashgate.

Andersen, Johannes & Jørgen Goul Andersen (2003). 'Køn, alder og uddannelse: De unge mænds sejr', in Jørgen Goul Andersen & Ole Borre (eds.), *Politisk forandring. Værdipolitik og nye skillelinjer ved folketingsvalget 2001*. Aarhus: Systime, pp. 189-206.

Bild, Tage & Jens Hoff (1988). 'Party System and State Dependents'. Arbejdspapir, Institut for Statskundskab, Københavns Universitet.

Bille, Lars, Hans Jørgen Nielsen & Steen Sauerberg (1992). *De uregerlige vælgere: Valgkamp, medier og vælgere ved folketingsvalget 1990*. Copenhagen: Forlaget Columbus.

Bjørklund, Tor & Jørgen Goul Andersen (2002). 'Anti-Immigration Parties in Denmark and Norway: The Progress Parties and the Danish People's Party', in Martin Schain, Aristide Zolberg & Patrick Hossay (eds.), *Shadows Over Europe: The Development and Impact of the Extreme Right in Western Europe*. New York: Palgrave/St. Martin's Press, pp. 105-34.

Christoffersen, Henrik (1995). 'Når velfærdsstaten bliver til transfereringssamfundet', in *Effektivisering av välfärdsstaten. Rapport från ett seminar 16-17. mars 1995, Reykjavik, Island*. TemaNord 1995:578. Copenhagen: Nordisk Ministerråd, pp. 102-16.

Citrin, Jack (1979). 'Do People Want Something for Nothing: Public Opinion on Taxes and Government Spending'. *National Tax Journal* 32, 2: 113-29.

Confalonieri, Maria A. & Kenneth Newton (1995). 'Taxing and Spending: Tax Revolt or Tax Protest?', in Ole Borre & Elinor Scarbrough (eds.), *The Scope of Government: Belief in Government* (Vol. 3). Oxford: Oxford University Press, pp. 121-48.

Dahrendorf, Ralph (1988). *The Modern Social Conflict*. London: Weidenfeld & Nicolson.

Esping-Andersen, Gösta (1990). *The Three Worlds of Welfare Capitalism*. Princeton: Princeton University Press.

Förster, Michael F. (2000). 'Trends and Driving Factors in Income Distribution and Povety in the OECD Area'. *OECD Labour Market and Social Policy Occasional Papers* no. 42. Paris: OECD.

Giddens, Anthony (1998). *The Third Way. The Renewal of Social Democracy*. Oxford: Polity Press.

Goul Andersen, Jørgen (1984). 'Udviklingen i sociale modsætningsforhold frem mod år 2000', in Jørgen Goul Andersen, Finn Kenneth Hansen & Ole Borre. *Konflikt og tilpasning*. Copenhagen: Aschehoug, pp. 13-89.

Goul Andersen, Jørgen (1993). 'Sources of Welfare State Support in Denmark: Self-Interest or Way of Life?', in Erik Hansen, Stein Ringen, Hannu Uusitalo & Robert Erikson (eds.), *Welfare Trends in the Scandinavian Countries*. New York: M.E. Sharpe, pp. 25-48.

Goul Andersen, Jørgen (1994). 'Samfundsøkonomi, interesser og politisk adfærd', in Eggert Petersen et al. (eds.), *Livskvalitet og holdninger i det variable nichesamfund*. Aarhus: Psykologisk Institut, Aarhus Universitet, pp. 15-136.

Goul Andersen, Jørgen (1997). 'Krisebevidsthed og velfærdsholdninger i en højkonjunktur', in Gert Graversen (ed.), *Et arbejdsliv. Festskrift tilegenet Professor dr. Phil Eggert Petersen*. Aarhus: Department of Psychology, University of Aarhus, pp. 151-70.

Goul Andersen, Jørgen (1999). 'Offentlig og privat', in Johannes Andersen, Ole Borre, Jørgen Goul Andersen & Hans Jørgen Nielsen (eds.), *Vælgere med omtanke. En analyse af Folketingsvalget 1998*. Aarhus: Systime, pp. 91-8.

Goul Andersen, Jørgen (2000). 'Borgerne og sygehusene'. *CCWS Working Papers 16/2000*. Aalborg: Department of Economics, Politics and Public Administration, Aalborg University.

Goul Andersen, Jørgen (2001). 'Skatter, velfærd og ansvarlighed. Vælgernes politiske dagsorden februar 2001 og prioriteringer mellem skattelettelser, velfærd og afdrag på statsgælden i et mellemlangt perspektiv'. *Working Papers from the Danish Election Project No. 12*. Aalborg: Department of Economics, Politics and Public Administration, Aalborg University.

Goul Andersen, Jørgen (2002). 'Work and citizenship: Unemployment and unemployment policies in Denmark, 1980-2000', in Jørgen Goul Andersen & Per H. Jensen (eds.), *Changing Labour Markets, Welfare Policies and Citizenship*. Bristol: Policy Press, pp. 59-84.

Goul Andersen, Jørgen & Peter Munk Christiansen (1991). *Skatter uden velfærd*. Copenhagen: Jurist- og Økonomforbundets Forlag.

Goul Andersen, Jørgen & Jens Hoff (2001). *Democracy and Citizenship in Scandinavia*. Houndsmills: Palgrave.

Goul Andersen, Jørgen, Per-Arnt Pettersen, Stefan Svallfors & Hannu Uusitalo (1999). 'The Legitimacy of the Nordic Welfare States', in Mikko Kautto, Matti Heikkilä, Björn Hvinden, Staffan Marklund & Niels Ploug (eds.), *Nordic Social Policy. Changing Welfare States*. London: Routledge, pp. 235-61.

Graubard, S.M. (1986). *Norden – the Passion for Equality?* Oslo: Universitetsforlaget.

Habermas, Jürgen (1975). *Legitimation Crisis*. Boston: Beacon Press.

Habermas, Jürgen (1981). *Theorie des kommunikativen Handelns*. Frankfurt: Suhrkamp.

Halvorsen, Knut (1999). 'Labour force status of married/cohabiting couples in Norway: Associations and explanations of (un)employment homogamy'. *CCWS Working Papers 9/1999*.

Holmberg, Sören (2000). *Välja parti*. Stockholm: Nordstedts.

Juul, Søren (2002). *Modernitet, velfærd og solidaritet. En undersøgelse af danskernes moralske forpligtelser*. Copenhagen: Hans Reitzels Forlag.

Knutsen, Oddbjørn (1990). 'Materialist and Post-Materialist values and Social Structure in the Nordic countries – a comparative study'. *Comparative Politics* 23, 1: 85-104.

Littlewood, Paul & Sebastian Herkommer (1999). 'Identifying Social Exclusion: Some Problems of Meaning', in Paul Littlewood et al. (eds.), *Social Exclusion in Europe*. Aldershot: Ashgate, pp. 1-22.

Mandag Morgen (2000). *Fra velfærdsstat til medborgersamfund*. Mandag Morgen Strategisk Forum. June.

Martinussen, Willy (1988). *Solidaritetens grenser*. Oslo: Universitetsforlaget.

Ministry of Finance (2000). *Finansredegørelse 2000*. Copenhagen: Schultz.

Nolan, Brian, Richard Hauser & Jean-Paul Zoyem (2000). 'The Changing Effects of Social Protection on Poverty', in Duncan Gallie & Serge Paugam (eds.), *Welfare Regimes and the Experience of Unemployment in Europe*. Oxford: Oxford University Press, pp. 87-106.

OECD (2004). *Taxing Wages*. Paris: OECD.

Petersen, Eggert (1996). 'Den samfundspsykologiske udvikling 1982-1986-1988-1990-1994', in Eggert Petersen, Henrik Albeck, Jørgen Goul Andersen, Jørgen Dalberg-Larsen, Knue-Erik Sabroe & Bo Sommerlund (eds.), *Danskerns trivsel, holdninger og selvansvarlighed under opsvinget*. Aarhus: Aarhus University Press, pp. 15-168.

Petersen, Eggert, Ole Steen Kristensen & Knud-Erik Sabroe (1987). *Danskernes tilværelse under krisen. Bd.2 Studier i den politisk-økonomiske udvikling 1982 til 1986*. Aarhus: Aarhus University Press.

Pierson, Paul (1994). *Dismantling the Welfare State? Reagan, Thatcher and the Politics of Retrenchment*. Cambridge: Cambridge University Press.

Pierson, Paul (1998). 'Irresistible Forces, Immovable Objects: Post-Industrial Welfare States Confront Permanent Austerity'. *Journal of European Public Policy* 5, 4: 539-60.

Rose, Richard & B. Guy Peters (1978). *Can Government go Bankrupt?* New York: Basic Books.

Rothstein, Bo (1998). *Just Institutions Matter: Theories of Institutional Design*. Cambridge: Cambridge University Press.

Rothstein, Bo (2001). 'Social Capital in the Social Democratic Welfare State'. *Politics and Society* 29, 2: 206-40.

Svallfors, Stefan (1989). *Vem älskar välfärdsstaten? Attityder, organiserede intresser och svensk välfärdspolitik*. Lund: Arkiv.

Svallfors, Stefan (1996). *Välfärdsstatens moraliska ekonomi. Välfärdsopinionen i 90-talets Sverige*. Umeå: Boréa Bokförlag.

Svallfors, Stefan, Knut Halvorsen & Jørgen Goul Andersen (2001). 'Work orientations in Scandinavia: Employment commitment and organizational commitment in Denmark, Norway and Sweden'. *Acta Sociologica* 44, 2: 139-56.

Svensson, Palle & Lise Togeby (1986). *Politisk opbrud*. Aarhus: Forlaget Politica.

Svensson, Palle & Lise Togeby (1991). *Højrebølge?* Aarhus: Forlaget Politica.

Taylor-Gooby, Peter (1995). 'Who wants the welfare state? Support for state welfare in European countries', in Stefan Svallfors (ed.), *In the Eye of the Beholder*. Umeå: Impello Själsupport/The Bank of Sweden Tercentenary Foundation, pp. 11-51.

Taylor-Gooby, Peter (1998). 'Commitment to the Welfare State', in Roger Jowell et al. (eds.), *British – and European – Social Attitudes. The 15th Report. How Britain Differs*. Aldershot: Ashgate, pp. 57-76.

Thomsen, Søren Risbjerg (1995) 'The 1994 Parliamentary Election in Denmark'. *Electoral Studies* 14, 3: 315-22.

van der Brugge, Jimmy & Henning Voss (2003). 'Mediernes dagsorden', in Jørgen Goul Andersen & Ole Borre (eds.), *Politisk forandring. Værdipolitik og nye skillelinjer ved folketingsvalget 2001*. Aarhus: Systime, pp. 119-234.

Wilensky, Harold (1976). *The 'New Corporatism', Centralization, and the Welfare State*. London: Sage.

Wolfe, Alan (1989). *Whose Keeper? Social Science and Moral Obligation*. Berkeley: University of California Press.

3 THE WELFARE STATE AND THE LABOR MARKET

Per H. Jensen

Introduction

Major changes occurred in Denmark's labor market during the 1990s. Between 1993 and 2000, the OECD standardized unemployment rate decreased from 10.2 pct. to 4.7 pct. (OECD, 2001). This decline in unemployment had no damaging repercussions on the economy as a whole. The inflation rate was unaffected and Denmark achieved a solid balance of payment surplus and a domestic public budget surplus. Thus, Denmark escaped many of the problems usually associated with rapid economic growth accompanied by a sharp decline in unemployment.

The changing labor markets of the 1990s can hardly be attributed to a single causal variable, especially because Denmark's small open economy is influenced by a multiplicity of factors. A series of labor market reforms in the 1990s undoubtedly contributed to the turnaround in employment patterns. The policy changes were carried out by a Social Democratic-led coalition government formed in January 1993. The coalition came to power promising to fight unemployment, which had risen dramatically in the early 1990s. The newly formed government redesigned labor market policies to combat structural unemployment. Danish labor market researchers unanimously agree that the reforms of the 1990s were profound and path-breaking innovations. This chapter analyzes the direction and dynamics of change, using the government coalition's rise to power in 1993 to define the definitive turning point in policy direction.

From the perspective of comparative welfare state analysis, the change in Danish labor market policies cries out for explanation. Welfare state research has been dominated by a historical-institutionalist regime approach (e.g., Esping-Andersen, 1990), leading to an emphasis on long historical trajectories that produced relatively stable welfare state configurations. Similarly, Danish labor market researchers have argued that the policy changes in the 1990s were profound, but the reforms did not exceed the boundaries of a Social Democratic welfare state regime type. From a welfare state regime perspective, then, the changes in Danish labor market policies during the 1990s constitute minor modernizations, adaptations and updatings of the existing Social Democratic welfare state regime.

Even in relatively stable regimes, change is bound to occur from time to time. Recent research contributing to our understanding of the logic and dimensions points to crucial variables that enable us to grasp and explain change in at least four dimensions (e.g. Pierson, 1994; Veen et al., 2000; Trommel & Vroom, 2002):

- *systemic* change, which refers to 'policy changes that alter the context for future spending decisions' (Pierson, 1994: 15), such as (a) de-funding, i.e., constraining the flow of revenues to future administrations; (b) shifting public opinion; (c) modifying political institutions; and (d) weakening interest groups;

- *programmatic* change, which refers to cutback of particular social programs. To clarify what we mean by changes in social programs, it is useful to make a three-part distinction between possible changes in these programs (Dahrendorf, 1988). (1) provisions, for instance unemployment compensation; (2) entitlements, which are benefits that require an 'entry ticket' or for which the beneficiary must meet certain eligibility criteria, e.g., the recipient must be a member of an unemployment insurance program for one year before he or she is entitled to unemployment benefits; and (3) program-specific requirements, which refers to programs for which an individual must be actively seeking employment in order to maintain his or her eligibility for benefits. By including requirements in welfare state programs, the state steers people's behavior not only through transfer payments, but also by exercising control via economic sanctions against those whose behavior does not conform to the conditions established to receive (or continue to receive) benefits. A comprehensive analysis of changes in social programs should take into account these three aspects of social welfare programs: provisions, entitlements and requirements;

- changes in program *configurations*, which refers to changes in the overall set of social programs, e.g., when several older programs are eliminated and replaced by new, less generous programs within a particular policy area, other programs may be established or existing programs expanded in another policy area to compensate for the loss. As an example of changes in program configurations in Denmark in the 1990s, programs that were established and later eliminated included early retirement schemes, leave of absence schemes and others, and these configurative changes reflected adjustments based on changing economic conditions that affected the size and composition of the labor force;

- changes in the *institutional design*, or changes in the institutional production of welfare, which refers to the implementation, administration and governance of welfare programs. As an example of changes in the 'institutional design' of labor market policies in Denmark during the 1990s, we can point to the decentralization of the policy system, along with the creation of a new policy instrument, the so-called 'action plan', which requires recipients of assistance to become much more involved in defining and solving their own problems. Thus changes in the institutional design were analogous to what Anthony Giddens (1994) calls 'life politics', a move away from standardization and productivism.

Policy changes may be spurred by perceived exogenous problems or they may be driven by changes in the political ideological power constellations. In Denmark since the 1970s, the welfare state has fallen under heavy criticism from neo-liberals and their companions, i.e., neo-classical economists who observed dysfunctional elements in the labor market and argued for the need to undertake systemic as well as programmatic retrenchment (Ministry of Labor, 1989; Jensen et al., 1992; Socialkommissionen, 1993). More specifically, in the labor market policy area, they demanded programmatic retrenchment in the form of a reduction in the amount of unemployment compensation (provisions), stricter requirements to qualify for unemployment insurance (entitlements), and stricter requirements on the availability of unemployed persons for work (requirements). Systemic retrenchment proposals included requirements for financing reforms for the unemployment insurance system, which aimed at restructuring the relationship between entitlements and contributions along with the inclusion of some kind of experience rating.

Labor market policy reform was put on the agenda after intense neo-liberal criticism of the labor market's performance in the late 1980s and early 1990s. But when the Social Democratic coalition government was formed in 1993, it resisted the demand to reduce the welfare state. Instead of following a particular strategy of systemic and programmatic retrenchment, the government opted for changes in the *configuration* and *institutional design* of social programs. In these efforts, the Social Democratic government built on experiences from the 1970s and 1980s, which – in contrast to the neo-liberal rhetoric – provided evidence that an extensive welfare state could be combined with considerable labor market flexibility.

When we discuss continuity and change in Danish labor market policies in this chapter, labor market policies are broadly defined as:

- passive policies such as unemployment benefits, social security benefits, etc., which are designed to mitigate the financial and social impact of unemployment;
- *policies designed to increase the effectiveness of the labor force*, i.e., to improve the productivity and capacities of the labor force, e.g., by stimulating geographical and occupational mobility through relocation grants, training programs, further education, etc.;
- *reintegrating policies*, i.e., programs designed to reintegrate the unemployed into paid employment by means of wage subsidization and other job creation schemes;
- *policies* encouraging *flows in and out of the labor force*.

Using this distinction among different types of labor market policies, this chapter provides a brief overview of the developments in Danish policies in the 1990s. To highlight both continuity and change in the four forms of labor market policies named above, we will make use of the distinction between systemic, programmatic, configurative, and institutional design changes.

However, this account requires that we first consider the historical context and emergence of labor market policies at the outset of the reform period of the 1990s. Therefore, section 2 describes how labor market policies were organized prior to the reforms. This is followed by a description of the lead-up to the reforms in the 1990s. Section 3 points out that the labor market was already highly flexible prior to the reforms. On the other hand, neo-liberals and neo-classical economists succeeded in putting labor market reform on the political agenda from the late 1980s on. The debate they encouraged helped construct 'the problems' that had to be addressed; these are discussed in section 4. In the meantime, the Social Democratic take-over contributed to a reformulation of the labor market policy debate, and section 5 describes how these reformulations manifested themselves in a series of labor market policy reforms in the 1990s. The lesson of the 1990s is that continuity and change along different dimensions occurred simultaneously in Danish labor market policies, and that the changes do not support an interpretation that a process of retrenchment has been underway. Thus, the Danish case may be characterized as 'change without retrenchment'. This will be reflected in *section 6*, which presents some concluding remarks and assesses a new set of concepts in Danish labor market policy, among them 'the golden triangle' and 'flexicurity'. We question whether these new concepts really reflect new materially different policies. From a broader perspective, this chapter tells several stories. The first is a tale about how the labor market wasn't as dysfunctional as the neo-liberals and neo-classical economists of the late 1980s and early 1990s claimed. The second is a tale about the renewal of labor market policy in the 1990s that was not as 'new' as the new terminology ('the golden triangle', 'flexicurity' etc.) would lead one to believe.

The historical framework

For many years, Danish labor market policy has had high aspirations. In 1989, for example, Denmark spent a higher percentage of its GDP on labor market measures than any other OECD member state (5.71 pct.). In international comparison, Denmark uses a comparatively high level of resources on 'active' labor market measures (Martin, 2000). Danish policy, however, spends an unusually high proportion of its resources on 'passive' income maintenance, which also explains the very low Danish poverty rate. In 1989, of the 5.71 pct. of GDP spent on labor market programs, 1.2 pct. was spent on 'active' measures, and 4.51 pct. on 'passive' income maintenance (OECD, 1990a: 52f, Table 14).

PASSIVE POLICIES

The unusually high dependence on passive policies has its roots in policies adopted in the beginning of the 1970s when a series of improvements in unemployment compensation were adopted under pressure from a very strong labor movement. For decades, more than 80 pct. of wage earners have been organized in unions that pushed politicians along a path towards very generous unemployment benefits. In 1992/93, entitlements were very extensive and provisions generous. Eligibility was contingent upon one year's membership in an unemployment insurance fund and 26 weeks of employment within the last three years. The benefit level was set at 90 pct. of previous earnings,[1] and the benefit period was stipulated as two years. It should be mentioned that the individual worker can freely choose whether to buy unemployment insurance. The principle of free choice arises from the fact that the unemployment insurance funds, while regulated and subsidized by the state, are affiliated with and administered by the trade unions.[2]

Unemployed who do not meet the criteria for unemployment insurance are entitled to social security benefits. In earlier periods, the amount of social security benefits was determined by a means test, based on a view of poverty as a relative concept. But the basis for determining the amount of social security

---

1 The actual benefits, however, are conditioned by a relatively low ceiling. That is, in practice the benefit system could be characterized as a flat-rate system.

2 In 2001, there were 33 unemployment insurance funds for wage earners and two unemployment insurance funds for the self-employed, with a total of 2.4 million members. In the second quarter of 2001, the labor force included 2,710,000 persons; of these, 204,000 were self-employed and 2,489,000 were wage earners (Statistics Denmark, 2001a).

benefits changed during the early 1990s favoring legal principles rather than relative measures as the guiding principle. For unemployed with high housing costs and/or many children, it would often be economically advantageous to rely on social security benefits rather than unemployment insurance. The fact that unemployed can opt for social security benefits indicates that Denmark has a two-tiered system that divides the unemployed population into two distinct groups. Accordingly, the functioning of the unemployment insurance funds is subject to national labor market legislation, with the Ministry of Labor as the central authority, while the social security benefits are administered by the municipalities and subject to social policy legislation; the Ministry of Social Affairs is the central authority.

Recipients of unemployment benefits and recipients of social security benefits must meet the program requirement that they are available for work and they must register as job seekers at the Public Employment Service. Thus, the most important task of the Public Employment Service is to establish contact between job seekers and employers. Historically, this activity has been administered quite liberally. The unemployed have therefore only been marginally required to be occupationally or geographically mobile as a condition for retaining their benefits. In this respect, we can speak of an unemployment insurance that has functioned as a form of career security in that unemployed were not required to take a job outside their former employment sector. Instead, they were entitled to income maintenance.

LABOR MARKET EFFECTIVENESS POLICIES

Besides this core activity of matching the supply and demand for labor, the Public Employment Service has functioned as the administrative body for the formation and development of the active labor market policies since the late 1950s (Jørgensen, 1985/86). The aim of active labor market policies in the 1950s and 1960s was to combat 'bottlenecks' and structural imbalances that generated inflationary pressures. This was primarily accomplished by means of supply side interventions like mobility grants and training and education measures intended to stimulate geographic and occupational mobility. Supply side intervention to improve economic performance thus has a long tradition in Denmark.

Since the appearance of active labor market policy in the early 1960s, labor market training has been favored over geographical mobility measures, in terms of both the number of persons enrolled in the programs as well as the size of public expenditures on the programs. In 1989, for instance, 5 million DKK were spent on mobility support, while 4,004 million were spent on labor market training (OECD, 1990a). In 1985, 91,744 persons participated in courses, most of which, about 72.4 pct., had a duration of less than five weeks (AMU Direktoratet, 1985: 25f, Table 6.2). The courses mainly target manual workers, and their main purpose is to upgrade the skill levels of the workforce. Almost all the expenses of these programs are paid by the state, and the training is a cooperative venture between the unions and local firms. The involvement of employers ensures that the content of the training matches the real qualifications required at firm level.[3] In addition, Denmark differs from most other OECD countries in that the courses are designed to appeal to all segments of the labor force; i.e., employed as well as unemployed. For decades, the relationship between employed and unemployed participating in the courses has been stable at a ratio of 2:1 (AMU Direktoratet, 1985), although in recent years there has been a decline in the relative number of unemployed reflecting the overall decline in the unemployment rate.

REINTEGRATING POLICIES

In 1974 unemployment began to rise and in 1975 a Social Democratic government was elected. One of the main priorities of the new government was to reintegrate unemployed persons into paid employment by expanding employment opportunities using a package of wage subsidization grants to private and public firms (Lind, 1985). The new schemes and measures mirrored the previously described two-tiered system of beneficiaries of unemployment benefits and social security benefits.

In 1977 a law was passed obliging municipalities and counties to earmark a certain amount of money per inhabitant to combat unemployment among social security recipients. These measures included subsidized employment in the private sector, training courses, education etc. Until the labor market reform of 1994, participation in the municipal employment programs counted as 'work' in terms of qualifying for the unemployment benefit system (i.e., social security beneficiaries could qualify for unemployment benefits by participating in municipal job creation programs).

In 1978, a 'job offer' scheme was introduced. Long-term unemployed (two years or longer) at risk of losing their entitlement to unemployment benefits were offered subsidized jobs. This program included considerable flexibility in the 'job offer' scheme to take into account the individual's needs and preferences. If, for example, an unemployed academic was able to find a vacancy at the university library, that position would then be recognized by the public employment service as a research librarian position. The salary in the 'job offer' scheme was equivalent to wages set by collective bargaining agreements, and the job offer lasted seven to nine months. Participation in a 'job offer' was thus

---

3 There are about 190 local vocational training centers in Denmark, i.e. about 13 to 14 in each county, offering about 2,300 different vocational education types.

an offer of at least 26 weeks of employment, which in turn allowed the unemployed person to re-establish eligibility to unemployment benefits. As such, a major purpose of the job offer scheme was to prevent unemployed persons from becoming disconnected from the unemployment benefit system, as the job offer scheme provided the opportunity to endlessly 'commute' between unemployment benefits and subsidized employment. In 1985, the scheme was supplemented with the options of receiving aid for self-employment or an educational allowance. By the end of the 1980s, the number of job offers which could be extended to the same individual was reduced to two. The effective maximum duration of unemployment benefits in the early 1990s was about nine years.

POLICIES ENCOURAGING FLOWS IN AND OUT OF THE LABOR MARKET

Since the 1960s, labor market policies have contributed to the recruitment and retention of women in the labor market (Jensen, 1996). It is characteristic of these policies that the emergence and development of labor market policies coincided with the massive entry of women into the labor force. In the three decades extending from 1960 to 1990, women's labor market participation rose from 43.5 pct. to 78.5 pct. (OECD, 1990b, 2000a). In the beginning, part-time employment functioned to a large extent as a 'bridge' to full-time labor market participation (Nätti, 1993). For example, 40 pct. of women employed outside the home were part-timers in 1980. Part-time employment was viewed as an integral part of the labor force. For over 30 years, part-time workers have been able to participate in the unemployment insurance funds.[4] From the 1980s on, women's employment patterns shifted considerably. In 1999, 75.8 pct. of women worked outside the home (OECD, 2000a), and approximately 17 pct. of these women were part-time workers (Statistics Denmark, 2001b). That percentage is even lower if we control for number of female students[5] (see also Goul Andersen, 2002a, 2002b). Thus there is a clear trend of women moving toward full-time employment. The flow of women into the labor market from the start of the 1960s reflects an attempt to mobilize the reserve army of potential workers in connection with the full employment economy that emerged at that time.

---

4 In 1999, 76.4 pct. of the workforce was insured for full-time employment, and 2.1 pct. for part-time employment.

5 The numbers are also sensitive to other limitations. Workforce statistics based on register data are somewhat lower than numbers based on survey responses. But comparisons of the measurements note that they are not entirely comparable because they are based on different criteria.

With the same objective in mind, the Folketing (the Danish parliament) adopted the 1960 'rehabilitation act' (Plovsing, 2000) that facilitated rehabilitation physically, mentally or socially disabled persons (Ebsen et al., 1998). Rehabilitation programs, administered by the municipalities, counteracted the labor market's exclusionary processes by assisting persons threatened by exclusion to gain a firmer foothold in the labor market.

As unemployment problems grew from the mid-1970s on, efforts to recruit new segments of the population into the labor market were de-emphasized. In fact, policy headed in the opposite direction by stimulating flows out of the labor force to combat unemployment. An early retirement scheme introduced in 1979 opened a new pathway out of the labor market for elderly workers (Olsen, 1985). The scheme gave unemployment insurance fund members aged 60 to 66 the opportunity to retire from the labor market prior to the ordinary retirement age, which was reduced from 67 to 65 years of age in 2004. The eligibility criterion was five years' membership of an unemployment insurance scheme. In 1992, the qualifying criterion was raised to 20 years, and the benefits paid were more or less equivalent to unemployment benefits. The early retirement scheme was supplemented by a 'part-time' pension scheme in 1987, and in 1992 the so-called 'transitional allowance' was introduced, making it possible for the long-term unemployed aged 55 to 59 who had been a member of an unemployment insurance scheme for at least 20 years to receive an early retirement allowance corresponding to 80 pct. of unemployment benefits (Pedersen, 1998).

The original early exit route from the labor market, i.e., the disability pension scheme, was adapted to the employment situation of the 1970s and 1980s via a major reform in 1984 that made it possible to qualify for a disability pension solely for non-medical reasons for people over 50 (Ministry of Social Affairs, 1992: 4). More women than men receive disability pensions, and the gender imbalance may be caused by the fact that women are more likely than men to have been in and out of the labor market during their working years. This would reduce their likelihood of meeting the minimum requirements to qualify for early retirement benefits.

NUMBER OF PERSONS ENROLLED IN PROGRAMS

Table 1 outlines the structure of social programs under the 'old system', i.e., before 1994, showing the distribution of persons in the various labor market schemes.

TABLE 1.
Number of persons (age 18-66) enrolled in labor
market measures or benefit schemes 1990

Job creation and job offer schemes	59,000
Adult vocational training	12,000
Unemployment benefits	211,000
Social security benefits and rehabilitation	137,000
Early retirement	101,000
Disability pension	250,000
Total	770,000
Total labor force (age 16-66)	2,794,000

Source: Statistics Denmark (1993, 1998).

As the table shows, the 'old system' relied predominantly on a passive strategy in dealing with unemployment problems. In 1990, 439,000 persons out of a total labor force of 2,794,000 persons received unemployment compensation, social security benefits, or early retirement allowances. But the old system cannot be characterized as exclusively passive, since 1.2 pct. of GNP was spent on active labor market policies in 1989, and in 1990, approximately 59,000 people were in job creation programs. But it must also be remembered that the main idea behind 'job creation' in the 1970s and 1980s was to prevent members of the unemployment insurance funds from losing their entitlements to unemployment benefits, or to help social security recipients to gain entitlements for unemployment benefits. The experience with job creation programs may thus be labeled 'passive' activation, inasmuch as it was the 'passive' policies, i.e., the rules laid down in the unemployment insurance scheme and the number of people at risk of losing their entitlements to unemployment benefits, which tended to determine the scope of job creation. This can be contrasted with adult vocational training programs that were designed to stimulate occupational mobility. This may have had a positive effect on the labor market because supply-side policies help eliminate structural imbalances in the labor market. However, as will be discussed in the next section, passive support and high benefit levels may actually contribute to the modernization and flexibility of the labor market and the economy as a whole.

High benefit levels and labor market flexibility

Some economists argue that an extensive welfare state has a negative feedback effect on the behavior of economic actors (e.g., Keeley, 1981). High unemployment benefits, for instance, are expected to increase voluntary unemployment. First, easily accessible unemployment benefits tend to push the unemployment rate upwards. The system encourages people to register as 'unemployed' even though they are not available for the labor market. Second, generous unemployment benefits may lead workers to quit voluntarily and/or prolong their job search period, thereby increasing the duration of unemployment. Third, generous benefits may encourage a job seeker to hold out for higher wages. As such, unemployment benefits may affect the adjustment function of the labor market and reduce wage flexibility by protecting the existing wage structure.

It is, however, questionable whether generous unemployment benefits solely act as a work disincentive,[6] just as it intuitively seems highly problematic to evaluate the labor market's operation on the basis of a single social program. Rhetorically, one might ask whether the effects of generous unemployment benefits don't also depend on the way the unemployment insurance system interacts with and reinforces other social programs. From this perspective, it is also worth noting that employment protection legislation traditionally has been very limited in Denmark (OECD, 1999: Ch. 2). In practice, some segments of blue collar workers can be dismissed from one hour to the next or with a few days' notice. Consequently, the fact that employers have been able to adjust their workforce quickly in accordance with changes in economic requirements may have paved the way for higher levels of efficiency in the economy as a whole. From the point of view of the wage earner, high job insecurity was offset by extensive welfare benefits (high levels of long duration benefits). Since workers have not feared unemployment due to high wage compensation, we might expect that workers have been willing to accept dismissals and adapt to changing markets and technologies (Schmid & Reissert, 1991: 101). It has thus been argued (Jensen, 1987; Goul Andersen & Christiansen, 1991: 177-80) that the combination of job insecurity and high benefit levels may actually have enhanced labor market flexibility.

The neo-classical perspective based on the assumption of preference maximizing actors frequently overlooks the fact that often it is not just material or pecuniary gains that motivate individuals – Danes – to work (Svallfors et al., 2001). The motivation to work is probably to a far greater extent based on the notion that an individual's identity is defined in large part by his or her job and in the collective identity created in the workplace. It is interesting to note that 10 pct. of the employed[7] in Denmark prefer a lower income from employment than they would have if they were to receive unemployment

---

6 Comparative studies from the 1980s demonstrate that the average replacement rate in unemployment insurance is unrelated to unemployment levels or productivity growth rates (Schmid, 1987; Korpi, 1989), and more recent comparative studies have not fundamentally undermined these insights (but see also Calmfors & Holmlund, 2000).

7 Here we refer to persons who are working and members of an unemployment insurance fund.

insurance, and 20 pct. of the employed workforce earn less than DKK 500 per month more (net) by working 37 hours per week than they would receive from unemployment insurance (Smith, 1998: 207). In 2001, the minimum wage for unskilled workers over 18 was DKK 82.40 per hour or DKK 3,048.80 per week. The fact that people work without achieving a financial gain over what they might receive from unemployment insurance offers very little support to the hypothesis that the unemployment insurance system breeds inactivity and locks the unemployed into marginal positions on the labor market.

Few studies have examined the linkage between insurance levels and flexibility at the firm level. One exception is Knudsen & Lind (1987), who investigated restructuring processes at Aalborg Portland cement factory. In the study, the chief operating officer pointed to the high unemployment insurance as a justification for restructuring:

> Our improved performance was due to the fact that we were able to close down some of our factories sooner than some of the other producers. This was possible first and foremost because ... in Denmark we have a tradition for tolerating the closure of factories that are no longer profitable ... This characteristic in Danish industry – when firms have to close down, making co-workers unemployed – makes it much easier to run a company here than in any other country in the world. (cf. Knudsen & Lind, 1987: 128f)

Thus, a generous unemployment compensation level reduces the potential for conflict between employers and wage earners in connection with layoffs. All other things being equal, this facilitates structural adjustments and better firm performance. The first studies of flexibility[8] throughout the economy were undertaken in the 1980s and they demonstrated considerable flexibility in Denmark. Brüniche-Olsen, for instance, showed that out of a labor force of 2.5 million, over 1 million persons changed jobs one or more times during the period from November 1980 to November 1981 (Brüniche-Olsen, 1987: 323). Another measure of flexibility is the fact that out of a total labor force of 2.9 million, about 775,000 persons were affected by unemployment in the period from 1994 to 1995. Most, however, only suffered short-term unemployment, since more than 50 pct. of the 775,000 persons were unemployed for less than 15 to 16 weeks (Ministry of Finance, 1995: 291). Other studies have shown that flexibility was quite high in the 1990s (Lind, 2000), and especially high if the Danish experience is viewed in a comparative perspective (OECD 1997).

---

8 Flexibility of labor markets encompasses several dimensions that complement each other (cf. Ganssmann, 2000: 245 and Lind, 2000: 8f). The following discussion focuses in particular on numerical flexibility, measured by job turnover rates.

The BEK project report argues that mobility in Denmark is in fact unacceptably high in some segments of the labor market because it leads to unforeseen transaction costs for employers, potential employees and the state. The problem of matching workers to job vacancies negatively affects productivity and effectiveness (BEK-projektet, 1992: 7).

We can establish without doubt that the developments in the economy and employment in Denmark during the 1990s occurred without producing changes in the replacement rate of unemployment benefits. This substantiates the conclusion that high benefit levels interacting with other labor market policy measures actually can increase the flexibility of labor markets inasmuch as a flexible labor market refers to the ability of labor market, organizations and individuals to adapt to changes in the overall economic environment.

The prelude to the labor market reforms in the 1990s

Already from the mid-1970s employers claimed that the generous unemployment benefits affected the recipients' economic behavior in an undesirable way. Employers believed that the reserve wage was too high. They first presented this as bottleneck problems, and later as 'paradox' problems, and from the late 1980s on they were viewed as structural problems. The employers' criticism remained relatively isolated up until the end of the 1980s when the scientific community in the form of neoclassical economists took up the employers' argument. They focused on the relationship between the minimum wage and unemployment benefits and asserted that the high social benefits would create incentive problems and counteract flexible workforce adjustment to structural demands (e.g., Ministry of Labor, 1989; Danish Council of Economic Advisors, 1991, 1992; Jensen, et al., 1992; Smith, 1998; Goul Andersen, 2002c).

The problem definition has one critical flaw: There is no clear-cut way to analyze benefit-induced unemployment in terms of concepts, methodology and data (cf. Reubens, 1989: 29). In other words, it is difficult to measure or prove the existence of incentive problems and structural problems in the labor market. The Danish Council of Economic Advisors points out that 'the need for workforce mobility is difficult to determine' (1992: 118). Instead of taking up these challenges, incentive and structural problems have been reduced to purely academic postulates. For example, economist Nina Smith uses a definition based on the claim that there are incentive problems for those who have less than DKK 500 per month in net gain from holding a job (Smith, 1998: 190). The question is whether one can identify *real world problems* via such arbitrary definitions. Economists tend simply to reason that a certain pecuniary incentive structure *must* translate into economically conjectured effects. Smith does not demonstrate how a small net gain concretely influences the way the labor market operates. In fact, many factors indicate that the economists have made a fundamental mistake in the incentive and structural problem debate. It appears that in reality there cannot be an incentive problem when 20 pct. of the employed in 1996, as mentioned earlier, had a net gain of less than DKK 500 per month by working 37 hours per week rather than collecting unemployment insurance benefits. The problems emerge only when the workforce stays home because it does not pay to go to work. Furthermore, as observed by Larsen & Stamhus (2000: 2f), structural unemployment in 1994 was 11 pct., but from 1993 to 2000 unemployment fell from 10.1 pct. to 4.7 pct. without creating serious bottleneck problems or inflationary pressures.

Even though the reality of structural problems is debatable, they were nevertheless from the late 1980s on discursively treated as real world problems that politicians had to address. From the beginning of the 1990s, the structural problem emerged as a serious agenda item. By December 1991, all the political parties in the Danish parliament agreed to establish the Zeuthen Committee, comprised of all the relevant corporatist actors. The committee was charged with undertaking an investigation to establish a comprehensive basis for legislation to address the structural problems of the labor market. According to the committee's charge, the proposals should concentrate on (a) better activation of the unemployed, and (b) changes in the financing of unemployment expenses. There was no 'experience rating' for either unions or employers in the system. The focus on the financing of the unemployment compensation system reflected the fact that the state increasingly bore the burden of the growing expenses related to increases in unemployment, in that both the employer and employee contributions were determined independently of the actual expenditures on unemployment compensation. The unemployment compensation system was organized so that the state contributed about two-thirds of the expenditures from general tax revenues, while the remaining third was financed by member contributions and employer contributions. The reform objective was to transfer responsibility for financing the program back to the labor market partners who should take on a greater proportion of the costs associated with unemployment compensation, and thereby also a greater proportion of the responsibility for the collective developments on the labor market.

Recent changes in Danish labor market policies

The Zeuthen Committee delivered a report in 1992 (Udredningsudvalget, 1992), but the parliamentary parties and politicians could not agree on a new labor market reform. In the meantime, the new Social Democratic government that came to power in 1993 decided to fight unemployment. With this objective in mind, the government presented a new law on active labor market policy that was largely based on the work of the Zeuthen Committee. It took effect on January 1, 1994. In conjunction with this reform, the government also stimulated flows out of the labor market, especially from the mid-1990s on.

This section briefly describes the strengths and direction of the labor market changes that took place in the 1990s. They were predominantly *passive policies* that amounted to minor programmatic changes in terms of provisions, entitlements and requirements. On the other hand, there were certain common tendencies in the reform to make the labor force more *effective* and to *reintegrate* workers via configurative and institutional design changes. Aside from these aspects, the policies designed to make the labor force more effective did not constitute major changes, while the reintegrating policies involved programmatic (especially in terms of provisions) changes. *Policies encouraging flows in and out of the labor force* required configurative and programmatic (entitlement) changes. Generally speaking, however, these labor market policies did not amount to systemic change.

PASSIVE POLICIES

The Zeuthen Committee's task was to present a proposal for a financing reform of the unemployment insurance system which put greater emphasis on the concept of 'experience rating'. Meanwhile, the new government chose instead to introduce the so-called 'labor market contribution', which largely amounted to another method of book-keeping (Lind, 1995). After the gradual implementation of this approach, all wage earners came to pay a gross tax of 8 pct., while employers now pay 0.6 pct. of their payroll. These contributions were expected to cover the expenses of unemployment compensation, sick day pay, and the active labor market policies. The government's original intent was to make these contributions less visible to the wage earner in order to counteract the tendency toward a tax and welfare backlash. In other words, rather than *systemic retrenchment*, the Social Democratic government aimed at *systemic enhancement*. However, the government failed to make the 'labor market contribution' invisible: it appeared as a gross tax on the wage earner's pay stub.

However, the government managed to push through a number of *programmatic* changes in the unemployment insurance system over the course of the 1990s.

- First, in terms of *provisions*, the unemployment insurance system remained relatively untouched. The benefit level remained unchanged throughout the 1990s, in that an unemployed worker still receives 90 pct. of his or her previous wage, though up to a ceiling, which in January 2001 was 588 DKK per day or 2,940 DKK per week, which on average amounts to a compensation level of about 60 pct., albeit with a higher compensation rate for low paid workers. Along with the decline in unemployment during the six year period, there were a number of adjustments in the duration of benefits. In 1993, the maximum duration of nine years was cut to seven years. In 1996, another cut was made, this time to five years, and subsequently, the duration was cut to four years in 1999. Throughout these years, various regulations have safeguarded workers so that recipients of unemployment benefits above the age of 50 would not lose their right to unemployment benefits. In 1998, these regulations were abolished for people between 50 and 54, while special arrangements for persons aged 55 to 59 were retained.[9]

– Second, in terms of *entitlements*, the qualifying conditions were tightened. With law no. 15/95, the employment requirement was raised from 26 to 52 weeks of work within the last three years.[10] In addition, as of January 1, 1994, it was no longer possible to extend unemployment insurance rights by participating in labor market policy programs; the right to unemployment compensation could only be established via 26 weeks of ordinary work within the last three years.

– Third, in terms of *requirements,* the duties and conditions have changed. First, the job an unemployed person can reasonably be expected to accept has been tightened, especially in terms of how far a person is expected to travel and the duty to accept a job outside his or her former trade. Second, in 1993, the duration of benefits was subdivided into two periods, and in 2001 the two periods were divided into the first year called the 'benefit' period, followed by an 'activation' period of three years during which the person has the right and obligation to be activated (for young persons under age 25, the benefit period is 6 months and the activation period is 3.5 years). There has been some criticism of the reform in that unemployed persons, according to the new legislation, are obliged to be activated during the 'activation' period, which has been interpreted as a shift from a 'right' to an 'obligation' rationale (e.g. Loftager, 1995). However, the reality appears

---

9 A member who has reached 55 years of age and who, through continued membership and payment of an early retirement contribution can fulfill the seniority requirement to qualify for early retirement when he or she turns 60 years old and retains the right to unemployment compensation until age 60. A member who has turned 60 can receive unemployment compensation for no more than 2.5 years.

10 There was no change in the provision that an individual can join the system through participation in an educational program. There are no work requirements for those who have finished an education of at least 18 months' duration. This group of unemployed, however, receives only 82 pct. of the ordinary unemployment benefits.

CRISIS, MIRACLES, AND BEYOND

to be the same now as under the old system. Under the old system, the unemployed were not obliged to accept a 'job offer', but it was an unspoken understanding that the unemployed would lose their right to unemployment compensation if they refused to be activated. In the 'new' system, this requirement is made clear and the activation offer is moved up by about one year.

Although the unemployment compensation system has experienced some programmatic changes, the Danish system – in a comprehensive assessment and compared internationally –remains one of the most generous in the world.

Social security benefits have also undergone some *programmatic* changes. Those who have been ill, unemployed or going through marital separation and are no longer able to provide for themselves or their family are eligible for social security benefits. Earlier the amount of social security allowances was based on a means test, but the basis for determining the amount of the benefit changed during the early 1990s with means testing replaced by legal principles. In 2000, persons over 25 with children receive DKK 9,317 per month, while those over 25 without children receive DKK 6,998. Persons under 25 not living at home receive DKK 4,489, and persons under 25 living at home are entitled to DKK 2,195. Thus even in the area of social insurance, there has not been sufficient change to constitute programmatic retrenchment.

IMPROVING WORKFORCE EFFECTIVENESS AND REINTEGRATING POLICIES

As has been shown, Denmark has a two-tiered benefit system, and this two-tiered system is also a constitutive structure in the system of labor market policies. Therefore, in the following description of workforce effectiveness and reintegrating policies, we must distinguish between 'labor market' policies (for the insured eligible for unemployment benefits) and 'social policies' (for the uninsured).

With respect to the 'labor market' policies, the governing principles since the early 1970s have been regionalization and decentralization (Jørgensen, 2000). The aim has been to make labor market policy more flexible and adaptable to regional, local as well as individual needs. It was not until the 1994 reform, however, that a regionalization of responsibility and competence in relation to activation of unemployed was fully implemented. This was accomplished with the creation of 14 regional labor market councils, one for each of Denmark's 14 counties.[11]

---

11 The 14 counties differ in size, ranging from 45,000 and 619,000 inhabitants (1995), with an average county population of 326,000 inhabitants.

The formation of the regional labor market councils marked a strengthening of corporatism and increased influence of organized interests on regional labor market policy. Thus, the labor market organizations, i.e., the organized interests of employees and employers, occupy two thirds of the seats, and the regional/local authorities, i.e., the county and municipalities, hold the remaining seats. It was expected that the quality of policy formation and implementation would increase by drawing on the knowledge of organized interests. That is, it was expected that employees and employers had first-hand insights into the functioning of the labor market, so that they could react adequately to the practical problems of regional unemployment. Moreover, the choice of corporatist arrangements was also due to the fact that organized interest groups, the enterprises and the local authorities are crucial for the implementation of activation measures. For instance, it is impossible to give an unemployed individual an offer of job training if private firms or local governments refuse to participate in the activation effort.

Like the regional councils, the National Labor Market Council, which was also established in 1994, has a corporatist structure. It functions as an advisory body to the Minister of Labor, and formulates general goals and output requirements for the regional labor market councils. In conforming to these centrally formulated goals, each regional labor market council commands a wide range of policy instruments, which they can draw on to compose an appropriate solution for their region.

With respect to changes in the labor market policy's *institutional design*, the reforms involved new *configurations*, including an instrument known as an *individual action plan*. The emergence of this instrument must be understood in connection with the fact that since 1994 the unemployed have both the right and the responsibility to be activated (Jensen, 1999). This new instrument means that an 'action plan' is elaborated for each unemployed person individually. An action plan outlines the goal of activation and the means by which the goal is expected to be achieved, i.e., activation will not occur abstractly but rather in conjunction with an individual appropriate skills and abilities (education, job training etc.). The plan is drafted and signed as a contract between the unemployed individual and the Public Employment Service. The formulation of an action plan must take its point of departure in the needs and wants of the individual. Thus the 'action plan' is designed to activate the individual by involving the unemployed person in shaping his or her own future.

As the new labor market reform introduced individualized and needs-oriented activation, we have seen a move away from rule-governed labor market policies. This has put pressure on the internal structure of the Public Employment Service, which functions as the Regional Labor Market Council's administrative branch, to adapt to the new circumstances. This has required a shift from a Weberian to a more professional organization (see, e.g., Mintzberg, 1983). Such changes require an internal re-education of the street-level bureaucrats. Standardization of outputs in a professional organization is conditioned by standardization of skills. However, such internal re-education measures have still not been fully accomplished (Haahr & Winter, 1996). This may pave the way for 'creaming' and arbitrariness in the treatment of the unemployed. Certain tendencies are reinforced by conflicts between national and local priorities, and conflicts between expectations and available resources.

In contrast to labor market policies, social policy has a long historical tradition of decentralized decision making because social policy is administered by the municipalities. As in the case of labor market policy, since the mid-1990s social security recipients have the right to elaborate an action plan.[12] The action plan for social beneficiaries must reflect the capabilities, needs and wishes of the social client. The goals of the activation must be outlined and the client must be offered a choice among various means and options. If employment or education is not a realistic goal, the aim of the action plan must be to stabilize and improve the general life situation of the individual (Law no. 455/1997 § 9).

CHANGES IN POLICY REMEDIES

No meaningful changes occurred during the 1990s in the area of policy remedies used to achieve greater workforce effectiveness. This is particularly true if we look at policies directed toward persons who are already employed or the most mobile and capable of the unemployed. In contrast there have been a number of changes in policy remedies regarding reintegration and they have the dominant characteristic of stricter *requirements*.

While there have been changes, these changes in reintegration policy are not new or innovative. The remedies that the regional labor market council has at its disposition were used in various forms prior to the 1994 reform.

The offers made to the unemployed and which are specified in the individual 'action plan' are, however, different with respect to the benefit period and the activation period. Offers during the benefit period arise from an individual assessment of whether the unemployed person is at risk of long-term unem-

---

12 A series of studies (e.g., Langager, 1997; Weise & Brogaard, 1997; Hansen et al., 2001) show that individuals who work out an action plan, whether they are unemployment insurance recipients or social security beneficiaries, believe that they had a decisive influence on the construction of their own action plan. More generally it can be concluded that those being activated have had a significant positive self-reported benefit from participating in the activation program, that the unemployed have improved their occupational and educational possibilities and that the unemployed have perceived activation as leading toward an improvement in their situation on the labor market.

ployment. The unemployed person has a responsibility to accept an offer and to be available for both state-subsidized and non-subsidized work. Unemployed persons who refuse an offer of training or work receive one week's quarantine while the termination of an offer or work results in five weeks' quarantine. During the *activation period*, the unemployed has the right and responsibility to a job or an educational opportunity, as well as a minimum income that corresponds to the highest amount of unemployment compensation for which he or she qualifies. The fact that the unemployed person runs the risk of having to work for a wage that corresponds to the unemployment compensation level, represents a clear *programmatic* diminution in the generosity of the reintegrating policies. Refusing an offer of work or education results in a loss of benefits.

The municipalities administer the social assistance system,[13] and the political remedies available to the municipalities are very similar to the instruments used in the labor market reform. The difference lies primarily in the legislation that since the 1980s has enabled activation of social security claimants. But it was not until the start of the 1990s that activation of social security recipients became much more salient. From the beginning of 1997, all recipients of social security under the age of 30 were obligated to accept activation after receiving social security for 13 weeks, and since 1998, people over the age of 30 have also had the right and been under an obligation to accept activation after 12 months of unemployment. From 1996 to 1999, the number of social benefit recipients dropped from 105,344 to 93,490, while the number of activated persons increased from 33,340 to 39,689. This obligation also applies to recipients of social assistance who have social problems other than unemployment. In such cases, however, the activation must mirror the capabilities of the social client, and the activation must be complemented by other forms of treatment. In general, 50 pct. of the expenses of the municipal activation come from the state; the remaining 50 pct. are financed by the municipalities from local taxes.

POLICIES ENCOURAGING FLOWS IN AND
OUT OF THE LABOR MARKET

The Social Democratic government had come into office by promising to reduce unemployment. To live up to these promises, the new government launched a series of initiatives to stimulate flows out of the labor market. First, in 1994 the government softened the eligibility criteria (*entitlements*) for early retirement. The segment of the population eligible for transitional allowances was extended to include long-term unemployed aged 50 to 54, who

---

13 In 1995, Denmark had 275 municipalities with populations ranging from 2,400 to 473,000. On average, each municipality had a population of 19,000 inhabitants.

CRISIS, MIRACLES, AND BEYOND

would now receive 82 pct. of the unemployment benefit. Second, a series of *configurative* changes in policies encouraging flows out of the labor market were adopted. In 1995, 'part-time' early retirement was introduced, and from January 1, 1994, a new law came into effect that had the effect of expanding the leave of absence schemes introduced in 1992. The 1994 law encouraged workers to take educational leave, sabbatical leave, or leave for childcare. Persons on educational leave received an allowance corresponding to the level of unemployment compensation, while those on sabbatical and childcare leave would be compensated at a rate of 80 pct. of unemployment insurance. Based on the compensation rates, these measures designed to combat unemployment were cheaper or cost neutral compared to the potential costs of unemployment compensation.

The general purpose of the leave of absence schemes was to reduce unemployment, which means that they may be viewed as an attempt to camouflage the actual extent of unemployment, and to redistribute the burdens of unemployment by means of job rotation and job sharing in the labor market. The hope was that vacancies generated by the schemes would be filled by unemployed people (Madsen, 1998a, 1998b, 2000; Olsen, 2000: 100). Another purpose was to improve the qualifications of the workforce (Landsarbejdsrådet, 1998: 156). In other words, workforce effectiveness measures were also built into the leave of absence schemes. This was particularly true of the educational leave option that would improve workers' opportunities for life-long learning. However, sabbatical and childcare leave also contain an educational dimension. That is, in as much as the schemes create job openings, they allow unemployed people to improve their skills by means of 'on the job training' in ordinary jobs. In effect, these people will become more employable.

The success of the leave schemes was instantaneous. Already in 1995, approximately 82,000 whole-year employed persons were on leave. Of these, 7,480 took sabbatical, 42,000 took childcare leave, and 36,000 went on educational leave (Jensen, 2000). The extensive use of the leave schemes is bound to have had an impact on overall unemployment. In 1999, for example, 36 pct. of the persons on leave were previously unemployed. But the schemes also indirectly affected unemployment in that 64 pct. of persons on leave in 1999 were employed prior to taking leave (Statistics Denmark, 2000b: 4). Furthermore, it is estimated that approximately 63 pct. of persons on leave from jobs are eventually replaced by substitute labor (Andersen et al., 1996: 21). In general, it is assumed that unemployment was reduced by 33,000 to 40,000 persons in 1994 and by 60,000 to 70,000 persons in 1995 due to the leave schemes. Nevertheless the job rotation effects were modest, since only few vacancies were filled by long-term unemployed (TemaNord, 1996: 25; Andersen et al., 1996: 22). The reason is, of course, that it is often very difficult to find a long-term unemployed person with the right qualifications to substitute for a person on leave.

Soon after the implementation of the 1994 reform, the leave schemes gave rise to bottleneck problems, especially in the public sector. The problem was most pronounced in the social and health care sectors, and partly in the primary and secondary school sector. The demand was greatest for nurses, pre-school teachers, social and health workers, midwives, physiotherapists, secretaries and school teachers (Landsarbejdsrådet, 1997, 1999). The Employers' Association therefore started to attack the leave schemes and demanded that childcare leave be conditioned on the acceptance of the employer (*Politiken*, 6 October 1994). Leading economists argued that if unemployment continued to fall, it would be necessary to reconsider the possibilities of maintaining the leave schemes (e.g., Niels Kaergaard, a member of the Council of Economic Advisors, in *Politiken*, 6 October 1994). The Minister of Labor argued that access to the leave schemes should be made more selective, depending on the employment situation in the relevant industrial and economic sectors. In other words, eligibility for leave schemes should be made dependent on the state of unemployment in each occupation, which could lead to a situation in which nurses, for instance, would be ineligible for the schemes. However, these ideas were not implemented. Nevertheless, the outcome was that, in order to increase the supply of labor it was made less attractive to take leave in 1995 and 1996 (Landsarbejdsrådet, 1997; Ministry of Labor, 1999a: 16). In terms of provision, for instance for sabbatical and childcare leave, benefits were first reduced to 70 pct., and then to 60 pct. of the unemployment compensation rate. Finally, in 1999, the sabbatical leave scheme was abandoned. In other words, the content and structure of the leave schemes succumbed to the concern for overall employment and the imbalances in the labor market. Consequently, the number on leave fell from 82,000 in 1995 to 34,000 in 1999.

With the same objective in mind, the transitional allowance scheme, which was very popular, was abolished in 1996. In addition the early retirement opportunities were tightened in 1999, with a complete overhaul of the system:

–   First, in terms of provisions, the new scheme involves strong incentives to postpone early retirement. (1) An early retiree will receive 91 pct. of unemployment benefits, i.e., DKK 130,605 annually, during the entire period of early retirement. If, however, early retirement is postponed until age 62, early retirement benefits will be raised to equal unemployment benefits, i.e., DKK 143,520 annually. (2) If a person postpones early retirement until age 62, s/he will be entitled to a DKK 8,600 tax exemption for each time s/he works 481 hours (which equals one quarter of full-time employment) between age 62 and 64. That is, people who do not use their right to early retirement will receive a tax exemption of DKK 103,200 when they reach the pension age. Taking contributions and benefits into account, the tax exemption award yields a net gain of DKK 45,000 for people who postpone retirement until the age of 65. (3) For early retirees (between 60 and 62) who have additional income due to individual pension savings, etc., 60 pct. of their additional income will be deducted from the early retirement benefit. However, if the person chooses to postpone withdrawal from the labor market to age 62 or later, only certain types of personal income are deducted from the retirement benefits.

– Second, in terms of *entitlements*, the eligibility criterion was changed in that that the mandatory 20 years' membership in an unemployment insurance fund was raised to 25 of the last 30 years. Earlier, the eligibility criterion was an integral part of membership in an unemployment insurance fund. Now in addition to the general unemployment insurance contribution, the member must pay an early retirement contribution if s/he wants to be covered by the early retirement scheme. This latter contribution is thus optional, and about 12 pct. of all unemployment insurance fund members have chosen to back out. The new contribution amounts to DKK 184 a month, and is expected to rise to DKK 322.

It is quite obvious that the early retirement scheme of 1999 created considerable economic incentives to postpone early retirement. It is, however, difficult to predict how people will actually react to the new structure of incentives. Life-cycle expectations are deeply rooted in individuals' own life histories, so dramatic changes in early retirement patterns should not be expected to occur overnight. The government expects that the new early retirement scheme alone will increase labor force participation about two percentage points among people aged 60 to 64 within the next three to five years, and four to five percentage points within the next 10 years (Det Seniorpolitiske Initiativudvalg, 1999: 49).

Parallel to these changes, i.e. from the mid-1990s, the government attempted to counteract flows out of the labor market by supporting the creation of an all-inclusive labor market. The Ministry of Social Affairs launched a campaign, 'It concerns all of us – an initiative on the social responsibility of companies,' the purpose of which was to encourage the two sides of industry (management and employees) to include social chapters in the collective agreements covering both the private and public sector in order to reduce exclusion from the labor market (Ebsen et al., 1998). Since 1995, an increasing number of collective agreements have contained so-called 'social chapters' that facilitate the local creation of new types of jobs in terms of wages and working conditions for people of reduced working capacity. About 4 pct. of private and public employers have established jobs in line with the 'social chapters' – in total 3,700 jobs, of which 1,100 are located in the public sector (Ministry of Labor, 1999a: 54). Correspondingly, efforts have focused on retaining people entitled to early retirement in the workforce. In 1998, the government initiated a major reform of the disability scheme. The main purpose was to prioritize the placement of disabled persons in so-called 'flex jobs' and 'soft jobs', which are subsidized by the municipalities (Ministry of Labor, 1999b; Ministry of Social Affairs, 1999). Other things being equal, these schemes may have had an effect on the awarding of disability pensions. In 1992, 8,000 persons were awarded disability pensions for non-medical reasons compared to 1,900 in 1999 (Den Sociale Ankestyrelse, 2000: 11). In addition, rehabilitation has come to play a more important role as a measure supporting the creation of an all-inclusive labor market (Regeringen, 2000). The purpose of rehabilitation is to help the individual regain lost work capacity due to physical, mental or social conditions – in other words to reduce the likelihood that an individual becomes a permanent recipient of disability benefits.

Finally, in 2000, the major political parties in parliament agreed to take one step further in reforming the disability pension system. The purpose of the reform was to ensure that persons capable of working are given real opportunities in the labor market. The reform stresses active efforts to integrate this group into the labor market rather than supporting them passively. The goal is that a disability pension should only be awarded when it is impossible for the person in question to remain in or re-enter the labor market either under normal conditions or in subsidized employment.

Conclusion

During the period from 1994 to 1999, the number of unemployed persons in Denmark fell from 343,000 to 158,000. In 1999, Denmark's unemployment rate was 5.2 pct., the lowest rate among all industrialized countries. Not surprisingly, Denmark has become the focus of considerable international attention (e.g., Auer, 2000; Ganssmann, 2000; Scharpf & Schmidt, 2000). Some authors actually refer to this as 'the Danish "employment miracle" of the 1990s' (Madsen, 1999: 74, 2000).

It is doubtful, however, if this is truly an employment miracle. First, the size of the workforce during the period from 1994 to 1999 fell by approximately 24,000 persons (Statistics Denmark, 2000a), which, everything else being equal, reduced the scope of unemployment. Second, since 1994 participants in labor market measures have not been registered as unemployed in the official statistics. Unemployment rates would have been much higher if the thousands of people involved in various active labor market schemes had been counted among the unemployed. As can be seen from Table 2, approximately 119,000 (whole year) persons were in activation schemes or on leave in 1999, corresponding to about a doubling of that number since 1990. Among the genuinely activated, about 45 pct. are enrolled in educational programs, while 55 pct. are enrolled in various kinds of job training, etc.

TABLE 2:
Number of (whole year) persons enrolled in labor market
measures or benefit schemes (ages 18 to 66). 1999

Activation: employment and 'other' activation	48,000
Activation: education	39,000
Numbers in leave of absence schemes	32,000
Early retirement/transitional allowance	179,000
Unemployment benefit	126,000
Social security benefit/rehabilitation	115,000
Disability pensioners	270,000
Flex/soft jobs	11,000
Total	820,000
Total labor force (age 16-66)	2,784,000

Note: The table is based on statistics that are not entirely comparable.

Source: Statistics Denmark (2000b, 2000c), Ministry of Social Affairs (2000).

It is noteworthy that the 'passive' programs still dominate the labor market policy measures. In 1989, Denmark spent 1.2 pct. of its GNP on 'active' measures and 4.51 pct. on passive measures. The corresponding proportions in 1999 were 1.77 pct. and 3.12 pct. (OECD, 2000b). The number of unemployed persons receiving unemployment and social security benefits has indeed decreased by 107,000 persons in the period from 1990 to 1999. On the other hand, the number of early retirees and disability pensioners rose by 98,000, and those taking a leave of absence add another 32,000 to the complete picture. It is not so strange, therefore, that Denmark still uses more resources on passive than on active labor market measures. But the relative importance of 'active' measures has increased.

There is no doubt that the labor market developments combined with a dramatic decrease in unemployment during the 1990s has led to the creation of a number of new concepts and buzzwords. These include phrases such as 'the golden triangle' (Ministry of Labor, 1999b; Madsen, 2002) and 'flexicurity' (Madsen, 1999; Auer, 2000; Ganssmann, 2000). The golden triangle refers to the relationship between (1) the high level of compensation and the long duration of the Danish unemployment compensation system, (2) the few restrictions placed on employment conditions, and (3) the use of active labor market policies. The term implies that the interaction among these factors contributes to increased flexibility on the Danish labor market. The question remains, however, whether the term 'golden triangle', gives us new insights and with what goal in mind? This question has been raised not only because the same insights were already part of the discussions in the 1970s and 1980s, even though they were not expounded loudly by social scientists and decision makers at the time the neo-classical economists' world view provided the dominant operational understanding of the policy system. The question arises because the golden triangle acquired a few scratches at its finish during the 1990s.

Turning to the passive labor market policies, we observe a number of programmatic changes, among others changes in provisions. Benefit levels have not changed significantly, but the duration of, for example, unemployment compensation (a central element in the golden triangle) has shrunk considerably. Similarly, a tightening of entitlements (including the conditions required to qualify for unemployment benefits, etc.) and requirements (what type of job an unemployed person must accept, etc.) has occurred. All else being equal, these restrictions have intensified the search process by unemployed and thereby contributed to making the labor market function more efficiently and effectively. Alternatively, the question of whether these restrictions correspond to a logic of necessity remains open. Danish wage earners have a very strong work ethic which manifests itself, for example, in the fact that a surprisingly large percentage (approx. 20 pct.) of workers go to work even though it doesn't really pay to do so. Considering the financing principles of unemployment insurance, however, we must add that the ambitions at the end of the 1980s to engage in systemic retrenchment of the unemployment insurance system ran out of gas, especially after the Social Democratic coalition came to power in the early 1990s.

The second leg of the golden triangle, labor market policies, was subjected to considerable changes with respect to their institutional design in the course of the 1990s. The management of labor market policy is now decentralized, regionalized and privatized in the sense that the labor market actors (organized labor and employers) are responsible for developing policy via the corporatist Regional Labor Market Councils. In terms of the institutional design of labor market policy, another new configuration is the introduction of the so-called 'action plan' that involves a specific adaptation of labor market policies to the individual person's situation. The 'action plan' involves the users in the shaping of their own future, i.e., the individual is given a greater degree of autonomy and possibilities to choose how to battle unemployment – a reflection of the emergence of the 'risk society'. A general problem facing most new constructions in institutional design is that they require personnel who are capable of implementing the policy. The existing staff is often not qualified to deal with the new conditions, so there is a tendency to 'cream' the more easily employable clients and/or to handle clients inconsistently.

More specifically, we can observe that over the course of the 1990s there was a quantitative expansion of labor market remedies. There have been no new elements added to the workforce effectiveness policies which date back to the 1960s. But on the other hand, reintegrating policies with roots in the 1970s and 1980s have been through a number of minor changes. In particular, we can point to programmatic changes that, for example, have taken the form of reductions in pay and working conditions for participants in activation projects.

Policies encouraging flows in and out of the labor force do not constitute an integrated element of the golden triangle, which is notable given that these policies have played a key role in efforts to reduce unemployment. Up until the mid-1990s when unemployment was high, policies were designed to stimulate flows out of the workforce by using configurative innovations such as the leave of absence schemes and programmatic improvement of the early retirement programs. When the economy improved, these programs were closed down (sabbatical leave). Policy was then designed to change the tendency from one of 'early exit' to one of 'late exit' via programmatic changes. In addition, policy makers favored a path toward an all-inclusive labor market. With this objective in mind, new programs were established, e.g., the creation of 'flex jobs' and 'soft jobs', and reorganization of the disability pension system. Generally, we can conclude that the configurative and programmatic changes in the 1990s steadily followed changes in the employment situation, and were manifested as frequent adjustments and adaptation.

'The golden triangle,' is largely old wine in new bottles. The same could be said of the concept 'flexicurity', although this is a more advanced and complex concept than 'the golden triangle'. 'Flexicurity' also refers to the existence of corporatist structures that function as confidence building measures to build relationship that function as a precondition for creating flexibility and changes without generating social conflict. From this perspective, it bears mentioning that Danish corporatism has deep historical roots and traditions. In other words, corporatism remains a strong component of Danish labor market policy. The dominant classes in the 1970s and 1980s laid most of the problems in the labor market at the feet of the corporatist system. But the experience of the 1990s demonstrates that this assertion was unfounded. Not only have change and adaptation been possible without significant reductions in the role of corporatist actors, it has also been true that corporatist actors have been drawn into the institutional redesign (Regional Labor Councils) to implement more effective labor market policies at the regional and local levels.

References

AMS (1999a). Surveyundersøgelse af effekten af aktiveringsindsatsen i dagpengeperioden. Copenhagen: Arbejdsmarkedsstyrelsen.

AMS (1999b). *Surveyundersøgelse af effekten af aktiveringsindsatsen i aktivperioden.* Copenhagen: Arbejdsmarkedsstyrelsen.

AMU Direktoratet (1985). *Arbejdsmarkedsuddannelserne, statistik 1985.* Copenhagen.

Andersen, Dines et al. (1996). *Orlov – evaluering af orlovsordningerne.* Copenhagen: The Danish National Institute of Social Research, Report 96:11.

Auer, Peter (2000). *Employment revival in Europe.* Geneva: International Labour Office

BEK-projektet (1992). *Sammendrag.* Dansk Teknologisk Institut.

Brüniche-Olsen, Paul (1987). 'Mobiliteten på det danske arbejdsmarked'. *Nationaløkonomisk Tidsskrift*, 3: 321-36.

Calmfors, Lars & Bertil Holmlund (2000). 'Den europeiska arbetslösheten', in *NOU 2000:21: En strategi for sysselsetting og verdiskaping. Vedlegg 4.* Oslo: NOU.

Dahrendorf, Ralf (1988). *The Modern Social Conflict.* London: Weinfeld and Nicolson.

Danish Council of Economic Advisors (1991). *Dansk Økonomi – November.* Copenhagen.

Danish Council of Economic Advisors (1992). *Dansk Økonomi – November.* Copenhagen.

Den Sociale Ankestyrelse (2000). *Førtidspensioner – Årsstatistik 1999.* Copenhagen: Den Sociale Ankestyrelse.

Det Seniorpolitiske Initiativudvalg (1999). *Seniorerne og arbejdsmarkedet – nu og i fremtiden.* Copenhagen: Ministry of Labor.

Ebsen, Frank, Jens Guldager & Bitten Kristiansen (1998). *Hvordan står det til med revalidering i krydsfeltet mellem aktivering og arbejdsfastholdelse?* Copenhagen: Center for Forskning i Socialt Arbejde.

Esping-Andersen, Gøsta (1990). *The Three Worlds of Welfare Capitalism.* Cambridge: Polity Press.

Ganssmann, Heiner (2000).'Labour market flexibility, social protection and unemployment'. *European Societies* 2, 3: 243-69.

Giddens, Anthony (1994). *Beyond left and right.* Cambridge: Polity Press.

Goul Andersen, Jørgen & Peter Munk Christiansen (1991). *Skatter uden velfærd.* Copenhagen: Jurist- og Økonomforbundets Forlag.

Goul Andersen, Jørgen (2002a). 'From the Edge of the Abyss to a Sustainable Welfare Model', in Jørgen Goul Andersen, Jochen Clasen, Wim van Oorschot & Knut Halvorsen (eds.), *Unemployment, Welfare Policies and Citizenship.* Bristol: Policy Press, pp. 143-62.

Goul Andersen, Jørgen (2002b). 'Velfærd uden skatter. Det danske velfærdsmirakel i 1990'erne'. *Politica* 34, 1: 5-23.

Goul Andersen, Jørgen (2002c). 'Work and citizenship: unemployment and unemployment policies ind Denmark, 1980-2000', in Jørgen Goul Andersen & Per H. Jensen (eds.), *Changing Labour Markets, Welfare Policies and Citizenship.* Bristol: Policy Press, pp. 59-84.

Haahr, Jens Henrik & Søren Winter (1996). *Den regionale arbejdsmarkedspolitik.* Aarhus: Systime.

Hansen, Henning, Jens Lind & Iver Hornemann Møller (2001). 'Aktivering som inklusion', in Jørgen Goul Andersen & Per H. Jensen (eds.), *Marginalisering, integration, velfærd.* Aalborg: Aalborg University Press, pp. 181-97.

Jensen, Per H. (1987). 'Tryghed i ansættelsen i Norge, Sverige, Storbritannien og Vesttyskland', in LO, *Tryghedsreform – tryghed i jobbet.* Copenhagen.

Jensen, Per H. (1996). *Komparative Velfærdssystemer.* Copenhagen: Nyt fra Samfundsvidenskaberne.

Jensen, Per H. (1999). 'Activation of the unemployed in Denmark since the early 1990s – Welfare or Workfare?' Aalborg University: *CCWS Working Paper No. 1/1999.*

Jensen, Per H. (2000). 'The Danish leave of absence-schemes – Origins, functioning and effects from a gender perspective'. Aalborg University: *CCWS Working Paper No. 19/2000.*

Jensen, Peter et al. (1992). 'Vedvarende arbejdsløshed i Danmark', in Karsten Albæk et al., *Kampen mod ledigheden.* Copenhagen: Spektrum, pp. 159-74.

Jørgensen, Henning (1985/86). *Arbejdsmarkedsnævn i arbejdsmarkedspolitikken – Forvaltning mellem stat og marked I.* Aalborg: ATA-forlaget.

Jørgensen, Henning (2000). 'Danish Labour Market Policy since 1994 – the New Columbus Egg of Labour Market Regulation?', in Paul Klemmer & Rüdiger Wink (eds.), *Preventing Unemployment in Europe – A New Framework for Labour Market Policy.* Cheltenham: Edward Elgar, pp. 108-36.

Keeley, Michael C. (1981). *Labor Supply and Public Policy.* New York: Academic Press.

Knudsen, Herman & Jens Lind (1987). *Rationalisering og relationer på virksomheden.* Aalborg: Aalborg University Press.

Korpi, Walter (1989). 'Aktiv og passiv arbetsmarknadspolitik i 18 OECD-länder', in Eskil Wadensjö et al. (eds.), *Vingarnas trygghet – Arbetsmarknad, ekonomi och politik.* Lund: dialogos, pp. 131-48.

Landsarbejdsrådet (1997). *Landsarbejdsrådets Arbejdsmarkedspolitiske redegørelse 1996.* Copenhagen.

Landsarbejdsrådet (1998). *Landsarbejdsrådets Arbejdsmarkedspolitiske redegørelse 1997.* Copenhagen.

Landsarbejdsrådet (1999). *Landsarbejdsrådets Arbejdsmarkedspolitiske redegørelse 1998.* Copenhagen.

Langager, Klaus (1997). *Indsatsen over for de forsikrede ledige.* Copenhagen: The Danish National Institute of Social Research.

Larsen, Flemming & Jørgen Stamhus (2000). 'Active Labour Market Policy in Denmark: Labour Market Reform, Crucial Design Features, and Problems of Implementation'. *Working Paper 3.* Aalborg: Department of Economics, Politics and Public Administration.

Lind, Jens (1985). *Arbejdsløshed og velfærdsstat.* Aalborg: Aalborg University Press.

Lind, Jens (1995). 'Unemployment Policy and Social Integration', in Nils Mortensen (ed.), *Social Integration and Marginalisation.* Copenhagen: Samfundslitteratur, pp. 183-205.

Lind, Jens (2000). *Hvor fleksibelt er det danske arbejdsmarked?* Aalborg University: LEO-serien No. 25.

Loftager, Jørn (1995). 'Magt, rationalitet og normativitet'. *Grus,* 45: 34-49.

Madsen, Per Kongshøj (1998a). 'Paid Leave Arrangements and Gender Equality – The Danish Experience in the 1990s'. Conference Paper presented at a High Level Conference organized by the OECD and the Ministry of Children and Family Affairs and the Ministry of Labour and Government Administration, Norway, Oslo, 12-13 October.

Madsen, Per Kongshøj (1998b). 'A Transitional Labour Market: The Danish Paid Leave Arrangements', in *New Institutional Arrangements on the Labour Market. Transitional Labour Markets as a New Full Employment Concept.* Berlin: Publications of European Academy of the Urban Environment, pp. 68-73.

Madsen, Per Kongshøj (1999). 'Denmark: Flexibility, security and labour market success'. *Employment and Training Papers 53.* Geneva: International Labour Office.

Madsen, Per Kongshøj (2000). 'Det danske jobmirakel – Fra massearbejdsløshed til fuld beksæftigelse'. *Søkelys på arbeidsmarkedet,* 17: 115-23.

Madsen, Per Kongshøj (2002). 'The Danish model of flexicurity: A paradise – with some snakes', in Hedva Sarfati & Guiliano Bonoli (eds.), *Labour market and social protections reforms in international perspective: Parallel or converging tracks?* Aldershot: Ashgate, pp. 243-65.

Martin, John P. (2000). *What works among active labour market policies: Evidence from OECD Countries' Experiences*. OECD Economic Studies No. 30.

Ministry of Finance (1995). *Finansredegørelse 95*. Copenhagen.

Ministry of Labor (1989). *Hvidbog om arbejdsmarkedets strukturproblemer*. Copenhagen.

Ministry of Labor (1999a). *Udviklingstendenser på det offentlige arbejdsmarked*. Copenhagen.

Ministry of Labor (1999b). *Arbejdsmarkedsreformerne – ét statusbillede*. Copenhagen.

Ministry of Social Affairs (1992). *Aktivering, Beskæftigelse, Førtidspension, Myndighedsstruktur – Bilag 1*. Copenhagen.

Ministry of Social Affairs (1999). *Sociale Tendenser*. Copenhagen.

Ministry of Social Affairs (2000). *Socialsektoren i tal: 2000*. Copenhagen.

Mintzberg, Henry (1983). *Structures in Fives: designing effective organizations*. New Jersey: Prentice Hall.

Nätti, Jouko (1993). 'Temporary Employment in the Nordic Countries: a "Trap" or a "Bridge"'. *Work, Employment & Society*, 451-64.

OECD (1990a). *Labour Market Policies for the 1990s*. Paris: OECD.

OECD (1990b). *Historical Statistics, 1960-1988*. Paris: OECD.

OECD (1997). *Employment Outlook*. Paris: OECD.

OECD (1999). *Employment Outlook*. Paris: OECD.

OECD (2000a). *Historical Statistics, 1970-1999*. Paris: OECD.

OECD (2000b). *Employment Outlook*. Paris: OECD.

OECD (2001). *Quarterly Labour Force Statistics*, 1. Paris: OECD.

Olsen, Bente Marianne (2000). *Nye fædre på orlov*. University of Copenhagen: Department of Sociology.

Olsen, Henning (1985). *På efterløn*. Copenhagen: The Danish National Institute of Social Research.

Pedersen, Peder J. (1998). 'Hvad vej går pensionsalderen?', in G.V. Mogensen (ed.). *Beskæftiget – ledig – på efterløn*. Copenhagen: Spektrum, pp. 122-40.

Pierson, Paul (1994). *Dismantling the Welfare State?* Cambridge: Cambridge University Press

Plovsing, J. (2000). *Socialpolitik*. Copenhagen: Handelshøjskolens Forlag.

Regeringen (2000). *Regeringens debatoplæg om det rummelige arbejdsmarked*. Copenhagen: Ministry of Finance.

Reubens, B.G. (1989). 'Unemployment insurance in the United States and Europe, 1973-83'. *Monthly Labor Review*, April: 22-31.

Scharpf, Fritz W. & Vivien A. Schmidt (eds.)(2000). *Welfare and work in the open economy*. Oxford: Oxford University Press.

Schmid, Günther & Bernd Reissert (1991). 'On the Institutional Conditions of Effective Labour Market Policies', in Egon Matzner & Wolfgang Streeck (eds.). *Beyond Keynesianism*. Hants: Edward Elgar, pp. 81-110.

Schmid, Günther (1987). *Systems of Financing Labour Market Policy: An International Comparison*. Stockholm: Institut för Social Forskning. Meddelande 11.

Smith, Nina (1998). 'Økonomiske incitamenter til at arbejde', in Nina Smith (ed.). *Arbejde, incitamenter og ledighed*. Aarhus: Aarhus University Press, pp. 179-209.

Socialkommissionen (1993). *Arbejde og velfærd – forslag til en ydelses- og aktiveringsreform for midtergruppen*. Copenhagen.

Statistics Denmark (1993). *Statistiske efterretninger – Arbejdsmarked* (1993:14).

Statistics Denmark (1998). *Statistisk tiårsoversigt 1998*. Copenhagen: Statistics Denmark.

Statistics Denmark (2000a). *Statistiske efterretninger – Arbejdsmarked (2000:13)*.

Statistics Denmark (2000b). *Statistiske efterretninger – Arbejdsmarked (2000:24)*.

Statistics Denmark (2000c). *Statistiske efterretninger – Sociale forhold, sundhed og retsvæsen (2000:19)*.

Statistics Denmark (2001a). *Statistiske efterretninger – Arbejdsmarked (2001:46)*.

Statistics Denmark (2001b). *Statistisk Tiårsoversigt, 2001*. Copenhagen: Statistics Denmark.

CRISIS, MIRACLES, AND BEYOND

Svallfors, Stefan, Knut Halvorsen & Jørgen Goul Andersen (2001). 'Work Orientations in Scandinavia: Employment Commitment and Organizational Commitment in Denmark, Norway and Sweden'. *Acta Sociologica*, 44, 2: 139-56.

TemaNord (1996:612). *Orlovsordninger i Norden*. Copenhagen: Nordic Council of Ministers.

Trommel, Willem & Bert de Vroom (2002). 'New Institutional Forms of Welfare Productions: Some Implications for Citizenship', in Jørgen Goul Andersen & Per H. Jensen (eds.). *Changing Labour Markets, Welfare Policies, and Citizenship*. Bristol: The Policy Press, pp. 85-106.

Udredningsudvalget (1992). *Rapport fra udredningsudvalget om arbejdsmarkedets strukturproblemer*.

Veen, Romke van der, Willem Trommel & Bert de Vroom (2000). 'Institutional Change of Welfare States. Empirical Reality, Theoretical Obstacles', in H. Wagenaar (ed.). *Government Institutions: Effects, Changes and Normative Foundations*. Amsterdam: Kluwer Academic Publishers, pp. 33-53.

Weise, Hanne & Susanne Brogaard, S. (1997). *Aktivering af kontanthjælpsmodtagere*. Copenhagen: The Danish National Institute of Social Research.

4 PUBLIC EXPENDITURES

Is the Welfare State Manageable?

Peter Munk Christiansen

Around the world, management of public expenditure has become a key political debate over the last 30 years. In this respect, Denmark is no exception. However, the dramatic growth in public expenditures is one of the most striking features of the development of the Danish welfare state. Although most OECD countries have experienced expenditure growth, the increase from a level of less than 25 pct. of GDP in 1960 to the present 50 pct. is close to a world record; at the very least, it is an OECD record (cf. Castles, 1998: 106). Danish crisis management during the late 1970s and early 1980s, in the words of the Social Democratic minister of finance at that time, brought the country to the 'brink of the abyss'. Although the Conservative-Liberal cabinets of the 1980s made management of public spending one of their main tasks, their results were meager compared to the goals they set. In the 1990s, the discourse changed, partly because Social Democratic cabinets came back to power, but also in response to a long and positive business cycle.

This chapter looks at the problems of managing welfare state expenses. What are the basic and overall political and managerial problems confronting Danish welfare spending? How are they dealt with and to what extent have they been solved? The conclusion – that problems of public spending management become more pronounced the more one approaches the micro-level – supports the findings of many studies that emphasize the incapacity to control public spending. However, the 1980s and 1990s did not leave the political and administrative apparatus without important insights about workable mechanisms for public budget management. The Danish case demonstrates that while controlling public spending is difficult – for political, bureaucratic, and economic reasons – it is not impossible. The experience in Denmark demonstrates that the collapse of the welfare state due to the structural incapacity to control spending is far from inevitable. We seek first to identify the potential capacity in the political and administrative apparatus to control and direct government spending. Then we turn to an analysis of the actual experience in Denmark to elucidate this perspective.

The political capacity to control welfare state expenses

Olsen (1978) formulated the ideal of a democratic system as one of parliamentary governance, in which government is portrayed as democratic and potent. If we add to this model the rationale for government intervention in the market place (i.e., market failure) and the rationale for welfare transfers and welfare provision of public services (i.e., equity), we get an ideal picture of government as democratic, potent and good.

For the last two decades, political science (and economics) has produced immense amounts of evidence challenging this ideal and naive view of government as purely benevolent. On the input side of the political system, aggregating individual preferences into collective decisions is now a classic problem. The operation of the government apparatus, the public choice literature has pointed out, raises the problem of controlling public bureaus by hierarchical means (Niskanen, 1971; Moe, 1984; Dunleavy, 1991; Lane, 2000) and the ensuing problems of securing the efficiency of public service production (Le Grand, 1991). Others have focused on the lack of validity of the causal models underlying public programs (Rose, 1981) and implementation failure (Pressmann & Wildavsky, 1973; Winter, 1990). This research could loosely be labeled as the 'policy failure' literature, although policy failures can also be formulated in a more precise way (e.g., Le Grand, 1991).

Together, these contributions point to the lack of capacity to control public expenditures and programs. Caiden (1990) contrasts two models, the capacity and the incapacity models of public budgeting. The models are not genuine models, but rather two collections of statements belonging to different paradigms of public budgeting.

The *incapacity model* emphasizes the basic aggregation problem in collective decision-making. When rational individuals pursue their self-interest, collective decisions will often be irrational. The result is what Caiden calls an '... intrinsic bias that ends by subverting the general interest. Whereas benefits are concentrated to accrue to particular interest groups, costs are diffused over the whole population, so benefits are easily perceived as outweighing costs' (Caiden, 1990: 237). Political decisions about spending are thus influenced by an asymmetrical distribution of incentives. Those who favor increased spending will resist cuts and are structurally placed in a much better position compared to those who fight increased spending and favor cuts (cf. Pierson, 2001). As a consequence, the incapacity model emphasizes the immobilism or inertia of the budget. Strong distributional coalitions (cf. Olson, 1982) and vested interests hold the budget in an iron grip. Finally, the incapacity model emphasizes the decline of norms that traditionally restrained the growth of spending. In sum, the incapacity model points to the favorable position of producer groups and other groups benefiting from public spending, as opposed to the rather disorganized taxpayers who have an interest in controlling spending. As a consequence, the political and administrative apparatus dealing with expense management is seriously constrained by the *status quo* and by a constant upward pressure on expenditures. The model thus emphasizes the incapacity of the political system to manage public expenses.

The contrasting *capacity model* is much closer to the Olsen (1978) ideal of parliamentary governance as briefly outlined above. The capacity model points to the manageability of the public budget. The capacity model sees the budget as an instrument to resolve conflicts and achieve consensus in the complex system of fragmented legislation and centralized budgeting. The budget is a product of political preferences and an instrument of whatever interests dominate at any given time. The budgetary system is neutral with respect to outcome and adaptive to changes in the political environment and responsive to other signals, although there might be some delays. In contrast to the incapacity model, the capacity model emphasizes the strength of the demand side of public expenses – and thus the political capacity to govern.

It is difficult to test the validity of the two models directly as they are both complex and represent an aggregation of multiple hypotheses and paradigms concerning public sector management. Here we use the two models to analyze the different types of constraints and the different levels at which the capacity to manage public expenditures must operate, as well as the political managerial tasks following from these. We therefore look for evidence in support of, or in conflict with, the two models at macro, meso, and micro levels.

The need to investigate all three levels requires justification. The incapacity model is clearly inspired by public choice thinking. Confessing to the principle of methodological individualism, the preferred – but not the only (e.g., Olson, 1982; North, 1990) – level of analysis is as close to the level of the individual as possible. Most studies thus refer to the level of the individual, the program or the policy sector level. Taking our point of departure in the micro world of policy failures and pursuing the goal of assessing the overall expense management, we run the risk of proving that the bumblebee is unable to fly. The capacity model – whose supporters are more difficult to identify – appears to be more concerned with the macro level, or at least founded in macro-thinking. Taking our point of departure at the macro level runs the risk of overlooking the problems at the micro level. The solution selected here is to contrast the two models of public expenditure management with empirical evidence at macro, meso, and micro level.

At macro level, i.e., total public spending, the incapacity model predicts ever increasing public expenditures. Public expenses are sticky downwards because groups adversely affected by cuts in public appropriations ally with groups seeking to advance their interests by demanding new or more appropriations (Pierson, 2001; cf. also Olson, 1982). Confronted with this organized opposition to budget cuts, decision makers generally tend to increase public expenditures when they want to add new tasks to the public sector agenda. The capacity models, on the contrary, view political managers as capable of resisting demands for appropriations beyond what they view as desirable.

The meso level refers to the composition of the budget. To what extent does the budget respond to shifts in political priorities? Or to what extent can the budget be reformulated in order to respond to such changes? Since budgeting is centralized in each unit responsible for public spending at the state, regional and local levels, the problem might seem simple. The budget is composed in precisely the way it is decided by those who are politically responsible. Formally, this is of course true. In the real world, however, political decision makers confront multiple restrictions in the pursuit of changing the composition of the budget. They may be left with relatively few degrees of freedom and strong rigidities that impede more than marginal changes.

In the case of service provision, we can be more precise in predicting the responses to changes in the demand structure underlying public budgets according to the incapacity model. For example, when demand in the education sector (measured by the number of school children) is increasing, appropriations tend to grow proportionally to increases in demand. When demand is decreasing, appropriations will tend to be reduced less than proportionally to the decrease in demand. The result may be asymmetrical adaptation (Christiansen, 1990), which is one of the mechanisms underlying the downward stickiness of public budgets. In relation to cash transfers, those in control of the budget must overcome the political barriers: budget cuts may impinge on the legal rights of individuals. Transferring resources from one program or sector to another may be difficult, if not impossible. In sum, the incapacity model points to very few degrees of freedom in deciding if and how to rearrange the budget.

According to the capacity model, the degrees of freedom are much higher. Budgetary changes occur as responses to shifts in political preferences, although one must of course expect time lags and problems with full adaptation.

The third prediction concerns the micro level. To what extent is it possible to impose budgetary mechanisms that allow the pursuit of efficient public service production? Taking the point of departure in the incapacity model, the predictions are quite clear. The traditional preference for governance of public service providers has been the use of hierarchical (bureaucratic) means (Lane, 2000: 59ff.). As government-supplied services have grown, a number of deficiencies have come to be associated with hierarchical governance: asymmetrical adaptation, low productivity, lack of customer responsiveness, etc. (Lane, 2000: 59ff.). In fighting these problems, most Western countries have imposed new methods of governance. According to the incapacity model, these reforms are likely to be rejected or distorted by bureaucrats in a way that makes their overall impact less predictable and often doubtful. Thus current reform measures to improve the efficiency, effectiveness, and responsiveness of public bureaucracies are likely to contribute only marginally to solving the problems of hierarchical control.

According to the capacity model, measures to increase efficiency should only pose problems insofar as their technical properties are deficient. Deciding and implementing reforms might be delayed during the initiation process. But provided they are the correct technical solutions to the problem, the reforms will be potent in contributing to the introduction of better and more efficient management in the governance of service provision.

Clearly the three levels are interdependent. The more we approach the micro level, the stronger our test of the two models. If we assume that government succeeds in restricting the growth of general government expenditures, this might be done with or without adapting the budget to changing sectoral demands. It might also be done with or without fighting efficiency problems at the micro-level. Where expenses are controlled without solving the problems at meso and micro level, fulfillment of the overall expense goal is reached by omitting otherwise desirable goals such as tax reductions or increased appropriations in needy sectors. A corresponding problem occurs if the problem of asymmetrical adaptation is overcome without solving the problem of efficiency of government service production. In sum, we must pursue the test of the two models at all three levels, but the real proof is at the micro level. The predictions of the two models are summarized in Figure 1.

FIGURE 1.

Predictions of the capacity and incapacity models in terms of responses to political demands

	Capacity model	Incapacity model
Macro level: Total government expenses	Follow political priorities except for variations due to market fluctuations	Sticky downward and ever increasing. Very difficult to manage
Meso level: Responses to shifts in policy priorities	Budget tends to follow political priorities, although with some delay	Difficult to pursue redistribution. Likely to follow a pattern of asymmetrical adaptation
Micro level: Efficiency	Efficiency will depend on the political strategies pursued, although with some delay	Difficult to enhance efficiency. Efficiency measures to be resisted by stakeholders.

Before examining the empirical evidence, we may consider whether the two competing models work independently of the context of public budgeting. Does scarcity (or abundance) affect the applicability of the two models? In a

CRISIS, MIRACLES, AND BEYOND

study of Danish municipalities, Mouritzen (1991) has shown that supply-side factors dominate in municipalities with resource abundance whereas demand-side factors dominate in municipalities confronting resource scarcity. The supply-side and demand-side factors seem to express the logic underlying the incapacity and capacity models. Mouritzen's argument can be summarized quite simply. In times of resource scarcity, politicians are forced to focus more intensely on the ways resources are used. In times of abundance, they confront fewer restrictions and relax their monitoring of the amount and disposition of resources. In a parallel argument, we expect the capacity model to have greater validity in times when resources are perceived to be scarce, e.g., when the governance of expenses and taxes is a salient issue among the electorate and politicians.

The incapacity model is easily justified by reference to the dominant literature on public spending, but it is much more difficult to find theoretically sound contributions in favor of the capacity model. In an extreme version, the capacity model could easily be confused with pure voluntarism, neglecting well-known problems of public budgeting. In this way, the capacity model could be a straw man argument making it easy to support the incapacity model. This makes it even more important to look carefully for evidence in support of the capacity model.

The 1980s and 1990s in Denmark provide a good testing ground for assessing the two models. The experiences from the late 1970s increased political and administrative attention towards spending management and continued pressures on public services brought permanent attention to service reforms. And we have witnessed that very different economic conditions prevailed during the period. A long recession ended in 1983, only to gain foothold again in 1987. 1993/94 marked the beginning of one of the longest periods of post-war economic growth in Denmark.

Public spending trends in Denmark

In the early 1960s, the level of Danish public expenditures was well below the OECD average and even significantly below the levels of Sweden and Norway (Goul Andersen & Christiansen, 1991: 28; Castles, 1998: 106). By 1970, Danish public expenses were not extraordinary compared with most other northern European countries. The end of the 1960s to the beginning of the 1980s, however, was a period of exceptional growth, with the Danish rate exceeding most other European countries. This period of unrivaled growth to a large extent followed the tax revolt, led by the lawyer Mogens Glistrup and his Progress Party, which took off during the election of 1973. Although the Progress Party challenged the apparent consensus on public sector development – and

literally threatened the established parties by gaining an unexpected proportion of the seats in parliament – the tax revolt had no visible or measurable
impact on public sector growth. However, it affected the public sector deficit:
taxes were lowered in the years following the entry of the Progress Party. But
outlays were not.

In order to understand the development of public expenses in the 1970s, the
changing international environment must also be considered. The oil shocks of
1973-74 and again in 1979-80 were followed by increasing unemployment and
an apparent weakening of traditional Keynesian economics (see contribution
by Nannestad & Green-Pedersen in this volume). The policies pursued by different Social Democratic cabinets attracted nearly every imaginable economic
problem: growing unemployment, high inflation, low economic growth, a large
and growing deficit on the balance of payments and very large public deficits
from 1979 onwards. Public debt exploded. In the four years between 1979 and
1983, public net debt increased from 57 to 359 billion DKK or from 10.2 pct.
to 64.9 pct. of GDP (Goul Andersen & Christiansen, 1991: 63).

The Conservative-Liberal cabinet that came to power in 1982 – and stayed
in power for more than 10 years under different coalitions – used the widespread
feeling of an imminent catastrophe to pursue the goal of reduced expenses and
taxes. And the cabinet appeared to be successful. Cuts in cash benefits, grants
to counties and municipalities, and a number of other state expenses signaled
the start of the 'restoration' of the Danish economy. In order to reduce the still
very large public deficits, a tax on pension funds was introduced and a number
of tax-like contributions were raised. Simultaneously the economy started
to boom. Interest rates fell, and investments and employment grew rapidly.
In 1986 the state budget showed a surplus for the first time in a decade. The
result was an impressive decline in government outlays as a proportion of the
GDP from 1983 through 1986. The balance of payments, however, deteriorated
seriously, mainly due to a strong increase in private consumption. New taxes,
restrictions on private borrowing, and a tax reform, which reduced the value
of interest tax deductions, were followed by a seven-year recession. The level
of public expenditures was thus largely unaffected by more than ten years of
Liberal-Conservative governments.

A new coalition cabinet led by the Social Democratic Party followed in
January 1993. In many respects the situation paralleled that of ten years earlier. In the words of the cabinet, a 'restoration' of the economy was urgently
needed. During 1993-94, the economy was 'kick-started' by increased public
spending and investment. And again the economy reacted positively. Contrary
to the situation in the mid-1980s, the balance-of-payments problem did not
undermine improvements in the economy. By 2000, the Danish economy was in
better condition than it had been for decades. The discourse on public spending

had changed, calls for 'cuts' and 'savings' had disappeared from Ministry of Finance documents. This does not mean that spending was allowed to grow out of control or that public sector reform came to a stop – on the contrary, as we shall see.

The Danish public sector is very decentralized. Municipalities are free to levy their own taxes, although not enough to cover all their expenses. Almost a fourth of all taxes are levied by municipalities.[1] With the addition of grants from the central state and income from services produced, regions and municipal expenditures account for more than half of all public expenses (Ministry of Taxation, 2007). The biggest part of citizen services – i.e., education, health and social services – are produced and delivered by regions and municipalities. Coordination between the central state, the 5 regions and 98 municipalities is an important aspect of the total system of expenditure governance. The many problems and details of the delicate balance between the different levels of government will only be discussed briefly in the following section (for a more detailed treatment, see Mouritzen in this volume).

The management of public expenditure

TOTAL GOVERNMENT EXPENSES

We now proceed to the discussion of the institutions governing public expenses. Some key figures concerning government outlays are listed in Table 1 for the period of Conservative-Liberal governments from 1982 through 1993. During the ten years of bourgeois reign, total public expenses grew by one-fifth in real terms. Growth was moderate in the first years primarily because of the economic boom, but the economic crisis from 1987 on had a negative impact on public spending.

The new cabinet of Prime Minister Poul Schlüter inherited a very large deficit in the 1983 budget, but the 1984 budget already reduced growth to almost zero due to cuts and reduced spending generated by increasing growth. After the initial years of Schlüter's government, some of the most pressing economic problems were reduced, and the time had come to implement lasting reforms. The new proposals were in line with previous budgetary reforms that started in the 1960s with the introduction of 'frameworks' for part of the budget.[2] These initiatives completed and refined what had been underway during the previous Social Democratic cabinet (Christensen, 1992;

---

1 After the local and regional government reform of 2007, that suspended the right of regions (former counties) to levy taxes. Prior to the reform local and regional taxes made up almost a third of all taxes.

2 This is similar to the debate over *unfunded mandates* in the US federal-state system (cf. Cammisa, 1995: 5).

Christiansen, 1999). One main idea was to include all types of state expenses except those related to unemployment benefits, interests on state debt, and contributions to the EU in expenditure frameworks. Increased spending in one area had to be offset by cuts in other areas and vice versa. Each minister was held responsible for not exceeding the framework within his/her portfolio. Another major innovation was to forbid real spending increases. Each year the budget would be based on 1984 expenditure levels with adjustments only for the rate of inflation and ups and downs in the business cycle. This system would bring down or contain government spending relative to the health of the private sector.

The budgetary reform was implemented with enthusiasm by the cabinet in general and by the Ministry of Finance in particular. However, no system functions better than the people who control it. Throughout the years, rules and norms gradually eroded. The basic goal of zero growth was maintained, but in practice it was undermined by allowing all kinds of tricks in the budgetary process. The Danish tricks are not substantially different from those described by Wildavsky (1980, 1988) and Meyers (1994) (cf. also Christiansen, 1990, 1999). Two examples demonstrate how the system was undermined.

In 1987, children's allowances were increased and all parents were made eligible. The allowances compensated for the reduced value of interest deductions due to the tax reform of 1987. These allowances entered the budget as negative income, and thus did not affect the so-called 'target number', which was the basic instrument to maintain the goal of zero growth. Another example was the gradual erosion of the core principle of finding compensating cuts in order to finance new expenses. In the late 1980s and early 1990s, the cabinet simply added new appropriations to each year's 'target number'. The 'target number' lost any accurate meaning. Other tricks are documented in Christiansen (1999).

It would be very unfair to say that the state budget grew out of control. What happened was rather a confirmation of some traditional problems of budget governance. Due to the asymmetrical distribution of costs and benefits of public expenses, the budget is sticky downwards. The Conservative-Liberal cabinets were all minority governments. Especially during the latter years they were in office, they lacked the parliamentary strength to pursue the goal of zero growth. During the 1980s, the budget increasingly became the object of tough political battles. The price for staying in power was to ease some of the budgetary restrictions.

TABLE 1.

State and total public expenses 1983-1992. Index in fixed prices
(1983=100) and total public expenses in current prices (bill. DKK)

	1983	1984	1985	1987	1989	1991	1992
Total state expenses Index (1983=100)	100	103	102	100	104	109	112
Total state expenses exclusive of un-employment benefits Index (1983=100)	100	104	103	103	106	109	113
Total public consumption expenses	100	99	103	107	106	106	108
Total cash benefits	100	99	99	104	117	125	130
Total public expenses Index (1983=100)	100	102	104	107	112	116	119
Total public expenses at current costs, bill. DKK	299.4	325.9	347.1	384.9	439.6	479.4	501.0

Sources: *Statistiske Efterretninger. Nationalregnskab, offentlige finanser og betalingsbalance*, various issues. Total cash benefits: Calculated from Green-Pedersen (1999). Consumer prices were used as a deflator except for consumption expenses that were deflated by the public consumption price index.

Table 1 reveals a structural development which is contrary to the one predicted by public choice-inspired theory and thus by the incapacity model. From 1986 through 1992, growth in public consumption in fixed prices almost came to a stop, whereas transfers continued to grow. The incapacity model emphasizes the strong supply-side forces in public sector spending. Since public employees have strong incentives to increase the budget allocations and are well organized, public producers are predicted to be in a strong position to combat cuts and pursue budgetary increases compared to other beneficiaries of public spending (cf. Pierson, 2001). As a consequence, consumption costs for services should be much more difficult to manage than transfer payments. Following this line of thought, consumption expenditures should increase or at least not decrease as a percentage of the budget. This is not what happened during the 1980s. On the contrary, consumption was kept at a level close to zero growth from the mid-1980s and dropped significantly as a proportion of total expenses. Recipients of transfer payments were clear winners in the battle over public expenditures during those years. The economic crisis of 1987 is not a sufficient explanation. The dramatic increase in transfers from the mid-1980s onwards by far exceeded the increase due to the long economic depression after 1986. Only half the increase in transfers between 1986 and 1991 was due to the downturn in the business cycle. The rest was mainly due to increases in transfers to retired people, students, families with children and tenants (Goul Andersen & Christiansen, 1991).

To what can we attribute the successful management of consumption expenditures and the failure to hold the line on transfers? The most severe economic restrictions had disappeared by the mid-1980s. The private sector boomed, and the public sector showed a surplus for the first time in a decade. The absence of significant economic constraints, however, explains only why it became more difficult to keep *total* expenses down. It does not explain the difference between consumption and transfers. That explanation probably lies in the political situation and the perceived distribution of political benefits flowing from different types of public expenditures (see also Green-Pedersen, 1999).

The Conservative-Liberal cabinets were, as already pointed out, rather weak, and they fought hard to stay in power. Simultaneously, the traditional norms in parliament changed. Traditionally, all 'responsible' parties voted for the annual budget, even if they disagreed substantially. It was not a tradition to challenge the cabinet on the budget vote. The Social Democrats changed that norm by voting against the 1984 budget. For the remainder of the 1980s, the vote on the budget would become a vote for or against the cabinet, which of course increased the level of party competition related to the budget. The Social Democrats and the Socialist People's Party argued more or less constantly for increased spending in a number of areas. In this highly competitive situation, two arguments favor increased spending on transfers: Most welfare state services are the responsibility of counties and municipalities and can thus only indirectly be affected by central government. Thus consumption expenditures yield less of a pay-off for parliamentary politicians, and inadequate appropriations can be blamed on local and regional governments (cf. Pierson, 1994: 19ff.). Direct transfers are, on the other hand, visible and directly controlled by the central government. This explanation is supported by the fact that the large increases in transfers were directed towards large groups of voters: retired people, parents, students, and tenants. Programs affecting parents and students brought the Danish model closer to a universal welfare state model and promised a good return at the polls (Green-Pedersen, 1999).

Despite appearances, the national cabinets nevertheless held a strong grip on consumption expenditures and on the budgets of counties and municipalities. It is true that the central government only indirectly controls total government outlays. Local and regional government, who are responsible for primary and secondary education and for health and social services, spends almost half of total public expenditures in Denmark. The very decentralized structure of the Danish public sector thus poses a coordination problem with respect to the governance of expenses. During the 1970s, real term growth in local and regional public expenditures was very high, partly due to economic incentives that favored growth. In the early 1980s, the Social Democratic cabinet tried to control the growth in local and regional expenditures to 3, 2 and 1 pct. for the years 1980, 1981 and 1982. Their tool was primarily the annual agreements between the central and local/regional governments. Subsequent

Conservative-Liberal cabinets went for zero growth from 1983 and onwards. The means were tougher compared to those used by the previous cabinets, and the goal was not only to reduce growth in local and regional expenditures, but also to improve the state budget. The cabinet broke at least the spirit of the so-called 'cooperation on the budget', an institution that had developed during the late 1970s on (Mouritzen, 1991: 122ff.; Christensen, Christiansen & Ibsen, 2006: Ch. 12). State grants were cut during the following years, and in 1985 the cabinet imposed sanctions on municipalities and counties that did not comply with the strict limits on expenditure growth. As a consequence, the level of conflict between central and local government was quite high during the mid-1980s.

After a conflict-ridden period in the mid-1980s, local expenses were contained through a system of negotiations and safeguarding mechanisms. On one hand municipalities and counties had to accept the state's goal of containing local and regional spending and, on the other hand, municipalities and counties exploited their position as part of a 'negotiating community'. If they had not entered into the annual agreements, the cabinet would have had to go to parliament, the outcome of which would be quite unpredictable. Consequently, the central government agreed to a principle of compensating counties and municipalities for expenses that are imposed by law and a guarantee against deterioration of local finances due to the economic cycle. These provisions were added to the annual agreements. The level of conflict was reduced compared to the mid-1980s, and growth in the appropriations to counties and municipalities was quite successfully brought under control. When controlling for the increase in local and regional tasks prescribed by law – and thus out of local and regional control – growth in local and regional expenses was very modest. The system, however, would not have worked had the basic interest of the government and the local political leadership – to keep expenses and taxes down – not been compatible.

The Social Democrats took over the prime minister post in 1993 after the longest period out of office since the party formed its first cabinet in 1924. The party had been severely punished by the electorate and by the important center party, the Social Liberals, for economic mismanagement in the late 1970s and early 1980s. The party – and thus the cabinet – consciously wanted to avoid making the same mistakes it had made during that period. The party had accused the Conservative-Liberal government of mismanagement of the welfare state, so welfare spending had to be restored from the poor condition of early 1993. At the same time, the government confronted the consequences of a seven-year recession and a very severe unemployment problem. But most other economic indicators were favorable, except the rapidly increasing public deficit.

The government's policy in 1993 was risky. Public expenses were significantly increased in order to 'kick-start' the economy. This reinvention of Keynesian economics was followed by a labor market reform and later by a tax reform. The strategy was successful; investments soon boomed, GDP grew, and unemployment fell. The economic policy was successful, and by the turn of the century the Danish economy was in better shape than it had been in as long as anyone could remember.

Table 2 shows that from 1993 through 1998, total public expenditures grew four pct. in real terms. Since the economy boomed during the same period, public expenses as a percentage of GDP dropped dramatically from 1993 through 1998 (cf. Budgetredegørelse 1999). The structural composition of the changes in the budget was inverted from the pattern of the 1980s. Cash benefits remained constant with a slight decline in 1998, but public consumption expenditures grew rapidly. If 1992 had been used as a base year – and one might argue that that is the relevant point of departure because the government increased consumption expenditures in 1993 despite the fact that the financial bill for that year had already been passed when the government took over – the index would have been 116 in 1998. In this sense, Denmark returned to its normal condition.

This means that the blame avoidance and voter popularity argument is difficult to apply to the 1990s, at least in the way it worked during the 1980s. Increases were devoted to public consumption and – as seen from Table 2 – local and regional governments have been free to spend. The first point is that there is not much blame to avoid. Very few groups have had to carry the burdens of budgetary cuts. Second, the cabinet had to follow up on the accusations of mismanagement of core welfare services. Consequently, significantly more resources were devoted to pre-school care and health care.

It is difficult to compare the bourgeois and Social Democratic governments because they ruled during very different economic conditions in the late 1980s and the late 1990s. But it is safe to say that Social Democrats have fared no worse in terms of overall expense management: actually, they have done quite well.

This conclusion is a bit surprising if one looks at institutional developments. The Conservative-Liberal governments had very strict budgetary goals, but were not able to implement them fully. The Social Democratic governments have had unclear and rather soft goals concerning total government outlays: the growth rate of government expenditures had to be 'significantly' less than the growth rate of the overall economy (cf. Christiansen, 1999). They still operate within expenditure frameworks, but these frameworks are not attached to some overarching goal. Nevertheless performance has been quite good. The Ministry of Finance is generally believed to have increased its already strong position vis-à-vis the other ministries, and there seems to be a general acknowledgment of the necessity of budgetary constraint among central decision makers. At the same time, the discourse emphasizing 'savings' and 'cuts' has disappeared from Ministry of Finance statements. The tough discipline of expense management has disappeared from the vocabulary of the ministry in favor of *quality*, *flexibility*, *adaptation*, etc. Yet, the results in terms of overall expense management have not deteriorated – on the contrary, they continue to improve.

TABLE 2.

State and total public expenses 1983-1992. Index in fixed prices (1983=100) and total public expenses in current prices (bill. DKK)

	1993	1994	1995	1996	1997	1998
Total state expenses Index (1993=100)*	100	101	100	100	98	97
Total state expenses exclusive of unemployment benefits Index (1993=100)*	100	102	102	103	102	102
Expenses of local/regional governments, Index (1993=100)	100	106	107	109	110	113
Total public consumption expenses Index (1993=100)	100	100	101	106	107	110
Total cash benefits Index (1993=100)	100	100	100	100	100	98
Total public expenses Index (1993=100)*	100	102	102	104	104	104
Total public expenses, current prices, bill. DKK	529.4	566.9	578.5	602.4	612.6	628.0

Sources: *Statistiske Efterretninger. Nationalregnskab, offentlige finanser og betalingsbalance*, var. issues. Deflated by the deflator of the ADAM-model.

* Due to changes in the tax status of cash benefits, it is difficult to compare the raw 1993 numbers with the following years. In order to make figures comparable, 15.09 billion DKK were added to the 1993 figures for cash benefits and total expenses (cf. Budgetredegørelse 1995: 148).

In sum, a comprehensive assessment of the governance of overall government expenses cannot be made independent of the standard applied. From a relative point of view, the management of overall public expenditure has been a success since the beginning of the 1980s in the sense that the growth of public expenses has been significantly reduced while services and benefits have been cut in only a few areas – and have been expanded in many others. In that respect, the development of the Danish welfare state does not differ from the norm in most OECD, and in particular European, countries. From the point of view of the Conservative-Liberal cabinets, the result of ten years of intense political attention to bring down expenditures and taxes must be disappointing. The management of public consumption expenditures proved remarkably successful during the 1980s, but transfer expenses wrecked the budgetary goals. During the 1990s, the relationship between these two types of expenses have reversed, but in a situation of smooth economic conditions.

CHANGES IN PRIORITIES

Few will disagree that managing government spending is a constant process of change and adaptation, successes and failures, trials and errors. The very dynamic process of public budgeting raises the question of how much freedom is left in the hands of parliamentary politicians and municipal and county councils who pass annual budgets. Even formally, the degrees of freedom are severely restricted by laws and collective agreements that make their claim on the budget. The degrees of freedom in budgeting are further constrained by the resistance and/or support they can get from groups with vested interests in public programs. Observing the annual budget negotiations in parliament (September through December) leaves one with the impression that the degrees of freedom are indeed very limited. Out of the more than DKK 650 billion state budget, the part which is the object of real political contention rarely amounts to more than 2-3 pct. of the budget.

According to the incapacity model, the budgetary system is characterized by inertia and immobilism because influential groups opposing any attempt to reduce appropriations monitor the budget. Building on the theory of incapacity, it might be argued that the asymmetrical distribution of incentives concerning public expenditure is particularly strong in cases of budget redistribution. The perceived costs of losing existing appropriations outweigh by far the financial value of the benefits derived from increasing appropriations (Christiansen, 1990). As a consequence, the electorate will punish losses more than they will reward gains (Pierson, 1994), and the real battles over the budget will take place when changes in priorities are followed by redistribution of resources. Asymmetrical adaptation is best measured in areas where demand is 'objective', such as in schools, universities, kindergartens, etc. With increases in demand, the budget is expected to increase by means of compensation, whereas reductions in demand are expected to be followed by less than proportional cuts.

The capacity model claims that it is possible through intelligent management to pursue politically demanded redistribution of the budget. In that sense, the budget institution in itself is neutral towards the outcome. Adaptation to changes in demand is not supposed to be complete, automatic or the result of pure will, but rather the outcome of negotiations.

It is extremely difficult to reallocate more than marginal parts of the budget from one area to another. Very strong vested interests maintain the status quo. Redistribution might also be defined in a less restrictive way, i.e., as uneven growth of the different parts of the budget. This involves allocating budgetary increases towards targeted areas while keeping the budget at zero growth in others. The political costs of this type of budget redistribution are smaller than direct reallocation, but it is also a more time-consuming endeavor. In the following, we look primarily for the capacity to pursue redistribution of the first kind.

The budgetary reforms of the 1980s aimed at controlling the overall spending level. In addition, during the 1980s, envelope budgets[3] were introduced at all levels of government and implemented to the level of institutions, and in large organizations such as hospitals even down to the level of the department (see Pallesen & Pedersen in this volume). Since, in principle, envelope budgeting gives the political level more control over the budget, politicians were left with more degrees of freedom in terms of pursuing redistribution compared to the traditional marginal budgeting system. Politicians don't have to consider how the individual organization will put together the budget in details – as was the case with old-fashioned budgeting – they only have to decide upon the size of the envelope.

In real life, things are more complicated. Envelope budgets and the other instruments introduced to create better economic management in the public sector (cf. also the following section) proved to be relatively impotent as a means of redistribution. Some of the redistributive decisions were moved from the Ministry of Finance to the individual ministries by demanding compensatory savings in order to finance new expenses. If ministers wanted to pursue more than marginal increases in spending, they had to be prepared to battle in the annual negotiations over the size of their framework for the coming year. In 1988, the Ministry of Finance introduced automatic reductions of 2.5 pct. of each ministry's budget in all areas that were not restricted by law. This was a primitive but effective way to create a 'fund' to finance new expenses. Nevertheless, it was not enough to keep the budget at the intended zero growth level, as shown in the previous section. Larger cuts to finance new expenditures proved to be more or less politically impossible after the cuts in unemployment benefits and reductions in transfers to municipalities and counties in the first half of the 1980s. Although appropriations were cut in some state programs, it is difficult to find evidence of substantial deviations from those predicted by a marginal budgetary system.

---

3 As opposed to the old budget system based on detailed and binding specifications, framework budgets increase the room for maneuver for public sector managers by leaving managers relatively free as to how appropriations are spent (cf. Christensen, 1992: 74).

As municipalities and counties are the major public service producers, their *service* production is perhaps the most interesting area in which to investigate the possibilities of pursuing budget redistribution.

Primary schools are a good example of some of the problems connected with changing priorities in public budgets because it is possible to measure responses to changes in 'demand' measured by the number of schoolchildren. From 1980 to 1990, the number of schoolchildren attending primary schools fell from 794,500 to 566,100 – a decline of 22 pct. From 1970 on, several public reports advised local governments to adapt expenditures on primary schools to the decline in the number of schoolchildren (Goul Andersen & Christiansen, 1991: 121ff.). At the same time, the teachers' organization – traditionally believed to be very strong – mobilized to combat a corresponding reduction in the number of schoolteachers.

The teachers won the battle. By constant marginal changes in collective agreements and formal and informal agreements with the individual municipalities, the teachers managed to transform the decline in student numbers into an increase in resources per pupil of slightly more than 10 pct. A more detailed analysis shows that the increase in resources was used to promote different compensation schemes for teachers rather than, for example, reducing the number of pupils per class, etc. (Goul Andersen & Christiansen, 1991: 123ff.; cf. also Ministry of Finance, 1994: 163ff.). This development could have been the result of a deliberate attempt to improve the quality of Danish schools, but it is difficult to interpret changes in local expenditures in the 1980s in this way. First, Danish schools appear to be among the more expensive in Europe (Goul Andersen & Christiansen, 1991: 125; Ministry of Finance, 1992: 98ff.); so Danish schools are hardly resource deprived. Second, the 1980s were characterized by a squeeze on local finances (Mouritzen, 1991). On the income side, cuts in government transfers to municipalities and the agreements on zero growth in expenses and later taxes, combined with the long recession in the Danish economy left the majority of municipalities with income growth significantly below that of the previous decade. On the demand side, there was persistent pressure in areas such as day care and eldercare.

Local governments thus had very good reasons to pursue reductions in school budgets made possible by the decline in student populations. As shown above, they did so only partially. It should be added that during the 1980s, an increasing number of municipalities changed their budgets so that appropriations were pegged to production. In primary schools appropriations were based on the number of pupils or the number of classes. But in most cases, the changes in the budgetary system came too late.

Envelope budgets make political steering much less detailed, but it hardly helps in setting budgetary priorities. *Taximeter budgeting* may be much more effective in binding appropriations and production together. The technical side of taximeter budgeting is that well-defined outputs are closely tied to the size of the appropriation. The major proportion of universities' appropriations depends on student performance. Each department carefully calculates how many full *student years* its students complete with passing grades. Each discipline has its own taximeter value, and appropriations are calculated on the basis of the number of student years times the taximeter value. Taximeters have been introduced mainly in higher education, but are also used in some parts of secondary educational institutions, and in vocational training. The taximeter approach became more widespread during the 1990s. In 1990, 0.2 pct. of the state's consumption costs were covered by taximeter budgeting compared to 22 pct. in 1998 (Buse & Smith, 1999: 273). From a governance perspective, the major advantage is that the problem of asymmetrical adaptation is reduced or eliminated, because appropriations follow changes in demand. A major disadvantage is that when changes in demand are more than marginal, it proves difficult to adapt smoothly to the new budgetary conditions. Long-term changes in demand raise the question of whether the budgetary consequences of the taximeter approach are politically acceptable. During the latter half of the 1990s, student enrollments in university departments in the natural and technical sciences dropped significantly. The accompanying decline in appropriations for these departments may conflict with other political goals such as maintaining a high standard of research and teaching in science and technology.

Not all problems of budgetary redistribution can be solved by such measures. Public service producers retain several ways to avoid cuts or to pursue marginal increases in appropriations. Good old marginalist mechanisms are still very alive, but moving appropriations from one area to another increased somewhat during the 1980s and the 1990s – but not dramatically. Strong supply-side forces are still at work in response to redistributive cuts. In the core areas of welfare services, these supply-side forces remain strong.

ENHANCING EFFICIENCY

Efficiency has been at the heart of public administration studies since the birth of the discipline. With the advent of the New Public Management school, efficiency has come to play an even greater role in discussions of public sector management (e.g., Hood, 1991). In the Danish case, the quest for efficiency is all the more pressing given the fact that a third of the country's economy is consumed by the public sector – a level only shared by Sweden – while other advanced welfare states run a public service sector that consumes between 20 and 25 pct. of GDP (cf. Christiansen, 1998: 280-281). It is no surprise, therefore, that efficiency has been on the Danish reform agenda since the beginning of the 1980s.

Efficiency has always been a tricky concept. For the sake of simplicity, *cost-effectiveness* – or X-efficiency – refers to the production of a given service at the lowest possible cost. Measuring cost effectiveness in public sector production is anything but trivial. The problems arise mainly because public services are only rarely sold in a market, and because it is sometimes difficult to define or delineate the output of public sector production (see Winter, 1994).

Although we concentrate here on cost effectiveness, a few remarks should be made on the problem of the *allocative efficiency* of public sector service production. Allocative efficiency exists when a commodity or service meets the demands of the customers as effectively as possible and is thus equivalent to the Pareto criterion (Le Grand, 1991). In a non-market system in which consumers are not asked to prove their willingness to pay for the service in question, the 'true' preferences of the consumer are not readily revealed. The problem political managers face is the question, 'Are we producing the right things in the right quantities?' A number of new instruments to detect what different types of users want are used more and more. For example, user councils, user boards, surveys, choices, etc. are now frequently employed to determine consumer demand. However, the effectiveness of these instruments is almost unknown. We therefore restrict our analysis in the following to the question of cost effectiveness.

The control literature (e.g., Niskanen, 1971; Moe, 1984, 1989; Pallesen, 1999) – which is theoretically in line with the incapacity model – points to the many impediments politicians or top-level bureaucrats must overcome in order to ensure the cost effectiveness of public bureaus. Competition can be used in some, but far from all, cases to reveal cost inefficiency. The complexity of many public services makes it difficult to get exact information on possible cost reductions. Political managers are thus in most cases left with less than satisfactory means to reveal potential savings. One solution is to define some kind of performance and then calculate its costs. Comparisons between different municipalities, locations or organizations may then be used to assess the *relative* efficiency of different producers (Winter, 1994).

The Conservative-Liberal cabinet that came to power in 1982 introduced the 'Modernization Program' (Ministry of Finance, 1983) in 1983. Its main elements were increased decentralization emphasizing greater flexibility in the disposal of appropriations (envelope budgets), deregulation of local and regional service provision by reducing central level demands on service producers, greater flexibility in wage setting, increased use of market mechanisms (i.e., privatization, contracting out and competition between public suppliers), more freedom of choice for users, increased responsiveness towards users, service management, better management and increased use of new technologies.

CRISIS, MIRACLES, AND BEYOND

As this short list of the main elements in the Modernization Program shows, the headlines are very much the same as those declared in a number of other countries (e.g., Aucoin, 1991; Hood, 1991; Olsen & Peters, 1996). The program was not the result of careful analyses of goals and effective means to achieve these goals. Instead, the new government gathered together a variety of goals and instruments that could demonstrate their commitment to serious policy change (in contrast to the 'soft' policies of the preceding Social Democratic government).

The program itself was, however, quite 'soft' in its implementation. Privatization as a reform strategy was abandoned very early and the other elements stressing different types of market mechanisms were never seriously pursued. Today the Danish welfare state continues to rely very little on market or semi-market mechanisms (Schwartz, 1994; Christiansen, 1998). The elements stressing decentralization of the budget to the level of the individual organization were pursued effectively in the sense that the budgetary institution was actually changed according to plan.

If there was any change in the overall strategy of the new Social Democratic governments from 1993 on, it was that the ideology and discourse of *New Public Management* tightened its grip on the public sector, with the Ministry of Finance as its strongest advocate. And in one area, the Social Democratic cabinets accelerated the pace of new reform measures. Following the slow privatization of state-owned enterprises prior to 1993, a large number of state-owned enterprises were created and some of them also privatized during the first five years of the new Social Democratic governments. As an example, the national Danish telecommunications company was totally privatized in 1997. Budgetary considerations undoubtedly played an important role in the sale of state-owned enterprises; from 1985-1998, the net effect on the state budget was an increase of 50 bill. DKK (Christiansen, 1999).

In the rhetoric of various cabinets, efficiency has come to play a core role in the discourse on the public sector. The validity of the underlying causal model, however, is dubious. The modernization plan did not really have a coherent, valid theory about how to affect (let alone control) efficiency. The main instruments implemented during this period – envelope budgets, decentralization, and new personnel policies – were more or less expected to automatically increase public sector efficiency.

By the end of the 1980s, it became clear that the Modernization Program did not automatically produce significant reductions in state expenditures or increases in the efficiency of service production. In 1993, the Audit Department (1993) released a report on the economic effects of the Modernization Program. The conclusion was clear: the program itself had no impact on economic behavior at departmental or lower levels. The Modernization Program was not without effects on state administration – but an independent impact on government efficiency was difficult to demonstrate.

In the early 1990s, new instruments were added. 'Contract agencies' were introduced to allow state agencies/organizations to contract with their supervising department on future goals and future appropriations. Contracting out was recommended to state as well as local and regional organizations, but was not enforced by hierarchical means. Benchmarking, quality assurance programs, etc. were introduced on different occasions.

At regional and local levels, new instruments for governing service production paralleled developments at the state level. The government has no hierarchical power to impose on counties and municipalities specific ways of managing public service production. Nevertheless, counties and municipalities to a large extent introduced a number of the core instruments launched at the state level. Envelope budgeting soon became common at the local and regional levels.

The effects on efficiency remain dubious. Envelope budgeting does not appear to have had a significant effect on efficiency. Even if the current budgetary systems contain inducements to pursue more efficient production, budgetary constraints are often softly implemented. The lack of political commitment to enforce budgetary rules leaves opportunistic agents in a good position to avoid the implementation of tough budgetary systems (Pallesen, 1997; Sørensen, 1994). In the course of writing a book on Danish public expenditures in an international perspective (Goul Andersen & Christiansen, 1991: 108f.), we collected all existing reports on efficiency and productivity in Danish state and local government production from 1985 through 1990. We were unable to identify any systematic improvement in efficiency. Instead, efficiency went up and down depending on the specific circumstances of the activity under scrutiny. Productivity in higher education increased due to an increase in the number of students enrolled; in primary schools productivity decreased due to decreasing enrollments. Taximeter appropriations reportedly have positive effects on productivity in higher education (Nannestad & Pedersen, 1998: 77ff.), but the underlying logic is not clear, since the very idea is to link performance and appropriations and thus 'freeze' the level of productivity.

In sum, when we look at explanations of changes in the efficiency of the public sector, factors beyond the control of political managers appear to be more important than deliberate measures to enhance efficiency. The economic efficiency of Danish public service organizations appears to have improved throughout the last decade, but it is extremely difficult to document, and it is definitely not a uniform development. The capacity to affect efficiency instrumentally is generally low.

Conclusion

A number of political, ideological and scholarly questions concerning the welfare state constantly recur in the richly faceted debates in Denmark as well as in other Northern European countries. Is the welfare state affordable in its present version? How should the organization and financing of the welfare state be adjusted to meet future demands? What are the effects on private sector growth and productivity, labor supply, etc. and how should they be dealt with? What about questions of legitimacy, especially in light of the moral effects of the welfare state on individual behavior (such as moonlighting, 'rent seeking' behavior among ordinary people, and the institutionalization of solidarity)? What happens to individual rights and preferences in a society with a large public sector?

These issues have not been discussed in this chapter, but they are not unrelated to the core question treated here: the capacity or incapacity to manage welfare state expenditures. The theoretical literature primarily supports the incapacity model. Public choice theory predicts the breakdown of highly developed welfare states just as Marxist theory predicts the unavoidable and approaching breakdown of capitalist society – including welfare states. However, the Danish case does not confirm either of these models. Welfare state expenses are not totally immutable. During the 1980s, changing governments succeeded in bringing down the rate of growth in public spending. Redistribution of the budget was pursued in some areas and a number of service areas experienced increases in productivity. In the 1990s spending declined relative to GDP and the whole issue of excessive spending, along with the need for cuts, has more or less disappeared from the public agenda. The bourgeois cabinets did not succeed in downsizing the public sector, but even the right wing parties abandoned the discussion of the bloated welfare state. Social Democratic cabinets have not proved their ability to manage overall spending in times of recession, but they did learn important lessons from the 1970s and 1980s. The political capacity to manage overall spending has increased. The development of new instruments is an important part of this capacity, but changes in the behavior of political elite based on lessons learned during the years of crisis has been the decisive factor. The result has been an apparent consensus that public expenses and taxes should not exceed certain levels.

On the other hand, redistribution within the budget occurred as a result of forces beyond the control of the government and municipalities, rather than as the result of a deliberately chosen strategy. The composition of public budgets has changed, but the differential growth rates across the public sector, not conscious reallocation of appropriations from one area to another, account for these distributional changes. The basic problems of budgetary redistribution have not changed, but inventions such as taximeter budgeting help decrease the level of conflict associated with gradual budget adjustments.

At the micro level – i.e., at the level of the individual public organization – the capacity to promote efficiency hardly changed; if it changed at all, it was in the direction of a modest increase in capacity. The results from the Danish experience are not very different from those of other countries. Politicians are only marginally interested in public sector efficiency and quality. Given the considerable asymmetry in the distribution of information concerning public sector services, the governance structures provide producers with a variety of ways to avoid responding to demands for greater efficiency and quality.

The years 1979 through 1982 were fateful ones for the Danish welfare state. Macroeconomic mismanagement brought Denmark to the 'brink of the abyss'. A combination of a sense of impending catastrophe and a commitment to re-establish a sound economy provided the political will to bring the Danish economy into the ranks of Europe's top performers a decade later. Big government and a generous welfare state are not incompatible with macroeconomic success. Paradoxically, it seems more difficult to create a 'sound economy' within the welfare state itself. Adaptation at the macro level – i.e., total public expenditures – is easier to accomplish than adaptation at the meso or micro level. In a relative sense, the most effective control measures were those applied at the macro level, while measures to promote redistribution and efficiency have been much less effective.

The relative success of macro management compared to meso and micro management explain one of the major paradoxes of Danish public spending. Even with taxation and expenditure levels approaching the highest in the world, Danes still share a widespread feeling that a number of core areas – schools, universities, hospitals, kindergartens, etc. – are underfunded. This may or may not be true. The problem is that it is difficult to see the relationship between appropriations, production and demand.

The basic problems confronting the political managers of public expenses in Denmark do not differ from those found in other OECD countries. With increasing taxation and expenditure levels, the pressure to pursue more effective political management increases. If managerial capacity does not increase with increasing spending, the problem of an expensive *and* poorly performing public sector becomes very real.

The Danish experience therefore suggests that we need a more nuanced assessment of welfare state capacity that examines the interactions among the various administrative levels of the welfare state and the overall political economy that both shapes and is shaped by the decisions of politicians. The future of the welfare state – at least in Denmark – still remains in the hands of democratically elected public officials.

References

Aucoin, Peter (1991). 'The Politics of Restraint Budgeting', in André Blais & Stéphane Dion (eds.), The Budget-Maximizing Bureaucrat. Appraisals and Evidence. Pittsburgh: University of Pittsburgh Press, pp. 119-41.

Audit Department (1993). *Beretning til statsrevisorerne om virkningen af regeringens moderniseringsprogram på udvalgte serviceinstitutioner.* Copenhagen.

Budgetredegørelse, various years. Copenhagen: Ministry of Finance.

Buse, Torben & Mikkel Sune Smith (1999). 'Taxameterstyring som budgetmodel – incitamenter og fristelser'. *Politica* 31, 3: 272-85.

Caiden, Naomi (1990). 'Public Budgetting in the United States: The State of the Discipline', in Naomi B. Lynn & Aaron Wildavsky (eds.), *Public Administration. The State of the Discipline.* Chatham: Chatham House, pp. 228-255.

Cammisa, Anne Marie (1995). *Governments as Interest Groups. Intergovernmental Lobbying and the Federal System,* Westport, CT & London: Praeger.

Castles, Francis G. (1998). *Comparative Public Policy. Patterns of Post-War Transformation.* Cheltenham: Edward Elgar.

Christensen, Jørgen Grønnegård (1992). 'Hierarchical and Contractual Approaches to Budgetary Reform'. *Journal of Theoretical Politics* 4, 1: 67-91.

Christensen, Jørgen Grønnegård & Peter Munk Christiansen (1992). *Forvaltning og omgivelser.* Herning: Systime.

Christensen, Jørgen Grønnegård, Peter Munk Christiansen & Marius Ibsen (2006). *Politik og forvaltning.* Aarhus: Academica.

Christiansen, Peter Munk (1990). 'Udgiftspolitikken i 1980'erne: Fra asymmetri til asymmetrisk tilpasning'. *Politica* 22, 4: 442-56.

Christiansen, Peter Munk (1998). 'A Prescription Rejected: Market Solutions to Problems of Public Sector Governance'. *Governance* 11, 3: 273-96.

Christiansen, Peter Munk (1999). *Ej blot til pynt? Om budgettets politik og politikernes budget.* Aalborg: Aalborg University Press.

Dunleavy, Patrick (1991). *Democracy, Bureaucracy and Public Choice.* New York: Harvester Wheatsheaf.

Goul Andersen, Jørgen & Peter Munk Christiansen (1991). *Skatter uden velfærd. De offentlige udgifter i international belysning.* Copenhagen: Jurist- og Økonomforbundet.

Green-Pedersen, Christoffer (1999). 'The Danish Welfare State under Bourgeois Reign. The Dilemma of Popular Entrenchment and Economic Constraints'. *Scandinavian Political Studies* 22, 3: 243-60.

Hood, Christopher (1991). 'A Public Management for All Seasons?' *Public Administration* 69: 3-19.

Lane, Jan-Erik (2000). *New Public Management.* London: Routledge.

Le Grand, Julian (1991). 'The Theory of Government Failure'. *British Journal of Political Science* 21: 423-42.

Meyers, Roy T. (1994). *Strategic Budgeting.* Ann Arbor: University of Michigan Press.

Ministry of Finance (1983). *Redegørelse til Folketinget om regeringens program for modernisering af den offentlige sektor.* Copenhagen.

Ministry of Finance (1992). *Udgiftsanalyser 1992.* Copenhagen.

Ministry of Finance (1994). *Budgetredegørelse 1994.* Copenhagen.

Ministry of Taxation (2007). http://www.skm.dk/tal_statistik/skatter_og_afgifter/495.html.

Moe, Terry (1984). 'The New Economics of Organization'. *American Journal of Political Science* 28, 4: 739-77.

Moe, Terry (1989). 'The Politics of Bureaucratic Change', in John E. Chubb & Paul E. Peterson (eds.), *Can the Government Govern?* Washington, D.C.: Brookings Institution, pp. 267-329.

Mouritzen, Poul Erik (1991). *Den politiske cyklus*. Aarhus: Politica.

Nannestad, Peter & Lars Dahl Pedersen (1998). 'Staten som driftsherre', in Jens Blom-Hansen et al., *Offentligt og effektivt?* Copenhagen: Gyldendal, pp. 61-96.

Niskanen, William A. (1971). *Bureaucracy and Representative Government*. New York: Aldine-Atherton.

North, Douglas (1990). *Institutions, Institutional Change, and Economic Performance*. Cambridge: Cambridge University Press.

Nyt fra Danmarks Statistik, various issues, Copenhagen.

Olsen, Johan P. & B. Guy Peters (eds.) (1996). *Lessons from Experience. Experimental Learning in Administrative Reforms in Eight Democracies*. Oslo: Scandinavian University Press.

Olsen, Johan P. (1978). 'Folkestyre, byråkrati og korporativisme', in Johan P. Olsen (ed.), *Politisk organisering*. Oslo: Universitetsforlaget, pp. 12-114.

Olson, Mancur (1982). *The Rise and Decline of Nations: Economic Growth, Stagflation, and Social Rigidities*. New Haven: Yale University Press.

Pallesen, Thomas (1997). *Health Care Reforms in Britain and Denmark: The Politics of Economic Success and Failure*. Aarhus: Forlaget Politica.

Pallesen, Thomas (1999). 'Institutionel teori og offentlig drift', in Anders Berg-Sørensen (ed.), *Politologi i praksis*. Roskilde: Roskilde University Press, pp. 159-85.

Pierson, Paul (1994). *Dismantling the Welfare State?* Cambridge: Cambridge University Press.

Pierson, Paul (2001). 'Coping With Permanent Austerity: Welfare State Restructuring in Affluent Democracies', in Paul Pierson (ed.), *The New Politics og the Welfare State*. Oxford & New York: Oxford University Press, pp. 410-56.

Pressmann, Jeffrey L. & Aaron Wildavsky (1973). *Implementation*. Berkeley: University of California Press.

Rose, Richard (1981). 'What if Anything is Wrong with Big Government?' *Journal of Public Policy* 1, 1: 5-36.

Schwartz, Herman (1994). 'Small States in Big Trouble: State Reorganization in Australia, Denmark, New Zealand, and Sweden in the 1980s'. *World Politics* 46, 4: 527-55.

Statistiske Efterretninger. Nationalregnskab, offentlige finanser og betalingsbalance, various issues. Copenhagen.

Sørensen, Rune (1994). 'Improving Government Resource Allocation: The Impact of Alternative Budgetary Methods'. *International Review of Administrative Sciences* 60: 5-22.

Wildavsky, Aaron (1980). *How To Limit Government Spending*. Berkeley: University of California Press.

Wildavsky, Aaron (1988). *The New Politics of the Budgetary Process*. Glenview: Scott, Foresman.

Winter, Søren (1990). 'Integrating Implementation Research', in Dennis J. Palumbo & Donald J. Calista (eds.), *Implementation and the Policy Process: Opening Up the Black Box*. New York: Greenwood Press, pp. 19-38.

Winter, Søren (1994). *Implementering og effektivitet*. Herning: Systime.

5 SMALL STEPS, BIG CHANGE?

Continuity and Change in The Danish Social Security System[1]

Jon Kvist and Niels Ploug

Introduction

As the Danish social security system celebrates its centenary, recent developments in the old age pensions system and in labor market policies together with the political rhetoric of a new welfare society signal fundamental changes in the system. This includes less social responsibility for the state and more social responsibility for employers and individuals.

Assessing changes in the Danish social security over the last twenty years offers a unique opportunity to answer a set of crucial questions related to welfare state reform. We investigate whether the politics of the Conservative-led coalition government (1982-93) and the Social Democratic-led coalition government (1993-2002) included changes in the social security system. If so, were these changes in the rules, the organization and the financing of the system due to political bargaining or, alternatively, were they largely in response to demographic and economic pressures? Furthermore, we examine whether there have been principal changes in the nature of the Danish social security system that constitute retrenchment or restructuring? If so, did the Right and Left coalition governments follow different policies in this regard?

In the first part of this chapter, we account briefly for the history and structure of the Danish social security system. The second part of the chapter presents measures of the changes in social security over the last twenty years. The historical overview sets out the timing as well as the nature of the principles behind the provision of social security which are, subsequently, used as a yardstick to evaluate recent changes. The chapter ends with a discussion of whether the recent changes to the hundred year old social security system constitute continuity or change to meet the demands and challenges of the new century, and whether there are cross-party differences. Much of the evidence seems supports an interpretation that piecemeal change has occurred. But

---

1 The results in this chapter are based on research published in Ploug and Kvist (1995, 1994a, 1994b). The authors would like to thank Dorte Boesby for technical assistance.

looking over a longer time span, fundamental changes to the Danish welfare state – most during the last 20 years – has occurred.

The emergence and development of the welfare state

The Danish welfare state and thus also the Danish cash benefit system were deliberately established as counterparts to comparable creations in Germany at almost the same time. Even before the German government had decided on a model in which a cash benefit system was financed by compulsory insurance schemes for wage earners, Danish political actors had rejected this approach (Petersen, 1985). Instead, a cash benefit system was established and developed according to principles which would later be perceived as fundamental characteristics of the Nordic welfare state: a system based on a universal scope of application, i.e., benefits for everyone (unlike the German system with benefits for wage earners only), and a system where benefits were largely financed by general taxation, not by earmarked contributions. In the Nordic states before the Second World War, the assessment of long-term benefits (such as pensions) depended on existing income – which meant that those who already had high incomes were not entitled to benefits. In 1956, the National Old Age Pension Act was adopted, launching a process of abandoning this principle by introducing a universal minimum pension irrespective of income. In 1964, this process culminated in gradual benefit increases that effectively made the national pension a universal flat-rate benefit from 1970.

The roots of the Danish welfare state are about one hundred years old. Its legislative foundation was established in the 1890s. Some social policies had been pursued prior to that time, e.g., poor relief in individual parishes, and special assistance funds more accurately described as self-help societies for journeymen. Nevertheless, no comprehensive legislation constituted a national social policy. In 1891, an Old-Age Pension Act and a new Poor Law were passed. The Old-Age Pension Act classified the elderly, defined as those over 60 years of age, as a special group within the 'deserving poor'. They became entitled to financial assistance from public authorities without poor relief restrictions such as the prohibition of marriage or loss of the right to vote. In 1922, recommended rates within the Old-Age Pension Act were replaced by a fixed pension formula. With the new Poor Law, the existing desultory legislation was transformed into a set of rules, which, among other things, outlawed maintenance in turns. Receipt of poor relief, however, still entailed limitation of personal freedom. In this way, it was made clear that poor relief was a last resort and the least attractive part of the social safety net.

The Sickness Insurance Act of 1892 was based on the principles of voluntary social insurance. Thus, membership in one of the more than 1,000 existing sickness funds was optional. In 1898, an Accident Insurance Act was passed. In 1921, voluntary sickness insurance was added with a compulsory disability insurance element.

The Unemployment Insurance Act of 1907 was extended in 1913 to include a public employment service. Together with Germany, Denmark was thus the first country to establish a state-governed cash benefit system – even though, as mentioned earlier, it was established on the basis of widely different principles than those in Germany.

In 1933, a social reform – 'the Steincke's social reform', named after the Minister of Social Affairs at the time – formed the culmination of social policy legislation before the Second World War. The reform was primarily a legislative simplification and resulted in the consolidation of the rules from 55 previous enactments into four new Acts. These acts covered social assistance, national sickness insurance, disability and old-age pensions, accident insurance and unemployment insurance. On the whole, the principles underlying social legislation remained unaltered with the reform. In principle, however, entitlement to poor relief no longer implied socially degrading consequences. Nevertheless, the discretion to deny poor relief claimants their right to vote was not finally abolished until the passage of a new Social Assistance Act in 1961.

After the Second World War, the cash benefit system continued to develop. In 1956, means-tested old-age and disability pensions were replaced by general national pensions, a decisive break with the former principle that long-term benefits should be reserved for those with low incomes. Now everyone was entitled to a pension regardless of other income or resources. At the same time, Denmark has retained the principle that the amount of the pension should not depend on previous attachment to the labor market or previous earnings. The only departure from this principle was the introduction of a wage earner's Labor Market Supplementary Pension Scheme *(Arbejdsmarkedets Tillægs Pension, ATP)* in 1964. ATP benefits reflect the length of the work record, but not previous income, as in other Nordic countries. Still ATP was an anomaly in the Danish cash benefit system with the exception of some pension schemes available to certain occupational groups, in particular persons employed in the public sector. However, in the late 1980s and early 1990s, the principle of previous attachment to the labor market was greatly expanded by the establishment of new occupational pension schemes for the private sector based on collective agreements. These are fully funded and benefits are actuarially based on the number and size of contributions (for a short overview, see ATP, 1995; Petersen, 1995; and Kvist, 1997).

In 1967/68, the remnants of the insurance principle were removed from the field of unemployment insurance through legislation which provided that future state contributions would fund unemployment benefits not covered by member fees. In other words, the marginal risk in the event of increasing unemployment was now the responsibility of the state. This arrangement was introduced at a time of very low unemployment, but subsequently entailed considerable state expenditures because of the increasing unemployment levels from the mid-1970s on.

The Social Assistance Act of 1976 simplified much of the social legislation and introduced a unified structure. The act was the final stage in a process that anchors responsibility for social policy in local government – the counties and, especially, the municipalities. A special feature of the Danish cash benefit system is that it has always been a part of the municipal system. This principle became even stronger with the introduction of the 1976 Social Assistance Act and the decentralization of services for people with disabilities in the early 1980s. Thus, an independent system to administer cash benefits has never been established, the exceptions being unemployment insurance funds affiliated with trade unions and pension funds for supplementary old age pensions negotiated in collective agreements.

In 1979, a voluntary early retirement pay *(efterløn)* was introduced to serve both labor market and social policy objectives. The labor market objective of the scheme was to combat unemployment by giving members of unemployment funds over 60 years of age the option to retire before the normal pension age of 67 years, thereby allowing younger people to enter the labor market in greater numbers. The social policy objective was to give older workers, many of whom had been attached to the labor market since leaving primary school, a dignified exit from the labor market.

The introduction of a number of leave-of-absence schemes in 1994 is the most recent major innovation in the field of cash benefits. These schemes gave employees the right to a leave-of-absence for parenthood, education, and sabbatical with some income compensation. The sabbatical scheme was an experiment, which only survived until 1999, but the leave-of-absence for parenthood and education persists, although at reduced levels compared to earlier initiatives.

The Basic Structure of Social Security

The historical development of social security in Denmark has produced a unified system in which the state plays a major role in financing and providing benefits and the entire population is covered in the event of social contingencies. This section describes the basic structure of the social security system – its organization, provision, financing and fiscal aspects (see also Plovsing, 1998).

ORGANIZATION

All social services are in practice the responsibility of the public authorities. In the case of cash benefits, the state and the municipalities share responsibility. In addition, the social funds, including the wage earner's supplementary labor market pension (ATP) and unemployment funds are part of social security provision. Unemployment funds are run by unions. This goes for a number of labor market pension funds, too, while other pension funds are run jointly by unions and employers organizations. In general, counties are not involved in administering cash benefits.

As in all areas where public authorities are involved, the Danish Parliament *(Folketinget)* has overall responsibility for social policy. Both the government and the municipalities must remain within the limits set by the majority of the parliament when implementing social policies.

Three ministries are involved in the administration of the traditional social policy areas (cf. ILO Convention No. 102). The most important is the Ministry of Social Affairs, which in the field of cash benefits manages benefits for sickness and maternity; disability pension; industrial injury insurance; the national old-age pension; partial pensions and family allowances; and cash benefits under the Social Assistance Act. The Ministry of Labor manages unemployment benefits including voluntary early retirement pay, while the Ministry of Taxation takes care of benefits to families with children. The ministries' roles have a more general character in that they provide guidance and supervision of the municipalities and social funds.

TABLE 1.

Tasks and burdens of social security and welfare, absolute in million Danish kroner and relative distribution in %, 1999

	Task	Burden	Task	Burden
	– % –		– DKK m –	
State	9.9	57.0	27,834	160,732
Social funds	15.9	6.1	44,936	17,140
Counties	4.7	4.7	13,385	13,318
Municipalities	69.5	32.3	196,085	91,048
Total	100.0	100.1	282,240	282,238

Source: Danmarks Statistik, Statistisk Ti-årsoversigt, 2000

The division of labor among the various parts of the public sector may be illustrated by examining the allocation of responsibilities for the provision and financing of welfare, i.e., a distribution of tasks and burdens (cf. Table 1). The task distribution shows the primary responsibility to provide the service, i.e., which entity is responsible for paying out the cash benefit or delivering benefits in kind to the beneficiaries. The distribution of burdens shows the proportion of expenditure met by the sub-sector concerned.

In the field of social security and welfare expenditure, including cash benefits and services as well as their administration, the majority of the tasks are undertaken by the municipalities. The heavier financial burden, however, is carried by the state (cf. Table 1).

Unemployment insurance is managed by a total of 36 different unemployment funds, 34 for wage earners and two for the self-employed. Unemployment insurance is regulated and the level of benefit fixed by parliament. The individual unemployment funds cover different employment areas and these generally parallel the major areas of union responsibility. The exception is the Christian Unemployment Fund *(Kristelig A-kasse)*, in which any employee regardless of employment type may be insured. Members of individual unemployment funds are not required to belong to the parallel trade unions, but most employees are members of both.

Unemployment funds may be either centralized, with a central administrative office, or decentralized, i.e., divided into a number of minor divisions with a common head office. The number of decentralized divisions varies from 293 (in the Danish Federation of Semi-skilled Workers, *SID*) to two (in the office and service workers' trade union, *HK*). Only five of the decentrally administered unemployment funds, however, have over 60 divisions. In comparison, the number of municipalities is 275. Thirty-two of the unemployment funds have some administration agreement with their parallel union. These agreements mean that the administration of unemployment insurance through the fund is either completely or partially managed by the trade union. Each unemployment fund has its own independent management that includes members' representatives and often representatives from the parallel trade union. Thus, the overlapping responsibility for the administration and management of unemployment benefits between the unemployment funds and trade unions is considerable.

The first two weeks of sickness benefits are administered by employers. At the end of this period, the claimant's municipality of residence takes over the administration of sickness benefits for private employees, while public employers continue to administer sickness benefits for their own staff. Municipalities also administer the optional sickness insurance schemes for the self-employed.

Administration of the disability pension is the responsibility of the municipalities of residence. The two highest levels of benefits are administered at regional level by rehabilitation and pension boards, as well as at a local level by the municipalities. Rehabilitation and pension boards consist of representatives from the Ministry of Social Affairs, employers, employees and the disability organizations. The award is made on the basis of medical opinions.

The national old-age pension is administered by the individual's municipality of residence. A council consisting of representatives of employers, employees and the state manages the Labor Market Supplementary Pension Scheme (ATP). Pension awards are made in response to requests to the ATP Fund. The contributions to the ATP Fund must be invested so that the fund grows as much as possible. This means that the investment policy must ensure the right balance between (1) scope and security and (2) the largest possible yield. Moreover, the ATP Fund is limited in the amount that may be invested in a single firm. The Danish Financial Supervisory Authority oversees the ATP Fund's legal compliance. The Labor Market Pension Funds are independent organizations with a board comprised of either representatives from a given union or representatives from both unions and employers' organizations.

The child allowance is administered and financed by the Central Customs and Taxation Administration under the Ministry of Taxation. The counties are responsible for the fulfillment of the allocation criteria. Finally, the municipalities of residence administer cash benefits under the Social Assistance Act.

PROVISION

For some people, cash benefits depend to some extent on earnings (current or previous), while other benefits are allocated independently of income. It is, however, characteristic of the Danish system that an upper ceiling applies to most benefits. This means that most wage earners will not receive 90 pct. of their prior income – the only exception is industrial injury insurance (see Table 2).

So, for example, unemployment, sickness and maternity benefits are payable at 90 pct. of previous earnings. However, the maximum benefit of 12,740 DKK (the 2001 level) per month means that only those with previous earnings of 14,156 DKK per month or less will receive 90 pct. of previous earnings. The tax system also has an impact on the actual compensation rates. In 1999, the net compensation rates varied between 80 pct. for a person previously earning 75 pct. of the average production worker's income (APW), about 63 pct. for an APW, and 37 pct. for someone earning twice as much as the APW (Hansen, 2000). In comparison to other Northwestern European countries, Denmark offers relatively high compensation rates for low income groups and relatively modest compensation rates for high income groups.

TABLE 2.

Benefit levels in the Danish cash benefit system, January 1, 2001

Benefit type	Monthly Benefit		
	In DKK	% of average workers wage	In PPP/US$
Unemployment benefit	Max. 12,740	56	1,483
Sickness and maternity benefit	Max. 12,740	56	1,483
Disability pension:			
- highest	13,487	59	1,570
- intermediate	10,625	47	1,237
- increased ordinary	9,636	42	1,128
- ordinary	8,552	38	996
Industrial injury insurance	28,750	126	3,347
National pension:			
- single person	8,552	38	996
- cohabiting/married person	6,264	28	729
Voluntary early retirement pay			
For those born before 1/7 1939			
- first 2½ years	12,740	56	1,483
- remaining years	10,443	46	1,216
For those born 1/7 1939 or after this date			
- first 2 years	11,592	51	1,350
- remaining years	12,740	56	1,483
Child family benefit			
- 0-2 years	1,008	4	117
- 3-6 years	917	4	107
- 7-17 years	717	3	84
Child allowances:			
- single parents	318	1	37
- one parent receives social pension	810	4	94
- both parents receive social pensions	1128	5	131
- orphaned children	1620	7	189
Social assistance under the Social Assistance Act:			
- breadwinners	10,245	45	1,193
- others	7,711	34	898
Parental Leave-of-absence	Max. 7644	34	890

Source: Forsikringsoplysningen (2001).

For those born before July 1, 1939, voluntary early retirement benefits are paid at a rate similar to the unemployment insurance benefit for the first two and a half years and subsequently at a rate equivalent to 82 pct. of previous earnings, although there is a maximum of 10,443 DKK per month. Recent changes in the voluntary early retirement pay have linked it not to previous income, but to the maximum unemployment benefit. For the first two years, voluntary early retirement compensation can be as much as 91 pct. of the highest possible unemployment benefit. Subsequently it rises to a rate similar to the unemployment benefit at 90 pct. of previous income with a maximum amount of 12,740 DKK per month. Social pensions – i.e., the various disability pensions and the national old age pension – are paid at a basic rate of 4,262 DKK. An income-tested pension supplement of 4,290 DKK for unmarried individuals and 2,002 DKK for couples is added per month. This makes the guaranteed total monthly amounts of these pensions 8,552 DKK and 6,264 DKK respectively for singles and cohabiting/married persons. More supplements may be added to the disability pension depending on the person's age and loss of work capacity with an overall maximum of 13,487 DKK per month.

Industrial injury insurance provides a compensation rate in the event of complete loss of capacity to work at 80 pct. of previous income, although the amount is subject to a maximum of 28,750 DKK per month. For partial loss of the capacity, the compensation rate is reduced proportionally.

The universal child family benefit varies with the age of the child (cf. Table 2). Moreover, child allowances are provided for certain children depending on the status of the parents and the family situation. Whereas child family benefits are paid to all families with children, child allowances are targeted to single parents and claimants of certain other social security benefits. Both the child family benefits and the child allowances are tax exempt and not income-tested.

Social assistance is allocated at a basic rate of 10,245 DKK per month for breadwinners and 7,714 DKK for others, which equals 80 pct. and 60 pct. (respectively) of the maximum unemployment benefit.

Since 1991, most cash benefits have been adjusted to take into account wage developments among workers organized in the Danish Confederation of Trade Unions *(LO)*. Unemployment benefits, sickness and maternity benefits, social pensions, voluntary early retirement pay and social assistance are adjusted on July 1 each year with the same percentage rate as the increase in LO workers' wages two years earlier. For example, on July 1, 1992, the rates were adjusted to match the percentage rate of the average wage increase for LO workers in 1990. However, this regulation does not extend to ATP. Individual ATP benefits depend on how much the person has paid in contributions and the current rate of return on the scheme's capital investments.

FINANCING

A main principle of the Danish welfare system is that the vast majority of social expenditure is financed by the public sector via taxes, while only a small proportion is financed through compulsory social contributions. Out of total expenditure for social cash benefits, income from compulsory social contributions amounts to approximately 8 pct. There are, however, only two areas where contribution financing is of any importance: unemployment insurance and old-age pensions, where ATP is financed via contributions. Most benefits are financed by either the state alone or the state together with the municipalities (see Table 3).

TABLE 3.
Financing rules as of July 1, 1999

Benefit	Rules
Unemployment benefit	State and member fees from the insured worker. Payments for the two first days of unemployment are made by employers.
Sickness benefit	First 2 weeks: employer 100 % Subsequent 8 weeks: state 100 % Afterwards: state 50 %, municipality 50 %
Maternity benefit	State 100 %
Disability pension	Basic amount: State 50 %, municipality 50 %
Industrial injury insurance	Compulsory insurance for all employers – with state reimbursement
Voluntary early retirement pay	As unemployment benefit. Recipients of early retirement only contribute half of the subscription rate to the unemployment fund
National old age pension	Basic amount: state 100 % Personal supplements: state 50 %/ municipality 50 %
ATP	Compulsory contribution from employer (2/3) and employees (1/3)
Child family benefit	State 100 %
Child allowances	State 100 %
Social assistance	State 50 %/municipality 50 %
Leave-of-absence schemes	State 100 %

Source: Plovsing (1998) with additions and updates.

ATP is financed by fixed rate compulsory contributions for all wage earners between 16 and 66 years of age who work over ten hours per week. The contribution, which is related to hours worked rather than earnings, is 2,332 DKK for wage earners in full-time employment, the equivalent of approximately 1.2 pct. of the average private sector wage. One-third of the contribution is paid by the wage earner and the remainder is paid by the employer.

Industrial injury insurance is financed by compulsory insurance premiums paid by employers to private insurance companies, which subscribe to industrial injury insurance schemes. However, employers are reimbursed by the state, at a rate fixed

CRISIS, MIRACLES, AND BEYOND

on the basis of the total expenditure for industrial injury insurance by all firms. Reimbursements are allocated as an average benefit so that employers with high insurance premiums still have expenses for industrial injury insurance while employers with low insurance premiums gain from industrial injury insurance.

Even though the Danish welfare system still can be characterized as a system in which most expenses are financed by general taxes, the recent trend has been to finance a greater proportion of the system via contributions. This applies to the Labor Market Pensions but more interestingly also – as part of a reform in 1999 – to the early retirement pay (*efterløn*) which for 20 years (from 1979 to 1999) was tax financed. It also applies to the compulsory supplemental old-age pension saving arrangement (*den særlige pensionsopsparing*) introduced in 1999.

FISCAL ASPECTS

In 1973, Denmark became world famous overnight in the academic literature on the welfare state because the new anti-tax party led by Mogens Glistrup won a remarkable number of seats in the parliamentary elections. However, as underlined in the introduction to this volume, there has been no major decline in support for paying taxes since then. Nevertheless, this has not stopped the search for new ways of financing, and, especially, ways to reduce the comparatively high reliance on personal income taxes and VAT. Thus, the tax reform of 1993, which came into force in 1994, followed a general trend (both nationally and internationally) of broadening the tax base and reducing certain tax allowances (Pechman, 1988).

The main objectives of the tax reform of 1993 were to reduce marginal tax rates, widen the income base and sources of taxation, make the costs of social protection more visible to the public, and increase the comparability and transparency of cash benefits (Danish Treasury, 1994). This was achieved chiefly by introducing earmarked social security contributions, increased emphasis on green taxes, and the reduction or abolition of certain tax allowances, especially for old age pensioners and recipients of social assistance (Ministry of Social Affairs, 1991).

As before the reform, taxes in Denmark are collected by the state, counties and municipalities. The state tax scale is progressive with three tax rates applying to different income brackets. The basic rate has been reduced gradually since the 1993 tax reform (cf. Table 4). The middle rate and the top rate have both been subject to slight changes in 1996 and 1997 respectively (see Table 4). As part of the transition period in the tax reform, a 3 pct. tax applied to high incomes was abolished in 1996. The tax scale for counties and municipalities (local government tax rates) is proportional to an average taxation rate of 29.5 pct.[2]

---

2 Members of the Danish National Church also pay church tax at 0.82 pct. on average.

TABLE 4.
Tax rates in Denmark after the tax reform, 1993-1999

	1993	1994	1995	1996	1997	1998	1999
Basic rate	22.0	14.5	13.0	12.0	10.0	8.0	7.5
Middle rate	-	4.5	5.0	5.0	6.0	6.0	6.0
Top rate	12.0	12.5	13.5	15.0	15.0	15.0	15.0
'6 pct. Tax'	6.0	5.0	3.0	-	-	-	-
Local government tax rates	29.5	29.5	29.9	30.4	31.2	31.7	31.9
Total tax rate	69.5	66.0	64.4	62.4	62.2	60.7	60.4
Tilted tax ceiling	68.0	65.0	63.5	62.0	60.0	58.0	59.0

Source: Danmarks Statistik (1999)

However, there are limits to how much an individual must pay in taxes. The tax ceiling establishes a maximum combined tax rate. For example, in 1999, no one pays more than 59 pct. of his or her personal income in taxes (cf. Table 4). However, the tax ceiling and the marginal tax rates do not take into account the social security contributions introduced as part of the tax reform. Since 1994, employees pay a gross tax on their wages in social security contributions that started at 5 pct. in 1994 and increased by one percentage-point per year to stabilize at 8 pct. in 1997. Already in 1994, revenues amounted to 23.3 billion DKK – 8 pct. of total government revenues with more than the 6 pct. deriving from corporate taxes (Statistics Denmark, 1995). Employers started paying social security contributions at 0.19 pct. in 1997 and rising to 0.33 pct. from 1998 on. At first sight, this is a fundamental change in the Danish financing system, away from the principle of general taxes towards contribution financing as found in neighboring countries like Germany and Sweden. However, because employees' labor market contributions are in no way linked to benefit rights, they constitute a *de facto* gross tax. In effect, nothing has changed but the label, except that tax allowances at the high marginal tax rates have been reduced. In other words, by using terms from traditional liberal and conservative social policy vocabularies (e.g., contribution-financing), the Social Democratic coalition government has managed to reform the tax system in accordance with their view of social justice.

Two income types are used to assess tax liability: personal and taxable income. Personal income is the tax payer's income in the form of wages, fees or profits from self-employment. Taxable income is personal income plus interest income from capital investments, if any, with allowances made for expenditure on, for example, contributions to an unemployment fund, commuting expenses plus any payments made to private pension schemes and interest payments on loans.

Since the 1993 tax reform, nearly all cash benefits are taxed. Before the reform, social assistance and, in practice, the national old age pensions were tax-free. In effect, the tax reform made the full national pension taxable and raised pension levels in order to compensate for the increase in the elderlys' tax liability. Similarly, social assistance was made fully taxable but benefit levels increased to offset the loss. The remaining exceptions to general tax liability are the supplements to disability pensions and the family benefits. The trend toward making cash benefits taxable has reduced the provision of welfare through the tax system – what Titmuss (1958) calls fiscal welfare.

However, there are still some tax expenditures and elements of fiscal welfare in the Danish social security system. Child family allowances are tax-free, as are a number of supplements for the disabled. Contributions to unemployment funds are deductible from taxable income. The most important types of tax expenditures, however, are found in provisions for old age where both the contributions from employers and employees to occupational pensions and private contribution to individual supplementary pensions are deductible. The interaction between the tax system and the private, supplementary pensions produces an effect known as 'the concealed multipliers of success.' The multipliers have taken on a more universal character in recent years due to the significant extensions in the coverage of occupational pensions as a consequence of collective agreements (see Kvist & Sinfield 1996, 1997; Kvist 1997).

The most significant tax expenditure in the Danish tax system is the right to deduct interest from the total taxable income. And this is the area where the most significant changes have taken place. Before the 1986 tax reform, 71 per cent of total interest payments on debt could be deducted from the total taxable income. This percentage has gradually been lowered and in 2001 it was 33 pct. As the majority of Danes live in owner-occupied houses, this has had a significant impact on the private economy of most Danes. A recent survey shows that the majority of Danes feels that housing taxes (an imputed tax) – as opposed to income taxes – is the major problem in the Danish tax system.

Developments during the 1980s and 1990s

The origins of the Danish social security system can be traced back to the end of the 19th century. However, the present system is very much the result of reforms and developments implemented in the 1960s and 1970s in particular. From 1970 to 1982, expenditures on cash benefits increased from approximately 11 pct. of gross domestic product (GDP) to approximately 17 pct. In other words, essential elements of the cash benefit system were established at a time when the economic situation was fundamentally different from the situation today. From the beginning of the 1960s, unemployment was very low. From the mid-1970s, the situation changed radically. Unemployment exploded and economic growth stagnated. Registered unemployment increased from 2.1 pct. of the labor force in 1974 to 10.0 pct. in 1982. This year marked the beginning of an eleven year period of Conservative-led coalition governments that repeatedly pronounced their intention to modernize the welfare state and cut expenditures on cash benefits. In the 1980s, social expenditure first went down and then up so that expenditures in 1991 were the same as they were in 1982. In 1982, expenditures on cash benefits expressed in constant 1990 prices accounted for 18 pct. of GDP; in 1986, they were 16 pct. of GDP; and in 1993 cash benefits accounted for 21 pct. of GDP. From 1982 to 1993, total expenditures on cash benefits rose by 39 pct., i.e., an increase of more than 24 pct. of GDP, measured in constant prices. In other words, the Conservative-led coalition governments' efforts did not result in cuts or a curtailment of expenditure in this crucial area of the welfare state.

The reason for this development can be found in the economic and political strategy chosen by the Government and its supporting parliamentary majority. Entering the 1980s the Danish economy faced two major problems – the deficit in the balance of payments and the high unemployment rate. Social Democratic governments in the 1970s had tried a twofold strategy to deal with both problems but failed. The Conservative-led government tried to continue this twofold strategy. But after historically high deficits in the balance of payments in 1985 and 1986, they revised the strategy. Therefore, to produce an improvement in the balance of payments, while allowing unemployment to grow, the tax reform of 1986 increased taxes and constrained domestic demand.

Unemployment peaked at 12.5 pct. in 1994. In January 1993, a new coalition government took power under the leadership of the Social Democratic Party. This was a majority government – a rare thing in Denmark. During 1993, the parliament passed a number of reforms by a narrow majority that did not include the parties in the previous coalition government. Crucial parts of the reforms where passed by a one-vote majority. The reforms included a tax reform (as described earlier) and a labor market reform, which took effect on January 1, 1994. Both reforms had a marked impact on the social security cash benefits and have been followed by policy changes in the same direction. The Government stated from the outset that its policy was not to reduce the level of cash benefits for individual recipients, but to obtain a more coherent and transparent system, to reduce unemployment, and to strengthen the bond between social rights and obligations. An economic upturn along with these policy changes led to a decline in the unemployment rate, which fell steadily from 1994 on, to a low of 5.3 pct. in January 2001.

During the periods from 1982 to 1993 and then from 1993 to the present, some benefit expenditures increased, while expenditures on other benefits decreased. On the whole, the changes in the level and mix of expenditures are caused by changes in legislation as well as changes in the number of recipients of cash benefits. The former may influence both benefit levels as well as how many people are entitled to benefits. The latter changes are partly due to economic conditions, and partly to demographic developments.

FIGURE 1.

Social Security Expenditure as a percentage of GDP, 1982-1997

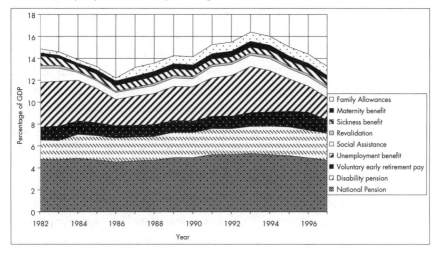

Source: Danmarks Statistik (1999)

FIGURE 2.

Whole-year Recipients of Social Security Benefits in Denmark, 1984-1998

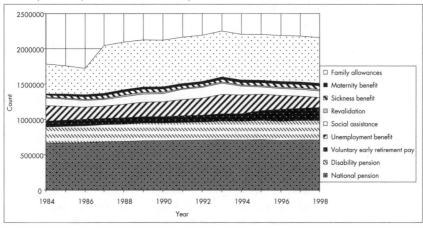

Source: Vip

In the following, central developments in the level of expenditure on cash benefits and the number of recipients within the field of cash benefits are examined for the period from 1982 to 1997 (see Figure 1 and Figure 2). In particular the aim is to see where the policies of the two types of coalition governments have made a difference to the nature of the system and where developments have been driven primarily by demographic and economic factors.

UNEMPLOYMENT BENEFITS

In the event of unemployment, Danes receive mainly one form of income compensation: unemployment benefits. An unemployed person who is not entitled to unemployment benefits may alternatively claim social assistance, but this is the case for only about one out of five unemployed persons.

During the two decades from 1970 to 1990, unemployment increased tremendously. From 1982 to 1987, however, unemployment decreased from 11 pct. to 8 pct. Unemployed persons drawing unemployment benefits decreased from 220,000 full-time whole-year recipients in 1984 to 174,000 in 1987. This decline was caused in part by the favorable economic situation that emerged as GDP and private consumption increased, which were in turn attributable in part to declining inflation and interest rates. Total employment figures in the period increased by approximately 200,000.

After 1987, unemployment soared to 264,000 people in 1994 – equal to an unemployment rate of 12.5 pct. This increase was caused by a series of political interventions that aimed to curb domestic consumption in order to improve the balance of payments situation. In 1985 and 1986, the deficit on the balance of payments current account reached historic levels of approximately 5 pct. of GDP. The political interventions included a tax reform that took effect from the fiscal year 1987. This limited interest deductions on private debt. A series of rules regulating consumer loans and credit purchases – the so-called 'Potato Cure' (*Kartoffelkur*) – further restricted private consumption,[3] and the subsequent slowing down in domestic consumption resulted in higher unemployment.

This development is also reflected in expenditures on unemployment insurance benefits. In 1982, unemployment benefits expenditures amounted to 18.9 billion DKK, or 4 pct. of GDP. In 1986, when public spending was at its lowest in the 1980s, unemployment benefits accounted for 2.4 pct. of GDP. Expressed in constant prices, spending was 24.1 pct. higher in 1993 than in 1982. In 1993,

---

3 The 'Potato Cure' was implemented in the fall of 1986, during the traditional period of the potato harvest, a staple of the Danish diet long before the advent of the welfare state and postwar prosperity. Thus, the 'Potato Cure' conjures up associations with former times of economic scarcity and more potatoes on the table.

expenditure on unemployment benefits accounted for approximately 20 pct. of total public spending on cash benefits. Only expenditures for the national pension exceeded those on unemployment benefits.

Expenditure per recipient slightly decreased from 1982 up to 1988. This too was the result of a series of political interventions designed to reduce expenditures on unemployment benefits and increase the distance between the level of benefits and minimum wages in the labor market. The maximum rate of benefit was frozen from October 1982 to April 1986. In 1982 supplemental unemployment benefits were reduced to 80 pct. of the maximum rate for full-time unemployed. In December 1987, the Conservative-led coalition government came to an agreement with the Social Democrats which resulted in a 10 pct. increase in benefit levels and the voluntary early retirement pay rate, effective July 1, 1988. This explains the increased level of expenditures from 1988 to 1989. In the spring of 1990, the Danish parliament decided that future cash benefits would be regulated in accordance with wage developments for workers. The purpose was to insert a mechanism that automatically gives social security claimants part of the wealth accumulation that is reflected by wage increases and to prevent benefit levels from being eroded due to inflation. In fact, to avoid recurrent political bargaining it also locks in benefits, keeping them separate and apart from the corporatist negotiations over wages.

Expenditures as well as the number of unemployment benefit recipients have fallen in tandem since 1994. For example, there were 140,000 full-time recipients of unemployment insurance in 1998, while in 1997 expenditures amounted to 23.0 billion DKK – equivalent to 2.0 pct. of GDP (see Figures 1 and 2). This reduction is the combined result of policy changes and improvements in the economy since 1994. A labor market reform in 1994 altered the organization of activation measures. Activation efforts were intensified, with an obligation for public authorities to offer some kind of activation opportunity to the unemployed. Unemployment compensation (and later social assistance) beneficiaries were reciprocally obligated to accept such 'reasonable' offers. In addition, a number of leave-of-absence schemes were introduced.

The cornerstone of the labor market reform was the stipulation of a maximum entitlement for unemployment benefits. In 1993, the period was fixed at seven years with a possible extension for up to two years for educational leave. Another year of parental leave per child and maternity leave of six months could also be granted. Since 1995, the maximum period of entitlement has slowly been reduced and is now four years. Recipients can continue to receive unemployment benefits after the age of 55. After the age of 60, the maximum entitlement period is reduced to 30 months. The reform changed the rules for unemployed under the age of 25. For this group unemployment benefits were halved. Together with improved educational opportunities, Danish policy resulted in one of the lowest youth unemployment rates in Europe.

The labor market reform also extended and improved leave arrangements. Employees may now take educational leave for a period of up to one year with the employer's approval. Both parents can take parental leave for a period of up to one year per child under the age of eight years. If the child is less than one year of age, the first six months of leave are a right; if the child is between one and eight years old, only the first three months of parental leave are a right. The rest of the time depends on the employer's acceptance. Finally, with the employer's consent, a claimant could receive a sabbatical leave for a period of up to one year. During a leave-of-absence, the recipient usually received cash benefits expressed as a share of the maximum unemployment benefit – 100 pct. for educational leaves or 60 pct. for parental leaves. The leave-of-absence reform was originally limited to a trial period of three years (1994 to 1996). However, the schemes proved immensely popular, especially the parental leave. In 1994, more than 80,000 people claimed parental leave, of which more than 4 out of 10 were unemployed. The popularity contributed to making leave-of-absence schemes (more or less) permanent with the 1995 state budget. At the same time, however, benefits for parental and sabbatical leave were reduced successively to 60 pct. of the maximum unemployment benefit in 1997 and the sabbatical scheme only survived until 1999.

The labor market reform also implied improved and more flexible schemes of job training and vocational training. These schemes are aimed at those out of work who receive unemployment benefits as well as social assistance. More flexible training schemes strengthen the opportunities for early job-training for those groups in the labor market who are vulnerable to long-term unemployment. Training offers used to be provided after a long period of unemployment and a great proportion of unemployed workers regarded the offers as an entitlement to a renewed benefit period. Today training offers do not qualify people for unemployment benefits.

The age of entitlement to the transitional allowance – which is an extension of the early retirement benefit for members of unemployment funds under the age of 60 – was lowered by the labor market reform from 55 to 50 years for a trial period of three years. As part of the 1995 state budget, the scheme was abolished altogether. This was the first time ever in the history of the Danish social security system that a scheme was abolished without something bigger and better being put in its place. The reason was a decline in unemployment and a beginning shortage of labor that coupled with the popularity of the scheme as measured by a huge influx of claimants made the scheme economically unsustainable. At least this was the opinion of the majority of political parties.

In 1999, due to the increasing shortage of labor and a decline in the average age of those leaving the labor market, the Social Democratic government adopted policy changes that made it more difficult to qualify for voluntary early retirement pay. For the same reasons, the eligibility age for the national old age pension was lowered from 67 to 65 years, which turns out to be a cost saving measure because the pension is smaller than the voluntary early retirement benefit. Due to the favorable economic situation and an expansive fiscal policy to finance the labor market reform, all these measures have contributed to a decline in unemployment.

SICKNESS AND MATERNITY BENEFITS

As a part of their collective bargaining agreements, the majority of employees in the Danish labor market are entitled to full pay during sickness. Those who are not entitled to full sick pay may claim sickness benefits from their municipality of residence. Spending on sickness benefits is modest. In 1982 and 1993, expenditures on sick pay amounted to 4.1 billion DKK or 0.9 pct. of GDP and 4.7 billion DKK or 0.5 pct. of GDP, respectively. The cost, expressed in constant prices, was approximately 8 pct. lower in 1993 than in 1982. The number of recipients increased from 29,500 full-time equivalent persons in 1984 to 38,000 in 1993.

Statistics on expenditures per sickness week reflect that the indexation of sickness benefits (as with unemployment benefits) was suspended from 1983 to 1986. Similarly sickness as well as unemployment benefits increased in 1988 as a result of political compromises. This is contributed to a slight increase in expenditures per week on sickness benefits at the end of this period, although total expenditure decreased, as mentioned above.

In the period of the Social Democratic-led coalition government, both expenditures and claimants increased dramatically. From 1994 to 1998, the number of claimants rose by 30 pct. from 38,600 to 50,200 full-time persons and expenditures increased by 16 pct. from 1994 to 1997, i.e. from 0.5 of GDP to 0.6 of GDP, respectively. This rise can primarily be ascribed to increased employment and hence a greater number of potentially sick-listed persons.

In 1997, the financing of sickness benefits was changed to increase municipalities' incentives to act earlier and more actively to reduce the number of sick-listed. Hence, municipalities became obliged to pay 50 pct. of the sickness benefit after eight weeks rather than the earlier 25 pct., the state covering the remainder. This eliminated the difference in the municipalities' share of financing of sickness benefits and disability pensions. Hence, the municipalities no longer had an incentive to keep people on sickness benefits for long periods have been diminished. This economic incentive has been some what weakened by the latest changes in the financing of disability pensions. But still the idea is to try to induce municipalities to take a more active part in the reintegration of those likely to become long-term sick-listed early in the period of sickness. This can be seen as yet another development in the activation approach taken by the ruling government.

At the end of the 1980s, large groups of workers (in particular public sector employees), gained the right to full pay during maternity leave as part of their collective agreements. Those who are not entitled to full pay may claim maternity benefits from their municipality of residence. During the 1980s, changes in the maternity benefit rules have affected the level of total expenditure. Maternity benefits, like unemployment and sickness benefits, were frozen in the period from 1983 to 1986. In the mid-1980s, the maternity period was extended by 10 weeks to a total of 24 weeks, and at the same time a two-week maternity leave for fathers was introduced. Together with an increasing birthrate this explains the striking rise from 1984 to 1985 in both the number of weeks of maternity leave as well as in the expenditure on maternity benefits. An increase in the labor market participation rate of women – and thus in the number of women who are entitled to maternity benefits – may also be of some importance. In the period from 1983 to 1999, Danish women's labor market participation rate increased from 74.2 pct. to 76.1 pct.

Total expenditure on maternity benefits is modest. In 1982, expenditures amounted to 1.3 billion DKK or 0.3 pct. of GDP, in 1993 4.5 billion DKK or 0.5 pct. of GDP, and in 1997 4.4 billion DKK or 0.4 pct. of GDP. Expressed in constant prices, spending has, however, increased by 102 pct. over the entire period. This is related to the various extensions of the maternity period and an increasing birthrate. The number of newborns rose from 51,000 in 1983 to 66,000 in 1998. As a result, the number of maternity leave claimants measured as full-time persons increased by 113 pct., i.e., from 16,400 full-time persons in 1984 to 35,000 in both 1994 and 1998.

DISABILITY PENSION

The disability pension system is a general, tax-financed system for all citizens. The system pays cash benefits in the event of invalidity and the loss of work capacity. There are three benefit levels depending on the evaluation of claimants' residual capacity for work. In the following we examine changes in the total number of disability pensioners and the amount of total expenditure on pensions at all three levels.

In 1984, the former disability and survivor pension schemes (i.e., invalidity, widow's and disability pensions) were reformed and from then on all so-called social pensions distributed to those under the age of 67 were gathered under the title of early retirement pension *(førtidspension)*. At the same time it became possible to award this pension on the basis of social criteria. This meant that a group of people previously receiving permanent social assistance was now entitled to a disability pension.

The result was a marked increase in the number of disability pensioners and expenditures on disability pensions. Two years before the reform (in 1982), 167,000 persons received disability pensions, whereas two years after the reform (1986), there were 246,000 persons. The increase continued, although at a reduced rate, reaching 265,800 disability pensioners in 1993. Total spending on disability pensions in 1982 amounted to 8.1 billion DKK equal to 1.7 pct. of GDP, and 21.7 billion DKK or 2.5 pct. of GDP in 1993.

The number of disability pensioners continued to increase even under the economic upturn during the Social Democratic-led coalition governments from 1993 onwards. Hence, the 273,500 disability pensions in 1997 were 3 pct. higher than in 1994. This generated much political discussion. Spending reached 27.3 billion DKK in 1997, equal to 2.4 pct. of GDP.

The disability pension system is the next system slated for reform after the unemployment benefit system and social assistance. A major reform with greater emphasis on rehabilitation and activation has been agreed upon and will be implemented starting in 2003. Steps to decrease the number of applicants for disability pension have already been taken. The municipality share of financing disability pensions has increased from 50 per cent to 65 per cent – and the individual's right to apply for disability pension has been abolished. Instead, citizens must convince the person at the municipality who is taking care of his or her case that application for disability pension is the right solution.

OLD-AGE PENSION

Senior citizens in Denmark are entitled to pensions from several different sources. The national old-age pension is a general tax-financed pension, which is paid to everyone who has reached the age of 67 for those born before 1 July 1939, or 65 for those born after this date. The Labor Market Supplementary pension scheme (ATP) is a compulsory, contribution-financed pension scheme for all Danish employees. Those above the pension age may also claim a pension from this scheme. In addition, large groups of employees are covered by occupational pension schemes that are determined by collective agreements between the unions and employers' organizations. And a great number of employees have individual pension savings. The Labor Market Supplementary pension scheme and the occupational pension schemes are funded by defined contributions schemes. Contributions to the ATP are paid on the basis on weekly hours worked while the contribution to the occupational pension schemes is based on wages. The following sections deal with the developments in the national old-age pension scheme.

The national old-age pension is – and will be for the years to come – the major source of income for Danish old-age pensioners. Occupational pension schemes have expanded to cover a greater percentage of the workforce has taken place since the end of the 1980s. As a result, the rules governing the national old-age pension have been changed in order to accommodate these new developments.

The national old-age pension is divided into two parts, a basic amount and a pension supplement. Until 1984, the basic amount was paid to every claimant, irrespective of income. After 1984, the basic pension was changed so that benefits were tied to earned income for those aged between 67 and 69 years. As part of the 1994 tax reform, additional changes where made. The age limit on the income test for the basic pension was abolished and the basic pension as part of the total national old-age pension was reduced while the pension supplement was increased. The pension supplement is reduced based on receipt of other sorts of income, i.e., income from supplementary pension schemes like the occupational pension schemes. In principle this means that national old-age pension is no longer universal.

The number of whole-year recipients of old-age pension has slightly increased from 664,000 pensioners in 1984 to 712,500 in 1993, and afterwards remained stable at around 710,000 pensioners. Increases are expected to continue up the year 2020 as a result of the aging of the population, as in most OECD countries (see, for example, OECD 1988).

The national old-age pension is the largest individual expenditure in the field of social security. As a whole, expenditures on the national pension have increased proportionally with the number of pensioners, although in the most recent years the former have increased more rapidly. This is related to the 1988 increase in basic pension amounts and pension supplements. Since 1988, the average pension has increased slightly as a result of this.

In 1982, expenses amounted to 22.2 billion DKK, which is equivalent to 4.8 pct. of GDP, while in 1993 these amounted to 46.4 billion DKK or 5.3 pct. of GDP. Expenses expressed as a percentage of GDP have fallen slightly since to 4.7 pct. of GDP in 1997. In the whole period covered, expenses increased by 41 pct. (in constant prices).

Reforms of the Danish old-age pension system in the 1980s introduced occupational pension schemes for the large part of privately employed workers who had no supplementary old-age pension except for the quite modest ATP pension. The Danish pension system was and is in many ways different from those in other Nordic and European countries. Denmark was not able (as were Sweden and Norway) to introduce an income related old-age pension system in the 1960s. Compared to Sweden and Norway, the Danish national old-age pension system has quite low replacement rates and was based on the 'male

CRISIS, MIRACLES, AND BEYOND

breadwinner' model, i.e., a household with one income prior to retirement was compensated with a national old-age pension for both man and wife. The one breadwinner model was left in place in Denmark until the end of the 1960s and the beginning of the 1970s. During the severe economic crisis in Denmark from the mid 1970s to the mid 1980s, pension reform was not as high on the political agenda as was the unemployment problem and problems with the balance of payments.

But during the 1980s, pension policies moved up on the political agenda (Ploug, 2003). In 1985, the Federation of Trade Unions proposed a pension reform. The idea was to create a supplementary, funded, defined contribution scheme covering everyone in the labor market. The Conservative-led government favored the idea of a funded scheme because it would increase savings and thereby contribute to solving Denmark's major macroeconomic problem at that time – huge deficits in the balance of payments. A tripartite commission was formed in 1988 to consider pension reform. For a number of political reasons, this did not lead to an immediate reform of the Danish old age pension system. The main reason was that the parties in the labor market had agreed that the negotiations in 1989 could only lead to general wage increases i.e. items like pensions was not at the negotiation table. Another reason was that the labor unions had to find a way to formulate the ideas of decentralized pensions schemes as they had originally argued for the creation of a central pension fund. But as a result of labor market negotiations in 1991, a number of pension funds connected to various trade unions were established. This new supplementary pension scheme was implemented in 1993 with a contribution of 0.9 per cent. As a result of the latest labor market negotiations, the contribution will increase to 9 per cent in 2003. Today the majority of workers are covered by supplementary, funded, defined contribution pension schemes. One of the reasons that Denmark was able to pass this kind of reform – one that so many other countries are currently attempting – was that the state old age pension scheme didn't have to be altered in order to adopt the reform. Thus the reform was a true supplement to the existing pension system where everyone in the labor market gained, while no one lost. The state old age pension scheme was left unchanged by the reform.

FAMILY ALLOWANCES

The two types of cash benefits for Danish families with children – child family benefits and the child allowance – are both tax financed, tax free and not subject to income-testing. Cash benefits to child families are one of the areas where the most important legislative changes took place during the 1980s. At the start of the decade, there was no universal benefit, only an income-tested ordinary child allowance. During the period from 1984 to 1986, the so-called child cheque was paid to all parents. In 1987, the universal child family benefit for all children was introduced. At the same time, the rules for the child allowances were changed so that today they are given to orphaned children, children of social pensioners, and children with single parents, without income testing. In the following, we examine the income-tested child allowance offered during period up to 1984. Then the child allowances and the child cheque are examined, and, finally for the period after 1987, we turn to the child family benefit.

The number of families that received the income-tested child allowance is obviously lower than the number of families that receive the universal child family benefit. In 1982, child allowances were distributed to 495,000 families with children. This number decreased until the mid-1980s, reaching 375,000 families in 1986.

In the period from 1982 to 1986, total spending on the child allowance, and in the period from 1984 to 1986 also for the child cheque, remained fairly stable. The introduction of the child family benefit resulted in an expected steep increase in both the expenditure as well as the number of child families receiving the benefit, see Figure 2. The increase in expenditure is higher than the increase in the number of recipients reflecting increased average benefits per recipient. Average benefits furthermore slightly increased, because subsequently a differentiation has been introduced so that higher benefits are given to children under the age of 6.

Total spending on child supplements amounted in 1982 to 1.7 billion DKK, which is equivalent to 0.4 pct. of GDP, while spending on child family benefits in 1993 was 7.2 billion or 0.8 pct. of GDP and in 1997 9,4 billion DKK or 0.8 pct. of GDP. In constant prices spending increased by 231 pct. The child family benefit is thus the benefit type that increased the most from 1982 to 1997.

MEANS-TESTED BENEFITS

Social assistance under the Social Security Act is paid according to an evaluation of the economic situation of the claimant and when applicable, the claimant's spouse. Social assistance provides the lowest level of support in the Danish social safety net. Social assistance is not paid until all other possibilities have been exhausted. In order to be entitled to social assistance, the claimant's situation has to have changed considerably from a previous situation where the claimant was self-supporting. Claimants are not entitled to social assistance on the grounds that they find their income level inadequate.

The number of whole-year recipients decreased from 105,600 in 1984 to 93,800 in 1987. The tax reform of 1986/87 and the 'Potato Cure' that curbed domestic consumption and thus increased unemployment, led to a marked increased in the number of persons relying on social assistance, peaking at

159,600 claimants in 1993. The number of claimants decreased from 124,000 in 1994 to 92,600 in 1998.

Expenditure on social assistance amounted to 6.0 billion DKK in 1982 or 1.3 pct. of GDP and to 9.1 billion DKK in 1993 or 1.0 pct. of GDP. The increase in expenditure is connected with the growth in the number of social assistance recipients, but also reflects benefit increases per recipient. The increase in the number of whole-year recipients of social assistance from 1987 to 1993 followed the same pattern as that for unemployment (see above). Since approximately two-thirds of all social assistance recipients receive financial assistance due to unemployment, this parallel development was expected.

A series of rule changes may also, however, contribute to the explanation of the development in the level of expenditure. In 1983, a rule was introduced that resulted in reductions in social assistance for those receiving assistance for more than nine months. The same year, social assistance to young people was reconfigured so that it would be equivalent to the level of educational aid from public funds given to students (SU). In the last half of the period, several changes were made to these rules, which may have contributed to an increased level of expenditure. In 1987, the setting of social assistance benefit levels was altered with a shift from partly mean-tested and discretionary benefits to so-called fixed rules, i.e., standard flat-rate benefits. This rearrangement was implemented so that child families receiving social assistance were given particular consideration. The rearrangement resulted in an increase in the expenditure level. In 1989, the gross rehabilitation allowance, the enterprise allowance scheme and the youth allowance were introduced. All these new allowances, at first, resulted in increased spending on cash benefits. Another part of the total increase in expenditure and the increase in average benefits per recipients may have been caused by the fact that recipients, as a whole, have received social assistance for longer periods of time.

During the economic upturn and the Social Democratic-led governments, the number of claimants fell from 124,000 in 1994 to 92,600 in 1998. From 1994 to 1997, expenditure fell from 10.7 billion DKK or 1.1 pct. of GDP to 9.3 billion DKK or 0.8 pct. of GDP.

Concluding remarks

The development of the Danish social security system is characterized not by sweeping reforms, but rather by incremental steps. Roughly two periods can be identified in the preceding century of social security. In the first fifty years, steps were taken to cover more groups in the population and to make benefits independent of income testing. This process culminated in 1964 with the advent of a universal national old age pension with a flat-rate benefit not subject to an income-test. This benefit was, like most benefits then and now, financed through taxes on a pay-as-you-go basis. These principles were refined during the subsequent fifteen years with increases in benefit periods and levels and consolidation of the decentralized benefit delivery system. The development of a comprehensive tax-financed social security system was thus a hallmark of the first period.

The year 1979 marks the start of the second period characterized by a restructuring of the social security system. In fact, this started in 1964, but only modestly with the establishment of the ATP scheme, the supplementary benefit scheme with an inherent logic that sharply contrasted with the national old age pension. Benefits are based on attachment to the labor market and financed through social security contributions on a funded basis. The size of ATP benefits depend on the amount of contributions made and their derived interest. So there is a direct linkage between contributions and benefits. This distinguished ATP from the civil servants' pensions in which benefits were expressed as part of previous earnings and financed like other cash benefits.

However, it was to take another 25 years before the supplementary schemes for working people really took off, i.e. with the addition of occupational disability pensions, survivors and old age pensions, as well as sickness and maternity benefits. And, with the introduction of 'new' schemes covering 567,000 people out of a labor force of approximately 2.8 million people, the expansion of occupational pension coverage to a larger and larger proportion of the labor force climaxed in 1993 (Ministry of Finance, 1995). There are no regular official statistics on the coverage of occupational pensions, but material from a recent survey shows that occupational pension schemes now cover 66 pct. of males and 71 pct. of females in the labor force. Other studies come to similar estimates, e.g., between 75 and 80 pct. of the labor force is covered according to an ATP study from 1994 (ATP, 1994). Occupational pensions and similar supplementary benefits are among the main bargaining points during negotiations over collective agreements. The second period of the development of social security in Denmark was defined by the addition of a second tier of cash benefits for the working population.

Most of these schemes are, like the ATP, financed through employers' and employee's contributions on a strictly funded basis. But the benefits are likely to be of a much more significant size compared to ATP, especially for middle and high income groups. Greater inequalities both within and between generations will occur as supplementary schemes mature and start paying out benefits. Whether the second tier will be complementary rather than supplementary to the state schemes of social security remains to be seen. In particular, middle and high income groups in 'old' schemes are likely to receive generous benefits while income-testing excludes them from the national old age pension benefits.

Nevertheless, occupational pension schemes may paradoxically be the instrument to damper inequality since they provide some form of mandatory income protection for low- and middle-income groups. In the absence of such collective schemes, individuals would have to save for retirement. By the early 1980s, there was a clear tendency towards a polarization of the Danish welfare state. Low-income groups relied on the national old age pension and higher income groups took up individual savings supported generously by the tax system (Vesterø-Jensen, 1985). Furthermore, the national old age pension supplement is income-tested, including income from other pensions. As occupational pension schemes mature and pay out more generous benefits than is the case today, more revenue will be collected in this way and contribute towards less income inequality. In this way, politicians installed a mechanism that does not affect many of today's pensioners and voters, but will gradually have a broader impact on society and the budget.

The development of a second tier of cash benefits constitutes the first element of the restructuring of the social security system. The changing nature of the first tier – the statutory schemes that have been the subject of this chapter – constitute the second element of the restructuring process. In 1979, the then Social Democratic-Liberal coalition government promoted changes to the cash benefit system to make it more 'active' by placing greater emphasis on active labor market policies and linking cash benefits more closely to participation in activation measures. The Social Democratic government that succeeded the coalition developed these ideas into a huge plan for employment creation by establishing what some called a third labor market (the first being private employment and the second being ordinary public employment) where people with problems getting a job in the ordinary labor market could find publicly subsidized work. However, due to adverse political and economic circumstances, this plan was never adopted. The Social Democratic government left office in 1982. And, as we have seen, the Conservative-led coalition that took office that year concentrated its efforts on general economic policy and (largely unsuccessful) attempts to curb expenditure growth. Labor market policy and fundamental changes to the cash benefit system were ignored during most of its reign. When the Social Democratic government took office in 1993, the external budget deficit was largely resolved and the internal budget deficit appeared as the next major problem to address. The Social Democrats and their coalition partners saw a window of opportunity to change the nature of the tax-benefit system, reduce unemployment and, thus, the deficit problem. The described tax and labor market reforms and the subsequent changes were the concrete policies aiming at this.

A retrospective account of the reforms reveals the following pattern of development. The Social Democratic governments of the 1970s and 1980s tried to pursue active labor market policies, but faced weak economic conditions. Entering the 1980s, the Danish economy was in trouble. After a short period of trial and error, the Conservative-led governments of the 1980s and 1990s decided to concentrate on improving the Danish economy, especially reducing real wages and consumption while increasing savings. But their ambitions with respect to active labor market policy were modest. They also faced fierce resistance from the trade unions. Learning from the Conservatives' approach to managing the macroeconomic situation, the Social Democratic governments of the 1990s have pursued active labor market policies on sound economic grounds. Thus, the-so called Danish miracle is not the work of one government's reforms, but rather the result of a long trial and error search for an appropriate strategy to manage the Danish economy in the wake of the general economic shift that accompanied the oil crises of the 1970s.

The question of whether the Danish social security system is in a period of change or continuity is therefore debatable. On the one hand, one could argue that the incremental steps reflect continuity. For example, the Conservative-led coalition governments from 1982 to 1993 did not manage to contain social security spending, nor did they cut the number of recipients. Instead economic turmoil was reflected in expenditure levels and the number of people on unemployment insurance, social assistance and, to a lesser degree, early exit schemes such as the voluntary early retirement pay and the disability pensions. Similarly, demographics played a role in this period and were reflected in increased expenditures on the national old age pensions and, to a lesser extent, on family benefits.

On the other hand, one could argue that the incremental steps constitute qualitative changes over time. The trend in the Danish social security scheme was first towards universalism and the removal of income-testing. More recently, the trend has been towards selectivism, e.g., 'special treatment' for youth, and income-tested benefits. The latter trajectory runs parallel with the development of the supplementary schemes. As these schemes mature, they may fundamentally change the whole nature of the Danish welfare state. This silent revolution is not so much a result of economic or demographic causes, but of political bargaining on the labor market.

Moreover, there is no shortage of debate at the most fundamental level about the future of the welfare state and, in particular, about the cash benefit system. In fact, social policy issues during the nineties became one of the most debated subjects in politics and in the media. This provides fertile soil for change. The increased emphasis on obligations and activation measures rather than rights and 'passive' cash benefits would not have been 'politically correct' fifteen years ago. For example, young uneducated people have been obligated to begin an education within six months of unemployment since 1995. This policy was adopted without a public outcry although, in principle, it broke with the much-praised tradition of equal treatment of unemployed irrespective of age. Social Democrats today advocate selectivism just as Liberals promoted universalism a hundred years ago. In fact, Liberals in Denmark were among the strongest proponents of universalism and state provision in the founding of the Danish welfare state. They sought to shift the burden of financing poverty relief away from the municipalities and real estate taxes and onto the state and income taxes (Dich, 1973). Today's Social Democrats include advocates of obligations as well as rights, of income testing rather than flat-rate benefits. Their objective is not to dismantle the welfare state, but to enhance the bond between rights and obligations, to target benefits to the needy, and to promote work and family life. Complete autonomy of the labor market is seen as morally wrong and a waste of human resources. Thus the Social Democratic project in Denmark is (no longer) only about wage and benefit increases, but also about quality of life. In such a project, targeting and activation become prominent policy tools. The story of the Danish social security system shows that the dichotomy between residual and institutional welfare states may serve as a summary categorization of welfare states at a given moment, but are inadequate to capture changes over time within a country. The Danish experience also demonstrates that the same tools of social policy can be used over time for different reasons by opposing political parties.

Will it be possible to keep the welfare state as it is? Seen from the outside, i.e., from more liberal countries, the Nordic welfare states seem destined to collapse sooner or later, as did the communist regimes of eastern Europe. Heavy tax burdens and huge deficits would prove unsustainable. The risk is indeed there, but recent political developments demonstrate a clear political will to reform and thereby adapt. Also, it should be kept in mind that in spite of its high taxes, this type of welfare state enjoys far more popularity than the communist regimes ever did and citizens have a voice in the direction of government policy.

References

ATP (1994). Supplerende pensioner i Danmark – en analyse af de lovbundne og de overenskomstaftalte supplerende pensioner. Hillerød: ATP.

ATP (1995). *Supplementary Pensions in Denmark: a description of the future pension system.* Hillerød: ATP.

Danish Treasury (1994). *Skattepolitisk redegørelse, juni 1994.* Copenhagen: Danish Treasury.

Dich, Jørgen S. (1973). *Den herskende klasse – En kritisk analyse af social udbytning og midlerne imod den.* Copenhagen: Borgen.

Hansen, Hans (2000). *Elements of Social Security*. Copenhagen: The Danish National Institute of Social Research.

Kvist, Jon & Adrian Sinfield (1996). *Comparing Tax Routes to Welfare in Denmark and the United Kingdom*. Copenhagen: The Danish National Institute of Social Research.

Kvist, Jon (1997). 'Retrenchment or Restructuring – The Emergence of a Multi-tiered Welfare State in Denmark', in J. Clasen (ed.). *Social Insurance in Europe*. Bristol: Policy Press.

Ministry of Finance (1995). *Pensionsopsparingens udbredelse og dækning*. Copenhagen: Ministry of Finance.

Ministry of Social Affairs (1991). Rapport om bruttoficiering af den sociale pension. Copenhagen: The Ministry of Social Affairs.

Pechmann, Joseph (1988). *World Tax Reform*. Washington DC: Brookings Institution.

Petersen, Jørn Henrik (1995). 'Leuven Lectures. Three Essays on Trends Towards a Transformation of the Danish Welfare State'. *CHS Working Paper 1995: 1*. Odense University.

Ploug, Niels & Jon Kvist (1994a). *Overførselsindkomster i Europa. Systemerne i grundtræk*. Copenhagen: The Danish National Institute of Social Research.

Ploug, Niels & Jon Kvist (1995). *Social Security in Europe. Development or Dismantlement?* Deventer: Kluwer Law and Taxation Publishers.

Ploug, Niels & Jon Kvist (eds.) (1994b). *Recent Trends in Cash Benefits in Europe. Social Security in Europe 4*. Copenhagen: The Danish National Institute of Social Research.

Ploug, Niels (2003). 'The re-calibration of the Danish old age pension system'. *International Social Security Review 56, 2*.

Plovsing, Jan (1998). *Socialpolitik*, 5th ed. Copenhagen: Handelshøjskolens Forlag.

Titmuss, Richard (1958). 'Social Division of Welfare', in *Essays on the Welfare State*. London: Allen and Unwin.

Vesterø-Jensen, Carsten (1985). *Det tvedelte pensionssystem*. Roskilde: Forlaget Samfundsøkonomi og Planlægning.

6 DANISH LOCAL GOVERNMENT

Poul Erik Mouritzen

Introduction

Like a guardian angel, Danish local government hovers over every Danish citizen from cradle to grave, ready to give a helping hand whenever the need is there. Midwives are available before you are born, visiting health nurses come to the home after your birth, professional pedagogues take over as soon as Mom and Dad have returned to their jobs, school dentists start a 12 to 15 year effort when you are three years old, teachers guide you through primary and secondary school, nurses and doctors – some in private practices others at public hospitals – are available free of charge throughout life, home helpers provide cleaning, shopping and personal care when you can no longer take care of yourself, and homes for the elderly are also available (although in short supply these days). A plethora of income transfer programs includes sickness allowances, maternity allowances, disability pensions, supplementary benefits, rent allowances and, finally, pensions for the elderly. Whatever your age and whatever your social conditions the municipality will always have an offer for you (recently, the author of this article – a well-paid university professor – took guitar lessons, the cost of which for the most part was borne by the other tax payers in his municipality).

Over one quarter of the Danish gross domestic product is allocated by the decisions made by some 2,700 locally elected politicians in 98 municipalities and five regions. No local governmental system plays a similar role in any other country in the world, although some come close, particularly in the Scandinavian countries. This system of local government is a result of incremental adjustments which have taken over several generations; however, it is also a result of two major reforms in 1970 and 2007. The purpose of this chapter is to describe these reforms in terms of their content, rationale and the political forces at work in the two periods; obviously, the latest reform is given more attention than the 1970 reform. The second half of the chapter describes the local government system in Denmark along dimensions like size, functions, revenue, the role of the local government associations and finally, the peculiar Danish institution labeled budget cooperation. It has now been in place for a generation, and the aim is to incorporate local government in the overall national economic policy.

The two grand reforms

THE 1970 REFORM

A system of local government may be organized around two quite opposing theoretical positions, termed the reform tradition and the political economy tradition (Ostrom, 1972; Mouritzen, 1989a). Danish local government was in 1970 completely reorganized based on the first tradition, according to which a local government system should be built on the following principles:[1]

> ... as far as possible in each major urban area there should be only one local government ...

> ... A second point upon which agreement is almost complete is that *the voters should elect only the important, policy-making-officers* and that these should be few in number...

> ... the functions of legislation and control on the one hand are so distinct from that of administration ... that *those who do the work of administration should* be a separate group of men and women, especially trained and adequately compensated for their work ...

> ... the *administration should be organized as a single integrated system* upon the hierarchical principle, tapering upward and culminating in a single chief executive officer (cited from Ostrom, 1972: 476).

Until 1970 a system of detailed central government control and narrowly defined categorical grants persisted in Denmark, leaving little room for local autonomy among the approximately 1,200 municipalities and 24 counties.[2] After more than ten years of planning, local government reform was implemented in 1970, starting with the amalgamation reform that reduced the number of municipalities to 275 and counties to 14. During the 1970s, decentralization of national programs to local governments also began, and in the same period the system of intergovernmental grants was gradually changed. Most of the categorical grants of the matching type have been abolished and a system of general grants with a high degree of equalization has replaced them.

These changes were largely structured according to the principles and goals of the reform tradition. The paradigms of the amalgamations in 1970 rested on the principle of 'one city-one municipality'. A system of a highly professionalized staff has been developed in all municipalities, with more and

---

1 The summary stems from an American textbook written in 1925.

2 The following descriptions are with a few changes from Mouritzen (1989b: 104ff).

CRISIS, MIRACLES, AND BEYOND

more university graduates entering the higher ranks of the bureaucracy. This contrasts with the situation in most local government bureaus before 1970, where the division between politics and administration was absent, if only because there were no administrators at all. One of the most experienced local politicians in Denmark (37 years in a local council) recalls his first year in politics:

> This was the time when the nine elected council members every two weeks crowded in a room under the roof of the home for the elderly and went through every single case in a fog of cigar smoke so thick that we now and then had to go outside to breathe some fresh air (Danske Kommuner, 1995).

Thus local government was transformed from an old boys system to a professionalized administration capable of taking on more complex tasks involving policy implementation and the provision of a wide range of social welfare programs. To a large extent, the reforms addressed the problem of the unequal distribution of costs and services via the 'one city–one municipality' principle in combination with the highly equalizing grant system.

The reform tradition also emphasizes the functional capabilities of the larger units.[3] Specialized services require relatively large populations because demand has to reach some threshold before institutional services can be provided economically. This was particularly an issue felt within the most important service of those days, public education. The many small localities of 1,000 to 5,000 inhabitants were unable to establish a school system that met the standards of the (then) modern society.

Also, conventional reform theory points to the existence of economies of scale: the larger the community, the more effective the production of services because the unit cost of production is negatively related to the quantity produced. The properties of large government add up to greater efficiency: citizens get more and better services for less (tax) money.

Greater efficiency may have consequences for local democracy. Larger units are able to do more; therefore citizens are able to control more (and more important) aspects of their environment. This was in fact the incentive held out by central government in the 1960s to induce local governments – and voters – to accept the amalgamations. Amalgamation became a prerequisite for the transfer of more tasks to local government and, as a consequence, for the strengthening of local democracy. According to this argument, larger units would improve citizens' incentives to participate in local affairs. Opportunities for individual participation were perhaps less likely to be found in the larger

---

3 For this description of the advantages of the larger units cf. Mouritzen (1989a: 662).

jurisdictions. But collective modes of interest representation were expected to be more prevalent in the form of active political parties and organized interest groups (cf. also Newton, 1982).

The sum of the reforms of the 1970s was the creation of a highly consolidated local government system (see Mouritzen, 1989b). It was territorially consolidated because jurisdictional boundaries correspond very much to the sociological realities of life ('one city-one municipality')[4] and there are very few boundaries that overlap other political-administrative units of government. It was consolidated in programmatic terms because most public services at the local level became the responsibility of the municipality or the county. Finally, the system was functionally consolidated because policy making, financing as well as service production became the responsibility of the same unit, the municipality or the country.

DANISH LOCAL GOVERNMENT UNDER PRESSURE

In the first 20 years following the 1970 reforms, the local government structure in Denmark was never questioned. However, by the end of the 1980s, the Conservatives questioned the sense of a continued existence of the counties. From 1995 to 1996, the debate was particularly intense in connection with the work of the Greater Copenhagen Commission to reform the Copenhagen metropolitan area (the assignment eventually failed due to political disagreement). That commission was followed by the Public Sector Tasks Commission, which in 1998 concluded that 'the existing task distribution between the three administrative levels basically must be considered efficient' and that it was 'the commission's expectations that, also in the years to come, the foundation of the task distribution will turn out to be robust towards the development of demands on the public sector'.

Not all municipalities agreed with that conclusion. Several groups of municipalities started discussions with a view to intensifying cooperation, in some places in the form of actual amalgamations. In one region, the island of Bornholm in the Baltic Sea, a popular referendum was held in 2001 leading to a decision to amalgamate the five existing municipalities as well as the county into one regional authority responsible for all local government functions. The merger took effect from 2003 and resulted in a local government with 45,000 inhabitants. Likewise, three small municipalities on the island Langeland held a referendum in 2001 in which a majority in all municipalities voted for an amalgamation. In other areas of the country where amalgamations were

---

4 It should be noted that the principle of 'one city one municipality' was never implemented in the metropolitan area of Copenhagen.

seriously considered, the efforts failed because of conflicts among the political and administrative elites.

THE 2007 REFORM[5]

The local negotiations all ended in the summer of 2002 when the new Liberal-Conservative government established yet another commission, the Commission on Administrative Structure. This time most observers, the local government associations and most municipalities and counties realized that the government was serious and that a reform of some sort was underway.

In hindsight, political decisions often tend to look more rational and planned than they actually were. The Danish local government reform is no exception – but it was in all likelihood not planned by the government from the day it took over in November 2001. A reform had not been mentioned in the election campaign preceding the new government, it was not part of the electoral platform of any of the political parties, and it was not part of the agreement between the two parties that eventually formed the government. Nevertheless it was decided to establish the Commission on Administrative Structure, which was commissioned with the task[6]

> of providing a technical and expert analysis to be used as a decision basis with respect to changes of the framework for the performance of public sector tasks

and further:

> … the Commission is to set up and assess various models for the distribution of responsibility regarding the performance of public sector tasks as well as for the appropriate sizes of public sector units.

The commission had a rather broad mandate, which involved all public sector functions at all three tiers of government (municipality, country and state). It was possible to suggest a reduction in the number of units as well as the number of government tiers. In fact, the commission was specifically asked to 'make an assessment of the advantages and disadvantages of reducing the number of administrations with directly elected leadership from a three-tier to a two-tier structure'.

---

5 For a more detailed account of the reform process see Mouritzen (2007).

6 The full text of the terms of reference (in English) for the commission can be found at http://www.im.dk/publikationer/struktur_uk/index.html

In January 2004 – after 14 months of work – the commission concluded that most municipalities were too small and too vulnerable given the complicated tasks that had been transferred to the municipal level over the years:

> The small municipalities have problems ensuring adequate professional sustainability in task performance in a number of areas and have higher expenditure per inhabitant (adjusted for differences in expenditure levels and financial capability of the individual municipalities). Furthermore, the smaller municipalities may find it difficult to ensure broadness in the options available to the citizens. The many relatively small administrative units are also unable to benefit fully from the advantages of digitalization. Likewise, most of the existing counties are too small to ensure optimal planning in the hospital sector. Finally, the limited geographical size of the counties in the region of Greater Copenhagen creates problems of coordination, especially within the areas of health care, transport and planning.[7]

It was found that a minimum size even without further transfers of functions ought to be around 20,000 inhabitants while the number of counties should be reduced to somewhere between three and eight depending on the distribution of functions. When it came to the specifics of the reform, the commission made no clear recommendations. Rather a number of models – ideal types – were put forward (Commission on Administrative Structure, 2004: 35f):

1. The status quo model with unchanged distribution of tasks, but with larger municipalities and counties.
2. *The broad county model* with three administrative levels with direct election where especially the counties and to some extent the municipalities are assigned new tasks.
3. *The broad municipality model* where especially the municipalities are assigned new tasks, whereas the task portfolio of the counties is reduced to responsibility only for tasks requiring geographical scope and a large population.[8]
4. *The state model* where all the tasks are placed at two directly elected, administrative levels – the state and the municipalities.

---

7 The full resume of the report can be found on the homepage of the Ministry of the Interior at http://www.im.dk/publikationer/struktur_uk/index.html

8 Some sub-models with indirectly elected county councils are left out from this description.

CRISIS, MIRACLES, AND BEYOND

Less than four months after the publication of the commission report the government was ready with its own proposal with the catchy title 'The New Denmark' (Ministry of the Interior and Health, 2004a). The proposal, in all its radicalism, took everyone by surprise. Central government and the municipalities more or less divided all county tasks between them, except one: health services. To run the hospitals, five regions were established with an elected council at the top but without independent power of taxation. From this point the term *counties* was not used any more. The government wanted to signal a major break with the past by using the term *regions*. Municipal mergers at a minimum size of 30,000 inhabitants were recommended, but allowing municipalities to be smaller provided they entered into binding agreements on cooperation.

The opposition, headed by the Social Democrats and the Social Liberal Party, had very early on, even before the Commission on Administrative Structure concluded its work, announced that they preferred a model where the counties kept most of their tasks, just as their independent power of taxation was made a crucial point. The opposition maintained that they were willing to change the content of the reform if they did not become party to the negotiation. On this basis – where the gap between the parties was considerable – negotiations for a broad compromise began. After one collapse of negotiations, contact was resumed only to result in yet another collapse in mid-June.

Throughout the negotiations, the government made several concessions to the opposition parties as regards the future tasks of the regions. Considerable parts of the tasks were maintained when only six days later, without major problems, the final agreement was successfully negotiated with the Danish People's Party (Ministry of the Interior and Health, 2004b). The agreement implied that the five future regions will continue to operate specialized institutions within the social area, prepare plans of regional development and be responsible for setting up transport authorities. However, they lose their independent power of taxation. The main task is still health services, which are financed by a combination of state and local government subsidies as well as a local fee for treatment of the municipality's citizens. A detailed list of tasks resting with the municipalities and counties can be found in Boxes 1 and 2 later in the article.[9]

---

9 See http://www.im.dk/publikationer/government_reform_in_brief/kap03.htm for the list and also for a more thorough discussion of tasks and financial arrangements.

As regards municipal size, the figure of 30,000 inhabitants is mentioned as a target; however, 20.000+ inhabitants is accepted. Finally, municipalities below that size may be allowed to continue provided they enter into binding agreements on cooperation with one large municipality.

THE POLITICAL PROCESS AT THE LOCAL LEVEL: WHO SHOULD WE MARRY?

As part of the June agreement all municipalities were asked to report to the Ministry of the Interior and Health by the end of the year how they wanted to respond to the requirements in the agreement. Obviously, municipalities with more than 20,000 inhabitants could go on as if nothing had happened, while municipalities with less had two options: find partners to merge with or enter into a detailed set of cooperative agreements with a neighboring municipality. This set off six months of analysis, decision making, negotiations in and between municipalities and finally a decision on the future of the individual municipality. For several reasons this involved a type of decision rarely faced by local politicians.

First, the decision obviously would have potentially large consequences for the citizenry as well as for the individual politicians, not least for a large number of mayors whose jobs were in danger. As a consequence, the decisions often involved a complex mix of economic calculations, partisan considerations, personal ambitions as well as positive or negative images of potential future partners. Often, the political parties were split in two or more parts, in many cases reflecting what part of the municipality the individual politician belonged to. Second, and maybe as a consequence of the reasons just mentioned, the decisions were in many cases left with the local citizenry. Altogether 73 referenda were held, in some municipalities involving only a particular part of the municipality where citizens wanted the municipality to be divided between two new larger units. Third, the decision made should in all cases be approved by the three parties behind the agreement at the central level. Also, the preferred marriage partner would of course have to say yes to the proposal, but in many cases this yes did not materialize. As a matter of fact one of the central elements of the decision was a sequential process where individual municipalities had to start more or less from scratch surveying new options when previous alternatives were made absolute by decisions in neighboring municipalities. Fourth, this type of decision was totally un-programmed. Nobody had ever been involved in a process of this type. Fifth, the decision had to be made within a short period of time and the normal option available to politicians – to finish the process by a non-decision – was simply not available. Finally, the decision was irreversible. Maybe the choice of partner was wrong, but once marriage was formalized a future divorce was absolutely out of the question.

CRISIS, MIRACLES, AND BEYOND

Given all the complexities of the decision, the process was surprisingly harmonious. Of course, dramatic and conflictual processes could be found here and there, but in most cases municipalities found the future partners after maybe one or two iterations. Also, the government and the partners of the agreements approved of almost all proposals from the local decision makers. Only in two cases did central government make a decision that was strongly in opposition to local wishes. In a few cases, the government decided to let an umpire resolve local conflicts.

Some observers have called the process 'voluntary'. This is true in the sense that the government did not dictate who should merge with whom in contrast to the situation for the counties, where the future borders as well as the location of the regional headquarters were decided centrally, often to the dismay of the regional politicians. However, it was not voluntary in the sense that municipalities under 20,000 inhabitants had a choice of whether or not to merge. Only two municipalities (well-off municipalities near Copenhagen) decided to continue with less than 20,000 inhabitants and entered into a co-operative agreement with one of the neighboring municipalities. So, the local politicians in fact had a gun to their head and had to make a decision rather quickly. Experiences from Denmark, Norway and Sweden seem to indicate that voluntary arrangements involving both questions of 'whether to merge' and 'with whom' rarely lead to municipal mergers since local opposition and personal ambitions act as effective veto points in the decision making process. By removing the option 'whether to merge' the government in effect removed those veto points.

The rationale of the reform

To understand the thinking behind the Danish reform of 2007 we may use the conceptual framework developed by the American scholars Robert Dahl and Edward Tufte (1973: 20ff). They distinguish between two dimensions, citizen effectiveness and system capacity. Citizen effectiveness in short is a question of how well democracy works: Is the political system effectively controlled by citizens, are citizens able to get access to politicians and communicate their wishes and is the system responsive to those wishes? System capacity refers to the ability of the system to solve problems and implement what citizens want in an effective way.

In many ways the Danish debate on the costs and benefits of a local government reform centered on these two dimensions. For many years it was considered part of conventional wisdom that the two dimensions were related in such a way as to present a dilemma for policy makers and reformers: It was possible to increase system capacity but at the cost of democracy; or, it was possible to improve democracy, but only at the cost of system capacity. This train of thought is illustrated by Line *a* in Figure 1. The belief in the existence of this trade-off was the major argument for the opponents of an amalgamation reform: Democracy would suffer if we abandoned the many small municipalities in order to improve system capacity. What effectively happened during the process was that the validity of this argument was questioned by a research report from the University of Southern Denmark according to which the trade-off between capacity and democracy was almost absent. Before we account for the democratic dimension, however, we need to take a closer look at the capacity dimension.

FIGURE 1.
System capacity and citizen effectiveness

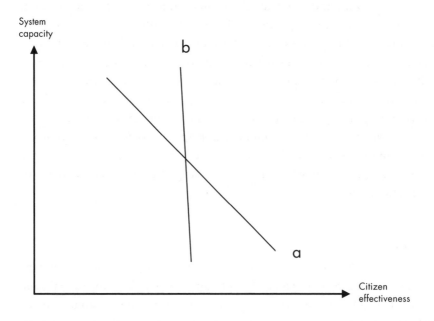

SYSTEM CAPACITY
Capacity concerns played a major role in the report from the Commission on Administrative Tasks. We may distinguish four different types of capacity problems discussed in the report.

Financial capacity may be defined as the ability to encounter and survive changes in the social and financial surroundings (the opposite of vulnerability). The report found that especially small municipalities had become more and more vulnerable towards changes in the environment, not least because the municipalities over the years had been given more and more complicated and expensive tasks to perform. One example suffices: Over the years more and more responsibility for pre-pensions had been transferred to the municipalities resulting in a situation in 2002 where municipalities had the full decision-making authority to decide whether or not a citizen (for instance a 30 year-old drug addict) should enjoy a public pension for the rest of his life (currently around 1,800 Euro per month). With the authority, however, came also the financial responsibility, since the municipality had to cover two-thirds of the expenses imposed by such a decision. Obviously, small municipalities with 5,000 inhabitants could be crippled by too many pre-pensioners.

The ability to produce good quality and inexpensive service represents a second aspect of capacity. This phenomenon was discussed in the report under the heading of *efficiency* or economies of scale. Previous research as well as research conducted by the Commission indicated that the relation between size and efficiency takes the form of a curve: At first, there are quite a few gains by going from small to somewhat larger municipalities, but gradually the gains flatten before they disappear at a municipal size of about 40,000 inhabitants. Above a certain threshold, however, costs start to increase slightly again. The overall conclusion of the Commission was that there are benefits of economies of scale in municipalities of up to at least 18,000-25,000 inhabitants and probably more. A recent analysis shows that the benefits of economies of scale have increased over the last ten years so that the municipality size with the lowest average expenditure per inhabitant has increased from 28,000 to 34,000 inhabitants. Some of the analyses also show that there are disadvantages of economies of scale in municipalities of more than about 50,000 inhabitants. In any case, there are very small differences in terms of efficiency in municipalities with between 20,000 and 50,000 inhabitants.

The ability to make decisions that meet the professional and legal demands and in this connection the ability to attract professionally qualified employees is a third aspect of capacity termed *professional capacity*. The argument against the small units of government was that a small staff was unable to specialize to the extent required by more and more complicated tasks and cases. Somewhat related is a fourth aspect of capacity, which may be labeled *implementation capacity* and refers to the ability of municipalities to implement legislation and the policies of central government. One example mentioned in the commission report was new legislation that required municipalities to engage in compulsive competitive tendering within the area of home help for the elderly. It was evident that, in particular, the small municipalities had problems living up to the requirement of the law.

DEMOCRACY

A few months before the commission report was published, a new comprehensive study of municipality size and local democracy was published by a group of researchers at the University of Southern Denmark (Kjær & Mouritzen, 2003). The study focused on citizens' perception of local democracy based on a large number of democratic aspects: affiliation, interest in and knowledge about local politics, participation in elections and other kinds of participation, political confidence and self-confidence as well as satisfaction with municipal services.

The main conclusion of the study was that large municipalities are no less democratic than small ones. Interest in local politics, affiliation with the municipality, knowledge about local government politics, the citizens' access to exert influence, and the perception of good local government have nothing to do with the size of the municipality. Only in terms of individual participation, participation in elections, satisfaction with local services and political confidence was there a small tendency that democracy suffers in the group of municipalities of more than 50,000 inhabitants. However, it was impossible to determine when this tendency starts. It is only possible to establish that in the range between 20,000-30,000 inhabitants and probably up to 70,000-80,000, there is a small reduction in individual participation, participation in elections, political confidence and satisfaction with municipal services. Conversely, the study shows that collective participation increases slightly as participation in for example political party activities is more common in larger than in smaller municipalities, where there is more personal contact with local officials and politicians.

Obviously, the study casts serious doubt on the assumption that a dilemma existed between system capacity and citizens' effectiveness or democracy. According to the study, instead of Line *a* in Figure 1, reality was better represented by Line *b* where the dilemma is almost non-existent. Politically, the study effectively, albeit unintentionally, removed the major argument of the opponents of an amalgamation reform, that democracy would suffer.

The political process behind the reforms

We can interpret the course of events in different ways, beginning with the consultation in the Danish Parliament on June 20, 2002, when the Minister for the Interior and Health categorically rejects a local government reform in the shape of a 'centrally determined, detailed and carefully prepared elitist plan'. Not quite two years later to the day, the same minister becomes the anchorman of a 'centrally determined, detailed and carefully prepared elitist plan', which radically transforms the administrative map of Denmark.

Contrary to the local government reform in 1970, we are at the start of the 21st century facing an extremely fast decision process without any preceding popular debate. Prior to the 1970 reform, there had been 12 years of preliminary work with several commission reports and with sufficient time to enter into voluntary municipal mergers. In 2002 the Commission on Administrative Structure is set up like a bolt from the blue. Prior to the November 2001 election, the leading government party, the Liberals, revealed absolutely nothing about such a reform being in the making, should they come into power. Nor were such considerations a part of the government program, which was decided between the Conservatives and the Liberals immediately following the election.

Prior to the 1970 reform it was evident that there were problems in the municipal structure at that time. It was problems that had been mapped out in thorough investigations throughout the country. There were two main problems: First the large municipalities had spread past their boundaries. The old town center was cramped as a municipality without chances of expansion, often with the affluent, employed part of the population living in neighboring municipalities. Second, the small rural districts, of which many had less than 2,000 inhabitants, had problems with sustainability, not least in the heaviest area of their budget, namely the running of modern municipal primary and lower secondary schools. The local government reform was a solution to these problems.

With the recent reform it is difficult to perceive such obvious problems. A major part of the Commission on Administrative Structure's work was actually to map out existing problems. The extent and consequences were disputed. It is no unjust interpretation that the solutions (larger municipalities and fewer, slimmer counties) in today's reform process came before the problems.

It was earlier mentioned that the 1960s local government reform was in preparation for twelve years. This is actually an understatement – by and large it only concerned the structural and financial part of the reform. With regard to what was then called the 'task reform', a gradual transfer of tasks to the municipalities and counties was only begun in 1970. Depending on when you set the final date, it took about 20 years before the process was concluded, and even up through the 1990s did changes in tasks occur. With a few exceptions, each task reorganization was the result of thorough, in-depth analyses and considerations in which were included research, expert knowledge as well as the interested parties involved. These reforms were not made without striking a blow, but at least they were well prepared. They came into being as true children of the Danish corporate society characterized by consensus, as it had developed over a century.

The processes during the 1960s and in 2002 to 2004 are thus fundamentally different. During the second period we have a closed, short process, turning up out of nowhere, without preceding popular debate. It is consistent with modern decision theory, where the term decision windows is used, i.e. brief periods during which it is possible to carry out major changes, and during which it is important to act quickly before the window closes again. The principal actors in the reform process specifically used this figure of speech. Modern decision theory also talks of 'policy entrepreneurs' who use such windows or even create them with a view to promoting their own interests and ideas (see Kingdon, 1984).

The Danish Minister of the Interior certainly acted as a policy entrepreneur once the window was open. He was able to orchestrate a process which allowed strong interests in society to form a coalition in favor of larger municipalities. For many actors in Danish society the establishment of the Commission on Administrative Structure represented a unique opportunity which allowed them to air solutions that had been hidden in the closet for many years just waiting for the right window to open, or for the right problem to which to connect. For many actors a possible reform could also be seen as a solution to a problem they had perceived for years: the Ministry of Finance predicted considerable pressure on public finances in the years to come and had for years perceived the small municipalities as inefficient. Amalgamation could be the solution. The Conservative Party, as the smallest party in the government coalition, had problems making itself visible. The party had for 15 years wanted to do away with the county level. Amalgamations were seen as a means because larger municipalities were a precondition for removing the county level. *Local Government Denmark* (LGDK) had among its members 110 municipalities who had formed their own fraction of poor and small municipalities. One of the requirements for joining was a population of less than 10,000 inhabitants. Amalgamations could be the solution to the problem perceived by LGDK. Also, LGDK was concerned about the increasing degree of state intervention in the daily life of the municipalities and saw the lack of capacity in the small units as one of the main reasons for this trend. Amalgamations were obviously the solution to this problem. Like several other business-related associations, the Confederation of Danish Industries was eager to improve the ability of the public sector to engage in the contracting out of services. Larger municipalities were seen as a solution. The mayors of big cities wanted to expand their kingdoms and a reform was the solution. All these interests, and several others, formed a latent coalition in favor of a reform.

Few actors were against. The Danish Regions obviously did not want to see the number of counties reduced; far less did they want the functions of the intermediate level to be transferred to other levels of government. Similarly, many mayors from the small rural municipalities were opposed to the reform, paradoxically decided and implemented by their own party in the government. The opposing forces were, however, too weak to go against the reform coalition and, as mentioned above, they lost their final ammunition when the report on size and democracy was published in the fall of 2003.

Danish local government at the start of the 21st century

The Danish local government system anno 2007 is thus a result of two major reforms. Below we describe the system as it stands in 2007, although pieces of the information used necessarily have to refer to the years before 2007.

THE SIZE OF MUNICIPALITIES

A comparison of size of municipalities and the size of the local government sector in Denmark and 13 other European countries is found in Table 1 in the form of three indicators: average size, median size and the proportion of municipalities with less than 5,000 inhabitants. The countries, which have been ranked according to the average size of municipalities, seem to fall into three main groups: The United Kingdom and Ireland stand out as one group; the two countries have very large municipalities of more than 100,000 inhabitants on average. There is another category of countries with relatively small municipalities (average under 12,000 and median less than 6,000). In this group of countries over half of the municipalities have less than 5,000 inhabitants. France is the most extreme example in this group: 19 out of 20 municipalities (95 pct.) have less than 5,000 inhabitants; in Switzerland it is 90 pct. and in Spain 86 pct. Denmark used to belong to the middle group, with Portugal, Sweden, the Netherlands and Belgium, characterized by medium sized municipalities and very few municipalities under 5,000 inhabitants.

TABLE 1.

Size of municipalities in selected European countries

	Mean	Median	Pct. below 5,000 inhabitants
Britain	137,000	119,500	0
Ireland	109,000	90,800	0
Denmark after 2006	**55,000**	**43,000**	**3**
Portugal	32,000	15,500	6
Sweden	30,800	15,500	3
The Netherlands	29,200	14,400	10
Denmark after 1970	**19,200**	**10,700**	**7**
Belgium	17,000	11,500	17
Finland	11,500	5,500	49
Norway	10,300	4,500	57
Italy	7,200	2,300	73
Germany	5,600	1,300	80
Spain	4,800	1,400	86
Switzerland	2,600	900	90
France	1,600	1,100	95

Note: The median indicates the 'typical' size of municipalities in a country in the sense that half of the municipalities have a size below this value. The last column shows the percentage of municipalities in a country which have less than 5,000 inhabitants.

Source: Average municipal is taken from Lidström (2003: 183). The median figures and share of municipalities with less than 5,000 inhabitants have been obtained from colleagues in the various countries via personal communications.

THE FUNCTIONS OF LOCAL GOVERNMENT

Often it is postulated that the functions performed by local government are closely related to how large the municipalities are – size being a proxy for the capacity to perform functions. A local government marked by many small localities cannot be trusted with functions that require specialized knowledge or large scale production facilities. This argument was central in the debate about the two Danish amalgamation reforms in 1970 and 2007. Empirically this relationship gains some credibility as indicated by Figure 2, where Denmark is represented by the system that was in place before the 2007 reform. When municipalities are small (i.e. on average approx. 15,000-20,000), the size of the local government sector is rather closely related to the average size of municipalities.[10] However, only when municipalities are relatively large does there seem to be some freedom of decision as to the degree of decentralization

---

10 What is important here is maybe not so much size per se, but rather the fact that a local government system with small municipalities on the average is also typically a system where a large part of the municipalities are rather small.

CRISIS, MIRACLES, AND BEYOND

in a country. In this situation the decision seems to reflect the north-south dimension in Europe: The further north, the higher the degree of decentralization.[11]

FIGURE 2.

Average size of Municipalities and Local Government Expenditures as Percentage of the Gross Domestic Product 1995

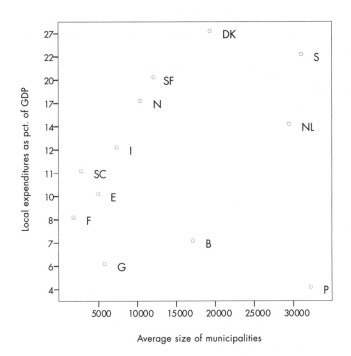

Average size of municipalities

Abbreviations: B: Belgium, DK: Denmark, E: Spain, F: France, G: Germany, I: Italy, N: Norway, NL: the Netherlands, P: Portugal, S: Sweden, SC: Switzerland SF: Finland. Great Britain and Ireland are excluded from the figure.

Sources: OECD National Accounts (1995 figures). Expenditures cover all local government expenditures, not just those that are in the municipal budgets.

Danish local government expenditures have been reduced by approximately 40 billion Danish kroner (old age pensions which are 100 pct. refunded by central government), equivalent to approximately 8 pct. of total public expenditures.

The main functions of municipalities fall into six categories, of which social and health services account for around 60 pct., education and culture for about 20 pct. and administration and planning for about 10 pct. The remaining 10 pct. are divided among urban development, public utilities, roads and capital expenses (2007 budget).[12] In programmatic terms, the four major tasks of

11 Britain and Ireland, which are left out of the figure because of the extreme values on the horizontal dimension, are both placed in the middle on the vertical axis (11 pct. of GDP).

12 Statistics Denmark, Statistikbanken, net expenditures.

municipalities are primary schools, day care programs, programs for the elderly and supplementary benefits. Although old age pensions are administered by the municipalities they are not normally counted as a local responsibility because they are reimbursed 100 pct. by central government and provided according to fixed rules.

The most important function of the counties in the pre-2007 system was the operation of hospitals, which accounted for 45 pct. of total county expenditures. The counties were also responsible for high schools, major roads and special social services. As mentioned earlier the five regions established by 1 January, 2007 merely have operation of the public health system as their main function. Expenses for those functions account for more than 97 pct. of total net expenses (2007).[13]

A list of the major functions of municipalities and regions after the 2007 reform is found in Boxes 1 and 2.

BOX 1.
Responsibilities of the Municipalities after 1 January 2007

Social services: Total responsibility for financing, supply and authority
- Child care
- Primary school, including any special education and special pedagogical assistance for small children
- Special education for adults
- Elder care
- Health care: Preventive treatment, care and rehabilitation that do not take place during hospitalization, treatment of alcohol and drug abuse, home care, local dental care, special dental care and social psychiatry
- Activation and employment projects for the unemployed without insurance in job centers run jointly with the state (10 pilot municipalities undertake the task for the unemployed with insurance on behalf of the state)
- Integration and language education for immigrants
- Citizen service regarding taxation and collection in cooperation with state tax centers
- Supplies and emergency preparedness
- Nature, environment and planning: e.g. specific authority and citizen-related tasks, preparation of local plans and plans regarding waste water, waste and water supply
- Local business service and promotion of tourism
- Participation in regional transport companies
- The local road network
- Libraries, schools of music, local sports facilities and culture

---

Source: http://www.im.dk/publikationer/government_reform_in_brief/kap03.htm

The few programs that have not been transferred to local government are historically linked to labor market organizations (i.e., trade unions and/or employers' associations). This is also true for the labor exchange (run by local

---

13 http://www.regioner.dk/upload/filer/økonomi/regionernes %20budgetter %202007. pdf. Expenses for institutions for exposed groups are not included since most of them are reimbursed by the municipalities.

CRISIS, MIRACLES, AND BEYOND

state offices and labor unions) as well as the occupational safety authorities, which are also run by local/regional state branches.

BOX 2.

Responsibilities of the Regions after 1 January 2007

- Hospital service, including hospitals. psychiatry and health insurance as well as general practitioners and specialists
- Regional development, i.e. nature, environment, business, tourism, employment, education and culture as well as development in the fringe areas of the regions and in the rural districts. Secretarial service for the regional growth fora
- Soil pollution
- Raw material mapping and planning
- Operation of a number of institutions for exposed groups and groups with special needs for social services and special education
- Establishment of transport companies throughout Denmark

Source: http://www.im.dk/publikationer/government_reform_in_brief/kap03.htm

REVENUES

When it comes to revenues, by far the most important source for both tiers of local government used to be the local income tax. In 2004 the municipal rates varied between 16.5 and 23.2 pct. with an average around 20.8 pct. The county rates varied between 11.4 and 12.5 pct. with an average of 11.9 pct. The first year of the new system led to an increase in the municipal tax rate as a consequence of the many new tasks transferred from the counties, and in 2007 the average municipal income tax rate reached 32.7 pct.[14] Local authorities are in principle free to set their own rate of taxation, however with increasing interference from central government (cf. the later section on macroeconomic policies). In 2007, i.e. after the last reform, taxes accounted for 57.3 pct. of total revenues, fees and charges for 18.6 pct. and grants from central government for 22.8 pct. Central grants were divided into two types, general grants and matching grants almost equal in size (Juul, 2007: 33).

VARIATIONS IN REVENUES AND SERVICES

One of the aims of a system of local self-government is that local preferences are allowed to be reflected in the policies pursued. To the extent that there are differences across localities with respect to preferences, we should similarly expect to find variations in policies – and there are quite large differences, cf. Table 2. These variations are based on the system in existence before 2007 (1998 figures).

---

14 Including the so-called health fee (*sundhedsbidrag*) which is fixed at 8 pct.

TABLE 2.

Variations in taxation and spending in selected areas in Danish municipalities, 1998

	Mean	Coeff. of var.
Income tax rate (pct.)	20.4	0.05
Property tax rate (per mille)	11.2	0.45
Day care expenditures (per 0-6 year-old)	24.292	0.22
Primary school expenditures (per 7-16 year-old)	37.137	0.12
Program for elderly (per +66 year-old)	34.448	0.11
Libraries, culture per capita	1.242	0.34
Roads per capita	746	0.25
Administration per capita	3.34	0.14

Note: All mean figures except tax rates are in Danish kroner.

In a comparative context the variations depicted in Table 2 are not dramatic, nor are they negligible. They are indicative (but not proof) of a system where localities are left with some autonomy that appears to vary from area to area. Variation is greatest in areas like day care, culture and roads, and lower in areas like primary schools and programs for the elderly. When it comes to taxation, there is relatively little variation in income tax rates (although the highest and lowest values are 22.8 and 15.5 pct.), while property tax rates vary considerably.

What accounts for such differences? One obvious explanation is that the differences in spending simply reflect differences in spending needs, which may, in principle, be tied to spending through a system of state regulations. In other words, variations per se need not be a sign of local autonomy. Previous research by the author clearly indicates that variations are only slightly reduced after controlling for spending needs (Mouritzen, 1991: 120).

The next obvious explanation is that spending variations are a function of local government wealth. Local taxable income varies quite a bit: in 1994 the coefficient of variation was 0.18. However, due to the equalizing effects of the grant system this figure overstates the actual differences. Taking the grants into account reduces the coefficient of variation to around 08. This is sufficient to be a major cause of service variations among municipalities. Over the last 20 years, many studies of Danish municipalities inspired by the policy output tradition as it developed in Great Britain and the United States have been conducted. They generally show that spending variations are strongly linked to the resource situation of the municipalities (as well as spending needs).

The third explanation focuses on the party political composition of the city council. Although there are nuances in the Danish findings, they seem to confirm the trends found in most other countries according to which party politics is far less important than socioeconomics as a determinant of public policy.

CRISIS, MIRACLES, AND BEYOND

Local elections are held every four years based on proportional representation; that is, each party or nonpartisan list obtains seats in the city council in proportion to the votes carried. In addition, representation on the important local finance committee and various standing committees is based on proportional votes in the council. Each municipality is a single district in electoral terms. While nonpartisan lists used to play an important role in small rural municipalities, the national political parties have gradually gained a near monopoly via their district and municipal organizations. Before the reform close to 10 pct. of the 4,685 municipal council members were elected on a non-partisan list. In the first election after the reform the nonpartisan lists obtained slightly under 6 pct. of the 2,522 seats in the 98 new city councils. Two parties dominate in local politics – the Social Democrats and the Liberal (or Agrarian) Party – and they hold about four out of five mayoral positions. The Social Democrats dominate in the bigger cities, while the Liberal Party has its strongholds in the rural areas of Denmark.

The form of government found in Danish municipalities (and previously counties) may be labeled the 'committee leader' form (Mouritzen & Svara, 2002: Ch. 3): One person, the mayor, is clearly the political and administrative leader of the municipality. However, executive powers are shared: the political leader may have responsibility for some executive functions, but others rest with collegiate bodies, i.e., standing committees composed of elected politicians, and with the CEO.

The political bodies in a Danish municipality are the city council, the finance committee and various standing committees. Committee members are elected by and among city council members on a proportional basis. Executive powers are shared among the committees and the mayor. The standing committees are responsible for the 'immediate administration' of affairs. The finance committee supervises all financial and administrative matters and prepares the budget.

The position of mayor is considered a full time position and is paid accordingly. The mayor is the chairman of the city council and the finance committee. He convenes the council, establishes the agenda, is responsible for the minutes and – most importantly – he is 'superior, daily leader of the municipal administration'. The mayor is thus the formal head of the total municipal administration. However, the mayor cannot interfere with or block decisions taken by the committees. Thus when it comes to specific, day-to-day administrative matters, the standing committees are fully in charge. This is a distinctive break with the reform tradition as presented above, which requires the administration to be organized as a single integrated system as found in e.g. the Southern European strong mayoral systems or the council manager systems in countries like Ireland, Australia and in many US cities (Mouritzen & Svara, 2002: Ch. 3).

An important aspect of participation outside the electoral channel in Denmark is what we refer to as 'institutional democracy' in the form of parental boards, senior citizen councils and consumer boards of various kinds. Perhaps the importance of municipal size diminishes as institutional democracy gains ground. The subsidiarity principle can be strengthened locally. In other words, citizens have day-to-day contact with their local authorities even though they may be physically or administratively farther removed than before the amalgamation. However, user participation has a number of disadvantages as well: It may make the powerful even more powerful and may lead to fragmentation of the local system at the expense of the overall view. A system with large municipalities and extreme use of citizen democracy may very easily lead to perpetual conflicts among organized bodies and interests, while the ordinary citizen is kept out (Andersen et al., 1998) or becomes frustrated with the internal battles.

THE LOCAL GOVERNMENT ASSOCIATIONS

A particular feature of the Danish local government system is the two associations of municipalities and counties. Local Government Denmark (LGDK) which organizes the municipalities and Danish Regions (DR) are among the strongest Danish interest organizations. The two associations are among the few associations in Denmark that are considered legitimate parties in more or less every policy area although the regional association obviously lost considerable influence with the 2007 reform. Their influence manifests itself in all stages of the political-administrative process, from identification of problems to the preparation and decision making stage to the implementation stage itself. The power of the associations is due to several factors.

The Danish inclination towards minority governments indicates an important external factor. Minority governments need support. Through negotiations with the associations, bills may pass more easily through the Danish Parliament. Another factor is that, on the one hand the local government associations make a point of being apolitical, while, on the other hand, they are dominated by two large 'local government parties' the Social Democrats and the Liberals. These factors give them some freedom of maneuver in relation to the political lobbying in parliament, a freedom possessed by very few interest organizations.

Besides this pre-legitimization of political decisions, the involvement of the associations has another important legitimization function. In as much as they have been involved from early on in the decision making process and have approved the outcome, it is expected that counties and municipalities support it. This subsequent legitimization rarely fails, first and foremost because the associations have built up a network through which they closely monitor what goes on among their members. This is taking place through the branches in each region, through the various political committees and through close co-operation with the various associations of municipal chief executive officers. Moreover, in particular the LGDK has built up a considerable consultancy division. Through many daily contacts to municipal actors the department has its finger tightly on the municipal pulse. Should the pulse be uneven, the association's top management will soon be informed and be able to react. The latter point indicates yet another reason why local associations have the power they have: They possess expert knowledge about municipal everyday life, a knowledge that is a commodity in demand among central government ministries.

The role of local government associations in the politico-administrative decision-making process is completely in accordance with Danish corporative tradition. Indeed, perhaps precisely these two associations, together with the Danish Federation of Trade Unions and the Danish Employers' Confederation, are the most striking examples of this tradition. Their important role implies that local government autonomy is not just something that is exclusively determined by government and parliament. On the contrary, through their associations local governments may greatly contribute towards influencing the conditions under which they exist and act. One example is the so-called system of budget cooperation, a distinctive feature of the Danish local governmental system.

MACROECONOMIC CONTROL IN A DECENTRALIZED SYSTEM

A completely decentralized system of government would leave little or no room for central government control of local affairs. But no central government in modern society completely refrains from intervening in local affairs. The ratio-nale for central control of local government may be grounded in concerns for equality or externalities, but in many countries it stems from the importance of the local government sector as a major player in the national economy as indicated by the fact that on average one-third of GDP today is spent by local government. Central governments in various countries have traditionally viewed local governments from quite different perspectives when it comes to control of the national economy. While the Danish local government sector is considered a major component of macroeconomic planning, the U.S. federal government, in contrast, traditionally does not engage the local government sector as a lever in national economic policy.

The experiences of several Western European countries during the last few decades – notably Denmark and Great Britain and lately Sweden and Finland –

have increasingly unveiled the potential clash between national macroeconomic goals and the values connected with local self-determination. The problem is not so much centered on the rationale as such for incorporating the local government sector into national economic policy making, although such a rationale has been and can be contested. More fundamental is the problem of how national governments can exert control over the local sector without serious implications for local governments' ability to adapt to local conditions. In other words, can central governments realize a welfare gain (through an optimal macroeconomic policy) without subsequent welfare loss caused by a consequently less adaptive, efficient, innovative and equalized local government sector?

From an international perspective, the relationship between central and local government in Denmark is distinctive. In Denmark, a special system regulates the total budgets of local governments, the so-called system of budget cooperation in which the local government associations play an important part.

Until the end of the 1970s, municipalities and counties were controlled by central government in three isolated 'pillars'. The first was the 'revenue-sharing pillar'. Here the principles of the present system of general grants were established and the size of the annual grants to counties and municipalities decided. The second pillar could be called the 'spending pillar'. Central government departments and agencies were active in this pillar. Through more or less detailed rules and regulations, demands were made on local governments, and sector planning systems were developed. These systems made it possible for government departments to gain detailed insight into the workings of local government business. The third was the 'budget cooperation pillar'. Through ad hoc agreements and intervention, the government controlled local government spending. This last pillar was the least important of the three. The 1970s were dominated by the introduction of the grant system and an explosive growth in services, while macroeconomic considerations and efforts to limit growth was of secondary importance.

In the first part of the 1980s, the picture changed. Led by the Treasury Department, budget cooperation now became the all important issue, determining what was possible in the other pillars. In practice, the change meant that grant policies and sectoral control were subordinated to controlling aggregate spending and revenue-generating activities of local governments. Since 1979, local government budgets have been regulated by negotiations in the so-called 'Contact Committee', where government representatives meet with local government representatives, i.e., Local Government Denmark, the Association of County Councils in Denmark, and the municipalities of Copenhagen and Frederiksberg. The committee is uniquely Danish. Every year for two and a half decades, only Danish government has been able to forge an agreement on the basic fiscal conditions of local governments. From this perspective, the budget cooperation between national and local governments can be considered a success.

Another criterion of success is whether the agreements have had their intended effect. The answer is probably not. An analysis of municipalities' compliance with the annual agreements for the years 1980 to 2005 shows that in only eight of these years have these agreements been kept (Lotz, 2007: 69). Thus, it is characteristic that the actors, both national and municipal, have had a remarkable ability to adjust the goals to what they actually believed possible. In part, they made exceptions so that areas of growth were kept out of the agreements, and also they were willing to overlook minor infringements. This particular flexibility may be due to a general cultural dislike of confrontation, but perhaps everyone knows that tougher forms of control, e.g. by way of sanctions imposed on individual municipalities, would in the long run lead to an unbearable situation for all the parties concerned.

Only twice in the period 1980 to 2005 (in the mid-1980s and in 2003) did the government intervene by punishing localities that did not meet the spending limits. Studies carried out by the author (Mouritzen, 1991) indicate that spending goals aimed at individual local governments are highly problematic, particularly if they are enforced by economic sanctions punishing governments that fail to live up to the established goals. Such instruments were used extensively in Great Britain during the 1980s and in certain periods during the same era by the Conservative-led Danish government. This policy instrument leads to a 'frozen' public sector with little or no adaptation to changes in local socioeconomic conditions and, perhaps even worse seen from a macroeconomic viewpoint, to little or no adaptation to regional shifts in the economy.

References

Andersen, Vibeke Normann, Rikke Berg & Roger Buch Jensen (1998). 'Omstilling og servicedemokrati i kommunerne – politikerrollen under forandring'. Politica 30, 3: 324-39.

Commission on Administrative Structure (2004). *Recommendation no. 1434.*

Danske Kommuner 12: 17-18.

Dahl, Robert A. & Edward R. Tufte (1973). *Size and Democracy.* Stanford: Stanford University Press.

Juul, Thorkil (2007). *Håndbog i kommunernes og regionerne nye økonomi.* Copenhagen: Jurist- og Økonomforbundets Forlag.

Kingdon, J.W. (1984). *Agendas, Alternatives and Public Policies.* London: Little Brown & Company.

Kjær, Ulrik & Poul Erik Mouritzen (eds.) (2003). *Kommunestørrelse og lokalt demokrati.* Odense: University of Southern Denmark Press.

Lidström, Anders (2003). *Kommunsystem i Europa.* Stockholm: Publica.

Lotz, Jørgen (2007). 'Spillet om kommunernes økonomi', in Svend Lundtorp & Max Rasmussen (eds.), *Rigtigt Kommunalt. Ledelse i kommunerne og amter fra reform til reform*. København: Handelshøjskolens Forlag, pp. 33-71.

Ministry of the Interior and Health (2004a). *Det nye Danmark*. See http://www.detnyedanmark.dk

Ministry of the Interior and Health (2004b). *Agreement on a Structural Reform*. See http://www.im.dk/publikationer/agreement/index.html

Mouritzen, Poul Erik (1989a). 'City Size and Citizens' Satisfaction: Two Competing Theories Revisited'. *European Journal of Political Research* 17: 661-88.

Mouritzen, Poul Erik (1989b). 'Fiscal Policy-Making in Times of Resource Scarcity. The Danish Case, in Susan Clarke (ed.), *Urban Innovation and Autonomy: The Political Implications of Policy Change*. Newbury Park: Sage Publications, pp. 100-27.

Mouritzen, Poul Erik (1991). *Den politiske cyklus*. Aarhus: Forlaget Politica.

Mouritzen, Poul Erik & James H. Svara (2002). *Leadership at the Apex. Politicians and Administrators in Western Local Governments*. Pittsburgh: Pittsburgh University Press.

Mouritzen, Poul Erik (2007). *Dinamarca El Govern Local: Preparat per a la Reforma?* (available at http://www.diba.cat/innovacio/fitxers/ml10_dinamarca.pdf

Newton, Kenneth (1982). 'Is Small Really so Beautiful? Is Big Really so Ugly?' *Political Studies* 30: 190-206.

Ostrom, Elinor (1972). 'Metropolitan Reform: Propositions Derived from Two Traditions'. *Social Science Quarterly* 53: 474-93.

7 HEALTH CARE IN DENMARK

Adapting to Cost Containment in the 1980s and Expenditure Expansion in the 1990s

Thomas Pallesen and Lars Dahl Pedersen

In the 1960s and 1970s, Danes considered their health care system to be one of the best in the Western world. They received high quality treatment delivered by well-trained physicians and nurses at high-tech hospitals densely scattered all over the country. Part of their pride stemmed from the health care system's general principle of free access for all and a vast array of expensive health care services available to anyone in need, irrespective of individual income or wealth. Two physicians phrased it this way: 'The best possible treatment was expected to be available for everybody regardless of costs and the Danes seemed willing to pay these costs mainly through taxation' (Søndergaard & Krasnik, 1984: 179).

But in the eyes of both the public and the producers of health care services, the happy days came to an end in the late 1970s. At this time attitudes changed as a consequence of public expenditure cutbacks in general and in the health care sector in particular, all of which had been triggered by the rapid increase in public expenditures in the 1960s and 1970s. In the early 1970s, the Ministry of Finance assessed the perspectives for the Danish economy in two major reports (Ministry of Finance, 1971, 1973) and concluded that the growth of public expenditures had to be restricted in order to eliminate the persistent balance of payment deficit and to avoid huge tax increases. Health care expenditure, one of the fastest growing items of public expenditure, received special government attention. A report by a government commission specifically addressed cost containment in the health care sector (Ministry of the Interior, 1977) and was only the first in a series of similar reports delivered in the 1980s. The 1977 commission recommended greater emphasis on prevention and further elaboration of planning and coordination in the health care sector in order to bring expenditures under control. In the short run, the report recommended introducing 'envelope' budgets with overall spending limits. This recommendation was echoed in commission reports in the 1980s (Ministry of the Interior, 1984, 1985, 1986, 1987).

In the eyes of the public, the Danish 'socialized' medical system was no longer as successful as it had once been. Not surprisingly, the public attitude was supported by health care providers: 'This sublime picture of what foreigners sometimes call the Danish case of successful socialized medicine is now beginning to wither away' (Søndergaard & Krasnik, 1984: 179). The public believed that efforts to contain health care costs had gone too far. Consistently more than two thirds of the electorate, irrespective of political orientation, favored increased health care spending. The political elite seemed satisfied with the results of the cost containment. Success came to mean something quite different. By the early 1990s, Denmark had one of the cheapest health care systems in the Western world (Ministry of the Interior, 1997).

By the mid-1990s, pressure from providers started to have an impact on the political elite. Policy makers increasingly found that the starving of the health care sector had gone too far and a series of supplemental allocations were channeled to the health care sector (Ministry of Finance, 1997). This policy change coincided with the change of government in 1993 when a Social Democratic cabinet took over after 10 years of right wing governance. However, it would be wrong to equate the change in health care policy with the cabinet change in 1993. The cost containment policy of the 1980s and early 1990s as well as the more lavish policy beginning in the second part of the 1990s were supported by a broad coalition of Social Democrats and right wingers.

The aim of the chapter is threefold. The first aim is to outline the basic traits of the Danish health care system. Although 'socialized medicine' is a catchy phrase, it is not very precise and it is often used polemically. The Danish health care system is indeed socialized, if socialized medicine is equated with public intervention in the health care sector. But the type and degree of public intervention vary significantly across health care areas. Furthermore, the Danish health care system is not very socialized if socialized medicine is equated with strong central government planning and control. Danish health care policy is only to some extent a national policy matter. Many important decisions are decentralized to lower administrative levels – the municipalities and in particular the regions (until 2007, the regions were called counties). The modes of public intervention in Danish health care services are described in the second section.

The second aim of the chapter is to discuss the widespread notion of a uniquely cheap, effectively cost-contained Danish health care system. The Danish health care expenditure figures support(ed) the image of Denmark as a low spender among OECD countries. However, a more comprehensive account of the health care system includes the structure of treatment and health care facilities. This is examined briefly in section three, which is a comparative inquiry that includes Denmark, Sweden, Germany, the United Kingdom and the Netherlands. This comparison indicates that cost containment in the health care sector has been pursued rather successfully in other countries as well and that cost containment in Denmark has had negative consequences for the volume of health care services and the capacity of health care systems.

In the final section of the chapter, we describe the shift to a more generous health care policy in the 1990s and point to the conclusion that from the perspective of national politicians, the decentralized Danish health care system is better suited to hidden cutbacks than visible service improvements.

Denmark – a case of socialized medicine?

As noted, the Danish health care system is sometimes characterized as an example of 'socialized medicine', but this is not how the Danes themselves would characterize their health care system. The term 'socialized medicine' gives the impression that right wingers prefer another way of organizing the health care system. This is not so. The basic goals and values of the health care system are not a matter of political dispute (Christensen, 1992). One of these undisputed goals is the principle of free and equal access to medical treatment based on need, regardless of age, sex, wealth, employment, prudent behavior, etc. Nevertheless, whether the Danish health care system is labeled 'socialized medicine' or characterized by its free and equal access, neither of these catchwords precisely describes the health care system.

Regardless of labeling, both catchwords refer to how the Danish health care system is financed. The core of the idea of free and equal access is that no one has to pay directly for health care services. Health care services are financed by general taxes, primarily income taxes, independent of the individual's actual or potential use of health care services. The introduction of user fees has been raised in the Danish health care debate. A few 'free' services have been singled out as potential targets for user fees: GP consultations, the 'hotel' costs of hospitalization, a few surgical procedures such as cosmetic operations and sterilization, and emergency room visits at hospitals. User fees for these services have not been introduced even though the suggested level of co-payment has been quite modest, e.g., a DKK 100-200 fee (approximately $20-$40) for a visit to a GP or a hospital emergency room.

Although proposals to introduce user fees have been rejected, it would be wrong to claim that no one has to pay in case of illness. The Danes do pay a share of the health care expenditure. The public tax-financed share of the total health care expenditures is high, but declining slightly. In the 1960s, the public share was close to 90 pct., while it was down to 83 pct. in 1995 (Ministry of Health, 2000). The out-of-pocket payment from each Danish citizen in 1997 was DKK 2,700 (approximately $540). The main areas of direct user payment are pharmaceuticals, dental care, and physiotherapy. The patient covers close to 50 pct. of the bill for dental care, but old, poor and chronically ill are to some extent exempted from co-payment. Physiotherapy outside hospitals and treatment by chiropractors are subsidized only up to a certain number of visits per year. Many, about one quarter of the population, is insured for out-of-pocket health care expenses by the private health insurance organization 'Danmark'.

Thus, 'free access' to Danish health care is modified in several ways. Free access to health care facilities and services applies only to core health care services: admission and treatment at acute care hospitals and the vast majority of services delivered by general practitioners. At acute care hospitals, there are no charges, and only very special GP services such as vaccinations for tropical diseases, medical certificates needed to get a driver's license, etc. are paid by the users.

The public share of total health care expenditures is about 80 pct., just one indication of the profound public commitment to the health care system. This figure does not, however, tell much about the mode or extent of the public intervention in the structure, administration, or delivery of health care. In principle, public involvement in the health care sector could be restricted to financing services and leaving decisions about how to spend the money to citizens and/or providers (including possibly private providers). At the other extreme, public involvement could entail not only financing, but also the production of services by institutions owned and managed as public organizations. A wide range of possibilities of mixed systems between these two extremes is conceivable as well.

In fact, public intervention varies significantly within the Danish health care system. Hospitals, the most expensive segment of the health care system, which absorb almost two thirds of total health expenditures, are organized as publicly owned and managed institutions. All employees, including medical specialists, are salaried employees. Furthermore, hospitals generally produce most of their support services in-house. Catering, laundry services, cleaning, technical services (building maintenance and other infrastructure tasks), and laboratory services are often an integral part of the hospital organization. When smaller hospitals lack this range of in-house production, most of these services are typically delivered by another public hospital, and only occasionally by a private firm. Larger hospitals often have a very broad range of in-house services, including notably the production and dispensing of pharmaceuticals. All in all, private firms deliver only a modest 4 pct. of total hospital outlays (Pallesen, 1997a).

In effect, Danish hospitals closely approximate the concept of 'socialized medicine', but the rest of the health care system is organized differently. Legally, GP and specialist practitioners are private entrepreneurs. Their private practice is, however, tightly regulated. The total number of GPs is not formally restricted, and anyone with the required educational qualifications and certification is allowed to practice, but entrance to the 'business' is *de facto*

CRISIS, MIRACLES, AND BEYOND

restricted. The right to pass the bill to the public health insurance system for services rendered is licensed only to a limited number of physicians. More than 99 pct. of a GP's income comes from public funds. The remuneration of general practitioners is a mixture of fees for services and per capita payments, while specialists and dentists are remunerated solely on the basis of fees for services. The GP receives a lump sum per capita payment for each patient listed with the practice. This per capita payment and the fees for service rates are determined in negotiations between the professional associations and a joint body representing the regions (Søgaard, 1991).

Remuneration of GPs accounts for only about 5 pct. of total health care expenditures, but GPs plays a key role as 'gatekeepers' to the specialized part of the health care system, e.g., the hospitals and specialized practitioners.

Hospital treatment and treatment by specialized practitioners normally require referral from a GP. There are only a few exceptions to this rule: direct admission to a hospital in case of acute emergency, and access to a specialized practitioner within a few specialties (ear, nose and throat; eyes). A small part of the population (approximately 2 pct.) pays a limited amount of the practitioner's bill in order to have direct access to all kinds of specialized practitioners without a GP referral. In addition, the GPs are important gatekeepers in relation to the consumption of pharmaceuticals. Most pharmaceuticals require a prescription from a medically trained person, normally a GP.

The pharmaceutical area represents still another kind of public involvement in the health care system. Central government tightly regulates production, distribution, and sale of pharmaceuticals (Juul et al., 1989). Production and distribution are publicly controlled in a number of ways. Pharmaceutical prices are regulated and subsidized. Although pharmacies, like private practitioners, legally are private organizations, the number of pharmacies is limited, and they have the exclusive right to sell pharmaceuticals (Ministry of Health, 1999).

In sum, public involvement in Danish health care takes a variety of forms, which can be described as more or less 'socialized'. Most people associate the term 'socialized medicine' with a centralized, central government health care system. In this respect, the Danish system is not 'socialized' because health care in many ways is a local government responsibility. The central government stipulates the overall legal framework for the health care system, including the regulation of patients' rights. Most importantly, central government interferes in the management of the hospital services by authorizing clinical specialties. This task is the responsibility of the National Health Care Board (*Sundhedsstyrelsen*), which is a professionally staffed directorate under the Ministry of Health (*Sundhedsministeriet*). The Board enjoys a *de facto* independent status in the central government hierarchy, although its decisions in principle are the responsibility of the Health Secretary. The Board is expected to apply professional standards to its planning decisions as well as the administration and authorization of the medical and paramedical professions, which is the second major function of the National Health Care Board.

Finally, the municipalities have responsibility for a minor part of the health care system. They organize visiting nurse services for infants along with dental care and nurses at primary schools. More importantly in terms of public expenditure, the municipalities organize other services in the gray zone between health care and social services, notably nursing homes and home care for the elderly. These services are considered social services rather than health care services in the Danish public sector.

While the term 'socialized medicine' has been used to characterize the Danish health care system, we would argue that a system with strong, but diversified public involvement is a more precise way to characterize the Danish health care system. Also from the perspective of the patient or consumer of the health care services the health care system is far from liberal. The main route of consumer influence is indirect via elections to the local, regional, and national government bodies. Patients' rights and choices are also somewhat limited. Patients can choose their own doctor among the licensed GPs, and it is the GP who decides if a patient needs hospital treatment or not. There is some choice of the specific hospital provider. GPs can refer their patients to all the public hospitals authorized for 'basic treatment,' while the most advanced, specialized hospitals are exempted. Elective patients, waiting for treatment, have the right to choose a provider, also private hospitals in Denmark and abroad, if the waiting time exceeds one month.

The patients' legal rights in cases of malpractice are also somewhat limited. Patient complaints are referred to the so-called Patient Board of Complaint, which is an independent public authority chaired by a judge, but dominated by regional and professional representatives. The Board is entitled to criticize medical staff and can submit serious cases of malpractice to the public prosecutor, who eventually may take the case to court. Although patients' rights and freedom of choice in an international comparative perspective may seem limited, most Danes accept this paternalistic organization of the health care system. The popular acceptance of the health care system is indicated by the fact that only 2 pct. of the population has opted for an unlimited right to change general practitioner and unrestricted access to specialists and second opinions, even though the price of these options is very modest. Most people also express satisfaction with health care system (Ministry of Health, 2001), and they consider the system to be economically rational (Ministry of Health, 2000). This widespread belief that the Danish health care system is comparatively cheap is critically discussed in the next section.

The Danish exception: A rich country, low spender

Table 1 ranks the OECD countries along three dimensions: per capita GDP, per capita health expenditures, and share of health expenditures in GDP in 1992. Not surprisingly, the United States spends the highest share of its GDP – 13.8 pct. – on health care. The ranking of per capita GDP generally corresponds with the ranking of per capita health expenditures among OECD countries. The rankings differ by more than three places in only six of the 25 countries.

TABLE 1.

Gross Domestic Product and Health Expenditures, OECD countries (1992)

	GDP per capita (US$)	Rank	Health expenditure per capita (US$)	Rank	Health expenditure as percentage of GDP (pct.)	Rank
Switzerland	34703	1	3249	1	9.4	4
Luxembourg	32404	2	2177	5	6.7	21
Japan	29477	3	2064	10	7.0	19
Sweden	28559	4	2166	6	7.6	15
Germany	27764	5	2398	3	8.6	7
Denmark	27380	6	1817	14	6.6	22
Iceland	26460	7	2155	8	8.1	12
Norway	26394	8	2178	4	8.3	11
Austria	23525	9	2107	9	9.0	6
France	23043	10	2159	7	9.4	3
United States	22396	11	3094	2	13.8	1
Belgium	21990	12	1783	16	8.1	13
Italy	21513	13	1821	13	8.5	10
Netherlands	21094	14	1797	15	8.5	8
Finland	21070	15	1972	12	9.4	5
Canada	19819	16	2031	11	10.2	2
U.K.	18005	17	1264	18	7.0	18
Australia	16960	18	1442	17	8.5	9
Spain	14772	19	1069	19	7.2	16
Ireland	14378	20	973	20	6.8	20
New Zealand	11888	21	911	21	7.7	14
Portugal	9481	22	672	22	7.1	17
Greece	7558	23	415	23	5.5	23
Mexico	3795	24	186	24	4.9	24
Turkey	2720	25	80	25	2.9	25

Source: Program OECD Health Data (Credes) (1995).

Note: Expenditure terms converted using exchange rates

Empirical studies generally show a close statistical link between the wealth of a country and the level of health expenditure (Kleiman, 1974; Newhouse, 1977; Gerdtham et al., 1992; Leidl, 1994; Pedersen & Maarse, 1995). This close link has been referred to as the 'iron law of health expenditure' (Culyer, 1989). Table 1 shows that Denmark seems to be an exception to the 'iron law' because the health expenditure rank does not correspond closely to its GDP rank. Denmark ranks sixth in per capita GDP, yet only 14th in per capita health expenditures. Thus the table seems to confirm the notion of a cheap and effectively cost-contained health care system in Denmark.

The picture of Denmark as a rich nation with low health expenditures can probably be carried too far. International comparisons of health care spending are restricted by the availability of appropriate and comparable international statistics. The OECD offers a set of fairly well-developed health statistics compared with available data concerning other policy areas. Nevertheless, Schieber and Poullier (1991: 9) have listed some of the specific difficulties with international health care statistics: 'data are generally not comparable; systems performance cannot be easily evaluated because of our inability to measure health outcomes; it is difficult to measure and control for social, medical, cultural, demographic, and economic differences across countries; and transferability of policies across countries is problematic'.

In this section of the chapter, we critically discuss the notion of Denmark as a 'rich country, low health care spender' by comparing the Danish health care system with some of the countries that normally serve as yardsticks for comparison: Germany, the Netherlands, Sweden and the United Kingdom. These five Northwestern European countries also happen to belong to two different groups of health care systems.

Provision of health care services stands out as a main government responsibility in modern welfare states. At a very general level, all Western European health care systems are financed by government-arranged compulsory, income-related, health care insurance or general taxation. Poor as well as better-off citizens, bad risks and better risks are all pooled together. Apart from this very general principle, the specific welfare state involvement in the health care sector differs from country to country. The arrangements can be divided into three groups (OECD, 1992).

The first model is the reimbursement model. Users pay for services directly to health care suppliers, but are wholly or partly refunded or reimbursed by publicly regulated insurers. In principle, the demand and supply of health services are left to the market. In the second model, the public contract model, the supply and demand of health services is determined by contracts between publicly regulated insurers and private providers. In the third model, the public integrated model, health care is directly provided at publicly owned institutions.

None of the health care systems in Western Europe completely conform to one of these three models. In most countries, the health care system is a mixture of elements from different models. Second, important characteristics of the health care systems are not included in the models. An important omission is the comprehensive and complex governmental regulation, which is present in all the Western European health care systems, irrespective of the predominant health care model. There are also various ways to fund and remunerate health care providers. This regulation can narrow or widen the real variation among health care systems.

Nevertheless, the three models point to important differences among the health care systems included in this study. Hospital services in Denmark, Sweden and the United Kingdom are delivered by publicly owned and financed institutions, e.g., the public integrated model, while Dutch and German hospital services are delivered according to the public contract model.

Taking into account Schieber and Poullier's warnings concerning the cross-national comparability of health care statistics, we focus not on expenditure figures, but rather on a number of basic health functions and activities. We compare how the countries studied in this section vary in these respects. National definitions of the health care system may differ, but certain basic functions and activities are part of any health care system. Hence, these basic functions and activities may serve as a more solid basis for comparison, or at least they help to shed light on different national health care system definitions.

TABLE 2.
Health care activities in Denmark, Germany, the Netherlands, Sweden and United Kingdom (1995)

	In-patient bed days per citizen	Acute in-patient bed days per citizen	In-patient admission per citizen	Acute in-patient admission per citizen	Acute staff per bed	Average length of in-patient stay
Denmark	1.5	1.1	19.8	18.8	3.2	7.3
Germany	2.9	2.0	21.9	19.2	1.5	14.2
Netherlands	3.6	1.0	11.1	10.3	2.3	32.8
Sweden	1.4	0.8	18.5	16.2	n.a.	7.8
U.K.	1.7	1.0	15.4	n.a.	3.7	9.9

Source: OECD Health Data (2000).

Denmark and Sweden have the lowest number of in-patient bed days among the five countries, 1.5 and 1.4 in-patient bed days per citizen, respectively. This is slightly less than in the United Kingdom, but only half the in-patient bed days in Germany and the Netherlands. The OECD also reports the number of in-patient bed days in acute care hospitals. Acute care hospitals are defined as institutions where the average length of stay is less than 30 days. Germany has the highest number of bed days in acute care hospitals, while the other four countries have only half the German number. The Netherlands stands out with a low number of in-patient admissions whether measured as total or only acute admissions. The other four countries have roughly the same number, but at a higher level than the Netherlands. In Denmark, Sweden and United Kingdom the average length of an in-patient stay is the same, while the average in Germany and especially the Netherlands is significantly higher. Also the staffing of hospital beds is at the same level in Denmark and the United Kingdom, while Germany and the Netherlands have fewer personnel resources per hospital bed.

These structural features of the five countries' health care systems point to the conclusion that the Danish health care system is in no way unique. Rather, Denmark, Sweden and the United Kingdom constitute a group of countries with a highly staffed, acute-oriented hospital system with a low number of in-patient bed days and a high turnover. Germany and the Netherlands constitute another group of countries with less personnel resources per bed and more and, on average, longer in-patient bed days.

Hence, the data concerning structural features of the health care systems in these five countries reveals considerable variation in the overall in-patient figures, both within and across the two groups of systems. The figures also indicate that the health care systems are defined differently, instead of functioning in different ways (see also van Mosseveld & van Son, 1999 for a similar conclusion). In terms of the core functions of the health care systems, i.e., the number of acute bed days and number of acute admissions, there are strong similarities among four of the five countries, and Denmark is one of the four in both cases. Hence, structural differences in these health care systems are related – not to the acute core of health care services, but rather in what constitutes hospital services. In Denmark – as opposed notably to the Netherlands – mental institutions and nursing homes are generally not included in statistics on health care facilities, because they are organized as social services. Thus, while the Netherlands includes a number of nursing homes as health care facilities, Denmark does not. The total capacity in nursing homes and other round-the-clock institutions was 7.6 beds per 1000 inhabitants in Denmark in 1992 (Statistisk Tiårsoversigt, 1994). This number is comparable to the capacity in other in-patient institutions in the Netherlands (7.2 beds per 1000 inhabitants).

In conclusion, the Danish peculiarity – the low health care expenditures compared to GDP per capita – is in part due to a different and narrower definition of health care. While total health expenditures and total number of bed days in the health care services are comparatively low in Denmark, the differences disappear when the main health care functions are considered.

Five countries adapting to cost containment in the 1980s

Most industrialized countries aimed to contain health care cost in the 1980s (Henke, 1992: 245). In the 1960 and 1970s, health expenditure gradually consumed an increasing share of the national income. In most countries, efforts to contain costs often did not mature until the early 1980s. Table 3 displays the changes in health expenditures as a fraction of GDP and the real growth in health expenditures during the 1970s and 1980s.

TABLE 3.

Health expenditures as share of GDP (pct.) and real growth in per capita health expenditures, 1970 to 1980 and 1980 to 1990

	Health care expenditures as a percentage of GDP			Real growth in per capita health expenditures (pct.)	
	1970	1980	1990	1970 to 1980	1980 to 1990
Denmark	6.1	6.7	6.5	+35	+16
Germany	5.9	8.4	8.3	+84	+20
Netherlands	5.9	7.9	8.0	+65	+ 17
Sweden	7.1	9.4	8.6	+54	+9
United Kingdom	4.5	5.9	6.0	+50	+36

Source: Program OECD Health Data (1995).

Note: Real growth is computed as absolute changes corrected by the GDP deflator.

The five countries developed differently in the 1970s and the 1980s. Throughout the 1970s, health expenditures grew more rapidly than GDP – but to a different extent, 35 pct. in Denmark and 84 pct. in Germany. In the 1980s, real growth in health expenditures was 9 pct. in Sweden, 16 pct. to 20 pct. in Denmark, the Netherlands and Germany, and 36 pct. in the United Kingdom. All countries experienced much lower real growth in the 1980s than in the 1970s, with health care costs rising roughly at the same rate as total national income. Thus, if reduction in real growth rates is a measure of success, cost containment was apparently achieved in all five countries. After expanding in the 1970s, health expenditures no longer continuously consumed a higher share of GDP in the 1980s. This is not a cutback in a more strict sense: health care costs continued to increase in real terms in the 1980s, but unlike previous decades, costs grew at the same rate as the overall economy.

If cost containment was a success in the 1980s, a directly related, but seldom posed question is how the health care systems in different countries adapted to cost containment. At least three ways of adaptation is possible: adaptation through structural changes; adaptation in services provided; and/or adaptation through changes in manpower and facilities (Pallesen & Pedersen, 1993). We now consider each option in turn.

TABLE 4.
Change (pct.) in per capita health expenditures for three major functions, 1980-90

	Total Health Care Expenditures	In-patient care	Ambulatory services	Pharmaceuticals
Denmark	+16	+ 9	+24	+14
Germany	+20	+20	+22	+31
Netherlands	+17	+11	+14	+49
Sweden	+ 9	..	..	+37
United Kingdom	+36	+12	..	+46

Source: Program OECD Health Data (1995).

Aggregate changes in health expenditures reveal differences among different categories of health care services throughout the 1980s. The three major categories in health care are shown in Table 4. In none of the countries did the three main categories of health care services decline. Yet, growth rates differed across the different services. Unfortunately, disaggregated data is not fully available for either Sweden with the lowest real growth in total health expenditure or the United Kingdom with the highest real increase in health expenditures in the 1980s. For the other countries, real growth rates are smaller for in-patient care expenditure than for the other categories of health services. Pharmaceutical costs increased considerably in all these countries, between 14 pct. in Denmark and 49 pct. in the Netherlands. With Denmark as the exception, expenditure for ambulatory services increased less than in-patient care expenditure in the 1980s. Apparently, cost containment first of all affected expenditure on in-patient care.

TABLE 5.
Change (pct.) in number of total in-patient care beds, acute care hospital beds and psychiatric beds, 1980-90

	Total in-patient beds	Acute care beds	Psychiatric beds
Denmark	-31	-19	-61
Germany	-7	-1	-14
Netherlands	-1	-12	-1
Sweden	-15	-16	-46
United Kingdom	-26	-20	-39

Source: Program OECD Health Data (1995).

CRISIS, MIRACLES, AND BEYOND

This observation leads us to scrutinize more closely the changes in in-patient services. One likely explanation of reduced relative cost is changes in the facilities. Table 5 outlines the changes in in-patient care beds. The number of in-patient care beds decreased considerably throughout the 1980s, with Germany as the only exception. However, the decreases in bed capacities were not uniform. Denmark and the United Kingdom reduced the number of in-patient beds by more than 25 pct. In Sweden the reduction was 15 pct., and in the Netherlands it was only 7 pct. Again with Germany as the exception, the number of acute care beds was reduced by between 12 pct. in the Netherlands and 20 pct. in the United Kingdom.

As far as the number of psychiatric beds is concerned, the Netherlands is the exception: throughout the 1980s, the number of psychiatric beds declined only 1 pct. In Germany, however, the number of psychiatric beds decreased by 14 pct. Most dramatic was the decrease in psychiatric beds in the United Kingdom (down 39 pct.), Sweden (down 46 pct.) and Denmark (down 61 pct.). The reduction in Denmark is quite dramatic. In just a decade, the number of psychiatric beds was reduced by almost two thirds, and the trend continued in the 1990s: between 1990 and 1992, the number of psychiatric beds was further reduced by one quarter.

One interpretation of Tables 4 and 5 is that cost containment was achieved in the United Kingdom and Denmark through a substantial reduction in hospital bed capacity. In-patient institutions in the Netherlands and Germany have not experienced similar cutbacks in bed capacity. Denmark stands out as the country with the highest reductions in bed capacity throughout the 1980s. One third of the total in-patient beds, one fifth of the acute care beds, and almost two thirds of the psychiatric beds were eliminated in the 1980s. These reductions resulted in lower growth rates for in-patient care expenditure than for other categories of health care services, and for the comparatively lower growth in in-patient care expenditure in Denmark than in the other countries.

Reductions in the number of hospital beds are possibly related to changes in medical technology. However, some medical technologies increase expenditure because certain treatments become possible, e.g., liver and heart transplants. Other changes in medical technology make cost reductions possible, e.g., therapies that reduce the demand for expensive in-patient care. One example is the treatment of stomach ulcers with pharmaceuticals instead of surgery. Medical developments tend to move quickly across borders among advanced industrial states, and we can expect implementation of new technologies to occur almost simultaneously in the five countries. Nevertheless, there seems to be no direct link between changes in medical technology, changes in health care facilities, and changes in hospital costs.

The impact of cost containment on output is difficult to evaluate. Output is difficult to measure in health care in general and in hospitals in particular (Pallesen & Pedersen, 1993; Pallesen, 1997b). In hospital services, two traditional output measures are used: the number of bed days and the number of patients admitted to hospitals. Used simultaneously, they are the best available proxies of hospital productivity. Table 6 shows that the two output measures point in different directions. If output is measured as number of bed days, then output has decreased – less in countries with increasing hospital costs, more in countries with constant or decreasing costs. If number of admissions measures output, the evidence points to the opposite conclusion. In all the countries except the Netherlands, the number of admissions increased throughout the 1980s. Furthermore, there is no direct correlation between changes in hospital costs and changes in the number of admissions.

TABLE 6.

Change (pct.) in output from in-patient institutions and in inpatient staff ratios, 1980-90

	Bed days per capita	Admission rates (pct. pop.)	Total staff per available bed	Nurses per available bed
Denmark	-26	+16	+52	+91
Germany	- 8	+11	+21	+43
Netherlands	-10	- 7	+18	+10
Sweden	-26	+ 7	..	..
U.K.	-17	+35	+48	+63

Source: Program OECD Health Data (1995).
Note: 1980-89. Estimate based on period 1980-86 and 1987-91, due to change in definition in 1987.

Table 7 shows the changes in employment within the health services. The Table indicates that cost containment in the 1980s was not associated with cutbacks in the number of professional health care employees. Total employment was higher in 1990 than in 1980 in all five countries. Germany had the most striking expansion of total employment in professional health care services (27 pct.); Denmark and the United Kingdom the smallest (3 pct. and 2 pct., respectively).

TABLE 7.
Change (pct.) in employment (full time equivalents) in health services, 1980-1990

	Total Employment	Physicians	Certified Nurses	Other Staff
Denmark	+3	+28	+29	-9
Germany	+27	+35	+29	+25
Netherlands	+8	+39	..	..
Sweden	+8	+34	+35	+1
U.K.	+2	+19	+23	0

Source: Program OECD Health Data (Credes) (1995).
Note: Germany 1980-89.

The change in total employment reveals considerable differences across the various health professions. The number of physicians increased considerably in the 1980s, by 19 pct. in the United Kingdom and 39 pct. in the Netherlands. The number of qualified nurses also increased, by 23 pct. in the United Kingdom and by 35 pct. in Sweden. These figures indicate that other professions and occupations shouldered cost containment while the number of physicians and nurses continued to expand. However, the countries differ with respect to the extent the increasing employment of physicians and nurses was counteracted by reductions in the employment of other staff.

The change in total employment and composition of health staffing in the five countries is an interesting puzzle. It raises the question why the increase in the number of nurses and physicians has been uniform while the development in other staff has not? One possible answer is that changes in employment are related to changes in the number and kind of health care services provided. In this way, the increasing number of admissions could explain the increased number of physicians because the number of admissions predominantly determines the physicians' workload. And it could be argued that the reduced number of bed days explains the reduced number of other staff members because many services provided by other staff, such as number of meals, cleaning, laundering, are directly related to the number of bed days.

However, this explanation is flawed in a number of ways. We can neither explain the Dutch case where the number of physicians increased despite fewer admissions, nor can we explain the German case in which other staff increased despite fewer bed days. Nor can we explain the increasing number of nurses in all the countries for which we have data because the workload of the nursing staff is determined by both the number of admissions and bed days, but more by the latter than the former.

It points to the conclusion that the health care system is also a political institution with internal power struggles. Traditionally, doctors have a greater say than other staff groups in this power structure. However, the figures of increasing nursing employment may indicate that the nursing profession is catching up. At least in the Danish case nurses have managed to raise their profile. The organizational changes in the Danish hospitals in the 1980s and early 1990s represent a milestone is this development: the nurses obtained representation on the hospital executive management board (together with the general manager and the chief physician) and got an equal say in the joint management team of a physician and nurse at the clinical departmental level. In this way the nursing profession may have obtained a platform for further increases in the number of nurses (Damgaard & Pallesen, 1999).

Different ways of cost containing

While a closer look at the international health care data makes it hard to sustain the picture of the Danish health care sector as a very special case, the analysis distills basically two ways of pursuing cost containment in the health care sector (Pedersen, 1996). One way is to allow total health expenditure to increase a bit more than total domestic expenditure combined with a rather modest reduction in the capacity and activity in the health care sector. This way Germany and the Netherlands have managed cost containment. Another way is to keep the growth in the health care expenditures below the growth in the total domestic expenditure combined with a considerable reduction in the capacity and activity of the health care sector. This way United Kingdom, Sweden and Denmark have managed cost containment.

This observation leads to – at least – two points. First, the Western European health care systems vary, although public involvement is present everywhere. Different forces are at work in the Western European health care systems, leading to different ways of adapting to cost containment. Second, the attempts to contain cost in the health care sector illustrate the severe problems of obtaining macroeconomic (i.e. keeping health care expenditure at a constant fraction of national income) and microeconomic efficiency (i.e. producing health care services at minimal cost) in the health care sector at the same time.

More specifically, the public contract model in Germany and the Netherlands seems to have drawbacks compared with the public integrated model in Sweden, the United Kingdom and Denmark in keeping health expenditure in line with the increase in total domestic expenditure. On the other hand, compared to the public integrated model, cost containment in the public contract model has more limited consequences for the capacity and activity in the health care sector.

The incentives built into health care systems probably explain why different health care models are more inclined to pursue some cost containment approaches than others. In the public integrated model, hospital costs are normally covered by a prospective budget. The budget is only accompanied by very general output guidelines, if any at all. This implies that there is no automatic adjustment to the budget when hospital activity levels change. Variations in output and the possible consequences for the budget are a matter of negotiation between the public hospitals and, in the last resort, the political leadership. Budgetary restraint has been the single most important goal for the political leadership in the era of cost containment efforts in the public integrated model while hospitals have not been punished for declining output levels. In this situation, it is not a surprise that cost containment has had profound impact on the in-patient capacity and average length of stay.

To state that the German and Dutch health care systems are public contract models does not say much about the output incentives of the systems. The contract between insurer and provider and the way it is administered are more important for the incentives. From a cost containment perspective, the incentives in the German and Dutch health care systems in the 1970s and early 1980s were difficult to determine. Hospital charges were negotiated between the insurers and the hospitals and approved by the government. The insurers were legally obliged to reimburse hospital costs. Although hospital charges were established by an agreement, retrospective payment for hospital services drove costs up because the budget only estimated demand for services. In the mid-1980s, both the Netherlands and Germany introduced prospective budgeting for hospital expenditures, i.e., comparable to the way public integrated systems finance hospitals. In order to avoid the possible drop in activity associated with prospective budgeting, the German reform also established a link between expenditures and activities at the hospitals: if the occupancy rates deviated from the contractually stipulated rate, the hospital budget would be – marginally – adjusted in the same direction (Altenstetter, 1986). Following the implementation of the Dekker reforms, the Dutch health care system has been heading towards a system of managed competition among insurance funds and providers. The aim of the reform is to give the insurance funds a financial incentive to contract for better and cheaper services with health care providers (Schut, 1992, 1995).

The public integrated health care systems of Sweden and the United Kingdom were gradually reformed in the late 1980s (Saltman & von Otter, 1992). The vertical integration of health care purchaser and provider has at least in formal terms been loosened. Rather than receiving a budget from the health authorities, hospitals must sign a contract with the same health authorities (and in the British case often also with the general practitioners) stipulating the amount and cost of health care services. But the purchaser is free to go elsewhere if the hospital's bid is not considered competitive.

Although there may be a gap between reform principles and practices (for a critical analysis of the British health care reforms, see Pallesen, 1997b), the reforms of the health care systems in Germany, the Netherlands, Sweden and the United Kingdom all constitute attempts to improve the micro efficiency of the health care system without jeopardizing the macroeconomic results of a decade of cost containment – and without altering the basic public traits of the health care system.

Unlike other countries in this study, Denmark has continued to support the public integrated model and prospective budgeting of hospital services even though the Danish health care system faces problems similar to those experienced by the other countries in this study. This calls into question the notion of a uniquely cheap and effectively cost-contained Danish health care system. If we insist on uniqueness in one sense or another, the lack of reforms is probably a more realistic singularity of the Danish system – although the reforms in the other countries may often be more apparent than real.

The new political agenda of the 1990s and beyond: Adapting to cost expansion

Although a closer look at the international health care data makes it hard to sustain the picture of the Danish health care system as especially low-funded, the notion has nevertheless gained a strong foothold in the public debate as an undisputed fact. But in the mid-1990s public opinion and provider pressure started to have an impact on the political elite, which found it increasingly difficult to defend 'cutbacks' in health care expenditure, and a stream of extra funds were channeled to the health care sector (Ministry of Finance, 1997).

Whether we focus on the activity or capacity of the health care system or on hospital staffing, the development in the 1980s continued in the 1990s. The number of discharges increased while the number of bed days decreased which, by definition, resulted in a continued shortening of the average length of stay. Bed capacity declined even more than the number of bed days, which implies that the turnover rate also increased. The total number of staff stabilized in the 1990s after a decline in the 1980s, but the changes in the composition of the workforce of the earlier decade continued in the 1990s. The number of doctors and certified nurses continued to increase while the rest of the work-force actually declined. The strong increase in the number of nurses reflects a substitution of uncertified nurses with certified nurses. But contrary to what many Danish nurses believe, this substitution only partly explains the increase. The total number of nurses, certified or not, increased in the 1990s.

TABLE 8.

Trends in activities, capacity, staffing and expenditure
in the Danish health system in the 1990s.

	1990	2000	2005
Activities	absolute numbers	absolute numbers	absolute numbers
Discharges (somatic)	1,057,000	1,029,000	1,102,000
Discharges (psychiatric)	33,000	39,000	40,423
Bed days (somatic)	7,097,000	5,567,000	4,998,000
Bed days (psychiatric)	1,532,000	1,406,000	1,280,000
Average length of stay, (somatic, bed days)	6.7	5.4	4.5
Average length of stay (psychiatric, bed days)	45.5	36.1	31.7
Capacity			
Somatic beds	23,879	18,484	16,410
Psychiatric beds	4,906	3,894	3,676
Staffing – Hospitals			
Total staff	81,928	84,622	86,914
- of which: Doctors	8,922	10,114	11,351
- of which: Nurses	23,578	28,668	30,401
Expenditure (in mill. 2005 Dkr)			
Total health	65,059	78,461	90,662
- of which: public health	53,146	61,425	71,566
- of public health: Hospitals	40,300	46,733	53,607
Private health	11,912	17,036	19,096

Source: Danish Health Care in Figures (Ministry of the Interior and Health, 2006).

The major change during the 1990s compared to the 1980s was the funding situation. Total expenditure increased by about one fifth in real terms during the 1990s. The largest relative increase was in private health expenditures, but in absolute terms, the increase in public health expenditures in the 1990s equaled the total private health expenditures.

The ongoing structural development of the Danish health care system and changes in funding policies in the 1990s raise a number of questions. One important question is why the Danish health care policy suddenly changed in the mid-1990s. The new expenditure policy coincided with the change of government in 1993 when a Social Democratic cabinet took over after 10 years of right wing leadership. The new health care funding policy also came in the wake of the Danish economic recovery in the mid-1990s, jump-started by Social Democratic fiscal policy. Their initial financial package, 'A new course towards better times' (*Ny kurs mod bedre tider*) launched in 1993 (Ministry of Finance, 1993) was an example of genuine Keynesian expansionary fiscal policy. Lower taxes and increased public expenditures, along with a dose of supply-side labor market policy produced economic growth and lowered unemployment. Hence, it would be tempting to conclude that the changed health care funding policy was due to the change in cabinet or the improved economic situation, or a combination of the these political and economic factors.

While the more favorable economic situation may have facilitated changes in health care financing, it would be wrong to assume a causal relationship between the change in health care policy and the change of cabinet in 1993. The cost containment policy of the 1980s and early 1990s, as well as the more lavish policy in the second part of 1990s and early 2000s were supported by a broad political coalition of Social Democrats and right wing parties.

The party political dimension is less important in explaining changes in health care finance than the political dynamic between the national and local government levels. However, the inter-governmental dynamic is different when cost containment rather than policy expansion is on the national health care agenda. As described above, the Danish health care system is to a high extent decentralized. Local governments have a major responsibility for health care service provision. At the same time, national politicians have always shown a strong interest in regional health care policy (Pallesen, 1999; Christensen, 2000). For national politicians this was a politically convenient set-up of the health care system when cost containment was on the agenda in the 1980s and early 1990s. The local financing system also proved to be a very efficient institutional arrangement for blame avoidance when health care funding had to be moderated in this period. Until 2007, the regional resources came from an income tax and a general central government grant. The income tax base stagnated due to the sluggish Danish economy in the late 1980s. Public expenditure cuts were part of the government's economic recovery strategy, and the central government added to the regional financial difficulties by instituting a series of block grant reductions in the 1980s. Meanwhile the government did not manage to reduce central government expenditures; transfer payment expenditures increased particularly rapidly (Blom-Hansen & Pallesen, 2001).

The local financial difficulties in the 1980s *de facto* strained health care expenditure severely. Health care is the single largest regional expenditure item, absorbing nearly two thirds of the budgets. The hospital area, which alone takes half of the regional budget, is also the policy area with the highest regional policy autonomy. Before the change in 2007, the other major regional policy tasks – primary health care, secondary education and special social services – were in various ways bound up in a complex web of central government regulation (secondary education), collective agreements (primary health care) and common county-municipal service provision (special social services) that make it difficult to reduce expenditure in these areas. Hospital services not only consumed a major part of the regional budgets, but also shouldered the lion's share of cost containment. Hence, while health care services in general, and hospital services in particular, remained among the most popular policy aspects of the Danish welfare state, they were financially stagnating. The hospitals' share of regional budgets declined in the 1980s to less than half of the total expenditures. However, the impact of the system of local financing given the institutional structures in the various county policy areas during the period of economic recession is a very complex matter. The average interested voter probably has only a limited understanding of the consequences of various decisions on the operation of the health care system, let alone the political authority ultimately responsible for the constraints that were imposed. For a central government looking for easy expenditure cuts it is a convenient arrangement: the reduction of the central government block grants in the 1980s was de facto targeted at the health care area, but it was not obvious to voters who are not familiar with the details of the arrangement. Of course, the regional authorities persistently claimed that the various problems of the health care system, especially the growing waiting lists, were caused by decisions made by the central government rather than themselves. But local governments use this excuse so frequently that voters often dismiss the excuse and seek additional explanations. The complexity of the interactions among the various elements of the health care system contributed to the opacity of the situation. The central government thereby managed to pursue a successful strategy of obfuscation (cf. Pierson, 1996).

When a consensus emerged at the national level to change the direction of health care policy, the same elements that allowed 'blame avoidance' now hindered 'credit claiming'. For the central government it would have been easy to prioritize health care policy further and increase health care funding by merely increasing the central government block grant to the regions. But framing a national political health care initiative in this way would have been as invisible to voters as the reduction of the block grants was in the 1980s. In order to overcome this symmetry of the system, national politicians had to find other, more spectacular ways to focus attention on their health care policy initiatives. National politicians also had to launch policy initiatives without compromising local government autonomy in the health care area. And so they did. The first major national health care initiative of the 1990s was the 'waiting time guarantee' of 1993, issued one month after the change of government, but prepared by the right wing government in 1992 (Blom-Hansen, 1998). Instead of pursuing a bill that would have impinged on local government autonomy, the waiting list initiative emerged from negotiations between the government and the county councils' association, now the Danish Regions. The aim of the waiting list initiative was to reduce the waiting time for elective operations to a maximum of three months by increasing the number of operations. The waiting list initiative was followed by another, similar initiative in 1994. Parallel to the waiting time campaign, a special effort to increase the number of heart operations ('the heart plan') was launched, and later psychiatry and oncology also received their own 'psychiatry plan' and 'cancer plan'. In general, these initiatives highlighted the role of the national government while requiring only a modest amount of central government financing and without disrupting local government autonomy in health care. Most health care initiatives have been settled in negotiations with the Danish Regions but have seldom reached their goals fully to ensure patients' rights, although the semantics of the agreements may have led some political observers or voters to believe so. For example, patients were not granted a genuine guarantee of a maximum waiting time for operations. In this respect, it could be argued that the government still counted on the strategy of obfuscation. However, this state of affairs is changing. While the new national expansive health care agenda of the 1990s respected the institutional and professional interests, the local autonomy has increasingly been circumscribed in the 2000s. By way of example, in the early 2000s, central government has gradually strengthened patients' rights without consultations with the local authorities (e.g. the right to choose another private or public provider after one month's waiting time).

The establishment of the new regional authorities in 2007 is another step in the direction of a stronger, direct national say in future health care policy making. The new regional authorities are amalgamations of the former counties and even more than the counties, the new regions' main task is the provision of health care. In contrast to the former counties, the new regions are financed mainly by central government funds that – in combination with stronger national planning of the hospital specialties – are a potential vehicle for more direct national governance of the regional health care policy. To what extent this potential is going to be realized is at the moment an open question, but the arrow is pointing at a more interventionist central government policy. However, the pendulum may swing back again if cost containment once more becomes a salient health care policy issue.

References

Altenstetter, Christa (1986). 'Reimbursement Policy of Hospitals in the Federal Republic of Germany'. International Journal of Health Planning and Management 1: 102-19.

Blom-Hansen, Jens (1998). 'Sisyfos på arbejde: Ventetidsgarantier i de skandinaviske sygehusvæsener'. Nordisk Administrativt Tidsskrift 79: 359-89.

Blom-Hansen, Jens & Thomas Pallesen (2001). 'The Fiscal Manipulation of a Decentralized Public Sector: Macroeconomic Policy in Denmark'. Policy and Government 19: 607-23.

Christensen, Jørgen Grønnegård (1992). Dansk Sundhedspolitik. Aarhus: Department of Political Science, University of Aarhus.

Christensen, Jørgen Grønnegaard (2000). 'The Dynamics of Decentralization and Recentralization'. *Public Administration* 78: 389-408.

Culyer, Alan J. (1989). 'Cost Containment in Europe'. *Health Care Financing Review* 10 (annual supplement): 21-32.

Damgaard, Jens Bejer & Thomas Pallesen (1998). 'Kommunalt selvstyre og organisering', in Jens Blom-Hansen et al., *Offentlig og effektiv*. Copenhagen: Gyldendal.

Gerdtham Ulf-G., Jes Søgaard, Fredrik Andersson & Bengt Jonsson (1992). 'An Econometric Analysis of Health Care Expenditure: A Cross-Section Study of the OECD Countries'. *Journal of Health Economics* 11: 63-84.

Henke, Klaus-Dirk (1992). 'Cost containment in Health Care: Justification and Consequences,' in Peter Zweifel & H. E. Frech (eds.), *Health Economics Worldwide*. The Netherlands: Kluwer Academic Publishers, pp. 245-65.

Juul, Svend, Svend Sabro & Ebba Holme Hansen (1989). *Det danske sundhedsvæsen*. Copenhagen, Aarhus and Odense: FADLs Forlag.

Kleiman, Ephraim (1974). 'The Determinants of National Outlay on Health,' in Mark Perlman (ed.), *The Economics of Health and Medical Care*. London and Basingstoke: Macmillan.

Leidl, Reiner (1994). 'Auswirkungen der EG-Intergration', in P. Oberender (ed.), *Probleme der Transformation im Gesundheitswesen*. Baden: Nomos Verlaggesellschaft, pp. 209-36.

Ministry of Finance (1971). *Perspektivplanredegørelse*. Copenhagen: Ministry of Finance.

Ministry of Finance (1973). *Perspektivplanredegorelse II*. Copenhagen: Ministry of Finance.

Ministry of Finance (1993). *Ny kurs mod bedre tider*. Copenhagen: Ministry of Finance.

Ministry of Finance (1997). *Budgetredegørelse 97*. Copenhagen: Ministry of Finance.

Ministry of Health (1996). *Sygehuskapaciteten i Hovedstaden, betænkning no. 1324*. Copenhagen: Ministry of Health.

Ministry of Health (1997). *Udfordringer i sundhedsvæsenet, betænkning no. 1329*. Copenhagen: Ministry of Health.

Ministry of Health (1999). *Danish Health Care Sector*. Copenhagen: Ministry of Health.

Ministry of Health (2000). *Danish Health Care Sector in Figures*. Copenhagen: Ministry of Health.

Ministry of Health (2001). *Patienters vurdering af danske sygehuse*. Copenhagen: Sundhedsminsteriet.

Ministry of the Interior (1977). *Prioritering i Sundhedsvæsenet, betænkning no. 809*. Copenhagen: Ministry of the Interior.

Ministry of the Interior (1984). *Sygehusenes organisation og økonomi*. Copenhagen: Ministry of the Interior.

Ministry of the Interior (1985). *Samordning i Sundhedsvæsenet, betænkning no. 845*. Copenhagen: Ministry of the Interior.

Ministry of the Interior (1986). *Praksissektorens organisation, betænkning no. 1080*. Copenhagen: Ministry of the Interior.

Ministry of the Interior (1987). *Amtskommunalt udgiftspres og styringsmuligheder, betænkning no. 1123*. Copenhagen: Ministry of the Interior.

Ministry of the Interior and Health (2006). *Danish Health Care Sector in Figures*. Copenhagen: Ministry of the Interior and Health.

Newhouse, Joseph P. (1977). 'Medical Care Expenditure: A Cross- National Survey'. *Journal of Human Resources* 12, 1: 115-25.

OECD (1992). *The Reform of Health Care*. Paris: OECD.

OECD (1995). *OECD Health Data*. Paris: OECD/Credes.

OECD (2000). *OECD Health Data*. Paris: OECD/Credes.

Pallesen, Thomas (1997). *Health Care Reforms in Britain and Denmark: The Politics of Economic Success and Failure*. Aarhus: Forlaget Politica.

Pallesen, Thomas (1997a). 'De danske og engelske sundhedsreformer: En test af New Public Management-bølgens indhold og betydning'. *Politica* 29: 279-94.

Pallesen, Thomas (1999b). 'Sundhedspolitik: Hvad udad tabes, må indad vindes', in Jens Blom-Hansen & Carsten Daugbjerg (eds.), *Magtens organisering – Stat og interesseorganisationer i Danmark*. Århus: Systime, pp. 127-45.

Pallesen, Thomas & Lars Dahl Pedersen (1993). 'Decentralization of Management Responsibility: The Case of Danish Hospitals'. *International Journal of Health Planning and Management* 8: 275-94.

Pedersen, Lars Dahl (1996). *The Politics of Cost Containment in Public Services. Hospital Budgeting in Denmark, Germany, and the Netherlands, 1979-92*. Aarhus: Forlaget Politica.

Pedersen, Lars Dahl & Hans Maarse (1995). 'The Iron Law of Health Care Expenditures: Do Health Policy and Politics Matter?' Maastricht: Rijksuniversiteit Limburg.

Pierson, Paul (1996). 'The New Politics of the Welfare State'. *World Politics* 48: 539-60.

Saltman, Richard & Casten von Otter (1992). *Planned Markets and Public Competition*. Buckingham: Open University Press.

Schieber, George J. & Jean-Pierre Poullier (1991). 'Overview of International Comparisons of Health Care Expenditures', in *Health Care Systems in Transition*. OECD Social Policy Studies, No. 7. Paris: OECD, pp. 9-15.

Schut, Frederik T. (1992). 'Workable Competition in Health Care: Prospects for the Dutch Design'. *Social Science and Medicine* 35, 12: 1445-55.

Schut, Frederik T. (1995). *Competition in the Dutch Health Care Sector*. Rotterdam: Erasmus University.

Søgaard, Jes (1991). 'Finance and Delivery of Health Care Services in Denmark,' in Tim Knudsen (ed.), *Welfare Administration in Denmark*. Copenhagen: Institute of Political Science, University of Copenhagen, pp. 325-56.

Søndergaard, Willy & Allan Krasnik (1984). 'Health Services in Denmark', in Marshall W. Raffel (ed.), *Comparative Health Systems*. University Park: Pennsylvania State University Press, pp. 153-96.

van Mosseveld, C.J.P.M. & P. van Son (1999). *International Comparison of Health Care Data*. Dordrecht: Kluwer Academic Publishers.

8 GROWTH BY RULES

The Case of Danish Day Care

Jens Bejer Damgaard

Introduction

Transactions involving goods or services from public or private producers to users or buyers involve at least two fundamental questions: 1) how *much* should be produced, and 2) *what* should be produced. A third question is formulated in the transaction cost literature: How should transactions be organized (Williamson, 1985, 1991)?

Standard textbook examples of market regulations often focus on the quantity aspect and usually answer the question of the appropriate output level as a function of varying price levels. The quality question is assumed to be answered by involving more than one producer. With many producers, buyers can shop around and find the quality they want or can afford. The market will provide a variety of comparable products at various prices, expressing buyers' preferences.

In a monopoly situation the market incentive to adapt to variation in buyers' tastes degenerates, leaving the buyers as losers in two ways. First, prices increase, bringing super profits to the monopolist. Second, the variety of products declines. From the buyer's point of view, the market narrows leaving it more difficult to satisfy individual preferences.

Analyzing the Danish welfare state's production of day care services, the questions of quantity, quality and organization provide a fruitful point of departure because they underline the basic questions related to public services: how much should be produced, what quality should be produced and how should the production be organized? Because the Danish system does not rely on market transactions to ensure the necessary quantity and quality of day care services, these questions are particularly relevant in analyzing the survival of the welfare state. Without market transactions local government are assigned with a planning job: First, establish the 'necessary' amount of day care and, second, set the price parents have to pay. The national Social Systems Act specifies the maximum percentage of the running costs that can be charged. After several changes the maximum percentage is currently set at 25 pct.

This also implies that an elected body (the local government) somehow can get information about parents' preferences and *shifts* in preferences (i.e., performs the allocation functions otherwise left to market forces). It further implies that the elected body is interested in efficiency and effectiveness and is also capable of implementing decisions through a hierarchical organized system to meet parental needs and wants.

Assuming that the pursuit of efficiency and effectiveness is somehow in the interest of politicians, achieving these goals may not be easy. Certain rules have to be followed by all actors involved in the game. By constraining actors' actions, these rules play a crucial part in explaining how and why the Danish day care sector has reached its present output and quality levels. Further, the rules ensure that all vital decisions about resource allocation to the day care sector are kept at the political level, and not negotiated by the producers and the users. Thus, rather than engaging in a simple discussion of how many hours our children should attend a day care institution and the price parents should pay for this service, these decisions have become a matter of debate at the local and national political level. Consequently, all municipalities discuss their day care policies. The results of these discussions vary from community to community, and local governments vary with respect to the amount of resources they assign to the production of day care and how these resources are used.

Basically, local governments are involved in two kinds of decisions. They may want a large output, measured as the covering percentage (the quantity question) or they may want a service with high quality, measured as the number of children per employee (generally accepted as the most important aspect of the quality question). A range of combinations is possible. However, it might be reasonable to ask whether the differences among municipalities are a result of a political process *where interests other than those of parents are represented*. Is this really an example of local politicians' capacity for fine-tuning to accommodate the needs of users in their local areas? An example will highlight this question.

The small island of Ærø has only two municipalities: Marstal and Ærøskøbing. In 1997, Marstal had 20.0 employees to look after 104 children in kindergartens and age-integrated institutions (5.2 children per employee). Ærøskøbing employed 20.2 'persons' in their two age-integrated institutions with 133 children (6.6 children per employee). The average for Denmark in 1997 was 5.4 children per employee (Danish Statistical Bureau, 1998). If the number of day care workers per child is a measure of quality, clearly Marstal's service was better. If we turn to the quantity side of the story between these two small municipalities, they also differ. The covering percentage in Marstal was 71.8 pct. for children between three and six years of age, whereas the same figure for Ærøskøbing was 82.7 pct. Thus Marstal offered better quality but for a smaller proportion of the community. How do we explain the differences between these two almost identical municipalities with a total population of only 7,704 people? (As of January 1, 2007 a major reform has changed the number of municipalities from 275 to 98. The small island of Ærø is now united in one municipality).

Do the differences between the two very similar municipalities reflect differences in parental preferences in the trade-off between quality and quantity? The answer is no. Although a market governance structure produces variations in day care provision, it would be difficult to imagine that two adjacent and fairly similar municipalities such as Marstal and Ærøskøbing, would have such different outcomes. Therefore, analyses aiming to explain variations in policy outcomes must focus on political priorities and the institutional arrangements within which decisions are made. Thus, we need to understand the institutional and political processes that allocate resources to the day care sector to explain differences in day care provision from municipality to municipality.

This means that political rather than economic explanations are more appropriate for understanding variation in the provision of day care services in the Danish welfare state. In Denmark, day care is mainly a service produced by local government institutions, pure economic theory cannot explain variations in quality and quantity. New institutional theory inspired by rational choice and economic theory (Ostrom, 1986; Williamson, 1985) combine political and economic perspectives. These micro-based theories offer a useful platform to analyze day care services in Denmark because these services are produced in a politically controlled, hierarchical governance structure comprised of many small units, each operating under a set of strict rules. Governance structures encompass two levels – the 'national part' negotiated among centrally placed actors and a 'local part'. Local governance structures vary across the municipalities. These local structures face varying demands and inputs, including differences in budget resources, the number of children in need of day care, and the level and type of parental involvement. Local authorities determine the opening hours and other operating conditions for each production unit (day care center).

This analysis of the Danish day care system falls into six sections. In the second section of this chapter, we examine the historical background of public involvement in the production of day care services. A social policy to provide relief for the poor in the 1930s evolved into labor market policy in the 1960s and 1970s. With women's entry into paid employment outside the home, day care for children became an essential element in facilitating their labor force participation. At the end of the second section, definitions of different kinds of day care are provided. Section three elaborates two aspects of the flexibility problem of publicly provided day care services; the quantity aspect of the flexibility question is given priority but the quality aspect is also addressed. Later, in section four, theoretical insights from new institutional theory are examined. First, the defense of institutional interests in the political decision-making process resulted in an amendment to the Social Systems Act allowing local governments to support purely private institutions but at that time institutional interests had implemented damage control. Second, the institutional arrangements provide corporatist actors a piece of the growing pie that an expanding public sector entails. This is the argument referred to as 'growth by rules'. Corporatist actors benefit from the current structure, while the 'losers' – the taxpayers – are enmeshed in a web of interests that leads to indifference or alliance building with potential opponents. This political process results in the lack of flexibility in the sector. Leaving the quantity side of the story, in section five we turn to the quality question to discuss whether the services delivered today are adequate. In section six, conclusions and recent reforms aimed at increasing flexibility in both quality and quantity terms to suit parental needs, are presented.

Day care becomes a publicly produced service

In 1933, a comprehensive social reform, initiated by the Social Democratic Party, was passed by the Danish parliament. The reform established the Ministry of Social Affairs, and placed day care institutions in that new ministry. Day care, then, was a part of the social policy of poor relief. Children from poor working-class homes needed decent care and good nutrition, and this issue united more conservative forces with social democratic concerns for their core voters (Siim, 1990: 84-6). In keeping with this spirit of the reform, public support was given only to existing private institutions that gave at least two-thirds of their places to children from poor homes (Knutsen, 1991: 19). Consequently, formerly private institutions became public in the sense that they began to receive most of their financial resources from the state. Today, some of these self-governing institutions remain private institutions, but since their prime income source is public, they must operate within the same rules as the public institutions that emerged after the 1933 reform. Thus, the 1933 reform was a political decision to 'contract in' rather than 'contract out' in the sense that a hierarchical governance structure replaced a market based system. Governments usually argue that supply-side imperfections in such cases require government intervention (Kettl, 1993: 31-33). The Danish government's position was that the market for day care services was too small to function effectively. It was therefore easy for the government, in 1933, to define day care as a public good which required public regulation.

CRISIS, MIRACLES, AND BEYOND

The Local Government Reform of 1970 decentralized political and administrative decisions from central to the local political authorities (Albæk, 1994: 1-4). Implementation of this change took years, and day care was not formally decentralized until 1976 when the Social Systems Act gave the local governments employer status (Ketscher, 1991: 102-4). The local government reform, however, did not change the political decision of contracting in; it just meant that a local governmental hierarchy replaced the central governmental hierarchy.

The late 1960s and early 1970s marked a turning point for day care as a purely social service. As women began to join the labor force, the demand for day care institutions rose (Borchorst, 1990). Day care was no longer viewed as a component of poor relief, but rather part of the government's labor market policy agenda. Denmark had entered a period of rapid economic growth and industry needed women's labor. As in 1933, two forces united to bring about policy change. First, industrial interests and the conservative/liberal parties wanted women to join the labor force and saw the necessity of providing as many public day care places as possible for their children. Second, the Social Democratic Party sought to increase access to day care for working class families, their core constituency (Borchorst, 1990: 171-75). For different reasons, therefore, otherwise opposing political forces could agree on one thing – an increase in the number of day care places.

As a result of this policy alliance, the number of children in publicly-funded day care schemes rose rapidly. And as the day care system grew, its character changed. It was no longer just for the children from poor homes (Ketscher, 1990). Instead, it became widely available to any family in society who met the qualification criteria. Universal access eventually had a positive impact on general attitudes leading to widespread support among the general public for day care institutions (Bertelsen, 1991: 49-51).

THE MANY FACES OF DANISH DAY CARE: SOME DEFINITIONS

Further analysis requires some definitions and identification of just which services we mean when we refer to 'day care'. 'Day care' and 'child care' are often used interchangeably. However, here the term 'child care' concerns all services (e.g., also services for disabled children) delivered to all children up to fourteen years of age. Thus 'child care' is too broad a term for the purposes of this chapter. Instead, the term 'day care' focuses on ordinary day care facilities available to children (Ministry of Social Affairs, 1993b: 3-6).

'Day care' in Denmark nevertheless involves a wide range of services. These services are delivered by a variety of different institutions, further complicating the overall picture of service provision (OECD, 1990: 126-29 & 149). The Danish decision to contract in, therefore, is largely responsible for the complexity of the service delivery system. In Denmark all kinds of institutions can be considered part of the public system, due to the political regulation, while in the US (or Canada) 'official' terms have been adopted because of the non-centralized approach in these two North American countries (Teghtsoonian, 1992, 1993). Table 1 provides an overview of Danish day care services. As the Table suggests, children up to fourteen years of age use a broad variety of institutions. A useful distinction is that of preschool and after-school day care. Municipalities usually divide their administration of day care institutions along this line. Note that Danish children start school at the age of seven, which is rather late compared to other European countries (Phillips & Moss, 1989).

TABLE 1.

Day care in Denmark – different types of institutions and different levels of organizations

	Pre-school (up to age 6)		After-school (age 6-14)	
Various types of day care	Publicly organized and self-governing institutions	Privately organized	Publicly organized	Privately organized
	• Supervised family day care • Nurseries (crèches) • Kindergartens • Age-integrated institutions	• Pool-scheme institutions	• School-care schemes (recreation centers)	• School-care schemes in private schools

Note: All terms used by either The Ministry of Social Affairs, (The Ministry of Social Affairs, 1993b: 4-6), or the Statistical Yearbook.

As shown in Table 1, the local government runs different types of day care (or incorporated and supported self-governing institutions).

Supervised family day care is mainly used for the smallest children (six months to two years of age). A private person signs a contract and nurses four or five children privately. The local government additionally makes routine inspections. This type of day care is not directly part of the local hierarchy. To parents, however, payments must still be made to the local government and not to the so-called 'day care mother'. Supervised family day care is indeed a flexible way of organizing day care, at least when it comes to adapting quantity to demand. No investments in buildings are needed and the 'day care mothers' are relatively easily hired and fired. This service can be used as a buffer if the number of children rises quickly or when difficulties arise in transferring a child from one institution to another.

'Competing' with supervised family day care, nurseries enroll children from six months to approximately three years of age. About half of the staff are professional day care workers who have received educational training of a duration of 3.5 years, while the rest of the staff is assistants with very short or no training (Ministry of Social Affairs, 1993a: 6). Nurseries are, to a larger extent, found in larger municipalities, while smaller municipalities rely on supervised family day care to a greater extent. In 2006, nurseries had 16,994 places available while the local governments had contracted to establish 65,666 places in supervised family day care (All figures in this section: Danish Statistical Bureau, 2007).

Enrolling children from approximately three years to six years of age, kindergartens are the next step for a child on his or her way into the school system. In 2006, 106,087 places were available. Staff composition is roughly the same as in nurseries, although the ratio between children and staff increases. Other institutions enroll children from six months to six (or more) years of age. These age-integrated institutions ease both children's and parents' problems related to shifting institutions. This has made them increasingly popular. Twenty years ago age-integrated institutions had only a few thousand places available; today they have 134,326 places.

Unlike supervised family day care, private pool-scheme institutions deliver a service comparable to the local governments' institutions. The difference is found in the contractual arrangement, which also make them distinct from self-governing institutions.

The long tradition of privately based day care made leeway for the Parliament to pass an amendment to the Social Systems Act in 1990. The amendment allowed the local governments to subsidize private day care by paying a monthly grant for each child. Negotiations between the private institution and the local government decide the size of the grant, but usually result in a *lower* cost than comparable services from public institutions. This being the fact (Pade & Glavind, 1993: 53), one might imagine that the local governments would support more of these institutions. As we shall see in section five, other institutional constraints prevent both local governments from supporting these institutions and parents from taking the initiative to establish them.

In the year a child becomes six years old, he or she is offered a place in a nursery class which are administered by the school system rather than the social welfare system. Children begin school in their seventh year, but this does not mean that day care ends. When school is over, child care begins. Two kinds of institutions accept school children for activities after school activities: those located within the school and separate institutions outside school. The first of these continues in the same buildings children attend for school while the others are located elsewhere in the community. The activities offered by these institutions, however, are roughly the same, although the total number of children in these two kinds of institutions has changed dramatically. After-school activity institutions outside the school used to be the most common form, but during the last two decades institutions within the school system have been given political priority since they are cheaper to run. One major reason for the price difference is that municipalities can charge a higher parental payment for institutions within the school system. In 2006, after-school activities outside school had 33,259 places available, while institutions within the school system offered 207,027 places. The staff in both kinds of institutions consists mostly of trained personnel.

Pre-school institutions consume far more resources than do after-school institutions. They also have a longer history and since pre-school institutions are not an *additional* service for parents in need of some care for their children during the day, the questions of output level and quality more directly reflect the degree of flexibility in the welfare state. In other words, while after-school care is optional for many parents, for working parents with pre-school children, day care is an essential service in order to participate in the workforce.

The evolution of the Danish day care sector – statistics

Day care institutions deliver a service demanded by parents. However, the actual level of *demand* is very difficult to measure. Most analyses start by asking why children are placed in day care. The rise in women's participation in the labor force has been one of the key factors driving the increased demand for day care. As more women went to work (and women worked more hours), more children needed more day care (Bertelsen, 1991: 25-37; Groes, 1991: 23-8; Jørgensen & Mouritzen, 1993: 66-69; Ministry of Social Affairs, 1993c: 25-30; OECD, 1990: 123-26). In explaining the number of places in day care institutions other independent variables are found: the wealth of the local government (high income – more places) and the number of children dependent on single heads of household (breadwinners). Most analyses illustrate the *political* dimension of demand. An economist would probably measure demand by asking, 'What is the *price* parents are willing to pay for day care and what is the total number of children in the relevant group?' In other words, demand is a function of the price of the service and the total number of potential service recipients (children of day care age).

The price parents have to pay for day care varies. Municipalities set different priorities which affects their pricing. In addition, the Social Systems Act specifies a maximum limit for day care charges. Thus, after decentralization to the local governments in 1976, the maximum fee was set at 35 pct. of operating costs. This rate was later reduced to 32 pct. and later 30 pct. (Ministry of Social Affairs, 1993b: 17). In 2003 the rate was changed to 25 pct.

Two social programs allow municipalities to reduce day care charges below the maximum limit established by national law. These include grants to day care institutions from the local governments themselves and a sliding scale for parental payments that depend on family income. The sliding scale is regulated by circulars attached to the Social Systems Act.

Figure 1 presents the enlargement of the covering percentage for children up to six years of age. The development is amazing. Increasing for more than 40 years, the covering ratio stands out as a clear indication of welfare services' institutionalization. The enlargement of the covering ratio, however, is not an effect of an expanding sector in *absolute* terms. In fact, the number of places decreased, a little, e.g. from 1981 to 1984. The covering ratio increased in this period because the number of children eligible for day care in the same period dropped dramatically (from approx. 450,000 to approx. 397,000 or more than 11 pct.; in the same period, the number of available places dropped 2.5 pct.). This illustrates the quantity side of the sector's flexibility problem.

The covering ratio for children from zero to six years of age in all day care schemes in Denmark is calculated as the number of children in day care compared to the total number of children in the mentioned age group, 1961-04.

FIGURE 1.

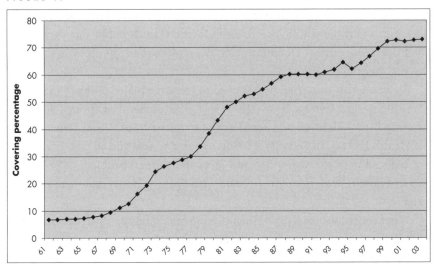

Source: Statistical Yearbook, various years.

The quantity side of the flexibility problem raises the question of governance structure. There is no doubt about the positive effects of a large day care sector (Vedel-Petersen, 1992: 9-12). But does it need to be (publicly) hierarchically controlled? At least two independent theoretical arguments could be put forward to support private provision. First, public choice theory would argue that day care should not be publicly produced because (1) it is a private good, (2) free-riders can be excluded, and (3) it does not create externalities

(Ostrom, 1983). Second, the theory of transaction costs would also support a non-hierarchical solution, mainly because the degree of asset specificity is too low to support a hierarchical (public) governance structure (Damgaard, 1998; Williamson, 1991). Although some capital investments in day care might lose value when converted for alternative purposes, these are almost exclusively connected to buildings. Many buildings, however, could be sold and used by private organizations to fill the gap created by a severe public retreat. The same line of argumentation could be used concerning the human asset specificity. Employees in day care institutions do, to some extent, increase their value from learning-by-doing functions. The point made by the theory of transaction costs, however, is that only if the degree of asset specificity is very high can a hierarchical governance structure be justified (Williamson, 1991). This is clearly not the case in day care provision.

Corporatism – a main institutional feature of Danish day care

Corporatism normally implies an iron triangle between unions, employer associations and the government. The iron triangle historically has divided costs and benefits among the players, who find it beneficial to negotiate these allocations without direct interference. In the Danish public day care sector the Local Government Denmark (LGDK) replace the employers' association leaving the triangle intact.

For years, this iron triangle has tried to solve the major problem facing the Danish day care system: to match supply with demand. Although so-called 'waiting lists' – children registered at the municipalities' Local Departments for Health and Social Security waiting to enter an institution (the LDHSS) – are reduced over the years, demand faces the general problem of providing services close to where parents live and with opening hours that meet parental needs.

What constrains local governments from matching supply to demand? The answer lies in the corporatist traits surrounding day care.

But there is a second aspect of the problem. If supply matches demand in the future, the day care sector will face another problem: productivity will decline. Since most of the production is carried out in institutions, budgets cannot be instantaneously adjusted to reflect the number of children attending daily. Thus, if the number of children drops and day care institutions do not fully use their capacity, the cost per child will increase.

The problem of productivity has yet another dimension: it is not just a problem for the local government (and for taxpayers). Supervised family day care, i.e., 'day care mothers', also pays a price for the deals struck by corporatist structures. They are the first to be fired. This redundancy might be an

CRISIS, MIRACLES, AND BEYOND

illustration of a flexible institutional arrangement that works. By maintaining a certain number of institutions and then using supervised family day care as a buffer for fluctuations in the demand, the system retains a higher degree of flexibility. This would be especially true if day care services provided in institutions constituted only a fraction of the total production. Unfortunately, the institutional arrangement does not work this way. More day care institutions are built at the expense of supervised family day care and day care institutions may turn out to be very difficult to close. Thus, by building day care institutions, local governments commit themselves to a specific way of producing day care services.

This political commitment is an outcome of corporatist negotiations. In market (or quasi-market) governance structures, unilateral commitments are rarely made because opportunistic actors would be likely to take advantage of such a move. Instead, one commitment must be met by a corresponding commitment by the other party, thus binding both parties to a mutually beneficial agreement. Such an arrangement reduces the uncertainty connected to transactions containing a certain degree of specialization (Williamson, 1983). This could be the case if the production of day care involved the employment of workers with a high degree of human asset specificity. Thus, if the employees were difficult to attract and retain (and difficult to replace), then local governments would have good reasons to make the facilities and working conditions attractive and to employ this rather complicated governance structure. Trained day care pedagogues can be hard to attract in certain areas/cities, but for other reasons. Once hired, they are not difficult to keep or replace because they are unlikely to find higher salaries outside the public day care sector and salaries within the public sector are regulated by union agreements.

The relatively low degree of human asset specificity should put the local government in a good bargaining position *vis-à-vis* employees. Again, interdependent institutional features impede bargaining for personnel cost containment. Although it can be argued that the salary for trained day care workers is low compared to other equivalent public sector professional groups (nurses, school teachers, etc.), they, too, benefit from the hierarchical governance structure. Day care pedagogues have a high degree of job autonomy because monitoring costs are high, and corporatist structures connected to public employment provide a high degree of job security.

This poses the interesting question: How is it possible for a group like Danish day care pedagogues to maintain and extend good working conditions when they hold a relatively weak economic bargaining position? A major part of the answer is the interdependence between institutional rules stemming from the corporatist tradition. Even if pedagogues have a weak *economic* bargaining position, they hold a strong *political* bargaining position (Moe,

1990). Local politicians are well aware of the popularity of day care (Pallesen, 2003) – national politicians add the positive effect on the supply of labor and together they admit influence on the sector to the other corporatist actors.

Private governance structures are very different from politically (hierarchically) controlled governance structures. In economic relationships, you gain something from trade; in politics it's all about winning and losing in the negotiations that allocate resources. And to win means to have and/or maintain a strong political base.

The political preference for day care institutions rather than supervised family day care probably did not originate in rational economic considerations. Day care institutions evolved within a political decision-making setting in which corporatist bargaining was the central element in the development of welfare state institutions. Three institutional settings illustrate how corporatism pervades the decision-making structures that regulate the day care sector in Denmark. These are: (1) unionization of day care workers and the corresponding constitution of the local governments as employers; (2) users' indirect influence; and, (3) the tradition of detailed regulation in the public provision of day care services. Corporatist bargaining structures are virtually absent from the supervised family day care segment and the public sector agreements do not take their interests into account. Thus political bargaining comes to focus on day care *institutions* and gives priority to services from public institutions.

Unionization

Two unions represent employees in Danish day care institutions: the Danish National Federation of Early Childhood Teachers and Youth Educators (BUPL), and the National Union of Nursery and Child Care Assistants (PMF). BUPL organizes trained pedagogues, who have three and a half years of education at special schools. Practically all trained pedagogues are members of BUPL because the union has – and needs to have (Olson, 1965: 66-97) – a set of selective benefits to offer members including access to jobs, job protection via representation, and access to strike pay. The collective agreement between the BUPL/PMF and LGDK is (almost) a closed shop arrangement allowing only union members to work in public institutions. Most pedagogues join the union during their period of education or before applying for jobs. Local shop stewards at day care institutions ensure that no one works without a union card (BUPL, 1990: 128-30). This system is so strong that practically all pedagogues working in public day care institutions are members of BUPL. Another way of keeping a high organization rate is through strikes. During strikes the union pays *members only* and recurrent conflicts certainly form an incentive to be a member. Other benefits from membership include experienced representation of the employee in any dispute or grievance against the employer (or from the employer).

Not all day care workers are trained pedagogues. In 2003, 58 pct. of those working in public day care institutions were trained (Danish Statistical Bureau, 2007). Nevertheless, unionization among untrained workers is also high, and for the same reasons. BUPL and PMF have the right to organize workers and the right to negotiate working conditions for these workers (BUPL, 1989: 29) at national level with their employer counterpart, LGDK.

Figure 2 illustrates the source of regulations governing working conditions at public day care institutions, including the legal basis (the Social Systems Act) and the local counterpart to the collective agreement. Every day care institution has a local agreement determining the specific working conditions in that institution. In this way corporatism at the national level is supplemented by a corresponding corporatist system at the local level.

The arrows in Figure 2 represent formal negotiation lines between central actors. Thus, BUPL and PMF representatives are consulted before political decisions are made, for instance regarding amendments to the Social Systems Act.

FIGURE 2.

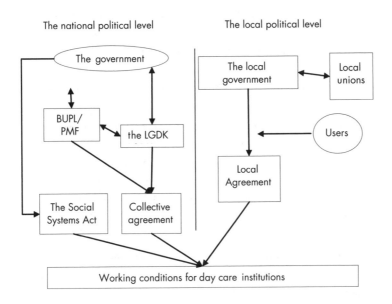

The national government – or national governmental officials – participates in negotiations between the unions and LGDK. A similar negotiation arena is found at local level (in the figure separated by the vertical line, between the local government and the local branches of the BUPL/PMF). These negotiations take place within the rules laid down in the Social Systems Act and the collective agreement. Users do not have direct influence in negotiations concerning the local agreement. But users do participate in hearings. The Parental Boards Act of 1992 clearly intended some parental involvement in shaping the content of the local agreement when authority was delegated to the boards.

Among the corporatist actors, the influence of the unions cannot be exaggerated. Working on the central and local level, unions hold several veto points in decisions concerning day care policy. For instance, when the Conservative-led coalition government took office in 1982, and the conservative Minister of Social Affairs, Palle Simonsen, floated a proposal to allow *private* day care *institutions* (pool-schemes) to receive public financial support, the unions were strong opponents. Using the argument that pool-scheme institutions would develop into discount institutions, the unions started a campaign that kept the proposal from passing parliament for eight years (Kyst & Tinning, 1992: 7-19). The real threat to the unions was that pool-schemes were outside their control. With their formal private status, the pool-schemes would not have been part of the municipal hierarchy and therefore not included in the collective agreement. The intention of the Conservative minister was not only to reduce costs per child and give parents more direct influence, but also to reduce union influence by not demanding pool-schemes employ organized and educated personnel. Instead of adopting the proposal in 1982, parliament voted to experiment with new organizational forms in the day care sector. During the subsequent five to six years, only twelve experiments were launched (Kyst & Tinning, 1992: 8). The green light for the pool-schemes came after negotiations between a subsequent Conservative-led government and LGDK in 1988. LGDK shifted its position on pool-schemes. Originally opposed to the idea, the municipalities were under increasing fiscal stress caused in part by the Conservative government's reduction of block grants to local governments.

Before local governments could subsidize private pool-schemes, however, the Social Systems Act had to be amended. This brought the debate right into parliament where the Social Democrats and the Socialist Peoples Party stood firm in support of union arguments. Social Democrat Jytte Andersen said:

> First we want [private] institutions, where collective agreements are signed with the unions [BUPL and PMF]. ... Third, we want to secure the pedagogical content, which mostly relies on the ratio between pedagogues and children. ... Fifth, we want the employees [in the new pool-schemes] to be trained pedagogues (*Folketingstidende 1988/89*, sp. 1831 – my translation).

The problem for the two socialist parties was that the government already had a majority in parliament favoring its proposal. On the other hand, the government knew that a proposal lacking the support of the unions and Social

Democrats would run into trouble in the implementation phase. Local governments would need union acceptance to establish pool-scheme institutions because employment of day care workers without such acceptance would be very difficult. Furthermore, when the Social Democrats eventually returned to power, they would modify the Social Systems Act to restore union power. Thus if the pool-scheme institutions were to survive, they had to be introduced with the consent of the unions and the Social Democrats.

However, outside factors helped corporatist actors to accept the amendment. Denmark was experiencing a 'baby-boom' and rapidly increasing demand for additional day care institutions. In addition, public day care became a right for unemployed parents as well. In short, demand increased dramatically. Given the pressure of increasing the overall capacity of the day care system, the jobs of trained (union) pedagogues were secure. Thus, pool-schemes were less threatening. So, although the proposal passed parliament in 1990, it remained a solid union victory in the sense that the union was able to stall it for eight years. During those eight years, the covering percentage of public institutions climbed steadily and steeply (see Fig. 2 in section 3). BUPL explicitly credits the assistance of the Social Democrats and the Socialist Peoples Party: 'Although BUPL views the proposal in the Social Systems Act with great skepticism, we must also recognize that the worst parts of the proposal were abolished due to BUPL's cooperation with the Social Democratic Party and the Socialist Peoples Party' (my translation, BUPL, 1993: 203).

Moreover, when the new private institutions started to emerge, the unions were ready. The reform required all new private institutions to register with the Ministry of Social Affairs. This made it possible for the unions identify when and where new institutions were established. With a network of representatives throughout the country, the unions met with leaders of the new institutions even before they had enrolled the first child. In negotiations between the new private institution and the union, the unions held a strong position. No trained pedagogues would work in an institution without an agreement specifying almost the same working conditions as in the public sector. Thus private institutions seeking to hire qualified personnel would nevertheless have to deal with union representation and union-negotiated working conditions. The unions retained the ability to control access to employment opportunities.

Attempts during the 1990s to contract-out day care services were prevented by earlier legislation passed by parliament. The only way private institutions could be established with financial support from local governments was via the private pool-schemes arrangements.

In this corporatist system growth by rules was established. Local governments could produce a service much wanted by parents (voters), unions were given more members and solid and secure bargaining positions and parents were given high quality day care services all financed by the tax system. So, even in times with larger demand than supply, local and central politicians maintained that an increase in day care services had to take place through the already established structure – it was just a question of getting more of the same kind of day care. This consensus may well explain the way adjustments (more day care institutions) were made during the period of the 1980s and early 1990s.

USER INFLUENCE

Parents have some formal and direct influence over day care institutions and day care in private households. In 1980, the Ministry of Social Affairs specified the range of parental influence (Circular letter, no. 693, 16 June 1980). So-called parental councils were established in all day care institutions, and joint councils were formed in supervised family day care. In 1993, parental boards replaced parental councils as part of a reform strategy to decentralized decision-making.

Day care users (parents) and employees shared a common interest in resisting attempts by local governments to reduce resources available to day care institutions. Often parents have physically supported employees by joining demonstrations against cutbacks. The latest events have been 'parental strikes', in which parents take their children *out* of day care institutions, leaving the employees with empty institutions, yet receiving the same salary. Other parental actions include 'boycotting' payments during employee strikes (Ketscher, 1991: 317-19). Parents argue that the local government is unable to supply the service parents have paid for. If the service is not delivered, then parents will not pay their share. As these examples illustrate, parental frustration or discontent with day care services is more often directed against local government, *not* the institution or the employees or unions.

Blaming the (local) government for any shortcomings in day care institutions, parents may also exercise another form of indirect influence when they go to the polls. If we add day care employees to the group of voters who may cast their vote at the local elections on the basis of day care issues, we can see that elected local government officials face a well-organized interest group with considerable resources. If local politicians value re-election either as a goal itself (Downs, 1957: 27-31) or as a means to achieve other ends (money, power, etc.) (Moe, 1990), they are probably inclined to listen to large, well-organized interest groups and voter blocks (Christensen, 2003; Christensen & Pallesen, 2001). Thus budget increases are more likely than budget cuts, because interest groups who might favor budget cuts or restraint are either politically marginal or unorganized as predicted by Wilson:

Programs that benefit a well-defined special interest but impose, or appear to impose, no visible costs on any other well-defined interest will attract the support of the organizations representing the benefited group and the opposition of none, or at best the hostility only of purposive associations having no stake in the matter (Wilson, 1973: 333).

At the local level, mobilizing individuals is relatively easily accomplished. The incentives are sufficiently strong to join in the collective action that free riding among parents and employees is not a significant problem. When local politicians face their demands, they almost always comply (Stone, 1988: 172-83). Even politicians of the Liberal and Conservative parties who normally favor reducing public budgets have split at the local level on this issue. The political environment facing local government, including considerable direct and indirect parental influence, along with the effects of the corporatist bargaining structure at both the national and local levels help explain – at least in part – the growth (and type of growth) of the day care sector. Any attempt by local politicians to cut resources is readily conveyed from day care workers to parents who are ready and willing to mobilize in order to exert influence over local political decision-makers (Christensen, 1990).

A TRADITION OF USING RULES

The local governments and the unions conclude local agreements specifying the exact operating conditions within day care institutions and supervised family day care. The local agreement complements rules generated at the national level, i.e., the Social Systems Act and the collective agreement (see Fig. 2). Thus, an important output of the corporatist structure is a set of '[formal] Rules ... that refer to prescriptions commonly known and used by a set of participants to order repetitive, interdependent relationships' (Ostrom, 1986: 5). However, local rules vary. Contracting is selective, meaning that in every municipality a local agreement is signed between the local government and the local branch of the BUPL/PMF. This explains some of the local variation in service delivery. It is possible to specify different opening hours, budget systems, sizes, etc. So, in principle, flexibility is built into the system.

THE CORPORATIST STRUCTURE – A POSSIBLE EXPLANATION?

The three sets of regulation mentioned in this section, however, are not independent: to run public day care means to obey *all* the rules. For instance, a local government can negotiate a local agreement in which a certain number of additional children attend a nursery. This does not violate the Social Systems Act, but it means that a new calculation of the institutions' workforce is needed. This, of course, seems fair enough. If an institution increases production, the agreement normally secures an automatic release of a larger budget. A closer look at the basic 'national level' calculation method, however, reveals a major problem in the flexibility of day care institutions:

No. of employee hours per week = Opening hours per week * No. of children/ Size of group * 2 + Time to open and close the institution + Time for administration (dependent on the No. of children) + time 'to do other work' (depending on the no. of children) (BUPL, 1985: 1019-21).

This calculation method reveals two significant features about resource allocation in public day care institutions: (1) work is calculated in hours, not dollars, and (2) they do not use marginal calculations. Using working hours instead of dollars suggests that each municipality cannot completely control the budget of its own institutions, since the employees' salary is negotiated between LGDK and the unions, and staff reductions are difficult to implement according to the formula of adding up employee hours. Moreover, all institutions within a municipality are equally staffed. Despite the fact that some institutions enroll children from socially strained city areas, the basis for calculating employee hours is the same as in more quiet countryside areas. This does not mean that actual staffing is equal, but it means that staffing does not necessarily stem from actual needs. Recall the example from the beginning of this chapter: institutions in Marstal were relatively better staffed than institutions in neighboring Ærøskøbing.

Unlike private firms, day care institutions make absolute rather than relative calculations. Thus, a day care institution generating economies of scale receives the 'profit' of the marginal gains. If day care institutions 'earn' extra resources based on marginal increases in the number of children they serve, one could imagine that day care institutions would try to attract as many children as possible. This is not the case. In fact, steps to increase the number of children, or to increase productivity by reducing staff, meet with heavy resistance from employees and their unions. If you ask employees and parents, they will tell you that existing institutions are filled to capacity. Instead unions, parents, and employees put pressure on local governments to build more day care *institutions*. The increasing covering ratio shows the success of this 'growth by rules' strategy.

The difficulty of adapting day care provision to meet parental demand illustrates the general managerial problem of planning production. How do we get day care institutions to produce exactly the amount of service parents want and how do we know the quality they require? The current institutional arrangement secures day care workers certain working conditions that make it virtually impossible to monitor staff. Giving monitoring responsibility to the LDHSS, a function based in the city hall does not make monitoring any easier. The incentives for LDHSS staff to monitor closely may also be small, because they are located politically between the institutions' employees and the politicians. Bureaucrats making strategic calculations in this situation are not likely to engage themselves in battles against day care institutions or workers who might seek political support in the local government – or among parents (voters).

Assuming that staff in day care institutions has an interest in shirking (Miller, 1992: 86-95), managerial dilemmas are evident in the sector. Complete surveillance of employees is prohibitively expensive. The interests of actors producing the service (union members) and those of the local government buying the service are in direct conflict. Theoretically it should be possible to design formal incentive structures that would work towards Pareto optimality. However, in a hierarchy the sponsor does not know the *real* price for the service or the commodity he is buying (Niskanen, 1971: 24-35; Miller, 2005). While there certainly is a continuum ranging from 'not knowing anything' to a 'situation of full information', the hierarchical solution points in a direction of knowing very little; *price* becomes less important. The only one interested in the real price is the taxpayer, and he or she is the last one to be heard.

Calculating in absolute figures, day care institutions have no incentive to initiate changes in the production. This can be illustrated by looking at productivity figures in the day care sector. Figure 3 shows the common way of estimating productivity – the number of children per employee. An interesting 'coincidence' emerges: quality and productivity can (to some extent) be estimated using the same measure. Knowing this, unions have a clear interest in stressing the quality aspect and trying to keep negotiations at the national level in order to secure minimum standards for their members. Thus, the collective agreement, established as a result of the Local Government Reform in 1976 and negotiated every second or third year between the BUPL/PMF and LGDK, can only be changed locally in the direction of 'higher quality'. The outcome of these negotiations was that the productivity level started to stabilize in the late 1970s, as illustrated in Figure 3.

In the early 1970s, kindergartens showed a significant increase in productivity. To reduce government spending during the economic recession in the mid-1970s, the Ministry of Economics implemented a new act fixing the ratio between employees and children: more children were put into existing institutions without increasing the number of employees. Time and motion studies formed the basis of the new ratios, leading to the '... notorious cutbacks in day care institutions' (BUPL, 1982: 1021, my translation).

FIGURE 3.

Productivity measured as the number of children per employee in the four different kinds of public day care in Denmark, 1974-99

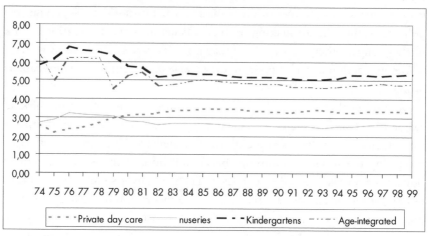

Source: Statistical Yearbook, various years.

At first, productivity grew, but after 1976, when the Social Systems Act was implemented and local governments were given employer status, productivity fell back to pre-1976 levels. An extremely stable productivity level emerged for all kinds of day care around 1982. This is not surprising, according to the growth by rule argument asserted in this chapter.

Changing institutional arrangements?

The above-mentioned 'Children's Package' was a political agreement between the leading parties in parliament. Apart from increasing public financing of the day care sector, the agreement also established parental boards in all day care institutions and supervised family day care. In addition, budgets were decentralized from LDHSS to the institutions. The intent was to increase responsibility and accountability among the institutional actors so that financial decisions would be more like that of an ordinary private firm (Ministry of Interior, 1994: 17-19).

The decentralization reform brings the focus of our analysis to the institutional level. What can we expect from more autonomous day care institutions? First, decentralization poses a problem for the existing institutional structure and rules because one important aim of the reform was to encourage many different institutional arrangements so that service supply could meet the local demand. Thus, institutions vary in (1) the delegation of authority to the parental boards, and (2) the budget system. The Parental Boards Act gave a certain degree of power to the parents, while also paving the way for more radical solutions. Empirical research suggests that parental boards usually are afforded only minimal formal competence. In other words, the boards have a right to be heard in employment cases; they receive an annual budget statement; and they have the authority to stake out the general pedagogical lines pursued in the institutions (Damgaard, 1997, 1998: 92).

Contrary to the rather limited extent of decentralization of authority to the parental boards, the budget system is undergoing larger reforms. Many municipalities have signed local agreements whereby institutions are allowed to carry over surpluses and deficits between budget years. In addition, institutions are given a framework budget with discretionary funds, thereby reducing LDHSS' formal budget control. The Parental Boards Act gives parents the authority to decide the general principles to guide resource spending. Whether this is actually happening and whether it has an effect on financial decisions in day care institutions are empirical questions, which so far have not been investigated.

The process of parental supervision and employee submission to inspection is presumably considered unproblematic because parents and employees are expected to have the same interests: high quality service. But high quality may imply low productivity. Thus, if parents and employees do not differ significantly in their views of what high quality is, the effects of monitoring are likely to be small. For instance, in market governance structures parents would be buyers and employees would be sellers with natural interests attached to each role. Due to the strictly limited delegation of authority to the boards, differences in the interests of 'buyers' and 'sellers' might not surface, because both groups benefit from a cooperative rather than competitive approach. Besides, parents and children presumably would benefit, like employees, from more resources.

By preventing parents from exercising an exit option, the current system leaves users with no direct authority to influence the provision of day care services by switching day care institutions. The LDHSS still makes all administrative decisions regarding the distribution of children among institutions.

Parents may also free ride from participation on, or interaction with, the boards. Why waste time on parental boards if other parents (with almost the same interests) are willing to do it? Thus, interest in serving on parental boards could fall to an embarrassingly low level, suggesting a negative *parental* evaluation of the board. In addition, once elected, which parent wants the unpleasant task of telling an employee charged with caring for one's child every day that he or she is doing something wrong or that he or she is making financial decisions in violation of the board's decisions? Thus, parents clearly have no incentives to discipline employees or enforce unpopular budget decisions. Knowing this, employees may be increasingly tempted to ignore board supervision. Loose budget control encourages employees to follow their own interests in daily decision-making. When budget cuts are required, the temptation facing employees to ignore board directives may be too great.

According to this line of argumentation, decentralization does not increase flexibility in the day care sector. On the contrary, the incremental institutional change is instead a step away from more flexible solutions because supervision from the LDHSS is not replaced by direct effective monitoring by parents. Parents are sidelined without effective jurisdiction to interfere or incentives to exercise what legal authority they have.

A NEED FOR CHANGES IN QUALITY?

Another aspect of assessing whether the day care system has the flexibility to meet parental demands requires us to determine whether parents actually want change. If institutions produce a service that satisfies parents, then no change is needed. In surveys, parents report that they are quite happy with the services as they are (Bertelsen, 1991: 42-5; Glavind, 1989). Asking parents what they want, however, is difficult because there are practically no existing institutional choices. This means that parents have no basis for preferring some other institutional arrangements. (This particular survey did not ask parents about the private pool-schemes). As a result, parents using public institutions *prefer* public institutions, and therefore seem to like what they get.

If public institutions produce the most wanted service, the private pool-schemes, which largely conform to public institutional parameters, should produce almost the same level of satisfaction. Surprisingly, they do not. At the end of 1992, Pade and Glavind counted 133 institutions (Pade & Glavind, 1993). Only a few of these pool-schemes produce a service found on the municipal menu. Instead, they reflect direct parental demands with respect to opening hours, activities, pedagogical content, and so forth. Many institutions also have built-in flexibility according to parental need for care. Thus, parents only pay for the number of hours children actually spend in the institutions. In public institutions, parents usually pay for full or part-time care, regardless of what they actually use.

Along with adapting to parental needs, the pool-scheme institutions have a contractual relationship with the municipality that secures a more efficient use of resources. The pool-scheme institutions' exposure to competition provides an additional incentive for efficiency as well as responsiveness to parental preferences. Although the real price of day care is unknown to the local government, they do know what they actually pay for the service. Comparing costs, local governments can ensure that pool-schemes remain cheaper than public institutions. Knowing this, pool-schemes have to produce their service at a lower price than public institutions, because the local government has an efficient and effective sanction possibility: it can reduce the grant to the private institution or decide not to extend the contract. This is a real threat to pool-schemes since they are not guarded by the corporatist structures. Besides, local governments can easily replace expensive pool-schemes with ordinary public institutions. From 1990 to 1992, eleven pool-schemes closed down, while 38 applications for public grants were rejected (Ministry of Social Affairs, 1992).

Empirically, pool-schemes are cheaper for the local governments (Pade & Glavind, 1993: 53; Damgaard, 1998: 203-12), partly due to the relatively larger financial contribution from parents, as well as their voluntary involvement in the institution. Of course these features reduce parental incentives to establish pool-schemes, and judging from the current number of institutions, the pool-schemes will never pose a real threat to the traditional public institutions.

Conclusions

It was a political decision in 1933 to provide public day care services within a hierarchical governance structure. Although several reforms have affected the sector, the fundamental decision to contract in remains unchallenged. The basic reason is now clear: actors involved in the iron triangle of corporatism in the sector allocate costs and benefits to actors involved in the production of day care services. By distributing costs and benefits accordingly, actors secure their institutional basis for seeking their own interests. Thus, regardless of outside factors such as the total number of children or unemployment, the covering percentage rose rather dramatically in Denmark. Proposals that might disrupt the balance of the existing system are either altered or postponed until they can be introduced under conditions conducive to allowing unions to retain control.

The decision to introduce private pool-schemes demonstrates the difficulties of changing institutional arrangements in sectors with well-defined and well-organized actors – even in the face of good economic reasons to do so.

Viewing the Danish day care sector in this way, the flexibility problems of hierarchically governed service production are evident. The paradox, however, is that the institutional arrangement might be so strong that users start to adapt to the service production rather than the day care institutions adapting to new parental needs or preferences. Separating the basic interests of the institutions from those of the users is, at present, unlikely. Public production of day services benefits both 'suppliers' (unions) and 'consumers' (parents) to such a degree that they are both likely to oppose any reform to alter the status quo. Who would initiate such a reform? Local governments do not use their authority to control day care institutions by advocating new private pool-schemes, although at first glance it might appear that they have strong incentives to do so. The dilemma for local government is that if parents are encouraged to establish private institutions, local government officials fly in the face of their relationship with already-employed public day care workers – who are unionized. Such a move would create an internal conflict that might cost them votes. For a politician seeking re-election this is not a well-considered strategy.

Are changes necessary? The day care system is very popular among parents (and employers), not only because it supplies them with a heavily subsidized service, but parents also appreciate the pedagogical content of the service. Day care does provide secure surroundings for children, and parents value the work done by the employees (Elsborg et al., 1995: 84-5). The point is, of course, that the governance structure does not affect the pedagogical work. Instead governance structures are – in a perfect world – designed to allocate goods and/or services at minimal costs. This implies that the choice of governance structure can change over time, regardless of whether the character of the service changes. Thus, even if the hierarchical decision of contracting in, taken by a Social Democratic government in 1933, was correct, efficient delivery of day care today might require another governance structure. Sixty years ago, the service supply was limited to a specialized service for poor people (Borchorst, 1990: 166-67). Specialized services may justify hierarchical governance structures (Williamson, 1985: 72-80). Today, the service is universal. There is nothing special about having your children in day care – on the contrary. The service and the administrative procedures are all standardized: parents know what to expect.

In spite of the dramatic changes in the character of the service that have occurred in the last seventy years, the governance structure remains (public) hierarchical. The reason is found in the corporatist structures that allocate benefits among central players involved in service production. Thus, the governance structure plays less of a role in the politically governed part of the day care system than in private institutional arrangements (Williamson, 1985: 35-8). The governance structure has become the gyroscope that keeps a safe course for the corporatist players in this part of the Danish welfare state, and given a chance the next goals are already lined up: a reduction (or removal) of parental payments, making day care a universal welfare service similar to that of the public school.

References

Albæk, Erik (1994). 'Denmark', in Lawrence Rose, Lars Strömberg & Krister Ståhlberg (eds.), Nordic Local Government: Developmental Trends and Reform Activities in the Postwar Period. Helsinki: The Association of Finnish Municipalities.

LGDK (1992). Kommunalstatistisk Årbog 2/92. Copenhagen: Kommunernes Landsforening.

Borchorst, Anette (1990). 'Political Motherhood and Child Care Policies', in Clare Ungerson (ed.), Gender and Caring: Work and Welfare in Britain and Scandinavia. London: Harvester Wheatsheaf.

BUPL (1992). Faglig Håndbog. Copenhagen: Forlaget Børn og Unge.

BUPL (1993). Faglig Håndbog 6. Copenhagen: Forlaget Børn og Unge.

Christensen, Jørgen Grønnegård (1990). Interest Groups and Public Bureaucracy in Danish Regulatory Policy-Making. Aarhus: Department of Political Science, University of Aarhus.

Christensen, Jørgen Grønnegård (2003). Velfærdsstatens institutioner. Aarhus: Aarhus Universitetsforlag.

Christensen, Jørgen Grønnegård & Thomas Pallesen (2001). 'Institutions, distributional concern, and public sector reform'. European Journal of Political Research 39: 179-202.

Chubb, John E. & Terry Moe (1988). 'Politics, Markets and the Organization of Schools'. American Political Science Review 82: 1065-89.

Damgaard, Jens Bejer (1997). 'How and Why Bureaucrats Control their Governance Structure'. Scandinavian Political Studies 20, 3: 243-64.

Damgaard, Jens Bejer (1998). Styring og Effektivitet: Organisering af dansk børnepasning. Århus: Forlaget Politca.

Downs, Anthony (1957). An Economic Theory of Democracy. New York: Harper and Row.

Elsborg, Steen, Ole Robenhagen & Vagn Rabøl Hansen (1995). Kan vi bestemme det? – Forældrebestyrelser i daginstitutioner. Copenhagen: Danmarks Pædagogiske Institut.

Folketingstidende (1989/90). The Official Record of the Danish Parliament. Copenhagen: Folketinget.

Glavind, Niels (1989). 'Forældreønsker & Holdninger'. BUPL-Rapport. Copenhagen: BUPL.

Groes, Eske (1991). Børnepasning i USA – Et privat marked. Copenhagen: AKF Forlaget.

Jørgensen, Torben Beck & Poul Erik Mouritzen (1993). Udgiftspolitik og Budgetlægning. Herning: Forlaget Systime.

Ketscher, Kirsten (1990). Offentlig Børnepasning i Retlig Belysning. Copenhagen: Jurist- og Økonomforbundets Forlag.

Kyst, Morten & Steen Tinning (1992). Puljeordninger. Copenhagen: Daginstitutionernes Landsorganisation.

Knutsen, Oddbjørn (1991). Offentlig Barneomsorg i Norden. (INAS-RAPPORT 1991:12). Oslo: Institutt for Sosialforskning.

Miller, Gary J. (1992). Managerial Dilemmas: The Political Economy of Hierarchy. Cambridge: Cambridge University Press.

Miller, Gary J. (2005). 'The Political Evolution of Principal-Agent Models'. Annual Review of Political Science 10: 203-25.

Ministry of Interior (1992). Indenrigsministeriets Kommunale Nøgletal. Copenhagen: Ministry of the Interior.

Ministry of Interior (1994). Fornyelse og Effektivisering i den Kommunale Sektor. Betænkning nr. 1268. Copenhagen.

Ministry of Social Affairs (1992). Notat om Udviklingen i Puljeordninger fra Maj 1990 til September 1992. Copenhagen.

Ministry of Social Affairs (1993a). Social Policy in Denmark. Social Policy in Denmark. Pamphlet Series. Copenhagen.

Ministry of Social Affairs (1993b). *Child and Family Policies*. Social Policy in Denmark. Pamphlet Series. Copenhagen.

Ministry of Social Affairs (1993c). *Parental Employment and Caring for Children – Developments and Trends in EC and Nordic Countries*. Copenhagen.

Mouritzen, Poul Erik (1991). *Den Politiske Cyclus*. Århus: Forlaget Politica.

Moe, Terry (1990). 'Political Institutions: The Neglected Side of the Story'. *Journal of Law, Economics, and Organization* 6: 213-53.

Niskanen Jr., William A. (1971). *Bureaucracy and Representative Government*. New York: Aldine Atherton.

OECD (1990). *Employment Outlook*. Paris: OECD.

Ostrom, Elinor (1983). 'A Public Choice Approach to Metropolitan Institutions: Structure, Incentives, and Performance'. *The Social Science Journal* 20: 79-96.

Ostrom, Elinor (1986). 'An Agenda for the Study of Institutions'. *Public Choice* 48: 3-25.

Pallesen, Thomas (2003). *Den vellykkede kommunalreform og decentraliseringen af den politiske magt i Danmark*. Aarhus: Aarhus University Press.

Phillips, Angela & Peter Moss (1989). *Who Cares For Europe's Children?* Brussels: The Commission of the European Communities. ECSC-EEC-EAEC.

Pade, Susanne & Niels Glavind (1993). *Rapport om Puljeordninger*. Bureau 2000. Copenhagen.

Olson, Mancur (1965). *The Logic of Collective Action*. Cambridge: Cambridge University Press.

Siim, Birte (1990). 'Women and the Welfare State: Between Private and Public Dependence', in Clare Ungerson (ed.). *Gender and caring: Work and Welfare in Britain and Scandinavia*. New York: Harvester Wheatsheaf.

Smith, Kevin B. (1994). 'Policy, Markets, and Bureaucracy: Reexamining School Choice'. *The Journal of Politics* 56, 2: 475-91.

Stone, Deborah A. (1988). *Policy Paradox and Political Reason*. New York: Harper Collins.

Teghtsoonian, Katherine (1992). 'Institutions and Ideology: Sources of Opposition to Federal Regulation of Child Care Services in Canada and the United States'. *Governance: An International Journal of Policy and Administration* 5, 2: 197-223.

Teghtsoonian, Katherine (1993). 'Neo-Conservative Ideology and Opposition to Federal Regulation of Child Care Services in the United States and Canada'. *Canadian Journal of Political Science* 26: 97-121.

Vedel-Petersen, Jacob (1992). *Dagtilbud for Børn under Skolealderen*. SFI-Rapport 92:8. Copenhagen: Socialforskningsinstituttet.

Williamson, Oliver E. (1981). 'The Economics of Organization: The Transaction Cost Approach'. *American Journal of Sociology* 87: 548-77.

Williamson, Oliver E. (1983). 'Credible Commitments: Using Hostages to Support Exchange'. *American Economic Review* 73: 519-40.

Williamson, Oliver E. (1985). *The Economic Institutions of Capitalism: Firms, Markets, Relational Contracting*. New York: Free Press.

Williamson, Oliver E. (1991). 'Comparative Economic Organization: The Analysis of Discrete Structural Alternatives'. *Administrative Science Quarterly* 36: 269-96.

Wilson, James Q. (1973). *Political Organizations*. New York: Basic Books.

CONCLUSION

*Erik Albæk, Leslie C. Eliason, Asbjørn Sonne Nørgaard
and Herman M. Schwartz*

The Welfare State: A political problem primarily and, only secondarily, an economic one

We started by asking what explained the remarkable resilience of the Danish welfare state, and what this told us about the future of the welfare state in general. We asked how this welfare state managed to survive during a quarter century that saw the collapse of Keynesian demand management and full employment, and a fairly successful and OECD-wide ideological challenge to the whole idea of the welfare state from the political right. We sought to present a comprehensive account and analysis of the institutional structure of the Danish welfare state in order to answer these important questions, and also just for the sake of presenting the first comprehensive account of the Danish welfare state and its situation in a specific set of macroeconomic policies, political institutions, and popular preferences. In this conclusion, we will not rehearse the details presented in each individual chapter. Rather, we will try to pull together a synthetic account that incorporates some of the most important findings from each chapter.

Recall that the Introduction argued, and some of the chapters demonstrated, that the theoretical literature on welfare state crisis largely over-predicted the severity and extent of constraints on the welfare state. Thus arguments that "globalization" or the collapse of the Bretton Woods system made large-scale welfare states impossible ignored the possibility that parts of the welfare state actually enhanced an economy's competitiveness or the possibility that rising external demand for a country's exports might help expand the revenue base on which the welfare state stood. Similarly, the remarkable reversal of Danish macroeconomic fortunes suggests that even if the Danish train neared the abyss, the engineers retained enough steering capacity to reverse course. Whether or not this reversal was purely the result of intentional action, the outcome suggests that there is nothing about the macroeconomic consequences of the welfare state that automatically produces disaster. Finally, the chapters nowhere suggest that European Union membership has forced a diminution or reshaping of the Danish welfare state. Indeed, the EU's influence is noticeably absent in virtually every chapter, except the one on macroeconomic policymaking, suggesting that as long as the fundamentals are right there is substantial room for maneuver in terms of domestic social policy goals. This book thus suggests that a largely tax-based, highly institutionalized, and welfare service-biased welfare state seems to be compatible with a more competitive and unstable world economy. While we are reluctant to generalize this into a claim of the welfare state as the solution to all, or even most, externally imposed economic problems, it is clear that the reverse is true: the welfare state is resilient in the face of external challenges.

At the same time, the various experts who authored the fine-grained case studies in this book all highlight the institutional and political dynamics at play in the sectors and areas they analyzed. As a collective enterprise, these chapters point out a variety of anomalies from the perspective of older crisis theories of the welfare state, while also suggesting an alternative conception of welfare state dynamics. First, they question the widely held assumption that continued welfare state expansion and support only occurs in good times. Second, they show that consistent Social Democratic backing and political power is not critical for the durability of the Scandinavian welfare state. Third, they reveal that the prevalent conceptualization of the welfare state as inherently involving social Keynesian full employment strategies and macro economic corporatism is misguided. Instead, it reflects a particular time-bound configuration of political, economic, and institutional dynamics.[1]

The chapters thus confirmed the introduction's intuition that the central problems of the welfare state were political problems – enduring problems of governance and governability. Could political actors shift the welfare state's funding priorities if and when the demand for services changes or as social demographics changed? Could political actors prevent welfare state producers from putting their own interests ahead of their clients' interests? Could political actors structure transfers in ways that maintained social solidarity and a willingness to work; or to put it in terms symmetrical to the prior question, in ways that prevented rent seeking not by producers but by concentrated groups of clients?

All of these questions lay at the heart of public choice theory critiques of the welfare state. Those critiques suggested three axes of decay for welfare states. The first two are economic: first by rent seeking producers desiring budget growth and work minimization; second by rent seeking client groups pursuing increased services and especially transfers. Both arguably should cause the welfare state's costs to rise inexorably and should make any redistribution of resources impossible. The third axis is political: the abuse of principals by

---

1 Przeworski (1985) is one important example of this kind of conceptualization, whose idea of social Keynesian compromise involves particular policies (full employment and equality), historically privileged actors (Social Democratic Parties), and specific institutional configurations (corporatism). For a similar conception cf. also Cameron (1984). For a critique, see Schwartz (1998).

CRISIS, MIRACLES, AND BEYOND

agents in the public sector – as distinct from simple rent seeking – should create public dissatisfaction with public provision and undermine popular support for the welfare state. All three axes of decay arise from fundamental asymmetries in the ability to organize collective action, and all suggest a long run incapacity on the part of politicians and the state to control the welfare state's fiscal and "legitimacy" deficits.

All of the chapters in some way touch on the asymmetry issue, and all indicate that rent-seeking and clientilism are critical causes of enduring governance problems in the Danish welfare state. Public Choice Theory (PCT) dynamics explain part of the incapacity to increase public sector efficiency, to make highly needed redistributions of public monies, and to make reforms that increase responsiveness to citizen demands and expand user influence. But taken together they also suggest that the very problems that PCT points to are sources of strength as well: precisely because privileged institutional actors want to maintain their privileges, they can be persuaded and compelled to accept budget restraint and high standards of client service. To be sure, central government politicians implemented government restraint in ways that did not upset delicate institutional balances among welfare service producers, and elected officials themselves were more than willing to share the mid-1980s and mid-1990s budget surpluses with their core constituents. But despite these increased transfers, the government's share of national income decreased, and the well-organized service producers of the welfare state failed to boost their budgets on their own accord. This finding has some external validation in the difficulties that Sweden's allegedly more resilient welfare state experienced roughly from 1988 to 1994. The strongly public choice based Lindbeck report on Sweden's crisis argued that typical PCT dynamics were bringing down the Swedish welfare state. Yet Lindbeck's scenario proved unfounded. In the end, Sweden's difficulties appeared to be mostly the result of macroeconomic mismanagement, and much like Denmark in the 1980s Swedish elites were able to negotiate a solution to their problems.

Empirically we must thus recognize that the welfare state is a highly complex and internally heterogeneous political entity. Theoretically, we have to appreciate that the welfare state cannot be conceptualized as a single stable political equilibrium that simultaneously meets all critical political demands and concurrently solves all governance problems. Instead the welfare state presents a heterogeneous collection of governance problems and dilemmas. The resolution of one problem inevitably generates new and sometimes unexpected problems. Thus our analysis below assumes that the welfare state and its problems involve enduring dilemmas, trade-offs, and the fulfillment of some goals at the expense of others. The welfare state is thus inherently political, and its problems can never be fixed with simple and unbiased solutions. The welfare state cannot be understood in technocratic or hagiographic terms.

Goul Andersen's chapter thus provides a partial explanation for the absence of a general crisis, showing that Danes generally like their welfare state, particularly because it supports their "way of life". This certainly facilitated efforts to find politically acceptable solutions to internal and external political and economic challenges. But in turn this facilitation neither dictated the form solutions might take nor forced producer groups to accommodate change.

Whence then arose adaptive capacity? We will argue below that adaptive capacity resides in the norms and interests embodied in the institutions of Danish corporatism. Both the failures and successes of the Danish welfare state are a function of popular goals and values derived from real life experiences, that is, of socially embedded norms. The collectivistic and democratic standards embedded in Danish corporatism not only hold producer group rent seeking in check, but also dictate the nature and scope of fair sacrifices. At the same time, this willingness to make some sacrifices can be invoked and exploited by policy makers in the service of public policy – if they can create or exploit the perception of crisis.[2] In such a situation, privileged producer groups will rationally sacrifice the fruits of the privilege for the sake of preserving privilege itself. Danish welfare state institutions thus represent a number of specific equilibria between, on the one hand, dominant norms "enforced by institutional and/or spontaneous collective intervention that overrides what self-interest and market power alone would dictate" and, on the other hand, the specific opportunities and incentives for rent-seeking and opportunism which those institutions provide for consumers and welfare state producers (quote from Swenson, 1989). These specific equilibria explain why Denmark escaped the abyss. But equally so, they also explain why problems of governability persist. All the chapters above located governability problems in political and institutional issues rather than in technical or economic problems. Success, failure, and crisis emerged from the intersection of popular norms and institutional politics.

Why the moral economy of the welfare state matters

We adopt our usage of a moral economy from Peter Swenson's comparison of German and Swedish industrial relations (1989: 1-4, 11-15). For Swenson the moral economy is a pattern of economic exchange relations whose bounds in large part are created by elites. These bounds express themselves in norms and customs but they are enforced by institutions and through collective and indi-

---

2 See Goul Andersen's and Christiansen's chapters in this volume; and also Cox (2001), Petersen et al. (1987: 325-335), and Goul Andersen (1994).

CRISIS, MIRACLES, AND BEYOND

vidual action. The pattern of social exchange relations thus cannot be predicted or deduced simply from market power and narrow self-interest. Intertwined informal social norms and formal political institutions also have an impact on the preferences (and values) the masses hold. Dominant popular sentiments and perceptions become politically germane because they set the range of feasible strategies for political elites. Public opinion and values are plastic and can be molded, but in the short run only to a limited extent. Simply put, Swenson's point is that the sphere of elite political action is embedded in and constrained by social norms shaped by past policies and today's institutions.[3]

The distinction between moral and political economy helps remedy the under-theorized relationship between elites and masses in classical PCT and most other theories of the welfare state. These theories either see elite-mass relations as unproblematic, with elites simply accommodating voter or member preferences to maximize votes, or they see leaders as entrepreneurs who can freely invent policies and incentives in order to mobilize support.[4] The moral economy approach on the other hand introduces a dynamic and diachronic relationship between the goals, values, and perceptions of the masses and the political action of elites. It stresses that popular expectations and demands are themselves shaped by past policies, rather than a mere reflection of economic interests derived from market positions, and that political institutions embodying these expectations constrain contemporary politics.

By stressing the diachronic nature of popular perceptions and policy preferences, a moral economy approach shows how the democratic dimension of policy making in modern welfare states creates path dependence. Policy making in democratic welfare states simultaneously involves coalition making, bargain-

---

3 This point has, from various vantage points, been "in" over the years. In his *Making democracy Work: Civic Traditions in Modern Italy* (1993), Robert Putnam shows how the predicaments involved in "the logic of collective action" can be overcome when institutions embodying traditions of cooperation and "social capital" establish reiterated games among political actors and shape their expectations to institutional performance. Making a similar point, Paul Pierson (1993) stresses the cultural feedback public policy breeds, and hence the subtle ways in which "policy makes politics" by shaping mass preferences and expectations. Cf. also Nørgaard (1996), more generally on the problems and advantages of a more dynamic conception of actor preferences and perceptions.

4 Two of the seminal books on political economy embody these competing conceptions. In Anthony Downs' *An Economic Theory of Democracy*, elected officials accommodate voter preferences to gain power and pecuniary benefits. Thus, mass politics is the pivot of policy making in modern democracies. In contrast, in the *Logic of Collective Action: Public Goods and the Theory of Groups*, Mancur Olson essentially argues that public goods and public policy is contingent upon the strategic action of political entrepreneurs. Paradoxically, collective action is possible only if elites do not act according to the theory Olson espouses for mass political behavior.

ing, and compromising among elites, and a continuous elite-mass interaction. This interaction with the masses includes legitimation and persuasion as well as aggregation and accommodation. So the way prior policy choices are institutionalized and legitimated produces a long-term drift in popular values and perceptions. Hence, public policy in liberal democracies always involves preference accommodation and preference shaping at the same time.[5]

Finally, a moral economy perspective helps overcome, though not solve, the somewhat artificial dichotomy between egoism and altruism. The issue is not so much whether people pursue their perceived self-interest, but rather what informs these perceptions. Past policies shape people's everyday social experiences, and individuals derive their preferences from their understanding of these experiences.[6] Policy preferences thus can merge selfish interests with norms of distributional equity. Although people do not habitually interrogate into the deeper sources of or reasons for their preferences, norms of fairness and equity impose a subjective constraint upon self-regarding attitudes. The most remarkable example of the impact of norms of fairness on economic and social behavior is probably the neoclassical anomaly reported by Pedersen and Smith in a paper prepared for but not included in this volume: Even in the face of marginal tax rates of around 100 pct., a full 70 pct. of low-skilled single mothers choose to work (Pedersen & Smith, 1995). Finally, as virtually all policies are sold by appeal to some distributional norm or some general good, the validity of the norms are recurrently reaffirmed in public discourse.

The fact that policy shapes popular preferences is particularly relevant for discussions of the welfare state. It implies that we cannot infer from historical evidence that support of a particular class or class-coalition is or will be the prerequisite for a viable welfare state now and in the future, just because it was so 25 or 50 years ago. Policy legacies make politics not only by structuring interests and incentives but also by structuring ideas about justice and equity as people arrange their lives in accord with given institutional structures and policies. This creates preferences that then form a dynamic constraint on pres-

---

5 The distinction between preference shaping and accommodation is discussed by Patrick Dunleavy (1991). It is unclear why Dunleavy insists on upholding the dichotomy between the two strategies. If preference shaping is part and parcel of electoral competition, logically preference accommodation must involve preference shaping too; that is, a particular shaping of preferences that reproduce and sustain the existing "aggregate distribution of preferences".

6 This point has been made convincingly by the late Aaron Wildavsky (1987, 1994). The general point is not as controversial as it might seem. Few mainstream theories in political science argue that people's perceptions and preferences are *unrelated* to institutional position and capacity, economic and social opportunities, or political and cultural context. Rather, the contention concerns how (and indeed whether) this relationship should be made the subject of academic inquiry and theoretical reasoning.

ent policy making. For most Danes self-interest and solidarity have become almost indistinguishable, as Goul Andersen's chapter reveals. This suggests – to misquote Jon Elster – that "if a reform is widely perceived as unjust, it is difficult to support it in more than a half-hearted way."[7]

Any explanation of welfare state politics thus requires analyzing both elite dominated horizontal negotiations between interest groups, and vertical elite appeals to and accommodation of the masses. Splitting moral and political economy into two casually independent variables for analytic purposes allow us to make better sense of the findings of the chapters. It also helps us develop a two dimensional predictive model of the character of welfare state politics, including the likelihood of crisis.

The (non-)crisis and the enduring governability problems of the welfare state, as well as reform, have to be explained at the intersection between the horizontal and the vertical dimension of politics. In the next section we sketch the particular dynamics of Denmark's crisis and recovery in the 1980s and 1990s. Then in the last section we will turn to the implications of adopting a combined political and moral economy perspective for the study of modern welfare states in general.

Why the political economy of the welfare state matters

Politics in general and welfare state politics in particular involves struggles in and around institutions. Institutions in general are ways to make solutions to various collective action dilemmas durable. From a political economy perspective and specifically a public choice theory (PCT) approach, collective action dilemmas are especially acute in the provision of public goods and social protection for risks that are manifested socially but of course always experienced individually. The well-known free-rider problem is the essence of this dilemma (cf. Olson, 1971). However, many goods provided by the welfare state are neither public goods in a strict economic sense, nor are they aimed at the social protection of risks. But because these goods have taken on the guise of rights and entitlements, from a PCT perspective they present the same political problem.

Some of the collective action problems involved in the provision of welfare services arise on the financing side, and others from their actual production. The public choice paradigm understands these collective action problems as efforts to free ride, abuse principals, and rent seek that arise from asymmetric opportunities and incentives to organize.

---

7 Jon Elster said: "If a reform is widely perceived as fundamentally just, it is difficult to oppose it in more than a half-hearted way" (1991: 135).

Tax financed, publicly provided systems for welfare services run the risk of moral hazard, namely that individuals will engage in behaviors that raise the risk that they will have to rely on the system, and thus that individuals will over-consume these goods relative to the norms on which tax contributions were calculated in the first place. The incentive to free-ride by understating the benefits and exaggerating the costs of the goods provided by the welfare state only intensifies the governability problems.

Welfare states run into trouble if the willingness to pay taxes or find work declines. At best, increased control and improved incentive mechanisms and sanctions can only solve part of the governing problems involved.[8] However as we noted above, the scope of the problem depends in large part on the moral economy in which a given welfare state is embedded.[9] As Per H. Jensen argues in chapter 4, the theoretically conjectured incentive problems are not necessarily found empirically.

However, monopolized public production of welfare services magnifies the risk of abuse and governing problems. The provision of publicly paid and produced welfare services, and in particular services produced by professional staffs, inherently involves some definition of the client's needs by the service provider (e.g. teachers shape the articulation of students' goals through curricular structures; doctors and hospitals define what is treatable as a medical problem). Increased autonomy for service producers thus creates a risk that they will maximize their own interests by shirking or rent seeking. On the other hand, the nature of professional work involves discretionary judgments. While these groups usually have to accept external limits on work behaviors that fall outside the scope of their profession, they will not accept tight administrative control over areas involving professional judgment from non-peers (and often not even from peers).[10]

So the production side involves a danger that producers will over-consume resources while under-providing services. On the other hand, the desire to preserve professional autonomy and institutional privileges may lead producers to trade away short term budget gains in order to preserve professional norms and organizational power which are the original source for budget gains. When governance structures themselves become politicized, institutional actors focus their attention on the more fundamental goals. Though they do not make the

---

8 The basic insight on this point rests on the seminal work by Kenneth Arrow and Mancur Olson, but it has been made with renewed force by Miller and Hammond (1994).

9 See especially Wolfe (1989) for a discussion of norm maintenance and erosion in Scandinavia; cf. also the chapter by Goul Andersen in this volume.

10 On professions in general, and professionals and welfare services in particular, see Wilensky and Lebeaux (1965: 283-334). Professionals also play a critical role in regulation; cf. Wilson (1989a).

argument explicitly, the service sector studies by Pallesen and Pedersen and by Damgaard are consistent with the argument that institutional privilege is a more fundamental goal than short term budgetary gains. Analyzed from the government's perspective, Christiansen's chapter adds that government capacity to curb budget growth increases when "the environment is hostile"; i.e. the capacity for steering is contingent upon critical contextual variables, which partially can be manipulated by the government itself.

The institutional structures of individual welfare states reflect different politically mediated answers to these antinomies. PCT would predict that an expensive, unfriendly and unreliable welfare state would emerge from the publicly funded and provided Danish institutional structure. Both producers and consumers should tend to over-consume resources and services respectively, driving up budgets. Indeed, Denmark's welfare state did grow markedly in the 1970s despite an early and traumatic tax revolt. Meanwhile producers and consumers should clash over the reliability and friendliness of services. And indeed, waiting lists did grow in, for example, health care in the 1980s.

However, a purely political economy analysis-cum-prediction of the antinomies of the welfare state ignores ways that political actors can use institutional structures to remedy the pathologies PCT predicts, and it largely ignores the moral structures governing people's behavior. The chapters in this volume suggest that the Danish welfare state's specific institutional terrain and moral economy are the keys to explaining both its survival and its limited adaptability. They also suggest that the all but consensual popular support for the welfare state can be a political resource that makes adaptation to shifting economic demands easier.

Putting the pieces together, or, why the Danish bumblebee doesn't crash

The combination of the political and moral economy of the Danish welfare state creates dynamics somewhat different from those predicted by a pure political economy approach, and these differences have helped the Danish welfare state to survive.[11] In particular three attributes of the institutional terrain are decisive:

- localization of public consumption, production, and financing
- corporatist structures dominated by professional groups and by government itself
- minority governments compensating for weak parliamentary support by negotiating solutions with strong meso-organizations

---

11 A slightly different explanation is presented in Schwartz (2001).

LOCALIZATION

Public consumption, the largest part of the welfare state, is extremely localized in terms of provision and financing. On the one hand this means the central government has less control over spending than it might desire, and thus only weak control over the total government deficit and, indirectly, the current account deficit. On the other, localization restrains local voters' appetite for spending and provides the center with some leverage over local politicians.

In welfare provision there is considerable local flexibility, in particular in the smaller localities. As Mouritzen shows, party politics explain only part of the local differences in tax level and mix, budget composition, and services. Instead, local officials translate "objective" needs and fiscal capacity into budget and service priorities. In this way, the localization of the welfare state increases all local politicians' responsiveness to citizen and producer group demands.[12] On the funding side, Denmark has one of the highest ratios of local to central employees in the OECD, and local self-funding covers about two-thirds of local expenditures through locally imposed income taxes. However localities are not totally self-financing, so local decisions over spending thus have consequences for the center's governing capacity and budget. While on the surface it seems that central government has few instruments to make sure that national fiscal priorities are implemented, the extreme localization of service delivery and the salience of local funding reduce the ability of local politicians and voters alike to indulge in fiscal illusions.

Moreover, while central transfers to localities make up a large part of total central outlays, these grants to localities are also so important for the localities that the central state exerts considerable influence on local budgetary discretion. Besides, the center also regulates most local responsibilities and the inter-municipal redistribution of revenue, which is important for poorer localities. Finally, the organization of welfare services is constrained by nationwide collective agreements, and even if local unions and professional organizations develop local strategies and make their own demands, they closely coordinate these activities with their national organizations. All this implies that the center is not as weakly positioned vis-à-vis the localities as a quick glance at comparative revenue and expenditure statistics would suggest.

All of this affects the most important central instrument for controlling localities: the yearly budget negotiations. The consolidation of local autonomy in the wake of the 1970 Local Government Reform was immediately countered by an innovation that increased the center's capacity to control the budgetary behavior of localities. The informal yearly budget negotiations were designed

---

12 On the extent of local and regional autonomy in service delivery see the chapters by Pallesen & Pedersen and Damgaard.

to increase the center's control over national fiscal policy, initially much to the regret of the localities (Blom-Hansen, 1999a). However, as Nannestad and Green-Pedersen show, during the 1970s Keynesian orthodoxy and then a "demand twist" strategy permitted considerable growth in the public sector and rising budget deficits. Hence, in the 1970s the fiscal policy context of the informal budget negotiations was markedly different from that of the 1980s.

The fiscally stressed Danish central government obviously had reasons to try to control local spending. The question was: could this be done? The center waged a long and quite successful budget battle with localities during the 1980s. In 1982 central government grants provided 35.6 pct. of funding for local government activities; by 1985 they provided only 28 pct. (Eliason, 1992: 569). The newly formed bourgeois coalition government cut block grants to localities by roughly 2 pct. annually after local governments had already drawn up their budgets, and then sequestered part of local government budgets to prevent tax increases.

In its efforts to control local budget behavior the center institutionalized the hitherto informal practice of annual budget negotiation. At the meetings between the Finance Ministry and Local Government Denmark (LGDK here, but in Danish, KL) the level and content of central transfers to localities were determined. However, the center not only played the block grant card to persuade and compel localities to comply with national policy goals. The Finance Minister also negotiated, and sometimes dictated, aggregate tax and spending limits. And on occasion the center even introduced individual sanctions against localities that did not meet the agreed targets. Though these measures impeded local autonomy and flexibility, they also increased the center's capacity to control public expenditures by showing that the agreed upon budgetary aims were to be taken seriously, cf. discussion in chapters by Mouritzen and Christiansen. Through negotiation and threat, the center managed to ensure local budget restraint. Throughout the 1980s the local spending growth was very low. Whereas public consumption, which is overwhelmingly local, merely increased some 0.6 pct. annually from 1982 to 1992, real growth in total public spending amounted to 2 pct. annually in the same period.[13] Thus the institutionalization of these negotiations formalized a peculiar public sector corporatism in which *governments*, not labor market actors, received representation and a say in national policy making. It increased the center's capacity to translate a tight fiscal policy into local budgetary restraint, even though formally it left the widely cherished local autonomy intact.

---

13 Cf. Christiansen in this volume; on the content of the yearly negotiations see appendix to chapter one by Nannestad and Green-Pedersen.

This governmental corporatism changed the incentives for local politicians, and helped them control producer demands. Binding agreements with the center on central transfers to localities changed the structural position of local politicians negotiating with producers, motivating local politicians to do the center's dirty work in imposing restraint on the welfare state. But as Christiansen and Mouritzen note in their chapters, the center's strategy probably would not have succeeded if local governments had been completely unwilling to control spending.

In general, local politicians are wary of raising local taxes. The center heightened local politicians' sensitivity by decreasing central transfers to local government and by shifting from rebates for services provided to fixed block grants. Besides, because of the widespread popular perception of fiscal crisis, local politicians were probably even more reluctant to skirt the agreed upon budget goals. On the other hand, block grants meant that local politicians were free to shift money to the most pressing – i.e. vote getting – local problems.

It probably would have been impossible to implement budget restraint unless the electorate accepted the need for some restraint. This obviously helped local politicians resist service producers' most reckless demands for increased budgets. But the negotiations with the state provided local politicians with the excuse they needed to stick to the budget goals. On its side, the central government could maintain that due to the shift from reimbursement schemes to block grants it was the localities themselves which decided how to use their budgets. Due to the numerous national policy mandates this is only partially true (Nørgaard & Pallesen, 2003). However, because of this "blame game" diffuse support for restraint (which declines when popular services are singled out) could be translated into cost containment in the service sectors.

Like Ulysses, local politicians used LGDK's negotiations with the center to tie themselves to the mast: the negotiations enabled them to hear professional groups' and citizens' demands for more resources and services, and yet effectively claim that they could not meet all their demands. Their budget deal with the central government precluded a general free for all at the public trough, while the concentration of central transfers into block grants gave them some flexibility to help different groups at the margin. Here the contrast with Sweden is instructive: localities and local politicians could free-ride on central spending because less local spending is funded by local taxes, and they thus did not feel the effects of rising consumption of public services as acutely as Danish local politicians and voters. Also, while Sweden had institutionalized bargaining up until 1976, the central government ended it when localities did not uphold their end of the bargain (Lotz, 1990; Blom-Hansen, 1999b). Hence, with an equally localized welfare state the central government lacked the resources to impose fiscal restraint on the localities.

Corporatism clearly is a system for sustaining and stabilizing collective action. Corporatism can help subordinate narrow interests to broader social goals, but it also can entrench the interests of specific organized groups. Theories of public choice suggest that interest groups are by nature rent seeking, and giving those interest groups a large consultative role verging on control risks opening the fisc to pillage and plunder (see Schwartz, 1994). Corporatism as a mode of interest intermediation and administrative organization characterizes the governance structures of all of the (small) European welfare states, though to different degrees.[14] Leaving aside here the ambiguity of the concept of corporatism, the question of "more or less" is apparently not as decisive for a government's capacity to adapt to changing political and economic demands as is the *kind* of corporatism. Danish corporatism differs from that found in e.g. Sweden, and these differences partially account for the larger capacity to accommodate external economic challenges and internal political pressures.[15] Danish corporatism differs in two ways from Swedish corporatism.

First, as often noted in the literature on the Scandinavian welfare state, Swedish (and Norwegian) labor market corporatism includes stronger and more centralized organizations than in Denmark. Danish income policies during the 1970s never included the same close consultation found in Sweden. Similarly, for historical reasons, the active labor market policies and the strong emphasis on manpower programs usually portrayed as the quintessence of the Swedish-cum-Scandinavian Social Democratic welfare state, have not been paralleled in Denmark. Traditionally, Denmark to a much larger extent has spent on passive support, that is, largely publicly financed unemployment benefits.

Plausibly the fact that the government was *not* held responsible for the persistent high unemployment, except as a guarantor of an acceptable level of family income, made it easier for the government to pursue a more conservative fiscal policy "according to markets" as Nannestad and Green-Pedersen note.[16] Although the trade offs between inflation and unemployment and between remedying the balance of payment and the budget problems were accommodated more successfully in Sweden than in Denmark during the 1970s, the

---

14 Cf. Katzenstein (1985); see also the review essay by Lijphart and Crepaz (1991).

15 For an overview of Danish corporatism, see Johansen and Kristensen (1982). For an analysis of the kind and scope of administrative corporatism in various sectors in Sweden, see Rothstein (1992). On the absence of corporatism in Danish industrial relations see Due et al. (1994). The difference in labor market organization and centralization is also emphasized by Katzenstein (1985: 50-52, 123-125); and by Esping-Andersen (1985) in his *Politics Against Markets: The Social Democratic Road to Power*.

16 On this aspect of Danish economic policy-making see Nannestad (1991); cf. also his chapter in this volume.

cumulative changes in the international political economy in the 1970s and the 1980s increasingly made the Swedish strategy of "social Keyensianism in one country" vulnerable. The disciplining forces of the international financial markets were not accommodated in Sweden, and the artificially low budget deficits – aided as they were by recurrent devaluations to keep the competitiveness – eventually became evident. In the fiscally conservative mood dominating the international political economy in the 1980s the Danish labor market institutions made it easier to adapt to the monetarist and EMU demands for low-inflation policies. The shift towards a "policy according to markets" was also embraced by the Social Democratic-led governments of the 1990s. And in the context of this fiscally more sound economic policy, a more active and supply-side oriented labor marked policy could also be established. Corporatism was utilized in labor market policy, but macroeconomic corporatism and income policy never became part of the equation.

Second, while labor market corporatism was less developed in Denmark than in Sweden during the 1980s, *government corporatism* was and still is more fully institutionalized in Denmark. The somewhat unusual public sector government corporatism described above, in which local governments bargain directly with central government over budgets, tax-increases, and the scale and type of central transfers to localities, increases the center's capacity to manage the budgets of otherwise highly autonomous local governments. This kind of public sector corporatism is not unique to Denmark, but because the Scandinavian local governments can levy taxes and constitute the bulk of welfare service expenditures, the institution is more salient (see Blom-Hansen, 1999b).

The significance of strong institutions is critical in the Scandinavian welfare states for another reason. Scandinavians like their welfare state, and they have become used to generous services provided by the public. Unless politicians can blame someone else for their unresponsiveness, it is difficult for them to resist popular demands for more and better services and for more resources to new and old transfer programs. As the Danish case shows, national politicians could not resist the temptation to buy votes and popularity when budget surpluses re-emerged in the mid 1980s and mid-1990s. The political pay off of improving welfare policies is practically guaranteed in Danish politics, and the only visible way national politicians could do so was by improving transfers, e.g. the introduction of the universal child allowance scheme, the 30 pct. increase in student grants, and better maternity leave. In contrast, national policy makers could never fully reap the political benefits of improved welfare services at the local level.

Hence, probably all elected officials would have liked to make popular policy decisions. But whereas state-local negotiations and state regulations incited the localities to pursue at least some budget restraint, nothing prevented national policy makers from dodging their own professed policy goal when the eased

CRISIS, MIRACLES, AND BEYOND

budget constraint enabled them to accommodate voter demands rather than international economic pressures.[17] In the 1990s in a context of less economic strain, the welfare services expanded again.

The rather unique combination of fairly weak labor market corporatism and strong government corporatism has produced some capacity to keep public expenditures from spiraling, while at the same time the welfare state has been kept intact, or even expanded. In contrast to what we might expect from a classical PCT perspective it is the *least* institutionally entrenched areas of the welfare state – social transfers – that have expanded most. This suggests that popular support – i.e. the moral economy of the welfare state – is as important a cause of welfare state expansion as the political economy dynamics usually emphasized in the literature. The absence of popular dissent is one of the most conspicuous features of the Danish welfare state, and it is a crucial factor when explaining the constraints and opportunities elected officials face.

However, even if local politicians had a clear incentive to curb the growth of welfare service budgets during the 1980s, the question still remains: why did the strongly organized and often highly professionalized service producers go along? Again we have to include a more explicit political and institutional dimension to the usual political economy dynamics to explain the outcome.

As in most other welfare states professional street-level bureaucrats exercise a considerable influence on policy implementation.[18] However, more so than in other countries Danish professionals are also deeply integrated into the managing and governing structures of the welfare state. In addition to negotiating pay and work conditions with LGDK and the state through their national unions, and in addition to lobbying political parties and local officials on issues that affect member interest, professionals (and semi-professionals) are usually also given a privileged position in the *management* of welfare services.

Thus, as Damgaard notes the managers of day care centers are trained day care teachers themselves – and generally many of the local bureaucrats regulating day care centers started as day care teachers. And as Pallesen and Pedersen

---

17 These policies are part of what Nannestad and Green-Pedersen report as "the year of fatigue and fumbling" in economic policy. The argument made here also accords Christiansen who argues that it is "difficult to have politicians manage themselves". Goul Andersen's study on the other hand provides the other part of the equation: in the face of widespread popular support for the welfare state – as informed by an entrenched welfarist "way of life" – electoral incentives provided the stimulus for politicians to enact more generous programs. See the chapter by Kvist and Ploug for a more detailed analysis of the costly improvement in various social transfer schemes.

18 The classical argument on street-level bureaucracy is Lipsky (1980). On the impact of professionalism on the development of the welfare state see Wilensky and Lebeaux (1965). On the tensions between democracy and professionalization and between bureaucratization and professionalization, see Wilson (1989b: 148-158, 168-171).

note, Denmark is perhaps the only country in the Western world where nurses (and doctors) take part in all levels of hospital management.

The organizations representing professionals are thus simultaneously unions and professional associations. Due to the lack of powerful centralized labor organizations, doctors negotiate as doctors, nurses as nurses, etc. on a number of issues broadly affecting member interests. All are conscious not only of working conditions and pay, but also institutional privileges and professional turf.

From a PCT perspective this *administrative corporatism* dominated by professional group control should open up the Danish welfare state to the kind of pillaging PCT suggests. Personnel levels should tend to go up while the success of administrative reform becomes a function of the strength of the professional organizations promoting or resisting it (nurses vs. nursing assistants; trained vs. untrained day care teachers; etc.), not a function of the gains in economic efficiency or service effectiveness. What, aside from professional norms, has constrained Denmark's professional groups and local government from abusing their position?

One answer from the chapters might be: nothing has. Certainly in the health sector effective professional organizations defended work norms and institutional prerogatives against changes in the 1980s. Moreover, as Christiansen shows, cutting budgets and shifting resources was virtually impossible to do short of freezing budgets and letting inflation take its toll. Thus, the fatal weakness in the center's ability to control spending in Denmark's welfare state that PCT points to is partially validated.

But this seeming lack of spending control is only superficially true. Due to the dual functions of professional organizations they pursue more goals at the same time. Short term budget gains – preferably in the form of improved working conditions and pay increases – is one of these goals, but long term institutional privileges and management prerogatives are the prerequisites for the professionals' capacity to protect their turf and to negotiate budget increases also in the future. Administrative corporatism, like all corporatism, institutionalizes "reiterated games" which tend to extend the time horizon of those presently enjoying a privileged position within these administrative networks. However, the fact that the organizations pursue more and potentially conflicting goals can be turned into a resource for policy makers who want to control spending.[19]

---

19 The argument that actors only want to participate in corporatist administrative structures as long as the institution constitutes a positive-sum game is misplaced and methodologically unsound. For fairly rational actors it is not decisive whether they can get an absolute distributional advantage from the game. Rational actors may correctly believe that long term net gains are maximized by staying within the institution although immediate economic sacrifices need to be made. Furthermore, rational actors will stay in the corporatist forum even if it is a negative-sum game *insofar* as the alternatives are perceived as yielding an even poorer result. Hence, depending on the alternatives it is consistent with PCT to argue that rational actors might forgo immediate economic gains.

Hence, Danish administrative corporatism is organized around professional organizations that have a strong presence at all levels of government, but it is not organized around central labor market organizations worried about macroeconomic outcomes. National professional organizations bargain with LGDK (and the Ministry of Finance), and LGDK may sign hundreds of agreements with different national organizations. The national professional organizations are just as concerned with professional prerogatives as LGDK are with pay packets and working conditions. Meanwhile LGDK is bargaining as a representative of "shareholders" (i.e. taxpayers and voters) and the central government, because management per se has been colonized by the professional organizations that actually control policy implementation.

Because professional organizations control policy execution, it has focused the local and central states' attention on gross budgets and general policy mandates rather than on detailed budgetary control and regulation of service delivery. For their part, professional organizations have been willing to accede to stagnant budgets in order to preserve their work place autonomy. Generally, professional groups protect professional turf, management prerogatives, and institutional privileges in preference to overall budgets.

As the two case studies on service production show, cost containment and a further drop in efficiency were obtained precisely when local and central government challenged professionals' institutional privileges. In the 1980s, for example, nurses traded away budget and pay increases for more control over hospital administration and over the allocation of work inside hospitals, effectively leading to an expansion of their professional turf. Though judged on their own terms the impact of the reforms has been negligible, the politicization of management structures does seem to have increased policy makers capacity to curb budget increases, whether this was intended or not. Thus, while in general the institutional terrain of administrative corporatism makes radical departures from past practices almost impossible, the political actors can use this institutional terrain to impose some of their own goals.

DIFFUSED POWER AND MESO-ORGANIZATIONS: STRATEGY AND CAPACITY FOR CHANGE

To complete the picture of the institutional terrain of Danish welfare state politics it is important to acknowledge that political power is highly diffused. Had a truly powerful political center been able to assert its priorities, the institutional dynamics discussed above might have been quite different. However, the contributions in this volume suggest that the central dog rarely barks in Danish politics, and that even when it does bark it does not bite. A highly fragmented party system – of both left and right – and constant minority government exacerbate the effects of administrative corporatism, government corporatism, localism, and the absence of centralized labor market corporatism.

What then counterpoises the pervasive power of professional interest groups at the sectoral and local level? Strong concentrations of power are found in meso-level organizations. The absence of powerful centralized organizations means that no one can hope to win distributional battles. No one wants to initiate US style distributional battles, and thus all change is negotiated among these governmental and organizational partners.

Within this institutional terrain a weak central government seeking fiscal restraint, redistribution, and service sector reforms has only two options that by and large tend to yield the same result. The government can try to forge a broad political compromise with all the dominant parties, in which case the very pursuit of a super majority secures the critical constituent interests of each party. Social Democrats usually will pay heed to the interests of day care teachers, school teachers, etc. Social Democrats and the bourgeois Liberals, who dominate local governments, will usually take keen notice of the interests of the localities. The list could go on. By implication the interests of the professions and the localities are observed indirectly, and radical departures from past practices are foreclosed.

The other option is simply to sidestep the parliament and negotiate directly with LGDK and the professional organizations. If all relevant organizational actors endorse the changes in policy, it is all but impossible in Denmark for opposition parties to obstruct the policy, even if they make up a comfortable majority. Besides, empowered with organizational support a minority government can often exploit the differences of opinion among the opposition parties to drive through a bill that none of these parties fully endorses.

While the result is largely the same as in the parliamentarist strategy, namely institutional stalemate, for the government this corporatist strategy has its advantages. First, the government can always take the issue on the table to parliament if the negotiations break down. Even if this does not guarantee that the government gets its priorities implemented, the professions' and LGDK's privileged access to the policy making process will be blocked. Though the outcome is highly uncertain, the localities and the professions loathe this uncertainty. Second, even minority governments can make some policy priorities without the active consent of parliament. Many statutes, for instance, give ministers broad discretion to issue regulations under the law.

It is important to note that it is the central government that is in a position to choose between the two strategies. This alone increases its leverage vis-à-vis organizational actors in general and the localities in particular. Government power, as the 1980s show, does make a difference. Thus, although central power is diffused the institutions of administrative and government corporatism actually help *re-empower the center vis-à-vis the localities and entrenched organizational actors*. So the diffusion of power into society and the concentration of power at the meso-level paradoxically imparts some flexibility to a Danish political system which for more than two decades has seen a string of rather weak minority governments.

Notwithstanding this central power, a minority government cannot use either of the two strategies to make radical reforms. In either case, countervailing forces prevent a radical rearrangement of welfare state priorities. Thus, since brutal or rapid change is impossible, *negotiated adaptation* occurs. The institutional terrain shaping the political interactions that constitute what we have coined negotiated adaptation, have helped the welfare state survive what is now a twenty year old "crisis".

As Nannestad and Green-Pedersen note, changes in macroeconomic policy did not substantially disturb the division of income between capital and labor after 1975. It was possible to get a cap on some kinds of spending but no party could effect a great departure from established patterns. But this stasis did not produce either economically or politically disastrous policies. Instead it seems that Danish immobilism produced policy outputs that were highly optimal in political terms even if they were sub-optimal economically – the situation in day care mirrors larger national processes. Politicians used the crisis of the early 1980s to put administrative reform on the table along with austerity budgets; professional groups accommodated austerity to protect their work norms and privileges from administrative reform; citizens and consumers got continued services; the budget deficit came down to sustainable levels; and local and central politicians were able to shift the blame onto each other. No one had cause to fear a sudden shift in the balance of power that might lead to an unfortunate distributional outcome. In the 1990s, of course, the easing of constraints permitted renewed spending.

With no clear policy mandate, nor vision, in the center and with a broad moral consensus favoring the welfare state, the Danish welfare state path continued during the 1980s and 1990s. So did many of its governability problems. But the center skillfully exploited the institutional terrain to impose budget restraint and better performance from public sector service providers. For their part, while still enjoying some flexibility, the localities could use central demands for fiscal austerity to contain local demands for greater spending without taking the blame for austerity, much as third world and European governments have sometimes used IMF conditionality agreements or the Maastricht criteria to escape responsibility for spending cuts and market liberalization.

INTERACTIONS AMONG THE THREE FEATURES

The combination of professional group corporatism and a fragmented parliament made changing welfare institutions or the entire welfare system quite difficult. The 1973 tax revolt thus ironically undermined efforts at comprehensive control over the welfare state. By fragmenting both the parliamentary left and right it enhanced the power of professional organizations, and in combination with the local government reform of the early 1970s, which consolidated the localities, the Earthquake election increased the leverage of professionals, local governments and their associations vis-à-vis the state.

As the case studies have shown, entrenched producer groups are well positioned to resist assaults on professional autonomy and prerogatives. Much as Esping-Andersen argues, universal provision and the institutionalization of welfare created entrenched constituencies to defend particular welfare measures (cf. Esping-Andersen, 1985, 1990). In addition to the generic middle strata that Esping-Andersen identifies as core welfare state supporters, it is also, and perhaps even more so, the institutional leverage of public sector producer groups that has secured the welfare state from external and internal challenges. However, by the same token, they have also obstructed the implementation of the few and feeble attempts to reinvent the welfare state.

In general, a central state run by minority coalition governments found it hard to articulate a coherent vision for change, despite the adverse budgetary consequences of producer control. And yet, they found it even harder to control themselves when budget constraints eased in the mid-eighties. The interacting corporatist institutions discussed above allowed them to impose fiscal restraint on the localities, and thus by implication on welfare service producers. In contrast, no institutions prevented the center from improving highly popular social transfer schemes. If welfare services were under the auspices of the central government, the costs of running these programs would probably have increased too.

In the absence of a central vision for change, the moral consensus favoring the welfare state meant that any effort to change it had to be sold as welfare preserving cost containment, not as a gutting and rebuilding. Well-positioned welfare service producers, who stood to lose from the few reforms that were introduced, skillfully challenged the wisdom of the reforms by arguing that they attacked not their privileges but the quality and scope of the welfare state. In combination, institutionally entrenched professionals and strong popular welfare state support are powerful incentives that almost certainly will induce weak minority governments not to pursue too radical reform ideas. In short, *negotiated adaptation* could not break the institutional stalemate of the Danish welfare state. But it did allow a resolution of some of the most pressing governance problems.

The Political and Moral Economy of Welfare State Governance: Beyond Denmark

The Danish welfare state's macro economic, political, and social/cultural difficulties have been managed fairly successfully despite considerable constraints. Obstacles to political control, public sector efficiency, and redistribution among programs endure, and discussions of how to meet present and future demographic and social needs are topical in the Danish debate on how to secure economic and political viability of the welfare state in the new millennium. An aging population is still a challenge to generous transfer schemes, and feeble but troubling signs of increasing polarization among the young might signal an emerging legitimation crisis. Demand overload and institutional inertia continue to constrain policy makers' efforts to reinvent the welfare state.

Despite all this, scholarly and political debate in Denmark does not revolve around "breakdown" or "crisis". Denmark achieved macro economic stabilization without making major cuts in the level or content of welfare services and transfer payments, and the overwhelming majority of the population still support their welfare state. Incremental negotiated adaptation led to the politically acceptable and marginal changes in the welfare state needed to assure its survival.

The Danish case thus remains anomalous for dominant crisis theories of the welfare state. While it is perhaps tempting to simply substitute Denmark for Sweden as the premier case of successful Scandinavian exceptionalism, and then revive the old theoretical truism of the feasibility of "Social Democracy in one country", this conclusion is empirically inaccurate and theoretically mistaken. As it is, numerous governability problems persist and only the future can tell whether these problems can be solved or contained. Theoretically the conclusion is misguided, because we thus simply reproduce some of the systematic flaws dominant in existing scholarship on the welfare state, and which we rebuked in the introduction: we would privilege the experience of one country while ignoring the differences that are found within clusters of "most similar" welfare states.

Viewing the Danish experience as a critical case rather than as an archetype or an exception, advances our comparative understanding of the political dynamics of the welfare state better. As an EU member, as a small open economy, as a highly institutionalized and generous welfare state with highly visible taxes, and as a country with a "postindustrial" class structure, Denmark should have crashed under its own weight. However, PCT theories of gravity neither explained nor predicted the right outcome. To us this suggests that domestic rather than international, and political rather than economic factors are the most critical determinants of welfare state viability. Put bluntly, international economic pressure, EU convergence criteria, and the break-up of the traditional class structure are neither sufficient nor necessary conditions of welfare state crisis. Domestic politics are. International economic stress per se does not cause a crisis of the welfare state, although it may be translated by domestic politics into one.

We can use the distinction between political and moral economy, and between the horizontal and the vertical dimension of politics, to generate a typology of welfare state politics that identifies and predicts dominant problems, styles of politics, and likely outcomes which can we tested. The typology lays out different political settings with distinct incentive structures for elected officials, and with different typical problems. Though the model is probably more accurate and useful if we regard its two dimensions as dynamic constraints and as continual rather than static dichotomies, we of course will initially present it in static terms. It is important to note that we are not presenting yet a typology of welfare states, but rather one of welfare state *governance problems*, stressing the constraints and opportunities for change and the probable political responses. Whereas the core of our argument rests on the firm belief that it is impossible to solve all problems at the same time, it is possible and indeed likely for societies to cycle through different quadrants as political struggles play themselves out.

FIGURE 1.

A Combined Moral and Political Economy Explanation of the Governance Problems of the Welfare State

Typical Problems		**Political Economy** Degree of welfare state institutional entrenchment	
		High	Low
Moral Economy Degree of popular welfare state support	High	*The hegemonic welfare state* Institutional stalemate: -redistribution difficult- -inefficiency/cost containment difficult	*The unmanageable welfare state* Institutional power conflicts: -inefficiency/cost containment difficult- -ineffectiveness
	Low	*The elitist welfare state* Institutional unresponsiveness: -redistribution difficult- -legitimacy problems-	*The degenerated welfare state* Institutional breakdown: -ineffectiveness- -legitimacy problems- -cycling among programs

Note: The moral economy of "support" pertains to the empirical welfare state, its institutions and practices, whereas the problem of "legitimacy" is a question of whether people endorse the normative foundation on which it rests and believe that a welfare state is a viable project. It is thus consistent to hold that presently the welfare state does a poor job in reducing social inequalities (or does it in a wrong way), which will be manifest in low support, and at the same time think that the welfare state is a desirable and feasible political project – indicating that welfarist aspirations are legitimate. Hence, it is two theoretically distinct variables and we can make the causal claim that low support for the empirical welfare state is likely to impact people's perception of the viability and desirability of any welfare state.

Each of these ideal typical situations poses different problems and challenges for politicians, while also imposing different kinds of constraints and opportunities. Whether narrowly self-regarding political beasts, declared ideologues, or creative political entrepreneurs, all elected officials in liberal democracies have to secure the support of critical constituencies to stay in power. Thus, depending on the moral and political economy within which they operate politicians face different incentive structures in the four situations. Even if elected officials defy the built in incentives and propose radical change aimed at remedying the most pressing governance problems, the ability of powerful interest groups to resist these changes depends on the extent to which they can rouse a public outcry against the reforms. So dominant popular sentiments and preferences are both a resource and a constraint. Combining the two dimensions we have the typology of the likely governance problems which modern welfare states faces.

In the "hegemonic" (upper left) cell, in which people like their welfare state and organizational actors are deeply entrenched in its institutions, the most powerful organizational actors participate in what they see as a advantageous game. These constraints make radical departure from past policies highly unlikely. Political interference and control is limited by the strong probability that professionals can muster popular support for the status quo, in particular by arguing that cost containment is a Trojan horse for reductions in service quality or quantity. Similarly, major efforts to redistribute money among programs threaten the delicate balance of power and privileges among institutional actors. For these actors, politicization of budget shares creates an uncontrollable process that might throw up new, unexpected priorities, and fearing this uncertainty they will try to obstruct efforts to redistribute public funds. This symmetry between the horizontal and vertical dimension of politics also works against efforts to fine-tune the welfare state in order to ensure its long-term viability. While this welfare state is hegemonic and effective, it is prone to inefficiency and institutional rigidity relative to market based service provision.

In the "unmanageable" cell (top right), welfare programs enjoy broad public support, but institutional politics are marked by conflict over privileges and professional turf. The sources of the conflicts vary. Often they are prompted by external (economic) events, but they can also be created by policy makers who inadvertently or intentionally have reinvigorated latent conflict of interests among institutional actors. Conflicts may also arise simply because institutional actors change strategies or develop new preferences. Political entrepreneurs, but also self-interested politicians navigating in a sea of mixed and partially inconsistent welfare demands, have an incentive to start or exploit such institutional battles, hoping that new programmatic priorities and the privileging of new organizational actors will forge a new institutional and popular base for their policy and party. But this situation is prone to effectiveness and efficiency problems since most service delivery involves cooperation among organizational actors and professions within and across sectors. (Consider the health care sector). Institutional actors confronted with extinction have little incentive to help others to perform well, and will take every opportunity to make other actors look bad by obstructing their work. Besides, institutional actors will try to convince the public that efforts to increase efficiency have detrimental consequences for the welfare state they still support. However, as producer groups fail to observe their political mandates, popular support for the welfare state as a whole may also begin to erode.

The "elitist" cell (bottom left) is PCT's ideal typical situation. Even though the populace may be unhappy with welfare state programs and provision, entrenched and contented institutional actors protect the status quo. The balance of power among institutional actors enables them collectively to resist popular demands for changes in particular programs or policy complexes. This also prevents any new division of responsibilities between public and private sectors. Status quo politics further alienates the populace, leading to an immanent legitimacy crisis for the welfare state. In this situation, political actors have conflicting incentives. They might try to persuade or force institutional actors to keep costs down and/or improve efficiency, and in this way balance the tension between strong institutions and an unhappy populace. But if discontent is profound, this strategy probably will fail and people will begin to wonder whether a welfare state is indeed feasible and desirable. Political entrepreneurs may then try to tap into popular discontent. Though a total lack of responsiveness probably is inconceivable if popular discontent is massive and intense, elitist welfare states with low but permanent discontent are in fact quite common. In the long run this is perhaps the greatest danger for the Scandinavian welfare states, although presently the level of political and economic polarization is far from critical.

In the "degenerated" cell (bottom right), the welfare state is neither capable of delivering its promises – effectiveness is low – nor does it enjoy popular support. This situation combines the worst features of the "unmanageable" and "elitist" cells: conflicts among institutional actors obstruct program effectiveness, while loud and unequivocal demands for change favor political entrepreneurs. Institutional actors and different groups in the population all have highly different agendas for change, leaving plenty of room for entrepreneurial action. Temporarily, elected officials may be able to force organizational actors who face the threat of extinction to do more for less, but in a welfare state on the verge of decay efficiency will eventually suffer as well. Weakly entrenched institutional actors fighting for their own survival, but confronted with new demanding policy mandates have nowhere to turn when appeals to the populace for support are worthless. The most likely outcome of this politics

CRISIS, MIRACLES, AND BEYOND

is an outright breakdown of the welfare state as support for specific programs withers away.

These static typologies underscore the constraints political actors in democratic welfare states face at any given moment of time. But since solving some problems only creates new difficulties and new challenges, a dynamic perspective is also useful. In a dynamic perspective, incentive structures created by the moral and political economies can be manipulated to a limited degree. Manipulation has its price, particularly as it is impossible to settle all types of problems at the same time. Welfare state politics, like all modern politics, involves trade-offs and imperfect solutions.

The Danish welfare state in the 1980s illustrates this well. Although rather serious governing problems were widespread during the seventies the Danish welfare state was institutionally entrenched and highly popular. To increase its capacity to ensure macroeconomic efficiency and cost containment the bourgeois government (and the last Social Democratic government before 1982) had to create and sustain a popular perception of crisis questioning the long term feasibility of the welfare state if left unchanged. Thus, the famous metaphor "Denmark is at the brink of the abyss" (which was actually coined by the last Social Democratic Minister of Finance, Knud Heinesen).

The moral economy approach cautions us that popular values and preferences are difficult to change, but precisely because the welfare state was held in high regard it was possible to create some support for an attack on what was perceived as an unsustainable path of fiscal recklessness. The support for a status quo welfare state thus declined. By creating a hostile environment and by politicizing institutional prerogatives, politicians were then able to change the incentive structure that institutional actors faced. Politicians raised popular awareness of and opposition towards entrenched institutional interests and continuous deficit spending, precisely in order to break that institutional deadlock. By politicizing institutional prerogatives, politicians changed institutional actors' hierarchy of goals, and thus created some room for maneuver on spending and efficiency issues.

However, though the crisis awareness was heightened in the early eighties, the Danish welfare state remained all but hegemonic and elected officials were reluctant to accept the consequences of a more radical strategy aimed at solving efficiency problems or the setting of new priorities. Thus as Nannestad and Green-Pedersen say, the economy was "tuned to the needs to keeping the welfare state viable" rather than the other way around.

But this effort reveals the limits to change in a hegemonic welfare state. It is hard to maintain popular dissatisfaction with a welfare state only by making efficiency issues politically salient. But expanding the attack to include policy effectiveness risks undermining the legitimacy of the welfare state as well and thus causes supporters of the welfare to rally in its defense. In Denmark at least, entrenched institutional interests would probably be capable of encouraging large segments of the population to stand up in their defense. Any weak minority government attacking core welfare state programs face an immanent risk of losing office. A Danish government that defies the strong built-in incentives to preserve the welfare state, *and* prevails while doing so, remains to be seen.

Whether from calculation or belief, few political actors were willing to risk what had become commonplace in neo-liberal assaults on welfare elsewhere. Furthermore, it was all but impossible to secure budget restraint, prevent further drops in efficiency, and sustain effectiveness while also making more than marginal redistributions among programs. Budget restraint and some efficiency gains could only be implemented with the cooperation of institutional actors, and they would not cooperate if major redistributions were also taking place. Redistribution – politicization – was a bargaining card politicians could trade for cost containment or efficiency gains.

Notwithstanding the partial easing of the constraints policy makers faced in the hegemonic Danish welfare state in the 1990s, service production efficiency and the difficulty of making new priorities remain enduring problems. On the other hand, macroeconomic efficiency, policy effectiveness, and welfare state legitimacy were all secured and even improved during the 1990s. Thus, *politically* the welfare state was, and still is, viable.

In Denmark, economic crisis was not a sufficient cause of crisis for the welfare state, and it is clear that the same was be true of the Swedish state in the 1990s. Swedish politicians solved inflation and fiscal challenges greater than those Danish politicians confronted in the early 1980s. However, as the Danish evidence suggests, doing so did not necessarily create a welfare state crisis. The governance problems Sweden faces today can be confronted in ways that are not antithetical to welfarist aspirations, contrary to the Lindbeck Commission report. A crisis of the welfare state is likely only if institutional problems are ignored and if popular support declines, as Bo Rothstein has argued (1992).

Combining political and moral economy explanations for welfare state politics highlights the mass bases of welfare state politics. While welfare states are unable to meet all challenges at the same time and achieve an administrative or economic equilibrium, they certainly can achieve and maintain stable political equilibria. By implication, even if welfare states are constrained by the international political economy the root of welfare state crisis, as well as its survival, is domestic politics.

The Danish case suggests that the crisis theories of the welfare state have been misguided. But it also cautions against the equally deceptive belief that only if a hegemonic welfare state is established, all problems of governance evaporate. In Denmark, certainly, "saving" the welfare state has not increased its capacity to make new priorities and set new goals. With an aging population, popular demands for more and better services, and a large public debt, the redistributional capacity of the Danish welfare state *has* to improve in the future. However, while we must hope that these problems will be addressed in the near future, it would be delusive and foolhardy to pretend that making these adjustments come without a price. Although politics is the art of the possible, not all things are possible at the same time.

References

Blom-Hansen, Jens (1999a). "Policy-Making in Central-Local Government Relations: Balancing Local Autonomy, Macroeconomic Control, and Sectoral Policy Goals." Journal of Public Policy 19: 237-264.

Blom-Hansen, Jens (1999b). "Avoiding the 'Joint-Decision Trap': Lessons from Intergovernmental Relations in Scandinavia." *European Journal of Political Research* 35: 35-67.

Cameron, D.R. (1984). "Social Democracy, Corporatism, Labor Quiescence and the Representation of Economic Interest in Advanced Capitalist Society", in John Goldthorpe (ed.), *Order and Conflict in Contemporary Capitalism*. Oxford: Clarendon Press, pp. 143-78.

Cox, Robert (2001). "The Social Construction of an Imperative: Why Welfare Reform Happened in Denmark and the Netherlands but Not in Germany." *World Politics* 53: 463-498.

Dunleavy, Patrick (1991). "Party Competition – The Preference Shaping Model", in Patrick Dunleavy, *Democracy, Bureaucracy, and Public Choice*. New York: Harvester Wheatsheaf, pp. 112-144.

Downs, Anthony (1957). *An Economic Theory of Democracy*. New York: Harper Collins.

Due, Jesper et al. (1994). *The Survival of the Danish Model*. Copenhagen: DJØF Publishing.

Eliason, Leslie (1992). "Reading the cards on the table." *Scandinavian Studies* 64: 544-581.

Elster, Jon (1991). "The Possibility of Rational Politics", in David Held (ed.), *Political Theory Today*. Stanford University Press, pp. 115-142.

Esping-Andersen, Gøsta (1985). *Politics Against Markets: The Social Democratic Road to Power*. Princeton: Princeton University Press.

Esping-Andersen, Gøsta (1990). *The Three Worlds of Welfare Capitalism*. Princeton: Princeton University Press.

Goul Andersen, Jørgen (1994). "Samfundsøkonomi, interesser, og politisk adfærd", in Eggert Petersen et al., *Livskvalitet og holdninger i det variable nichesamfund*. Århus: Department of Psychology, University of Aarhus, pp. 15-136.

Johansen, Lars Nørby & Ole P. Kristensen (1982). "Corporatist traits in Denmark, 1946-76", in G. Lembruch & P. Schmitter (eds.), *Patterns of Corporatist Policy-Making*. London: Sage, pp. 189-218.

Katzenstein, Peter J. (1985). *Small States in World Markets: Industrial Policy in Europe*. Ithaca: Cornell University Press.

Lijphart, Arend & Markus Crepaz (1991). "Corporatism and Consensus Democracy in Eighteen Countries: Conceptual and Empirical Linkages." *British Journal of Political Science* 21: 235-256.

Lipsky, Michael (1980). *Street-Level Bureaucracy: Dilemmas of the Individual in Public Services*. New York: Russell Sage Foundation.

Lotz, Jørgen (1990). "Controlling Local Government Expenditures: The Experience of Five European Countries," in Rémy Proud'homme (ed.). *Public Finance with Several Levels of Government.* Brussels: Proceedings of the 46th Congress of the International Institute of Public Finance, pp. 249-262.

Miller, G. & T. Hammond (1994). "Why Politics is More Fundamental than Economics: Incentive-Compatible Mechanisms are not Credible." *Journal of Theoretical Politics* 5: 5-26.

Nannestad, Peter (1991). *Danish Design or British Disease: Danish Economic Crisis Policy 1974-79 in Comparative Perspective.* Århus: Aarhus University Press.

Nørgaard, Asbjørn Sonne (1996). "Rediscovering Reasonable Rationality in Institutional Analysis." *European Journal of Political Research* 29: 31-57.

Nørgaard, Asbjørn Sonne & Thomas Pallesen (2003). "Governing Structures and Structual Governing: Local Political Control of Public Services in Denmark." *Journal of Public Administrative Research and Theory* 13: 543-561.

Olson, Mancur (1971 [1965]). *Logic of Collective Action: Public Goods and the Theory of Groups.* Harvard University Press.

Pedersen, Peder & Nina Smith (1995). "The Welfare State and the Labor Market." Conference on the Negotiated Adaptation and the Danish Welfare State, Aalborg.

Petersen, Eggert et al. (1987). *Danskernes tilværelse under krisen II: Studier i den politisk-psykologiske udvikling 1982 til 1986.* Århus: Aarhus University Press.

Pierson, Paul (1993). "When Effect Becomes Cause: Policy Feedback and Political Change." *World Politics* 45: 595-628.

Przeworski, Adam (1985). *Capitalism and Social Democracy.* Cambridge: Cambridge University Press.

Putnam, Robert D. (1993). *Making Democracy Work: Civic Traditions in Modern Italy.* Princeton: Princeton University Press.

Rothstein, Bo (1992). *Den korporativa staten: Interesseorganisationer og statsforvaltning i svensk politik.* Stockholm: Norstedts.

Schwartz, Herman (1994). "Public Choice Theory and Public Choices: Bureaucrats and State Reorganization in Australia, Denmark, New Zealand, and Sweden." *Administration & Society* 26, 1: 48-77.

Schwartz, Herman (1998). "Social Democracy Going Down vs. Social Democracy Down Under? Institutions, Internationalized Capital, and Indebted States." *Comparative Politics* 30, 3: 253-272.

Schwartz, Herman (2001). "The Danish Miracle: Luck, Stuck or Pluck?" *Comparative Political Studies* 34, 2: 131-155.

Swenson, Peter (1989). *Fair Shares: Unions, Pay, and Politics in Sweden and West Germany.* Ithaca: Cornell University Press.

Wildavsky, Aaron (1987). "Choosing Preferences by Constructing Institutions: A Cultural Theory of Preference Formation." *American Political Science Review* 81: 3-21.

Wildavsky, Aaron (1994). "Why self-interest means less outside of a social context: Cultural contributions to a theory of rational choices." *Journal of Theoretical Politics* 6: 131-159.

Wilensky, H.L. & C.N. Lebeaux (1965). *Industrial Society and Social Welfare.* New York: Free Press.

Wilson, J.Q. (ed.) (1989a). *The Politics of Regulation.* New York: Basic Books.

Wilson, J.Q. (1989b). *Bureaucracy: What Government Agencies Do and Why They Do It.* New York: Basic Books.

Wolfe, Alan (1989). Whose Keeper: Social Science and Moral Obligation. University of California Press.

CONTRIBUTORS

Erik Albæk, professor of political science and journalism, University of Southern Denmark. Chairman of the Danish Social Science Research Council 2001-2005, chairman of the Nordic Political Science Association since 2005.

Jørgen Goul Andersen, professor of political sociology and director of Centre for Comparative Welfare Studies, Aalborg University, Denmark.

Peter Munk Christiansen, professor of political science, University of Aarhus, Denmark. Member of the steering committee of the Danish Power and Democracy Study 1998-2004. Editor of *Scandinavian Political Studies*, 2008-2011.

Jens Bejer Damgaard, PhD, chief of section (intersectional negotiations between local governments, general practitioners and hospitals), Central Denmark Region.

Leslie C. Eliason, until 2004 when she sadly passed away, was associate professor in the Graduate School of International Policy Studies, Monterey Institute for International Studies, USA. Autumn 1999 Fulbright visiting professor at the Department of Political Science, University of Aarhus, Denmark.

Christoffer Green-Pedersen, research professor, Department of Political Science, University of Aarhus, Denmark. Editor of Scandinavian Political Studies, 2008-2011.

Per H. Jensen, professor of social policy, Centre for Comparative Welfare Studies, Aalborg University, Denmark, and chair of the board of the Danish PhD Research School – 'Welfare State and Diversity'.

Jon Kvist, professor of social policy, University of Southern Denmark. His research interests include comparative social policy and welfare state research, methodology, and the social divisions of welfare.

Poul Erik Mouritzen, professor of political science and public administration, University of Southern Denmark. Author (with James Svara) of *Leadership at the Apex. Politicians and Administrators in Western Local Governments*, Pittsburgh: Pittsburgh University Press, 2002.

Peter Nannestad, professor of public policy, Department of Political Science, University of Aarhus, Denmark. Author of *Danish Design or British Disease? Danish Economic Crisis Policy 1974-1979 in Comparative Perspective*, Aarhus: Aarhus University Press, 1991.

Asbjørn Sonne Nørgaard, professor of political science, University of Southern Denmark. He is head of the PhD-programme in political science at the University of Southern Denmark and chairman of the Danish PhD Research School in Political Science, *Polforsk*.

Thomas Pallesen, professor of public administration, Department of Political Science, University of Aarhus, Denmark. Former employment in Aarhus County Hospital Administration.

Niels Ploug, research director at SFI – The Danish National Centre for Social Research. He is an economist and his research covers comparative and historical analysis of the development of the Danish welfare state with a special emphasis on labour market and pensions policies.

Lars Dahl Pedersen, PhD, head of department, Department of Health Care Planning, Central Denmark Region.

Herman M. Schwartz, professor of politics, University of Virginia, USA. Autumn 1990 Fulbright visiting professor at the Department of Political Science, University of Aarhus, Denmark, and Autumn 1999 Fulbright Chair in North American Studies at the University of Calgary, Canada.